A Celebration of Young Poets

Illinois – Spring 2000

Creative Communication, Inc.

A Celebration of Young Poets
Illinois – Spring 2000

An anthology compiled by Creative Communication, Inc.

Published by:

CREATIVE COMMUNICATION, INC.
90 NORTH 100 EAST
LOGAN, UT 84321

ISBN 1-58876-008-1

Dedicated to the youth of Illinois

Foreword

Recently I was asked by a newspaper reporter what Creative Communication does as a business. My first impulse was to say that we are a publishing company. On second thought I responded by saying that we are in the "dream fulfillment" business. Over the last eight years I have read the poetic dreams, hopes and fears of thousands of students. The joy in reading these poems is hard to describe. My imagination has been filled with images of nature. I have laughed along with poets who describe their humorous antics. I have cried with poets who describe the pain in their lives. In reading these poems, I know that behind every poem is a poet and behind every poet is a dream.

Creative Communication has received numerous letters and calls from parents, teachers and poets. Many of these have told about a life that has been changed when a poem was chosen to be published; a poet who was experiencing a difficult time in his or her life and needed a feeling of success. It might be from a divorce, a death in the family or a student who was struggling in school. In each of these cases, the publishing of a poem became a dream fulfilled. As you read these poems, visualize the poet and the message that he or she is trying to convey. But most of all, read and enjoy.

I want to thank each of the poets in this book for allowing their poem to be published. I want to thank my staff. Behind the scenes of each book are judges, typists, editors, desktop layout specialists and numerous other individuals who have provided thousands of hours to this project. Without all these individuals this book would not be possible.

Gaylen Worthen, President
Creative Communication
September 2000

Future Poetry Contests for Young Poets

There are two contests available for each school year. The Fall contest deadline is December 1st. The Spring contest deadline is April 17th. Over $2000 in prizes will be awarded in each contest. To enter, poets in grades 4-12 should submit one original entry, twenty-one lines or less. Each poem must be submitted with the student's name, grade, and home address, as well as the student's school name, Language Arts teacher's name, and school address.

Mail each entry to:

Creative Communication, Inc.
90 North 100 East
Logan, UT 84321

Or enter online at:

www.poeticpower.com

Table of Contents

Poetic Achievement Honor Schools   1

Section I: Grades 10-11-12   5
    Top Poems   6
    Poems of High Merit   16

Section II: Grades 7-8-9   61
    Top Poems   62
    Poems of High Merit   72

Section III: Grades 4-5-6 219
    Top Poems 220
    Poems of High Merit 230

Index 333

Poetic Achievement Honor Schools

The following schools are recognized as receiving a "Poetic Achievement Award." This award is given to schools who have a large number of entries of which over fifty percent are accepted for publication. With hundreds of schools entering our contest, only a small percent of these schools are honored with this award. The purpose of this award is to recognize schools with excellent Language Arts programs. This award qualifies these schools to receive a complimentary copy of this anthology. In addition, these schools are eligible to apply for a Creative Communication Language Arts Grant. Grants of two hundred and fifty dollars each are awarded to further develop the writing and appreciation of poetry in our schools. Last year's Language Arts Grants were awarded to:

Grant Park Middle School – Grant Park
and
St. Mary Star of the Sea School – Chicago

Spring 2000 Poetic Achievement Honor Schools

* Teachers who had fifteen or more poets accepted to be published

Althoff Catholic High School
Belleville
 Betty Henry*

Beckemeyer Elementary School
Beckemeyer
 Mrs. Ahle*
 Sandra Jansen
 Mrs. Reckling*
 Mr. Strieker*

Blessed Sacrament School
Belleville
 Michelle Janes*

Channahon Middle School
Channahon
 Lisa Klover*

Clay City High School
Clay City
 Ms. Pheghly*

Clifford Crone Middle School
Naperville
 Kathy Nickelman*

Diekman Elementary School
Dolton
 Carol Bodnar*
 C. McRoberts

Emerson Elementary School
Berwyn
 Darlene Tomanich*

Fenwick High School
Oak Park
 Mr. Sullivan*
 Fr. Paul Whittington

Finley Jr High School
Chicago Ridge
 Jane Nolan*

Forest Trail Jr High School
Park Forest
    Ferbie Claudon*

Francis Granger Middle School
Aurora
    Ms. Parent*

Francis Xavier Warde School
Chicago
    Brigid J. Cashman
    Ms. O'Rourke*
    Ms. Reese

Grand Prairie Elementary School
Joliet
    Judy Crowhurst
    Peggy Dillinger

Grant Park Middle School
Grant Park
    Melissa Ducat
    Mary Guertin
    Christie Keller

Harrison Elementary School
Wonder Lake
    Deborah Draper*

Holden Elementary School
Chicago
    Ann Gubricky*

Holy Angels School
Aurora
    Ms. Séguin*
    Mrs. Waegner
    Mrs. Williams

Iroquois West Upper Elementary School
Thawville
    Mrs. Swan*

Jonesboro Elementary School
Jonesboro
    Pam Gawrych*

Laraway Elementary School
Joliet
    Mrs. Dodson
    M. Doody

Manteno Middle School
Manteno
    Ms. J. Grimes*

Marian Central Catholic High School
Woodstock
    Kay Hansen*

Marshall High School
Marshall
    Kay Bolinger*

Meridian Middle School
Buffalo Grove
    Judy Buchheim*

Morton East High School
Cicero
    Sharon Kman*

Morton High School
Morton
    Carol Reiser*

Most Holy Redeemer School
Evergreen Park
    Mrs. Wazio*

Newark Community High School
Newark
    Ursula Goldman*

Nichols Middle School
Evanston
    Mrs. Bertocchi
    Judith Ruhana*

North Elementary School
Marshall
    Mrs. Cutshall*

North Park Elementary School
Chicago
    Laurel Johnson
    Leigh Ellen Ludwig

Owen Scholastic Academy
Chicago
    Mrs. Laschober
    Patrick Sullivan*

Parker Jr High School
Flossmoor
    L. Fehrenbacher*

Parkview Jr High School
Lawrenceville
    Rita Rynder*

Pope John XXIII School
Evanston
    David Onofrey*

Queen of Martyrs School
Chicago
    A. Tasler*
    Mrs. Turkowski

River Trails Middle School
Mount Prospect
    Mr. Harmon*
    Karen Seeberg
    G. Zitis

Schaumburg High School
Schaumburg
    Mrs. Breaux
    Mrs. Prochaska
    Karen Spering

Schiesher Elementary School
Lisle
    C. Enger*

Schurz High School
Chicago
    Ms. Cichowski
    Mrs. Enstrom
    Mr. Rychlewski
    Ms. Scott
    Catherine Wrenn

Smithton Elementary School
Smithton
    Rhonda Hatridge*

St Ferdinand School
Chicago
    Rachel Gemo*

St George School
Tinley Park
    Mrs. Aranda
    Mrs. Bujan
    Ms. Pries*

St Gerald School
Oak Lawn
    Mrs. Thompson*

St Irene School
Warrenville
    Maureen White*

St John Fisher School
Chicago
    Robin Creevy*

St John Of The Cross School
Western Springs
    Mrs. Kannry
    Mrs. Mahoney
    Miss Trick

St Joseph Catholic School
Harvard
    Laura Wicaryus*

St Mary Of Czestochowa School
Cicero
Mrs. Helie*

St Mary School
Alton
Karen Crites
Lora Wagner

St Mary's Of Kickapoo
Edwards
Mrs. Stender*

St Mary-Dixon School
Dixon
Mrs. Gingrich*

St Matthew School
Champaign
Mrs. Gumbel
Mrs. K. Marietta
Karen Pickard*

St. Richard School
Chicago
Karen Smith*

St Vincent De Paul School
Peoria
JM Davis*

Stratford Jr High School
Bloomingdale
Fotini Abou
Ms. Hennessey*

Sullivan High School
Sullivan
Brett Gayer*

Tri-City Jr-Sr High School
Buffalo
Kaysha Simpson*

Young Poets
Grades 10-11-12

Death by Acne

Death, of course, as we all know
can come in many ways.
It may claim your youthful legs
or lover's loving gaze.

But any nervous schoolchild
preparing for the fall
can tell you that a social death
is swiftest of them all.

Once inside the teenage world
of bustling passageways,
a pizza face or pimple chest
can number all your days.

Take heart, young child, and be assured
that someday it shall clear,
and those that this day shun you not
should be your friends most dear.

So stroll outside with youthful pride
and look towards the sun!
For death by acne, you should know,
is not an eternal one.

Benjamin Cherry
Charleston High School
Charleston
Grade 12

Vanishing Impressions

My toes sank deeply into each cool grain
grasping to form the footprint
that I so hoped would remain

But the waves, they were strong that sweltering summer day
and with two or three currents
my print was wiped away

I ran along the beach and encountered what I feared
one by one each footprint
had gradually disappeared

Each one was engulfed in the sand it was made
my impression wasn't deep enough
and thus, it had to fade

Though some legacies vanish,
while others will withstand
we all are merely
footprints in the sand

Beth Duncan
Willowbrook High School
Villa Park
Grade 12

Who But You

Who but you could hold me
　and keep the world at bay
Who but you could scold me
　in the nicest kind of way
Who but you could take my hand
　and step into a dream
Who but you could bring me joy
　enough to make me scream
Who but you could lead the way
　through fantasies, part by part
Who but you could make me love
　and open up my heart
Who but you could bring to Earth
　each and every star
Who but you would tell me
　"I love you just the way you are."
None, not a single one
　could do the things you do
I could never love another
　the way that I love you

Dana Fritz
Newark Community High School
Newark
Grade 11

Watching Heaven

Sitting on a moonbeam,
Hanging on a star,
Dancing on the planets' rings
With the sky as black as tar.

Don't look down,
It's a long, long way to fall.

Dodging flying comets,
Watching meteors explode,
Talking with the astronauts.

Don't look up,
There's still a long, long, way to go.

Looking at the sun burn,
Running with the rays,
Wishing on falling objects;
Doing this for days and days.

Don't look up and don't look down,
There's a great distance either way.
You're right in the middle,
Right where you belong.

Stacey Huber
Midland High School
Varna
Grade 10

Forever Remembered

Preserve me
in your mind
like wild flowers
between plated glass.

Preserve my image,
my warm eyes,
and see purity, and truth
and an ear for your sacred thoughts.

Preserve my words,
my soft voice,
and I will guide you
through the darkest of life's midnights.

Preserve my laughter,
my flavored humor,
and you will always
have reason to smile.

Preserve my mistakes,
my flaws,
and you will learn
more than I ever could imagine.

Alyssa Rzeszutko
Prospect High School
Mount Prospect
Grade 12

Luna

Bewitching moon
A kiss of grace to the copious blackness of the night sky
She winks...and stars dot the sky, her seed scattered like fairy dust...
     Dollops of cream in God's coffee
She modestly reveals herself in fractions,
     Causing unrest when bare
She summons romance and aberration alike,
     And beguiles every eye whose view she snares
She is subdued as the night grows stale, and the sun commands her throne...
     Yet her whisper remains upon the sky,
          Promising her return

Lauren Scalzo
Providence Catholic High School
New Lenox
Grade 11

My Foolish Cat

The greasy gray Persian walked toward the window
With eyes full of promise; a hunter closing in on its prey
Three squirrels appeared outside, ascending toward their "holy grail": the bird feeder.
Pandora ran toward another window to get a better view of her possible meal
One of the squirrels became visibly weary of being harassed by the cat
And pitched a backward glance at the window
After pawing and meowing toward the squirrels for some time
I awaken, and prepared to banish the noisy feline to the basement
By this time Pandora had given up
Realizing that surmounting this challenge would require an open door
I give her a questioning look, as if to ask, "Why do you have to keep me awake?"
I point at my watch, vainly attempting to explain the concept of time to a feline
Realizing my intentions, Pandora reluctantly marches toward me
I pick her up, and carry her to her dungeon
But to compensate for her missed meal opportunity, I donate a can of cat food

Nate Stonewall
Morton High School
Morton
Grade 11

The Bridge of Love

When your skies are gray
And the rain comes down
And you just can't seem
To get rid of that frown.

Call on me and I'll be there
Forever to listen
Always to care.

I'll be around
To dry all your tears
And be your shoulder to cry on
For the next million years.

No number of miles
Can keep us apart
For love builds a bridge
Between two friends' hearts.

We can meet on that bridge
Any time of any day
So I'll never be
But a few steps away.

Heather Wagner
Gibault Catholic High School
Waterloo
Grade 11

What Goes Around Comes Around

A convertible, a fishing pole,
The groundwork had been laid.
With a gleam in his eye that forecasts the future,
My father holds his first fishing pole
With his shiny new convertible behind him.

In a sailor suit his mother made him wear
He still manages to look delighted on Christmas Day.
Living in a cramped Chicago apartment
The gifts seemed to be unusual choices.
It turns out they made sense,
The move to suburbia soon followed.

Thirty-seven years later the picture holds true.
Though the sailor suit is gone,
My dad drives a convertible,
And still enjoys drowning some worms.

Ryan Walter
Schaumburg High School
Schaumburg
Grade 11

The Bag of Time

We ran around
Pushing each other, laughing,
Giving piggy-back rides, two at a time.
A big stony stage in the middle of a dark park,
Where I ate Lucky Charms, and learned how to do an Irish Jig backwards.
We were so loud, the four of us, the three girls and me,
Playing 007, smoking cigarettes,
Saying things we actually meant.
Hopes were up, because we put them there, because we had actually found
something to do with the time that we so desperately wanted to keep.
We opened the bag that we kept it in, we spat into it, we pulled the drawstring
tight, and then we, all four, sat on it, bouncing up and down, taking no heed
that the contents were leaking out.
The park was ours,
The memory is mine.

Michael Warren
Oak Park River Forest High School
Oak Park
Grade 12

Awaken My Dreaming Eyes

Awaken my dreaming eyes.
Rid yourself of the remnants of sleep and open to see the world anew.
Look not through your young, unblemished lenses
Fashioned of ideals and innocence, but with ones of reason and foresight.
Ones which have been earned through experience and time.
Remember wondering eyes, harbor not the nightmares you once faced.
Do not let them dwell in the depths of your soul.
But in turn, remain wary of the comfort and solace of sweet dreams as well;
That which gave you peace during the blackest of nights.
For in our enchanting world of endless possibilities
Both exist in equal roles; the good and the bad.
Neither is subject to time or circumstance and neither guarantees the dawning of a new day.

Mace Boshart
Charleston High School
Charleston
Grade 12

Spindle of Dreams

The spindle in my mind is turning,
weaving the most delicate of threads.
It spins the thread of hope, the thread of dreams,
that shines like gold, locking into a web of fantasy.
Each night a new strand is added,
and shimmering with delight, is the fabric of wonderful thoughts my mind weaves during the night.
I wish that I could reach out, and hold it close to my heart,
But my fingers come close, so close!
Yet never close enough.
My mind alone holds the key, to unlock my spindle of dreams, that winds effortlessly in my head.
It holds my inspiration, it keeps my fantasies dear,
for the day that I am ready to finally venture there,
to gaze upon my fabric of dreams, and remember, and remember.

Laila Siddiqui
Lisle Sr High School
Lisle
Grade 11

Dancers in the Breeze

We come up and then we die
We dance to the soothing music of the wind
Dull, no existence of color, one of a kind
Confidently swaying from side to side
Every gust of restless wind slaughtering me to death
Our creation of fluffs, our protector from the secret depths that linger in our shadow memories
Our body chipping away like glistening night chalk
Moonlit at night, shined on by sun
Picked in a moment of admiration and dispersed in the whirling maze of our wind
Our unique beauty to you we bring and your superiority to us you give
We watch your children grow
We exist in your tattoo memories
Our collected voices travel in the wind
Our bodies dream through the breeze to kiss your rosy cheeks goodbye
We came and now we die

Esther Yambo
Schurz High School
Chicago
Grade 11

Springtime Lullaby

Fiddley dee dum, fiddley dye
Hush now little one, don't you sigh.
The rain beats hard and tears will fall;
A shameful weight for shoulders so small.
But don't you worry and don't ever fret;
He who made the rain will not forget
To care for, look after, and cherish His own.
Come summer you'll see you were not alone.
So hush now little one, don't you sigh.
Fiddley dee dum, fiddley dye.

Kelly Davis
St Clair Christian Academy
Dupo
Grade 11

Leslie

A girl is dead
we're not sure why
we don't know what happened
it's too late now
there are no answers to our questions
she's dead
and her boyfriend lives
he knows what happened and he's holding out
he's going to court
instead of speaking out
he would rather spend time
in a place full of hate
whatever happened that night
we will never really know

Nicole Willette
Newark Community High School
Newark
Grade 10

The Monster Within

In the home hath have no fear
The comfort of my love is near
She doth have the monster inside
She hath have no place to hide
A monster she has in her body so sweet
A monster tucked away nice and neat
It eats away from inside out
Slowly creeping taking no route
This disease begins to take its toll
Eating away, making her body empty as a hole
No light will scare this relentless beast away
Once it comes it is here to stay
The monster knows not the rich nor the poor
When it comes death comes knocking at your door
But in the home hath have no fear
Good-bye my friend, my mother, so dear

Garrett Laschinski
Grant Community High School
Fox Lake
Grade 11

Food

Food has everything to give,
All sorts and colored shapes,
With tasty icing on a cake,
Bright fruits that are sweet and sour,
And vegetables that are green,
Like broccoli that looks like a tree.

Food has everything to give,
Lemons like a sun of gold,
Smell of lasagna in the oven,
Cheese that melts, apples that glow,
And for your stomach's delight,
Wonderful sweets that fill the mouth.

Give all you have for your body,
Eat and never give in;
For one moment of health
Eat many a fruit of different kinds well-tasted,
And for a time in your life
Give all you have, or will be.

Kristy Kash
Marshall High School
Marshall
Grade 10

Boys Don't Cry

Dear Teena,
I've heard there's a fine line
Between what you are and what you want to be.
They say they know who you are
And what you ought to be.
I've heard you can never run away from yourself,
Because she can always find you.
You shouldn't have to hide your heart
Because it makes them cringe.
In an eerily open field they question,
But you don't have to answer why.
Because here transgender isn't an issue.
It's a sin.
It's an invitation to death,
A welcome mat for fists and feet.
They said they knew,
That is was better to make you leave this place,
Torn and bleeding, than to let you live a lie.
If you can still listen, hear them.
Dear Brandon,
Boys don't cry.

Brian Spencer
Schaumburg High School
Schaumburg
Grade 11

Thoughts on Thoughts

Death comes upon me,
and it becomes my shadow,
my friend,
my enemy within my soul.

Fear comes upon me,
and it becomes my death,
my afterlife,
my courage within my heart.

I thank the Lord above
for my life,
my times here on earth,
my spirit within my mind.

Virginia Hunt
Glenbrook North High School
Northbrook
Grade 12

Windsong

The oldest song the world knows,
Is that which whispers through the trees.
That's been here since the dawn of time,
Voice of the earth, the blowing breeze.
It has outlived the dinosaurs,
And spanned the stormy reign of men.
Though we may last ten million years,
It will be there to see our end.
Coriolis, take me away,
And bring me to my destiny.
I want to hear your song on land,
And echoed off the bluest sea!

Matthew Born
Tinley Park High School
Tinley Park
Grade 11

The Willow

With its poignant, striking beauty,
Under starry skies above,
Stands the mighty weeping willow,
A symbol of unrequited love.

Its leaves droop to the ground,
Where they hang in mournful sorrow,
She never realized that I loved her,
Today, nor will tomorrow.

In the branches a whippoorwill sings,
Its said, melodious song,
I yearn for your love evermore,
As passing time grows long.

Brent Furrow
Maroa-Forsyth Sr High School
Maroa
Grade 12

Feelings

I like you
But you don't like me.
I asked you out
Yet you said no.
Your life seems to go on
Unaltered by this knowledge.
It's plain to see that you don't have feelings for me.
Why then must I still have feelings for you?
Every time I see you my heart starts pounding.
I even start to sweat.
Why must I still have feelings for you?
I receive none in return.
You exist in my world every day.
Why then am I helpless to change your feelings for me if this truly is my world?

Ryan Herdes
Clay City High School
Clay City
Grade 12

The Summer Is Gone

The summer is gone; it has gone away for good.
Now the winter is here, and at times I should
forget about the old, and the past,
because when I think about those things, it makes me sad.
When the summer was here, there were bad times as well as good,
but I never guessed the summer ever would, dwindle away,
like it was never here.
I tried to fight it, but I can't hold back the tears.
Before it left, the summer whispered regretfully,
"Their winter must come, it's the end for you and me."
Maybe I got attached too strongly to the warm and sunny days,
but who could blame me, who wouldn't do the same?
So now as I see the first snowflake starting to fall,
I think about how much I still love the summer through it all.
The summer is gone, maybe one day it'll come back,
but until then I have to deal with the winter, with my wool hat.

Marquita Powell
Eisenhower Campus High School
Blue Island
Grade 12

July 7, 1996

I suppose what I wanted was a comfortable feeling,
To lay out in the grass with our heads touching,
Pointing out the constellations, and making up wild stories,
To be unaffected by the spectators that built up a young relationship.
I guess I wanted you to let me know, continually, what you were feeling,
And have complex conversations about life, love, and the ceremony of intellect,
As if our words weren't cliched thoughts.
I saw in you a special person that was to change my way of thinking
And invent the smallest part of me, take away the headaches of growing up,
And be mine.

Catherine Morrison
Mascoutah High School
Mascoutah
Grade 12

The Fading Star

Just a speck of life in a vast eternity,
Enclosed in the depths of a dark reality.
The cold, never-ending spiral of time.
Shining bright, you will soon fade away into the night.
But not a soul will notice that you are missing.
You are just a number; a statistic.
No one knows your name; you have no identity.
Your life is equivalent to that of a star: You are one of billions.
There are too many to miss any at all.
Though you shine more than all the others,
It gets you nowhere. Nothing. No one. You are one.
As you continue on in a futile attempt to be recognized,
You notice that there is nothing to strive for.
So you allow yourself to become dimmer.
You unite with your surroundings.
A once flaming, now lifeless pit of existence.
You are eternity. You no longer shine.
The light that you once gave now lights the lives of others.
They are one, as you once were.
Now, as you have meshed with all existence, you are united.
And although you are only one, you are many.

Amy Meglio
Glenbrook South High School
Glenview
Grade 12

Taken for Granted

Earth has a beauty to admire.
All nature and wind that whines;
Burning like branches on a fire;
Cool water that sparkles and shines;
And forests that whisper and rejoice,
Rustling like a calm voice.

Earth has a beauty to admire.
Soft like a pair of doves,
Roughness of cliffs in the desert,
Smooth seas that envelop you, that everyone loves,
And for small things of beauty, small things of joy,
Moments that shape that soul like a toy.

But all you see for miles around,
Changes and never stays tamed,
For one season of warm summer,
Turns to many a day of snow well named.
And for a moment, stop and look,
At all you didn't see, or just glances you took.

Jessica Powell
Marshall High School
Marshall
Grade 10

Cooled Emotion

Anger flaming beyond control,
With each moment growing more intense.
Coals of feeling too hot to touch,
Unattended, it burns on and on.
Hidden back-drafts engulf the soul,
Create a spark to soothe within.
Heavy rains destroy this fire.
Showers of love,
The anger evaporates.

Kristen Waspi
Grant Community High School
Fox Lake
Grade 12

Grandma

I remember the last time I saw her
She was lying in a hospital bed
She was hanging onto life
I remember my mom the night she told me
She cried softly and said Grandma Lillard died
I was so sad
I sat and cried for hours
I remember the funeral; so hard to get through
As I sat in the small church
I thought of the times I had come with Grandma
Every Sunday we sat and sang hymns
I will never forget the day my Grandma died

Cara Piatt
Tri-City Jr-Sr High School
Buffalo
Grade 10

Foot Fetish

Sometimes the sun smiles at me,
Or sometimes it is the rain.
But I think most of all it's the
Tornado in me,
That wants to overcome this disdain.
Whirling around like a dervish,
In some exotic desert locale.
Blowing winds uncontrollably,
Like the ones Ulysses knew well.

I wonder whether wishes will walk
Right out from under my feet.
My toes, thinking they're being tickled by white sands,
Don't acknowledge them; my defeat.
Perhaps I should always wear high heels,
So my precious dreams will never escape.
And they'll kick and they'll scream to be let out,
But the heels will keep them prisoner,
Never to be released.

Lauren Hanson
Marian Central Catholic High School
Woodstock
Grade 12

Somewhere Today

Somewhere today
in a place not far away,
a young woman was killed
and her destiny left unfilled.
Somewhere today
in a place not far away,
two people fight
about which one was right.
Somewhere today
in a place not far away,
a little child has left,
a fallen victim to theft.
Somewhere today
in a place not far away,
a person lies dying,
the family left crying.
Can't you see?
These places aren't happy.
You may not shed a tear,
but what if those places were here?

Shanna Wieneke
Pana High School
Pana
Grade 10

The Noodle

A noodle went to Paris
And bought himself a cat.
He said "Do not compare us
We're not normal—that is that."

The cat then said, "Sir Noodle,
I do not like it here.
If I see another poodle
I think I'll lick my ear!"

The noodle had to leave that place
He called to get a plane.
The pilot had to fly through space
Through lightning, snow and rain.

The noodle and the cat arrived
At their final destination
When the cat stared with eyes alive
At the noodle with anticipation.

The noodle tried to run away
But had no arms or legs.
The cat jumped upon him right away
He tasted just like eggs.

Nathan McMillan
Momence High School
Momence
Grade 11

Wherever I Go

Wherever I look
I see her face
Wherever I go
I feel out of place

My heart does cry
When she's gone
My heart does sing
When I hear her song

The sky seems bluer
When she is with me
The sky seems darker
When she sets me free

My life is joy
When I'm holding her near
My life is pain
When she leaves me with all this fear

God help me through
Every day that she's gone
God help me through
Just help me hold on

Jake Becker
Althoff Catholic High School
Belleville
Grade 12

Lips

Ruby red
Tender
Voluptuous
Pulsating
Vain
Vulgar
Rough
Sweet
Gentle
Misleading and deceiving
As you utter the words
"I love you"
I love you
Piercing my mind
Flooding my soul
And overpowering my common sense
Another fool
Fed a lie
Another lover
Hung out to dry

Sandra Zieren
William Fremd High School
Palatine
Grade 10

The Eagle

Over the mountains
Soaring into the sun
Looking for
The catch of the day
Talons sharp
And ready to clasp
Hunting viciously for fish
In the river
You spot your prey
So gracefully you swoop
Down to the river
Congratulations
It was a success

Amanda Urban
Tri-City Jr-Sr High School
Buffalo
Grade 11

Strong

My soul is a burning flame,
What stories it can tell.
My life is full of pain.
Can anyone help me at all?
My heart is full of shame;
But love will break down the walls.
You may think I am so weak,
But all this has made me strong.
Strong enough to keep standing,
Strong enough to love one and all.

Bob Berry
St Edward Central Catholic High School
Elgin
Grade 10

Never Mind

Never mind the things I see.
Day after day,
They say these things to me.
Day after day,
Nothing left to be.

I try to walk away.
But it follows me.
Everywhere I turn,
It's there greeting me.

Never mind the pain.
Forget what's left of me.
Until it all goes away,
There's nothing left to see.

Brett David McCarthy
Tri-City Jr-Sr High School
Buffalo
Grade 10

Untitled

The flower blooms in the springtime air.
Its color growing with the hue of love.
With untouched beauty, it stretches its petals.
Its stem reaching toward the blue sky.
The gentle breeze kisses the soft blossom.
Breathing the gift of life through the open petals.
The breathtaking view of splendor,
Attracts the songs of birds to take a flight.

Nikki Berry
Plainfield High School
Plainfield
Grade 12

A Woman

A woman is the soul of a man,
The voice of freedom.
A woman is a mother of a child,
The lover of the brother
That we call man.
A woman is the tears of happiness,
The joy in our step
The love in our hearts.
A woman sometimes must take the place of the man,
She must be the strong and gentle hand.
When a woman is hurt and must cry,
She holds it in and looks to the sky.
A woman is many things wrapped into one.
Learn to be proud, independent, and count on no one.
To all women, let your pride
Be your guide.

Shannon Tugle
Vincent Gray Alternative High School
East St Louis
Grade 10

Masquerade

Tonight the masquerade ball begins
at the strike of eight
Each guest in their own world
hiding behind their superficial facade
All with smiles upon their lips
but never allowing their faces to be seen
They look back at the visions of truth
leaving only deception to dictate
Superfluous conversations envelop the room
until it comes time for the guests to depart
Descending the stairs some remove their masks
and for the rest fear fills their hearts
So they continue to dance in the darkness
with their masks upon their face
Living a life of masquerades
until the day they pass away

Brooke Wells
Charleston High School
Charleston
Grade 12

Drawn By a Dream

Hauntingly familiar, I hear a voice,
And it speaks to me in the night.
This ghostly speaker knows me.
In his fist, my soul he holds tight.
I can't escape him, and yet I don't wish to.
I feel safe when in his presence,
And yet I can't shake this other feeling,
This guilty, scared lack of confidence.
I feel the throbbing heat of my blood,
Pounding through my veins with fear.
I dread his coming, and yet, sometimes,
I mourn when he is not near.
I do not know this ghostly visitor,
I could not tell you his name,
For when he calls, all he calls is my name,
And he is as silent and unknown as the grave.
So many conflicting emotions,
I can barely understand them.
In my dreams, he promises me peace.
I cannot refuse his call, I am drawn by a dream.

Jessica L. Tosetti Winsloff
Nokomis High School
Nokomis
Grade 12

The Sound of a Runner

The sound of a runner is easy to hear.
Just close your eyes — it will be very clear.

Snap-pop-pop
As he rolls out of bed.
Sore joints moan — they would rather be dead.

Beep and beep
His little watch chimes
Announcing the start of today's race against time.

Slap-slap-slap
Crunch and splash
From pavement to gravel to puddle in a flash.

Hiss-hiss-huh
His breaths come in pairs.
His mind is free from all worries and cares.

Now listen with care as he ends the last mile.
Didn't you hear it? The sound of a smile.

Catie LaBracke
Marian Central Catholic High School
Woodstock
Grade 12

Winter

The sun shines brightly
through the bare trees.
Snow begins to fall
slowly to the frozen ground.
Wind blows forcefully,
unaware of the mess it causes.
The lake sits still and motionless.
The playground abandoned
by children who wait for winter's end.

Nikki Oestreich
Althoff Catholic High School
Belleville
Grade 12

Thinking of You

I'm in my room thinking of you
And I know you think of me too.
I remember the things we did,
And the things we hated too.

I think of the time I first laid eyes on you,
The first time we went out,
Remember our first kiss,
And when I told you I loved you.

I think of the time,
We were together.
When people said we wouldn't last,
I thought we won the battle.

I think of the time,
When you said it was over.
You left me thinking,
Thinking of you.

Gustavo Rosales
Morton East High School
Cicero
Grade 12

A Message to the Multitudes

War has clipped the wings of the dove
In a world where hope is a slave,
Chained to silence deep in her grave,
Bleak as night, blocked from above.

Soon the shroud will be lifted up.
Churning the earth, hope will emerge,
Halting the crowds chanting their dirge;
Soothing softly spills from her cup.

She gathers every nameless face.
Misguided minds recover their place.

Natalie Lauren Hyser
Belvidere High School
Belvidere
Grade 12

All By Myself

B eing on a basketball court
A ll by myself.
S hooting, running, dribbling, just practicing,
K eeping my eyes on the goal.
E very day, I just play,
T rying to get better one shot at a time.
B eing out in the cold or sweating in the hot sun
A lways practicing no matter the conditions.
L istening to people ask if I ever quit playing
L oving it, enjoying it, just being on a basketball court all by myself.

Gina Reinburg
Woodlawn High School
Woodlawn
Grade 11

Remember

Remember when your eyes met with mine and we became one.
I have so many memories of our love that are good and bad.
Remember the roses you gave me one day.
With time they died and so did your love.
Your love is like the roses, it grew to be such a beautiful thing,
but like the roses our love had to die sooner or later.
Now is that time for this rose to die.
Remember I was just trying to keep us together the way we once were.
Now the roses are dead and you went away
forgetting the love I gave you one day.

Guadalupe Cisneros
Schurz High School
Chicago
Grade 12

The Soul

The soul has colors to share,
All beautiful and unique,
Like the colors on a rainbow,
Hues of splendor that share and speak,
And warm the heart with
Magnificence like a shooting star.

The soul has colors to share,
Tranquil like a breeze of spring,
Love of friendship in the world,
A friendship that brings voices that soothe,
And for every color that you see,
A friend that brightens the world.

You'll have a friend which is all you need for life,
Change your attitude and never let go of your values,
For one obstacle of life,
Has many a lesson of truth well taught,
And for a moment of silence
You will have achieved all you need to know about colors or friendship.

Amanda Bridgeman
Marshall High School
Marshall
Grade 10

Peace

The world has peace to share,
All wonderful and exciting things,
The clear sunset on a summer night,
The whirling wind that whispers and sings,
And colorful leaves that fall to the ground,
The wildflowers that grow like magic.

The world has peace to share,
Colorful like a rainbow full of skittles,
Clouds are like a big ball of cotton,
Adults that care, and children that share,
And for people around the world,
People that give the happiness to everyone.

Enjoy all you can share for some aren't that fortunate,
Smile and never start fights,
For one can make a world of difference,
Peace many a year of work well done,
And for a moment of glory,
Share all you can, or make peace around your community.

Amanda Meehling
Marshall High School
Marshall
Grade 10

She Is My World, She Is My Life

Eyes that twinkle like the heaven's stars
A smile as bright as the sun's golden ray
Hair as beautiful as the faint glow of a winter's fire.
Such hurt she has endured,
Yet I will always be her shoulder.
She has brought me such joy
She is my world she is my life.
Twice she has slipped away
Our days apart were like death,
But love has brought her back.
No distance will keep us apart
For our love is thicker than blood.
Some think we are too young,
Yet my heart says different
It says she is the one for me.
She is my world she is my life.
Fate has given her to me,
And I will never let it take her away.
She has given me happiness,
She has given me love,
She is my world she is my life.

Eric Gimber
Coulterville High School
Coulterville
Grade 10

As Long as I'm Me

Wonder to me
What I will be
Will I be an athlete or doctor
Will I be an architect or a teacher
Will I be a good listener or a caring friend
Will I be a fast runner or a brilliant scientist
Will I be the one to discover a cure for cancer or for AIDS
Will I be an interior decorator or a math whiz
Will I be there for you through and through
Will I be the one you run to if you have a question
Will I be a good parent and a responsible adult
Whatever I do I'll do it well
As long as I can be me

Kelly Lynn Terry
Newark Community High School
Newark
Grade 10

Patrick

P ain has never touched him
A twinkle is always in his eyes
T ough when he wants to be
R unning constantly from responsibility
I nnocent in spirit
C omical at heart
K ind, even to his antagonizing older sister

Katherine Weiler
Marian Central Catholic High School
Woodstock
Grade 12

Life

Life has nothing to lose,
All mysterious and twisted at times,
Enjoy life's memories on a high note,
It has times that you can cherish and share,
And you never forget the people who were there,
Life is like a short dream.

Memories have good qualities to express,
Fresh in your mind like a time of happiness,
Remembrance of moments in the past,
Good times that unfold that tell a story,
And for yourself treasure,
Memories that linger in the mind.

Live all you can for happiness,
Love and never hate,
For one time of laughter
Is worth many a time of cheer well spent,
And for a minute think of life's joys
All you receive, or return.

Kandis Ramsey
Marshall High School
Marshall
Grade 10

The Gift

When a friend comes into your life
They change it in so many ways
The good times—
The bad—
All measure out so the good outweigh the bad.
A life without a friend
Is like a sky without clouds
Is like spring without flowers.
Thank you for helping to outweigh the bad times
For letting the clouds fly high,
And the flowers bloom.
Thank you for being you.
Most of all,
Thank you for being my friend
Because that, truly is the best gift of all.

Sara Schield
Naperville North High School
Naperville
Grade 11

God's Creation

The sun begins to set over the horizon,
with vibrant colors filling the sky.

The autumn breeze makes my hair dance;
it is crisp, cool and refreshing.

I smell nothing but crisp air,
and I hear nothing but nature.

Soon there will be no more colors to fill the sky,
for the moon's glow will be the only light.

Patricia Galbavy
Christ Lutheran High School
Buckley
Grade 10

Plot

Now is a sea of nothings, filled either
With ash of past glories burnt or promise of pain,
But holding happiness neither
Detached, I stop from thinking about this
Instead, I eat bitter, unripe peaches
And keep messy rooms cluttered by cleaning
I sleep to escape the creeping reaches
Of the mundane present without meaning
Then, breaking sleep's stillness, the nightmares come
To haunt me, a failing, tortured future
Until I wake and am once again numb,
Ignoring my heart held by a suture
Love twists and glitters above in the sky
A faint hope that I will escape this lie

Christine Stepanski
St Francis High School
Wheaton
Grade 11

Dragonfly

Hey dragonfly,
where did you get that disguise?

A disguise this is not,
but a mask of beauty here lays,

Brilliant shade of blue,
shimmering in the sun's rays.

A disguise in your mind,
a masterpiece in mine.

A color so royal,
oh, how ever divine.

Your disguise is my treasure,
while your treasure is my disguise.

With this beauty,
I'll raise up the skies.

I got this from the fairies,
the gnomes, the flowers.

The sun and the hillside,
are my true powers.

The earth and Mother Nature created me.
My masterpiece, your disguise
...how wonderful can that be?

Shireen Groleau
Holy Angels School
Aurora
Grade 12

A Disease*

Your year is gone
Your months have vanished
Your weeks are forever lost
Your days are numbered
As you meet the reaper face to face
You know death is near, your color is pale
Your body is weakened from an incurable disease
Your fight for life has been rough and hard
In your last days you put up your strongest fight
The doctors say your condition is worsening
These might be your final nights
Your family and friends are close to your bed
You see the fear and horror in their eyes
You are determined to beat this disease and say
I am a survivor of cancer

Tracie Purdy
Morris Community High School
Morris
Grade 10
*Dedicated to all cancer survivors

Only You

Once upon a time you said we'd always be two
But I said some hurtful things and now I don't have you
Can you ever forgive me? My heart's in pain
When you walk by me now I know I'll never be the same

You act like you're fine with there being no us
But all I want is to gain back your love and trust
I remember the touch of your sweet embrace
Oh tell me why did I have to make that mistake?

I want to go to you and take your hand
But I need to know if it's in *your* plans
Baby, you and me, can't you see?
It has always felt so right to me

Tell me what should I do?
Because for me there will be *only* you
We're apart but I know deep in my heart
That we are meant to be together

I'm never going to give up on you
It seems so wrong with all we've been through
Can you find it in your heart to come back to me?
For I'll always love you eternally

Stacy Slatton
Newark Community High School
Newark
Grade 10

Procrastination

Yards have grass to be cut,
All tall and darkest green,
Blowing, swaying in the wind,
Stately stalks that bend and lean,
And bright sunlight shining
Sparkling off all like small lights glittering.

Yards have to be cut,
Going to seed like a field uncontrolled,
Growing fast in the time,
Since it was last mowed,
And for the sun, it has turned to rain,
Another chance that was missed to cut the grass again.

Mow all you can for if you don't,
It will grow and never slow up,
For one day of rain
Will many a day of sun mess up,
And for a weekend of fun,
All you can do is wish that it had been done.

Alan Schroeder
Marshall High School
Marshall
Grade 10

A Mother

She is a part of me, and together we are whole
She is a piece of my puzzle of life
Without her I am incomplete.
A guardian from danger,
Yet she shows me joy.
She knows the path of the world better than I,
And strives to guide me through.
My friend, she is,
And together we share our feelings.
I am a rose and she is my stem.
I am a sapling and she is the sun.
I am the student
And she is the teacher in the class of life.
She puts her life into me
And therefore I succeed.
A friend; A teacher; A guide.
I am her and she is me.
She
is my mother.

Marci Fiedler
Ida Crown Jewish Academy
Chicago
Grade 10

The Pond

Peering into a pond one day,
I saw the image of a stub nosed turtle.
She smiled at me and went on her way
But where do turtles go on holiday?

With this the mallard replied, "Quack,"
And he took off on his own journey.
I pondered his response and was taken aback,
Where do mallards go to get back on track?

The answers to my questions are simple!!
After the turtle has taken her break,
She walks home without a quarrel.
For she knows happiness lies in every ripple.

The mallard too cannot avoid his place
He flies back home lacking a quibble.
He missed his life and many a smiling face.
It is his home that he longs to embrace!!

Now, you may question my rational
I know nothing about their past course.
But does that matter at all,
If I know that they are again joyful?

Brian Krueger
Schaumburg High School
Schaumburg
Grade 11

Some Days

Some days I feel like flying
Other days I feel like dying
Some days I am happy
Other days I am snappy
Some days I am ready to go
Other days I just don't know
Some days I feel like walking
Other days I feel like talking
Some days I really don't care
Other days I am on a dare
Some days I have no fun
Other days I get nothing done
Some days I am so clever and cool
Other days I am just a funny fool
But everyday I am so grateful
Because I am beautiful, colorful,
Delightful, graceful, peaceful,
And not to mention bountiful!

Tim Degner
Grant Community High School
Fox Lake
Grade 12

Nicole

Soft and sweet she is to me
Beautiful from inside to out
Making the world smile
Never in her mind one doubt
Her positive words and feelings
Encouragement to the final end
Being the best to me and the world
Being everyone's best friend

Justin Carlson
Newark Community High School
Newark
Grade 12

Winter

I hate winter more than any season.
I do not like it, here is the reason.
I like the heat. I hate the cold.
I bet it will be twice as bad when I'm old.

When winter comes I want to cry.
It makes me wish that I would die,
Or at least move to a warmer place.
Winter, I never want to see your face.

I wish that I could go far away,
To a place where it is warm all day,
And where I would never have to greet
Another flake of snow or sleet.

Scott Holman
Beardstown Sr High School
Beardstown
Grade 12

Melted Expression

The life slid out of her as he broke the news:
"I'm sorry."
Her arms hung limp at her side.
She could not clench her small, delicate hand;
Her throat tightened into a large lump.
The crimson blush in her cheeks faded to a pale white.
A large rubber mallet hammered at her heart.
She stared down at his old gym shoes tossed in the corner.
Her own breath remained still in her throat.
He gave her a sympathetic look, but he could not *know* the pain.
He had not lost his son.
He could not understand.

Kate Serling
Prospect High School
Mount Prospect
Grade 12

Loneliness

Droplets of water, descend from the dark sky
Silence is overthrown by the pitter patter of rain
Clouds loom over my head
My clothes, soaked by the rain, made my body feel cold and dead
I dropped to my knees and let out a scream that sounds for miles
No one hears my cry for help
The blood gushes from the wound in my side
I feel light-headed and dizzy, my vision is corrupted
There is no feeling left in my hands and legs
I fall face forward into a puddle
I have no memory of anything after that
Everything is black

Adam Thompson
Newark Community High School
Newark
Grade 11

Storm

laughter and small talk cease to exist
thunder is heard in the distance
an ever familiar mustiness becomes apparent to me once again
(you know that smell before the rain)
the scratchy, confined feeling jogs his memory
my plastic face that once held everything together
is lost in the darkness
lightning flashes reveal the sad eyes of truth
glances of understanding replace words of nonsense,
and entire conversations are held in silence
tears turn into rain, and through the storm his hand appears
I know it will be comforting, but I can barely touch his fingertips
the flood washes me away, and my arms are too short
the water becomes numbing, and my insides begin to melt
in the distance I see the silhouette of a man in a familiar plaid jacket,
and he saves me from myself

Cassandra Hatzfeld
Plainfield High School
Plainfield
Grade 12

The Day

Before I went to lunch I went to my locker
Concerning my friends they went with me.
Along with my buddies we went to lunch
Among ourselves we were talking.
After walking to lunch we got in line
But the line was very long.
In front of the line there were other friends.
Regarding other people they were not happy because we cut
Near me a friend said, "Don't worry."
Until security caught me and got me out of line.

Ruben Ruiz
Morton East High School
Cicero
Grade 12

Sailing Away

An inch wide, a hundred feet long
Tiny in comparison, yet how very strong.
I bring in your catch, I tie down your sail
For hundreds of years you've relied on my skill
I'm fragile, yet tough, but forget me not
Columbus couldn't even sail without me in his thoughts.
Blackbeard could not commit so many crimes
Without me coiled together like a pile of slime.
I fit together in my own special slot,
Tying it all together with life's invisible knot.

Michael Piskule
Morton High School
Morton
Grade 12

Butterflies

God has hope to offer,
All sons and daughters receive,
Together boldly flying on a Chrysalis,
We've learned to trust and believe,
And to rely on Him throughout our lives.
We show Christ like butterflies.

God has faith to offer,
Faith like a grain of mustard seed.
We're a beam of light in the darkness,
Lights that never face, faith that takes heed.
And for those who are lost or afraid,
There are Christians that shine the light of God.

Receive all you can for your future.
Hold on and never let go of love,
For one little seed of love planted in one person,
Helps many see the beauty of Christ like a dove,
And for a life full of faith, hope, and love,
Receive all you can of God, or reject it.

Jaleigh Dennis
Marshall High School
Marshall
Grade 10

Things Change

I thought you were the one I want.
But I have been mistaken.
You gave me love that's so untrue.
I feel it's time to move apart.
I know it seems very selfish
How can I help the way I feel
I'm not the kind of person to be and stay in love
Face the fact we're way too young.
You know others will be along
I guess there is no easy way.
We should have guessed it would happen
This is not for some other guy
I've got a change in feeling
I'm afraid of commitment
But also afraid of loneliness
My life is such a mess
I feel so confused
I don't know what to do
If we stay together I'll only hurt you.
It is so hard to tell you how I feel.
Though you'll always hold a place in my heart.

Amanda Turley
Tri-City Jr-Sr High School
Buffalo
Grade 10

Sociability

Sociability has friendliness to share,
All nice and splendid things to say,
Silently, peacefully on a summer evening,
They think of things that rhyme and sway,
And share with each other stories of the past,
Reaching for thoughts like a fisherman throwing his cast.

Sociability has friendliness to share,
Laughing like a child of a younger age,
Talking of thoughts in the heart,
Hands that grab you after that turn of the page,
And for the thanks of thoughtful wishes in the night,
Courage that gives the body strength and might.

Be friendly all you can for kindness,
Be sweet and never change a single positive thought,
For one spoken word of kindness,
Causes many an abundance of presents well bought,
And for an utterance of kind words,
Speak all your happy thoughts, or wishes.

Jenny Fouts
Marshall High School
Marshall
Grade 10

El Cielo

"Soy el cielo,
Clear and lonely as
An empty glass.
Yet full of galaxies.

I'm magical and moody,
Wonderful and mysterious
As Pandora's Box.

I am dark.
I am bright.
All depending
On the light.

One star here.
One star there.
Stars surround me,
They're everywhere."

Take a look at my cielo
One last time,
And find the figures
Of future life.

Leslie Palma
Schurz High School
Chicago
Grade 11

Mirror, Mirror on the Wall. . .

Do you lie to us all?
Do you abuse your power and distort what's real?
Could we really be walking around with the wrong image of ourselves?
Our perception on everything would change drastically.

Do you abuse your power and distort what's real?
How would we know the truth about images seen in you?
Our perception on everything would change drastically.
You'd be labeled a nasty liar. . .

How would we know the truth about images seen in you?
If day after day we are lied to by you
You'd be labeled a nasty liar. . .
And people would throw things at you out of rage

If day after day we are lied to by you
Your job would be done
And people would throw things at you out of rage
Pack your bags you lousy mirror— You're through!

Your job would be done
Your once indispensable job would be useless
Pack your bags you lousy mirror— You're through!
CRASH!

Courtney Wade
Fenwick High School
Oak Park
Grade 11

I Wish I Knew...

I wish I knew a special poem,
    that I could say to you,
You'd listen and smile,
    and think of us,
And how we fit as one.

Joined at the hip,
    joined at the heart,
This poem would tell the truth,
    of how I feel,
And how I loved,
    every moment I spent with you.

I wish I knew a special song,
    that I could sing to you.
Of love and war,
    and something much more.

About the way I feel,
    my heart so heavy.
My soul so empty,
    and all I can do,
Is think of you.

Julie Martin
Durand High School
Durand
Grade 12

Vehicles

Vehicles have people to carry,
    All shapes, colors and sizes,
    Racing quickly down a highway,
    A highway that falls and rises,
    And how fast they all whiz by
Like an airplane in the vast open sky.

Vehicles have packages to carry,
    Things like Christmas presents from Uncle Fred,
    A mountain of suitcases in the trunk,
Packages that make noise and some that smell like freshly baked bread,
    And much to the driver's delight,
There is a chance he will reach his destination, before the fall of night.

Remember all you can from these journeys,
    Enjoy the ride and try to never fight,
    For one road trip of pleasure,
    Brings many a passenger memories of delight,
    And for all the trips yet to come
Take time to remember all you have seen, all you have done.

Jason Parks
Marshall High School
Marshall
Grade 10

Perfection

Perfection has many levels to climb,
Some hard and others easy,
Few have it, while most don't,
Strive for your goals that are far and short,
And you may practice very hard,
Doesn't mean you'll play the winning card.

Perfection has steps to climb,
Just like a ladder of tests,
Blocks of failure in the way,
Play all that you can, but make sure that you rest,
And for those that have rough times,
Remember that practice is the key to success.

Make all you can of it, for it may not last,
Enjoy it and never regret it,
For one glimpse of perfection,
For many may not make it,
And for a few who may,
Make all you can of it.

Dustin Kile
Marshall High School
Marshall
Grade 10

Lost

As the dagger pierces my heart,
I bleed for love–
For love that I can never return.
Friends who needed me,
And me not able to give them a hand.
As I lay here dying,
I know true happiness–
Friends before and friends long ago.
I had the perfect life–
Love and happiness were mine.
And then, in the blink of an eye,
The beat of a lonely heart–
They were gone.
I know he yearned for love–
Love that I could not give,
For my lonely heart knew only loneliness–
Not love or happiness but hate and despair.
He was my brother who,
At last I turned away.
There he died alone and sad–
Knowing that I was all he had.

Seth Miles
Payson Seymour High School
Payson
Grade 12

Journey into the Imagination

Come fly on the wings of a dragon,
Into the depths of your imagination.
Where starlit pools ripple and gleam,
And the moon beams, into a fallen stream.
The airborne dolphins leap and cry,
In noble attempts to touch the sky.
I soar high above them, flying fast;
Set free from present, future and past.

Kelly Smith
Marian Central Catholic High School
Woodstock
Grade 12

Angels

Angels have wings to polish,
All shiny and sparkling bright.
While floating softly on a cloud,
Watching below that day and night.
And guarding the children as they play,
Shining from above like a sun ray.

Angels have wings to polish,
Halos like a circle of gold,
Heavens of beauty in the sky,
Thankful we are watched over and we are not cold.
And for the guardian angels floating above,
That look out for the ones we love.

Watch all you can for angels that fly.
Look up and never grab their wing.
For an angel of love,
Has many a song of praise to sing.
And for an angel who looks over
All you hope for, or hoped for.

Malerie Harper
Marshall High School
Marshall
Grade 10

I Hate You So Much

I hate you so much right now...
for always making me angry
I hate you so much right now...
for always putting me down
I hate you so much right now...
for always putting me aside
I hate you so much right now...
for never paying attention to me
I hate you so much right now...
for never believing in me
But most of all I hate you so much, so much
for being my mother and never loving me...

Maria Palacios
Bowen High School
Chicago
Grade 12

If These Walls Could Talk
If these walls could talk...
To whom they might talk to would be shocked.
The walls would speak of who I am, who I want to be, the things I do, and
the things I wish I could take back.
If these walls could talk, I would be in trouble for the things I did and said.
It's a good thing the walls can't talk.
But the walls can listen, better then any other friend.
I can trust the walls with all my secrets and thoughts.
Because I know for a fact, that the walls can't talk.

Lauren Strozewski
Grant Community High School
Fox Lake
Grade 11

The Autumn After
In the autumn after
The leaves turn beautiful shades of purple, gold, and red
They glisten in the midday sun
As you let their leaves reflect sunlight onto your face
When the light hits them just right, they turn silver, silver like that of a new quarter
They tell you that winter is coming
Autumn leaves slowly begin to fall
All their beautiful colors fall, fall, fall
Winter is here now
They have been blown away by October's cold chill
Spring comes
Summer passes by
Ah yes, it is autumn again
Only can you see a sight like this
Only in the autumn after

Heather White
Central Community High School
Breese
Grade 10

The Life of a High School Student (And You Thought Being a Teenager Is Easy)
I can't take this pressure anymore!
From term papers to history notes; homework is a burden.
After school activities take up too much of my time, but I can't back out of a commitment.
If you make one mistake, there is always someone there looking down upon you.
To try to relieve some of the stress in my life,
I try to make plans for Friday night which normally fall through.
And that is not the least of my problems.

I have to worry about my grades, my future, and what college I want to attend.
I wish I could go back to preschool; my most complicated problem was picking out a toy to play with.
My life was simple and easy.

NAP TIME! What a wonderful word.
Now I am so sleep deprived because of my many responsibilities; plus I have to meet many expectations.
In preschool, I was only expected to learn the alphabet and get along with other children.
Now I am supposed to be valedictorian, get into an Ivy League University, and deal with life.
The pressure is TOO MUCH!

Lisa Marie Haas
Schaumburg High School
Schaumburg
Grade 11

Vision

This vision of mine,
It was clear in my mind.
It played over and over; it was trapped in my mind.
I saw flashes of light and colors of brilliancy,
Things I could have never imagined occurred.
It was magnificent, marvelous, amazing as can be.
It was a dream come true, all that I wanted to see.
I would tell you this vision honestly,
But there is one problem you see.
When I awoke it was gone,
This vision of mine.

Amit Bhambri
Schaumburg High School
Schaumburg
Grade 11

Fight

It starts out like any other conversation.
Then it changes
To something more.
Provoked by a word or an idea—heated words.
I tire of it all
And close my eyes to the world.
He gets mad
And slams out the door.
I flinch at the sound
But I know
He's coming back
Because it's his house.
And the irony of it all
It's usually over
Something stupid.

Jennifer M. Bangert
Clay City High School
Clay City
Grade 11

When a Wish Comes True

I wish I could spend forever with you,
If I had one wish that's what I would do,
I wish you knew how much I think of you,
If I told you that, you would know my feelings are true.

When I wake up in the morning, you're always on my mind,
When I go to bed in the evening, I wish you to be mine,
When I'm alone and feeling down,
You somehow manage to bring me around.

I love to take you out and show you the town,
When we're together there's never a frown,
I wanted to let you know wishes do come true,
Ashli, I love you.

Jeffrey Garofolo
Webber Township High School
Bluford
Grade 12

What I Like

I like to sleep I like to walk
I like to eat I like to talk
I like to sing I like to dance
I like to give new things a chance
I like to look beyond the skin
And see what's waiting deep within
I like my family I like my friends
I like summer days that never end
I like the sun I like the stars
I like the privilege of driving a car
I like to laugh I like to daydream
I like the icy trees glistening through golden sunbeams
I like cookies I like shoes
I like the trips we took to the zoo
I like to win I like TV
I like it when my mom makes me tea
I like to hug I like to shop
As you can see I like a lot

Ashley Hopp
Newark Community High School
Newark
Grade 10

The Gift of Life

Donate an organ
You could save a life.
Give a dying man
One last pitch.

Surmount all the fear
And think of the pure joy
Of knowing a small piece of you,
Will live on in someone else.

I don't want to point fingers,
Or harass about what you should do
But think about that one dying man,
And what you could do for him.

You could give that person
The wonderful opportunities in life;
To walk, to run, to live again.
The wonderful things we take for granted.

What if you were that one dying man
Wouldn't you want someone to appear
To care enough to give you the greatest gift of all;
The gift of life!

Steve Amstutz
Morton High School
Morton
Grade 11

The Sun in the Sky

The sun in the sky
The light of the stars
The shape of the moon
Or the belt around Mars

Is nothing compared
To the way I see you
The way that you smile
The things that you do

You make me happy
I'd never be sad
If I lost everything
And you're all I had

Brad Cearlock
Vandalia Comm High School
Vandalia
Grade 11

Children

Children are the hope of this world.
We need them if we want to survive;
We need to protect their innocence
And not let go without a fight.
Children have such simple faith;
We need to be more like them.
Those who can keep it will go on,
They'll make it to the end.
Why can't people understand,
The need of our children today;
To build and help and nourish them,
And keep them going the right way?

Elizabeth G. Smith
Kankakee Trinity Academy
Kankakee
Grade 12

Free Spirit

Running wild and free,
With no where else I would rather be.
Living in the moment,
With nothing to hold me back.
Containing a unique and special spirit,
That no one else can capture.
Wandering through the torrents of life,
Hoping and waiting for some relief.
But keeping a smile and walking tall.
Living life for all it's worth.
Now I am laying down a path,
On which will rise a legacy.
With more than a cloud of dust,
To follow me when I'm gone.

Ashley Henrichs
Christ Lutheran High School
Buckley
Grade 10

A Fragment of Your Imagination

In a fragment of your imagination
you see whites, blacks, Asians, and Jews holding hands.
You picture children growing up happy and safe
and able to play in their own backyards without fear.
You see no poverty in the streets;
everyone has enough food to last them years.
You see all criminals caught in their own acts of stupidity
and you see them thrown into dark cells where they will live the rest of their lives.
You picture public schools as a place where kids can go
to learn and expand their minds, a place where kids can fit in and make friends.
You believe that all people have the capability of knowing right and wrong.
You see racism and prejudice as acts of the past.
You see the government as truthful and fair,
a machine that cleans up the world and unites all.
You see some goodness in every person.
And you see every person, man, woman, and child, black, white,
and everything in between, holding hands,
rejoicing in and sharing the laughter of happiness and love.
But all this, my friend, is merely a fragment of your imagination.

Amy Lazar
Schaumburg High School
Schaumburg
Grade 11

twilight

standing at the edge of my driveway,
where it is neither day, nor night,
i look up at the darkening sky,
now sprinkled with stars. it is twilight.

facing the heavens, how infinite i feel.
the beauty of the in-between
surrounds me, envelopes me,
the flaming reds, streaks left over from the setting sun,
fade into deep purples and indigos.

the breeze, alive, blows in and through me,
it takes out the stresses of the day
to tangle with the silhouettes on the cement

the hair untucks itself from behind my ear
to dance with the breeze upon my face.
it brushes my nose, and into my eyes,
but i let it dance, feeling the music within.

the sprinkled stars in the purple haze pour reflections into my eyes,
each eye embracing a separate universe.
i close my eyes, and they go unharmed, galaxies away
i am here, on my driveway where it is neither day, nor night.
it is twilight.

Alyssa Grenning
Schaumburg High School
Schaumburg
Grade 11

Flowers

Flowers have colors to look at,
All pretty and delightful ones,
Standing very tall in a pasture,
Like flowers that move and twist,
And dancing with the wind
Swaying back and forth like a rocking chair.

Flowers have colors to look at,
They are like a field of dreams,
Dreams of actors in the movies,
Pine trees that smell, and that move,
And for your eyes to focus on,
Flowers that stand out like the sun.

Enjoy all you can see for blind
Can't see it and never take advantage;
For one flower of the world
Can brighten many a places of the world well done,
And for a glance at the nature
Enjoy all you see, or smell.

Ashley Dill
Marshall High School
Marshall
Grade 10

For My Mother

A mother has love to give,
All she says and everything she has done.
Helps you out on a bad day.
You look at all that she has done
And you feel you have won.
And when you see her down,
You are there to help her not frown.

A mother has love to give,
She's like a friend of old,
She helps you out of the storm of life,
Arms that love, hands that hold,
And for all the times she makes you laugh
And want to hold on tight,
Just like the movie you two watched last night.

Share all the love you have for your mother,
Show it and never be afraid of it,
For one thing you need all of your life is a mother,
And many days of your life you will think it is well worth it,
And for a mother like her,
You will have all you want, or need.

Leslie Hendrix
Marshall High School
Marshall
Grade 10

You Are My God Given Angel

My life revolves around you!
God put us together and that is how we met!
How does it feel to be an angel sent from heaven
To be with me?
I love you so and he knew to send you to me!
You are the angel I want to be with!
That will never change!
You will always be my God given angel!

Marci Allen
Milford Township High School
Milford
Grade 12

Cancer

After 2 weeks the doctor gave us the bad news
About my grandfather, he had cancer
With my grandfather was all of our family
Without thinking we went to another doctor
Together with the doctor we talked to grandfather
For some test the nurse took blood
In one week they started the surgery
Since that day we cry and got together
To give my grandfather new hope for life
Since that day we started to fight against cancer
Along with other doctors we are fighting,
To get more time for my grandfather.
Against cancer we are fighting.

Jose Baltierrez
Morton East High School
Cicero
Grade 12

What Is Left

Hope slips away
Elusive
Sliding like oil
Skimming along on the crest of a puddle.

Hope flies away
Unobtrusive
Gliding like a hawk
Soaring beyond, supported by the singing wind.

Hope trickles away
Exclusive
Draining swiftly like water
Oozing away through grains of sand.

And what more is left
When hope is gone
Than a wet oil spot
On a dropped hawk's plume?

Kearney Gunsalus
Urbana High School
Urbana
Grade 10

For Molly

What causes a teardrop to fall
Tracing it's way down a cheek
Like spilled milk dripping to the floor

Is it pain of the body
Of the mind
Of the heart
Of the soul

The loss of a
Death of a
Pain of a
Friend

What causes a teardrop to fall
Tracing it's way down a cheek
Like spilled milk dripping to the floor

It is life
It is memory

Jessica Anderson
Evanston Township High School
Evanston
Grade 12

I Was Once Told. . .

I was once told that
if you believe in yourself so much,
you can do anything.
I was once told that
if you love someone so much,
you had to let them go,
and if it comes back,
you know it's yours.
I was once told that
if you stop willing,
stop hating,
stop desiring,
you could truly find peace.
I was once told that
with true love comes
a happy ending.
I was once told that
we would be friends forever.
I was never told that
you would leave.

Erik Olson
Newark Community High School
Newark
Grade 10

Silence

I'm quiet.
I lie still with my hands
Folded over my chest.
And as I watch
My friends, my family
Pass by.
One by one—
I cry,
But I'm quiet.

I'm silent.
I drift over
Land and water,
Leaving my potted prison.
And as I pass
Over the place I lived,
The places I've loved—
I cry.
But I'm silent

I'm settling in the grass—the very grass
I used to tread—
And there's silence.

Reece DeFrees
Lanphier High School
Springfield
Grade 11

Playing with Fire

You play with fire.
You grow weary of our warnings,
But I can't stop thinking:
One day you'll get burned.

Burned, but how badly?
What will it take?
How great will the scar have to be?
How deep will it need to run?

Run so deep that you never forget?
Is that what you need?
It pains me to see you, dear one.
Oh! How my heart hurts!

It hurts with your pain,
That pain that I know you feel
In the secret place where you cry,
And no one knows but I.

For I know your tears;
They are my own.
Your fears are mine, too.
Please, dear one, come home.

Gracey Amico
Marian Central Catholic High School
Woodstock
Grade 12

That Heavenly Night

To dream is pure heaven,
To love is pure bliss,
And when I close my eyes,
I simply think of this ...

A sweet romantic evening
With my true love right here,
We sit out by the pond
And the moon and stars appear.

As we warmly embrace,
We take a sideways glance,
And see the moon and stars
Putting on a dance.

The moon is in the center
With stars on either side,
They dance a slow waltz
Haste is not applied.

As we lovingly look skyward,
Together we unite,
That when the moon and stars dance,
How romantic is that night!

Rhonda Small
Christ Lutheran High School
Buckley
Grade 10

Modern Chivalry

No heroes remain in my world
They are extinct
I have wandered too far out of our
Current culture of extremes

The demons rip out my heart
But no one will come to my aid
They replace it with machinery
Trying to convert me
To the iron-laden technologized society
Striving to demean my humanity

Every being that enters its boundaries
Succumbs to its demands
But I will not let it.
In one sweeping act of desperation
I resort to the brutal force of nature
To abet me

I have been spared
But it will not salvage all!

Chris Gross
Loyola Academy
Wilmette
Grade 11

Heavenly Creature

Lift your soul and be free,
Release the ties that bind you to this earth,
Rise up to heaven and protect us with your love.
From your heavenly domain.

We love you and we'll miss you,
But you have been called upon
By a higher power than our love for you.

Be happy, because we are happy,
That you have risen to heights that you deserve,
Wait for us in heaven,
Because one day we will see you again.

Go with God and live your eternal life
As a heavenly creature.

Shawna Simmons
South Central High School
Farina
Grade 10

I Said No

It was in my face, it really was,
I said no just because...
You brought me up right mom, you and dad,
I really didn't want to make you guys mad.
They really wanted me to try it,
Someone even had it lit.
They all encouraged me a lot,
They wanted me to smoke some pot.
Everyone laughed and called me names,
They all had their fun and games.
I thought about what you guys told me, so...
Mom and dad, I said no.

Emilie Schilling
Gibault Catholic High School
Waterloo
Grade 11

Drifting in Dreams

Quietly, in the darkness, drifting in dreams,
Glittering in stars, chase endless moonbeams,
And while the moon crosses the velvet black sky,
Thoughts of you in mind, in sleep I sigh.
Drifting away in deepening silence, the night,
Your arms still around me, holding me tight,
We are so far apart, but our souls touch so near.
Barely a whisper, in dreams, your gentle voice I hear.
Comes the dawn, I awaken, unfolds the new day.
I've been drifting in dreams, the whole night away.
The morning sun rises, roses kissed by dew.
I've been drifting in dreams... just loving you.

Linsey Schnepper
Clay City High School
Clay City
Grade 10

The Gift of Love

Love cradles you in its arms.
It rocks you to sleep
And puts your mind at ease.
Comfort, security, and trust.

Love rocks your boat.
It scares you
And changes your whole life.
Vulnerability and fear.

Love tells you all its secrets.
It opens you up to touch
Another's soul.
Clarity, honesty, and freedom.

Love takes away your map.
It confuses you
And clouds your thoughts.
Wonder and confusion.

Love takes us in its palm and changes us.
We grow, we feel, we experience, we live.
Nothing impacts us so much as the gift of love.

Marinne Lorch
Marian Central Catholic High School
Woodstock
Grade 12

Deep in Thought

In my mind I gaze at your eyes
To see the sadness, I then sigh
Deep in thought
I wish I would have caught
All those memories in my mind
I rewind those times
Hoping to get one last glimpse of you
But as they closed the casket
I knew that you were so cold and blue
I didn't want to leave you
But I knew I had to
And as they anchored you into the ground
I fell down and started to cry
Deep in thought I will forever keep you
You were my love
But now the time has come
To say good-bye
And to put all my anger aside
Deep in thought you will forever be mine

Ashley Browning
Willowbrook High School
Villa Park
Grade 11

You Don't Know Me

When
you see me sitting quietly
Like a exceedingly still snake
Don't think I'm acting funny
I'm just keeping to myself.

When
you see me looking cheerless
Like a little lost child
Don't think I just want attention
I'm just thinking of old times.

When
you see me smiling and laughing
Like a kid getting tickled
Don't think I'm being goofy
I'm just trying to cover up pain.

Don't assume you know what's going on with me.
Don't assume you know my pain.
Don't assume you know me.
You really don't know me or my pain.

TaSheka Jones
Perspectives Charter School
Chicago
Grade 11

Live for Today

Sometimes I want to turn back time
Things were so much simpler then
We can't go back, we can only move forward
Live for today.

Things were so much simpler then
The memories will stay with me forever
I'll try to live for today
But the future is so uncertain.

The memories will stay with me forever
I don't know what's up ahead
The future is so uncertain
What is meant to be, will be.

Sometimes I want to turn back time
I don't know what's up ahead
What is meant to be, will be
We can't go back, we can only move forward
So I'll live for today!

Elizabeth Parr
Marian Central Catholic High School
Woodstock
Grade 12

Rolling Stones

You can't always get what you want
Seems like a reoccurrence that
Happens in everyone's life

You can't always get what you want
Should be a motivation
For what you want no matter what the odds

You can't always get what you want
Could also be a sign
That it wasn't meant to be

You can't always get what you want
But by living up to your full potential
You might get what you need

Adam Szudarski
Marian Central Catholic High School
Woodstock
Grade 12

Shades of Paradise

The paradise that they paint into my pupils untouched
is the yellow of sun
the orange
the silky red of autumn leaves
about to blow over.
so flicker, flicker
little candle on the window sill
spill your contents into me;
the flame and wax and every other part
which lets you light up
all embroidered corners.
The things doting on this world all end
Even candles bend
and I long to find a friend who sees
the blueness which the eyes behold.
Welcome to rustling skirts and champagne and paper smiles.
Welcome to paradise.

Olga Levinzon
Niles North High School
Skokie
Grade 11

The Race

To start the engine I turned the key,
Before I knew it, I was in the lead.
My gauges read hot,
But I felt the need to proceed.
I looked in my rear view, and saw my opponent,
No matter what could happen, this was my moment.
I kicked it into fifth, and dumped the clutch,
I looked in my mirror and didn't see much.

Jared Friestad
Newark Community High School
Newark
Grade 10

Attention

When my soul begins to speak
I go and sit down in a pink-gray theater
with sticky floors
The ceiling a white hard soundproof barrier
Stereos on each side of my head
Watching through my eyes the play
around me

Felicia Stodden
Marian Catholic High School
Chicago Heights
Grade 10

1984 – Bilbo Butterbean

We have lost to the strong;
All freedoms and personal privacy,
Are meagerly eyes on a dish,
Cold and primitive, that slows and stops,
And begins to fall to the floor
Like a carved stone.

The Party has ideals to imprint,
To form us like a pile of sand,
Minds of hollow people in the still world,
Repeat that which they were told, that which has always been.
And for protection, we were petrified,
In a forest that narrows the path set before us.

Life for all who cry for freedom,
Stay and never turn back,
For one that rebels of the party
Has many a torture of mind well ahead
And for a time you will live,
Until all you have is life, or forfeit.

Jim Bumpus
Marshall High School
Marshall
Grade 10

Fog

Thick, sharp, dark, obscure
It's aroma surrounds me
I feel my hairs stand on end
My mind jumps
My heart races
turning turning twisting wriggling confusion
where am I?
I am lost, that is all
the fog closes in
Suddenly, I feel no more
I fall to the ground
My eyes close
The fog lifts

Kristen Kaminski
Schaumburg High School
Schaumburg
Grade 11

We Get What We Give

Do you know who died today?
The crowd sits in the church, patiently
With frowns turned upside down.

Do you know who died today?
No one knows the answer, or asks
Except the one painted up in a fake mask.

Do you know who died today?
She had so many hopes,
And so many dreams.

Do you know who died today?
It was too soon
And this wasn't meant to be.

Do you know who died today?
Do you take thee?
Now say the vows.

Do *you* know who died today?
Me, with the sparkling gown knows.
And a part of my soul is left unknown.

Crystal Shevlin
Coulterville High School
Coulterville
Grade 12

John Deere: the Green Machine

John Deere tractors have power to spare,
All green and yellow outside,
Huge tires spinning on a wet field.
Mud sticking that flips and flies.
And this all happens while listening to the music of Hi-99
It sounds like a good thing to me.

John Deere tractors have power to spare,
Beautiful like a flower of gold,
The smell of dirt in the field,
Tires that hold you, engines that pull,
And for your hearts desire,
Diesel smoke that fills the night.

Give all you have for happiness,
Stay green and don't buy red;
For one mistake will make a lot of regret,
Count many a year of money well spent.
And for a good life,
Do all you can, or you will lose out.

Aaron Farris
Marshall High School
Marshall
Grade 10

The Opening

Through the opening
I never saw anything so bright
Like the flash from a camera
It lasted all night
With warmth it tantalized
This thirsty soul of mine
At last I realized
The purpose of my life
To shine

Will Zingrone
Marian Central Catholic High School
Woodstock
Grade 12

Untitled

White — the bones of creation
That engulfs a golden heart
Which may be touched
By only the gentlest
Flighty creature.
The foundation of its existence
Lies solely on one small stem.
With limbs that branch out.
Reaching towards the sky,
Towards the celestial beings.
But even its beauty
Cannot defy nature.
The icy glares will fall
From the descending heavens.
Its structure wilts: dies
And becomes the earth
It once thrived in.

Corin Potor
Mascoutah High School
Mascoutah
Grade 10

Lost in Love

Your eyes are like the ocean,
Pulling me in deep,
Just seeing you today,
Is like a vision in my sleep.

Your beauty shows around you,
Touching everyone,
Now you've got me thinking,
You could be the one.

Now I think I've fallen,
Deep in thoughts of you,
But I can't stop wondering,
Do you feel it too?

Kyle Shreffler
Clay City High School
Clay City
Grade 11

Waiting

Every morning my grandmother sits quietly
on the balcony outside her apartment,
sipping her coffee and nibbling her toast—a ritual.

She watches the waves repeatedly splash
against the rocky shore
they are completely predictable, dependable.

Casting her gaze over these youthful, immortal waves,
she longs for a comparable life
and yet she knows that as each day progresses,
her days dwindle.

When her presence has vanished,
when the balcony remains barren, the coffee unmade, and the toast uneaten,
the waves will still be splashing against the rocky shore
for they are completely predictable, dependable.

Emily Jacobs
Charleston High School
Charleston
Grade 12

Friendship

Friends are people just like you.
Real friends know how to make you smile when you are feeling blue.

A true friend is someone you can trust
with all of your secrets.

Friendship is a gift from God
and should not be taken for granted.

Friendship is worth more
than any piece of gold or silver.

Friends know just what to say
when there is nothing to say.

Friendship is so precious
that it cannot happen overnight.

Friendship must be handled with care
for at times, it can be sensitive.

Friendship can always make you laugh
even when nothing is funny.

Friendship is a blessing
and I am blessed with so many wonderful friendships.

Kendra Becherer
Althoff Catholic High School
Belleville
Grade 12

Friends Forever

Friends forever, you promised.
Always together, right?
You were always by my side.
We took friendship to new heights.

When I was sad, you hurried near.
When I was stressed, you calmed my fear.
When I needed a shoulder to cry on, you were there.
You could always fix the tear.

You were my best friend.
Always knew the right words to say.
You made everything seem okay.
As long as we were together,
Our problems would be put aside.

But somewhere along the line,
He came into your life.
He was always on your mind,
You didn't have time for me anymore.

Losing your friendship made me cry.
Things are changing though.
And I am moving on,
But you will *always* be my friend.

Erin Meirink
Althoff Catholic High School
Belleville
Grade 12

Music

Music has melodies to weave,
With a gentle and flowing gait,
Sweet voices lifting on a strain,
Deep tones that sing and resonate.
Big and showy or very small,
Crashing waves like a waterfall.

Music has harmonies to sing,
Ominous like a dark rain,
Flashes of lightning in the night,
Winds that blow, sobs of pain,
And for your spirit's quiet delight,
Stars that shine through the clouds of night.

Give all you have for music,
Make it first and never last,
For one moment of beauty,
Spend many an hour of practice well past.
And for the satisfaction it will give you,
Give up all you know, or knew.

Sarah Marrs
Marshall High School
Marshall
Grade 10

Sanity in Insanity

I'm insane.
I hear voices in my head, you see.
They are my parents, my teachers, the commercials on TV,
and countless others.
They tell me to do things.
They tell me what music to listen to,
what clothes to wear, and to get ready for college.
I hear them all the time,
with my ears and in my sleep.
The maddening collage of voices
is always there, whispering in one ear,
screaming in the other.
I must know the nature of this situation.
The voices get so angry
when I don't do what they say.
I realize that they are legion, and they are many,
but I'm not too worried.
I am who I am, and with this realization
they have no power over me.

Joshua Dearing
Quincy Notre Dame High School
Quincy
Grade 12

Mob Love

A friend in need is a friend indeed,
Or so the saying goes,
But the truth is in the type of help
Given against the mightiest foes.

When the heart is attacked by the average Joe,
Broken to pieces by the tease,
True friends step up and let everyone know
Joey will swim with the fishes.

If a cat chooses to pounce on dignity,
Claws out and hissing false cries,
The loyal ones put out the word.
The kitty will pay for her lies.

It's nice to know that someone's there
To lend a hand through trouble's blame,
But the real comrades will give an arm
To help shift what's inside the frame.

The ones that'll push, see the light through it all,
On their hearts you can depend.
They'll make the last effort, they'll take the shot,
In the action till the very end.

They will always be the forever friends.

Angela Corpus
Schaumburg High School
Schaumburg
Grade 11

A Beautiful Me and You

My eyes had not seen
Until I saw you
My skies were gray
And rarely ever blue
My heart would beat
But my soul was not there
You are the angel
That answered my prayer
Your eyes shine so bright
Your smile shows your soul
My heart now does love
And this I sure know
The day that we met
I knew it was true
There was always meant to be
A beautiful me and you

My heart you shall hold
In the palm of your hand

Adam Williams
Indian Creek High School
Shabbona
Grade 10

If I Had...

Innocence
But no childhood
Sleep
But no dreams
A name
But no personality
A face
But no beauty
Age
But no wisdom
Life
But no purpose
I had nothing.

Dina Rachford
Marian Central Catholic High School
Woodstock
Grade 12

Seasons

The winter snow is all but gone
Kids now play out in the sun
School gets out very soon
We know this by the flowers' bloom
After winter comes the spring
Insects will sting and birds will sing
Every year without reasons
Comes wonderful changes in our seasons

Anthony Mitchell
Althoff Catholic High School
Belleville
Grade 12

Stories

Everyone has a story to tell,
All unique and special tales,
Of love found on a summer's day,
Of he who tries and fails,
And maybe he can say it all with just a look
Because you can read his face just like a book.

Everyone has a story to tell,
Memories like a movie of the past,
Thoughts of your one day in the sun,
Days that come but never seem to last,
And for those who would rather forget,
Decisions made that didn't seem to fit.

And all you can do for yourself,
Is remember and never regret your life,
For one memory of happiness
Makes up for many a hardship of days past, and is well worth the strife,
And for a life worthy of admiration
It is all you can do to live up to your potential and his dedication.

J.C. Howard
Marshall High School
Marshall
Grade 10

gathered water splashes when disturbed

the rain rolls down the window as the car drives down the street
    and the puddles on the road are disturbed

the tears roll down the cheek of the child with swollen stomach
    but the ones who've not known hunger aren't disturbed
the lies roll from the tongues of those caring just for self
    but not a single ear that hears them is disturbed
when it doesn't cumulate fast enough or pile up high enough
    then the ones who truly want for nothing are disturbed

leaves fall from the trees as an old season dies and the beasts search for shelter
    the summer life they knew is disturbed

innocence dies in crimes of hate and somewhere someone is crying
    but in the small world of self, they aren't disturbed
young blood is spilled in senselessness, men fight and children die
    why does no one notice – why are none disturbed
when actions are harsh and cruel and wrong and they are the ones affected
    only then is the multitude disturbed

but still the rain rolls down the window of the car moving down the street
    and the gathered water splashes, is disturbed

Kristin Hunter
Boylan Catholic High School
Rockford
Grade 11

Hero

You try to be my Superman,
And do everything in your power for me.
You try to be my Batman,
And rid my Gotham City mind of evil.
You try to be my Quasimodo,
And claim sanctuary for me.
You try to be my knight in shining armor,
And slay all my dragons for me.
You try to be my conquistador,
And rid my mind of heathen ideas so I may go to Heaven.

Don't try to be my Superman.
I can do things for myself.
Don't try to be my Batman.
I must conquer my own bad habits.
Don't try to be my Quasimodo.
I have to face the world.
Don't try to be my knight in shining armor.
I need to fight my own battles.
Don't try to be my conquistador.
I'm already in Heaven when I'm with you.

Don't try to be someone you're not: You are already my hero.

Kari Gilbert
Newark Community High School
Newark
Grade 11

Memories

Memories have stories to tell,
All smiles and tears have been cried,
Swimming in the pond on a summer day,
Family vacations that were fun and exciting,
And though those days have been long gone away,
To me it seems like yesterday.

Memories have stories to tell,
Myths like the ancient of days,
Faces of laughter in the photographs,
Smiles that remember the fun of that place,
And for as many years as we will live,
It will remain a present the heart will always cherish.

Remember all you can of the memories you make,
Don't regret and never long for the past,
For one moment of happiness and joy,
Consider many a day of life well lived,
And for memories that make you smile,
Share all you will remember, or lest you will forget.

Sara Ledermann
Marshall High School
Marshall
Grade 10

Moving Day

I think I was too young to know what I was feeling.
Was it sadness? Happiness? Anger?
No one knows.
I knew something was coming though.
As her mom finished packing and they had their yard sale.
As we played on her jungle gym for the last time
(Little did I know it would be the last.)
The next day came along with the moving van.
Then those dreadful words were heard,
"Honey, it's time to go now."
As I watched her leave in the car with her mom,
We waved good-bye and began to cry.
We saw each other once or twice in the next year.
Little did I know it would be the end
Of one of my best friendships
Because that was the last time I ever saw her.

Aimee Koblitz
Althoff Catholic High School
Belleville
Grade 12

The Time Is Now

How can you sleep–
The hour whispers breathlessly
"Time will not stand still!"
Let not life lap at your toes
But plunge into the crystal water;
Every second you look into the mirrored glass
You see nothing but lost moments.
Death is nothing but a secret shadow
Creeping towards the aimless wanderers;
Stop not to think for a moment
But explore the world like the wind.
Arise from melancholy sleep–
Those dreams will only hinder you
True ecstasy lies in consciousness!

Elizabeth Moritz
Willowbrook High School
Villa Park
Grade 12

The Night of My Life

The night of my life we shared a dream
And oh, how real did it ever seem.
The night of my life we walked hand in hand
Laughing like we never had
Watching the water overlapping the sandy land.
The night of my life we stared at the midnight sky.
You told me how you would never lie
Swearing on the stars that you wouldn't break my heart.
The night of my life came to an end
When I found out you were seeing my best friend.

Alma Rodriguez
Morton East High School
Cicero
Grade 12

December

in the midnight eve,
the twilights cease
and fall.
pick them up
one by one
as they fall.
violinists play
from their resin souls.
I'm the china doll.
watch me dance.
I'm an Asian celebration.
the sky is tall.
flowers bare
the souls of
all.
the planned escape
of the night;
music from the walls.
winter too slow; circle the ice.
no more leaves—
watch

Lauren Faye Cruse
Minooka Community High School
Minooka
Grade 12

Heavenly Child

I know this little girl, she made me think of heaven.
She came to earth one afternoon,
On a sunny day, in the month of June.
Innocent and sweet with a smile like mine.
So I made her my goddess as if in ancient times.
I knew it had to be God who sent a gift so special from above.
For besides His Son, Jesus, He could have given no greater love.
With a glow that reflected, like blossoms that bloom.
I thought what shall I give her, the sun or the moon.
I could give her my world, but you might not understand.
She would know that I'm her passageway through to the mother land.
Knowing for her I'd be thick as blood or erosion through the wind.
Knocking down fortresses just to let my princess in,
That's why she makes me think of heaven,
'Cause her face is like the light.
The entrance way to the Golden Gate
So people call her Paradise.

Ruth Parker
Arts of Living School
Chicago
Grade 12

The Ocean

dive into my ocean
drink before you drown
life's much better
when you're going down

the water's rich
like the comforts below
liquid eyes contrast and contradict
everything we know

shake bubbles from your hair
they rise like broken dreams
break onto the surface
deluding subtle screams

sun sets on another day
as crimson waves rise and fall
good tidings of times past
wash away in alcohol

the sky falls to the ocean
heaven sinks into the sea
gods and heroes drown
as they fall down
and all that's left is me

Nick Moore
Maroa-Forsyth Sr High School
Maroa
Grade 11

The Little Soldier Boy

As the people cheered and yelled,
I heard the laughter and happiness amongst the crowd.
The children waved flags and banners in their little hands
back and forth in the air.

As I kept walking with the others down Washington Street,
I heard the beautiful words, "The war is over!"
The hugs and kisses being tossed around,
the fresh smell of popcorn, the happy smiling faces
that gave me the feeling of being proud to be an American.

I walked straight with my back lifted upright, and my head held high.
I saluted my officer and walked slowly up the stairs
to a platform in front of the White House.
I began to feel nervous at every step I took.
My name was called, and I stood forward to shake the president's hand.
I received a shiny medallion, and as the crowd went quiet,
I looked at my audience of about 100,000 people,
put my mouth to the microphone and said,
"It is good to be home in America, my country, I missed you."

Then the crowd roared and clapped,
and the little kids sat on their fathers shoulders.
One boy said, "Daddy, I want to be a soldier just like that brave man."

Kathy Gross
Prospect High School
Mount Prospect
Grade 11

Drifting

As I sit and watch the rain
A hundred thoughts race through my mind

......and then ten
......and then one
......What was it?
Slowly I drift off to sleep

Tom Keefe
Althoff Catholic High School
Belleville
Grade 12

Night Skies

Night skies have secrets to uncover,
All shining and glorious lights,
The moon's glow on a tree,
Twinkling stars that light and guide,
And meteors streaking through the dark
Giving beauty like a lark.

Night skies have secrets to uncover,
Silence like a piece of tranquillity,
Scent of clouds in the air,
Blackness that surrounds you, quiet that calms,
And for everything to be right,
Swirls of wind that rustle the night.

Take in all you can of the dark,
Cherish it and never fear it;
For one moment of utter peace
Makes up for many a day of stress well handled,
And for a sigh of relief
Absorb all you can, or want.

Heather Fonner
Marshall High School
Marshall
Grade 10

My Love

I was sitting near the harbor with
my beautiful love,
looking up to the sky, holding hands
both of us thinking about our love.
He is the only one I trust
I confide all my secrets to him.

Alone with him I feel protected
like if he was going to be with me forever.
Not even my parents can sever
the true love we feel
I love him; he loves me.
True Love.

Mayra Vargas
Morton East High School
Cicero
Grade 12

Self-induced Insomnia

Eyelids of brick tremor and fall
Aching limbs plead and beg
Not now, I must concentrate!
I have had no sleep.

Aching limbs plead and beg
My brain switches to tunnel-vision, eliminating excess work
I have had no sleep
Stuck in this rut, trying to claw my way out.

My brain switches to tunnel-vision, eliminating excess work.
Sobs well up in my throat
Stuck in this rut, trying to claw my way out
My body's running on empty.

Eyelids of brick tremor and fall
Sobs well up in my throat
My body's running on empty.
Not now, I must concentrate!

Rachel Sierminski
Marian Central Catholic High School
Woodstock
Grade 12

The Road of Life

There is one road you walk—
Straight or curvy, you decide.
You keep on pressing forward,
Though you want to run and hide.

If the road be straight,
You walk a lonely path.
If the road be curvy,
You had better get off fast.

For broad can be deceiving,
So narrow should you go;
You make your own decision,
But you just ought to know:

To find true happiness at last,
Not just a bunch of lies,
You've got to take that narrow path,
Not follow your heart's desires.

I pity you who walk,
Not seeing down the way;
For if I had to choose,
Narrow I would go today.

Rachel Lindsay
Vienna High School
Vienna
Grade 11

Equals

If I could tell you how I felt, it would all be okay
But if I could tell you just one thing, I'm not sure what I'd say

There is so much to tell you, if you only knew
I could talk to you forever, but then what would we do

After what I'd tell you, I'm not sure what you'd think
Would you like me for who I am, or would our friendship sink

I'd like to think that we'd become, the best of friends there'd be
But I don't think that's very likely, knowing you... then me

You are everything I've always wished to be
You're popular and pretty the opposite of me

Whenever I've been with you, when we talked that once or twice
I noticed how great you were, and how you were so nice

I've also noticed that when we're together, it's me that changes—not you
You treat me as an equal, which many people don't do

I want to embrace these moments, to never let them go
I want to be your equal, and tell you what I know

I suppose that will never happen, I guess that will never be
But I'm happy to have known you, I hope you're happy for knowing me

Brittany Becker
Regina Dominican High School
Wilmette
Grade 10

First Love

I remember when we met in second grade, for that memory shall never once fade.
It was the start of a beautiful thing, which really began when you gave me a ring.

The next time we met was at thirteen years old, the way you felt about me had never been told.
I never had liked you the way you liked me, but that would change too, we were meant to be.

I also recall, you were my first dance, sooner or later I would have my chance.
A couple more years would have to fly, before we would find each other near by.

Then that summer had come to us, now there would be a lot less fuss.
Under the stars was our first kiss, at the park we were filled with bliss.

Every day, together, we grow stronger. This has caused our minds to ponder.
Being in each other's presence has filled us with so much essence.

You have been there when I cried, you are always by my side.
With you I would forever stay, I never want you to be away.

When I see those beautiful blue eyes, shining brighter than the wonderful skies,
All I want you to know, is how much I love you so.

Aimee Scardina
Plainfield High School
Plainfield
Grade 10

Growing Up

There are so many choices ahead in life,
searching for that right husband or wife,
finding the career just right for you,
hoping that you can be happy no matter what you do.

The world should slow down,
and people should stop to look around.
And enjoy life in the fullest degree
and forget about the power and the money.

Growing up is a toilsome race,
we should slow down this raging pace.
And take the pressure off of people to succeed
and focus on what it is they really need.

Which is merely to do the things we enjoy best,
and not worry about passing life's grueling test.
So talk, laugh, love and play,
and get the most out of life now and everyday.

Keisha Richardson
Webber Township High School
Bluford
Grade 12

Wheel of Steel

Round and round I go,
In a circular motion, that never stops.
A motion that he can change.
He can make me go faster,
Slower or even leave me spinning until the world's end.

Either way,
It makes no difference to me.
Not at all.

It appears as if I have done something to him,
But I haven't.
It seems like he has some kind of rage towards something,
Though it isn't me.
It is as though someone has shut him down,
But they haven't.
Not at all,
He is just getting started.

He knows where the train is going
Working me like tomorrow's dawn will never come.
For he knows that if he does not,
His time spent can never be replaced.

Tom McGrath
Evanston Township High School
Evanston
Grade 12

Lonely Air

I have experienced every second of your life
Felt your love and hate
I'm part of history
Kept your ancestors alive and well
When you breathe me in and out
You let go of something inside you

People don't think of me
Even though I'm everywhere
I cry every single night and day
Soon my healthy surface will vanish
And everyone will experience
The last second of my life

Rafael Altamirano
Schurz High School
Chicago
Grade 11

Life

Life, what does it mean to you?
Do you know you have the privilege
to live on an earth that is designed
by one creator, God. Many people take
life for granted or as a joke.

Life, what does it mean to you?
Does it mean living your life the best you can.

Achieving your goals, does it mean taking
drugs, being in gangs having the "me first" attitude.

Life, what does it mean to you?
Does it mean life is full of turmoil?

Life isn't a meaningful thing, it's a purpose.

A purpose in life you should take in mind.
Does it mean anything to you?

To me, life is living for the good things
that life has to give me.

Life is not a choice, it's a privilege that
we all can share, if you live the life that
God has chosen for you.

Life would be something special,
as it is to me.

Marsean Campbell
Proviso West High School
Hillside
Grade 12

See it Through

When you are up against trouble
Meet it squarely, face to face
Lift your chin up to the sky
All you have to do is try.
Do the best that you can do;
You may fail or you may conquer
See it through!

Your future may not look so bright
We can only do what we feel is right
If the worst is bound to happen
In spite of all that you can do
Running away will not save you
See it through!

Drew King
Libertyville High School
Libertyville
Grade 12

Oma and Opa's Place

A house.
With small windy steps,
  a creaky old floor,
and a pool of fall leaves
  made to play in all day.
Where fruit means dessert,
  the main dish is toast—
and each time you leave
the scent of forgotten memories
    lingers in your brain.

Christine Bonheim
Plainfield High School
Plainfield
Grade 12

Hushed

Hushed, hushed
within me lay
a passion,
quiet over the years,
waiting, hushed, more beautiful
than a lake in the summer,
waiting to speak,
hushed, waiting to
fly forth from my fingers,
to soar on wings of ecstasy
with the purity of ivory,
hushed, but not denied,
quieted, quieted and not abused,
but now singing, more beautiful
than new snow in December,
now on wings of golden joy.

Raphael Ginsburg
Evanston Township High School
Evanston
Grade 11

What I Learned from Me

I began the trail with crayons and glue
I listened, I played
I did what they told me to do.
I passed with brilliant colors and striding forth I went,
Up the ladder with my pencils I climbed
Learning to read and write and rhyme
They smiled at me and I beamed with pride.
"It's not the things you do, it's the person on the inside."
On I went, that first life lesson chiming in my head
Dreaming of what was to come as I lie asleep in bed.

One morning I awoke to find that they were gone,
The ones who cheered me on, the ones who made me strong.
I was by myself, to become what I could.

I stumbled, I faltered and sometimes I fell
On the winding, twisty highway of life.
My times of joy inspired me.
I learned what I could from my strife
In the end my realization came to be
It's not what they will help me to become, but what I make of me.

Kimberly Bayley
Althoff Catholic High School
Belleville
Grade 12

Ode to the Cordoba

Your body is horrendous. You move so awfully slow.
Your insides are so ugly, I'm surprised you even go.

Your bumper is all saggy, wheel wells full of rust.
Your brake lines are a-leaking, and a dashboard full of dust.

Urine yellow paint, with a light touch of white.
Roaring down the streets, you're such an awful sight.

No working radio, or a single luxury.
I don't know what I like, or what in you I see.

You are my special baby. You've been so good to me.
Even when I put you in a ditch, you were the best car I could see.

I love you my Cordoba, with all of my heart.
Even though I am famous at the local Auto Mart.

In the end of my Ode, I just wanted to say,
You're worth every dollar of the 200 I had to pay.

Brian Rakers
Quincy Notre Dame High School
Quincy
Grade 12

Looking for Help

I am the lake,
washing from front to back.
Trying to reach you for help,
plastic and cans are polluting my water.

I am the lake looking for help,
so I could be clean every time you come and visit me.
I want people like you,
to come and clean me out.
Nooo! you have polluted me,
and I wish you hadn't.
Think about it,
you come and swim in me,
and you have polluted me with dirty cans,
imagine all the germs and diseases you might have,
you are not only polluting me but yourself also.

My hands cannot reach human life,
to come and clean me out.
Come and help my precious water,
be free from all the junk,
and you will see the pleasure of swimming,
in my clean precious water without any dirty cans.

Dulce Garduno
Schurz High School
Chicago
Grade 11

Look Past

I keep a lot of things to myself
All my secrets and thoughts I tell no one else
I just get a pencil and paper and write on and on
When I'm done, I throw the paper away and let it be gone
And when someone asks me what's wrong
I put on my mask like a clown

My poems have a lot to say
Some are happy like a nice summer's day
Or dewdrops of rain in the grass
Some that are funny and that make people laugh
And for the other ones, they're not about happiness
Those are the ones that get thrown away

Try all you want for you will not see
You'll never know the real me
For just a moment of thought
Many of you do not know
And for a few of you who look past
I thank all of you who look past the mask

Mandy Siverly
Marshall High School
Marshall
Grade 10

Spring

The bitter cold begins to fade,
As warmer days begin to persuade
The snow and sleet to go away.

The bright yellow sun, shines longer and brighter,
Slowly but surely the days become lighter.
And barren lands begin to bloom.

Birds are free to sing and fly.
The days are endless, the limit's the sky;
And warm carefree days chase all troubles away.

The grass becomes greener, the trees become taller,
The leaves on the ground keep getting smaller.
New life is in the air.

Spring is now officially here!
Good-bye, cold winter, we won't shed a tear,
For we know you'll return the same time next year!

Areta Ljubicic
Regina Dominican High School
Wilmette
Grade 10

Anger

"BOO HOO, WHY DON'T YOU CRY ABOUT IT, BABY."
The words ring out through the school yard
Laughter fills the air as pain strikes the heart of one
Anger builds and sits, stockpiling more anger on top of it
Until one fateful day when it explodes like a volcano
The newspapers read "13 DIE IN SCHOOL SHOOTING"
While the anger is released
The pain is still there and spreading.

Mike Grant
Marian Central Catholic High School
Woodstock
Grade 12

Maine

Maine can only be described one way...beautiful...
The evergreens that's smell fills the air...
The cool, clear, running waters...
The river is so clear you can drink from it...
The mountains that rise high in the sky...
To be on top feeling free...
The birds, bears, and moose...
King's Highway...my family...
Bethel...Mason...
The old farm on the hill...
Where the family near and far always come together...
Every summer I will got there
To Maine...my second home....

Jessica Thayer
Willowbrook High School
Villa Park
Grade 12

Relentless

Climbing up a shaky ladder,
Believing in one's self.
Taking a risk, completing the test,
Without a shred of doubt.
Not letting pressure get to you,
Ignoring the one putting you down.
Striving to become the best,
To be more than a face in the crowd.

Emilie Yount
Trinity High School
River Forest
Grade 12

New Beginning

Change.

Open the door to a new world,
endless possibilities.
Find oneself buried here,
dig and release,
Set upon the new day,
new possibilities,
new faces.

Awake from here and set out
to a place unknown,
land unsettled,
found here to see.
Lie upon here,
see the sights and live away.

Embrace my change.

Colby M. Hanik
Willowbrook High School
Villa Park
Grade 12

Loneliness

Another day has gone
And yet I don't belong;
Everyone walks by
And I still wonder why,
Why we too can't be
Like everyone we see;
Why can't we have a place
Like every human race?
I too have a heart
And only want to be part....
Of everything around;
My tears have now drowned
The way I always feel;
Because I too am real.

Teresa Sutton
Amboy High School
Amboy
Grade 11

Choirs

A chorus has songs to sing,
All pitches, chords, and tones,
Singing for a school or church,
Is where their pride is shown,
And how lovely their voices are sounding
They sing like beautiful angels, until their hearts are loudly pounding.

A chorus has a message to deliver,
Using songs to encourage and praise,
Not a dry eye in the house
As the choir sings songs of the good old days,
And for the members of the choir
Seeing the smiles and shining faces, are their only true desires.

Learn all you can from these members,
Enjoy the melodies and never make fun,
For one day you could be a member
Singing songs for the people that have come,
And for the church at which you sing,
For you, the bells will always ring.

Heather Bounds
Marshall High School
Marshall
Grade 10

Bitter Poem

Bitter.
I thought we were friends.
I don't understand. What did I do wrong?
Confused.
You said that you cared,
I said this wasn't the end. Did you say you agreed?
Betrayed.
You were so important to me,
I let you into my life, I gave you all my affection.
Lost.
How do I go on?
How can I trust again? Your absence makes me construct a fortress.
Angry.
Was I misled?
Did you lie to me? Was I a tool for your conniving ways?
Lonely.
I miss our talks, I miss your confidences, you made me sanguine.
Bitter.
I don't understand you. Friends are misleading.
Anger fades, and I am back, where I began,
Alone.

Elizabeth Martinez
Marian Central Catholic High School
Woodstock
Grade 12

Fantasy

Rainbows in the moonlight, flowers in the sky
Trees coated with cotton, rain that feels dry
Thunder made of music, lightning like the sun
Snow made of glitter, bubbles that are fun
Running like a stream and over a mountaintop
Up and over a rainbow, running past the golden pot
Hail made of candy bouncing off your windowpane
Swimming in a sea of sugar where chocolate falls like rain
Clouds above are dancing, the sun is smiling down
Children here are prancing and running all around
No one knows the time of day, or even has a care
If they could pick where to stay, they know it would be here

Kara Wiley
Clay City High School
Clay City
Grade 12

I Donated a Minister

One day I did run down the street.
The sun did harass and mix me up by its heat.
I made it to a certain point and began to walk.
An old minister came near and began to talk.
"I will ordain you," he said in a loud voice.
I began to point, for on a billboard I saw a choice.
I will donate my little brain to science for fun.
I then will appear at the hospital, then soon they will be done.
My achievements are many my deeds are good.
This will surmount to nothing for now I am dog food.
My head is an empty log, no more do I think.
I am one in a chain I am that weak link.
I do not run I do not walk.
The ordainment is done the minister will not talk.
The sun will no longer harass this body of mine.
For now my consciousness is in another place divine.

Benjamin Theobald
Morton High School
Morton
Grade 11

Clouds

I can be as soft and white as cotton.
I can be as mysterious and dark as night.
I can block the sun when you've had too much.
When I cry, it's only rain.
Have no fear, I won't hurt you.
When I get mad, I throw you hail.
When it's cold and I cry, the smallest
Tears turn into what you think is snow,
Shaped in all different kinds of geometric forms.
Big and small, thick and thin
Can be all my many sizes.
When you watch me, I can change into several shapes.
And after all of your pollution, I can be no more.

Chandra Weathersby
Schurz High School
Chicago
Grade 11

Friendship

There is a thing called friendship that dwells within the heart
you don't know how it happens, or how it gets its start...
but the happiness it brings you,
it always gives a special lift,
and you realize that friendship
is God's most precious gift.

A friendship is fragile like a snowflake
but almost never beyond repair.
If you have one true friend
you've had more than your share,
one person in a lifetime to whom your soul is bare.

Friendship means trusting
deeply in someone else, without a question or a wonder.
It takes knowing in your heart, without skipping a beat
that in this game of life
love is a two way street.

The heart sometimes has reasons,
that reason cannot understand,
but faith thrives on believing,
when it is beyond the power of reason to believe.

Lisa M. Hacker
Newark Community High School
Newark
Grade 10

Effigy

Listen to the sound of unborn children crying,
And the question,
Can you die, never having lived?
The smell of camphor in the air,
A half-empty Coke bottle,
God save this world.
Liquid pain, streaming down my face,
It is not raining,
Are these tears?
I did not think tears were red,
Simpletons, we are mere fools,
Trespassing in the darkest forests,
Pleading for our trespass again,
What good is it to fear?
Hiding in the half-deserted streets,
Amidst the sound of remorse dying,
The black of night entraps us,
Escape, and I have,
Listening to the sound of unborn children crying,
God save this world.

Ryan Swan
Iroquois West High School
Gilman
Grade 10

The Deer Hunt

I was up early
To set up my stand
And find the best tree
The best in the land.

I sat in for an hour
To wait for the light
And prepared my bow and arrow
For the first deer in sight.

From over the hill
Came a 10-point buck
I said to myself
I must be in luck.

I put in my arrow
And pulled back my bow
My aim and accuracy
Were soon to show.

I released the arrow
And watched him fall
That 10-point buck
Now hangs on my wall.

Brian Pittman
Clay City High School
Clay City
Grade 11

Every Day

You gave me birth,
and let me go.
Something inside
told you so.

Why did you leave
and let me stay?
Where people don't
and can't obey?

Then you felt
you had to go
and left me here
to be alone.

I'll never know
why you died.
Or if you're living,
could you have lied?

The pain inside
won't go away.
It comes and goes,
almost every day.

Amy Moore
Christ Lutheran High School
Buckley
Grade 10

Wild Thing

Addiction is a wildflower
Sprouting, growing, spreading
Through every thought
Planting new frustration
Suffocating any hope

Addiction is a wild animal
Biting, scratching, clawing
At the soul
Preying upon guilt
Consuming any pride

Addiction is a wildfire
Burning, scorching, destroying
All signs of life
Igniting anger
Combusting any joy

Addiction is a wild thing
Confusing, entrapping, controlling
Humanity
Giving birth to pain
And nothing is more painful than
Addiction

Gordon Schermer
Marian Central Catholic High School
Woodstock
Grade 12

Heartless

Vast a tearful cry has spoken,
Aloud with a heart that's broken,
For a nonuseful tool that's token,
Of its need of nothing.
Can live without a heart,
End of life with no start,
His soul split apart,
For no need is something.
But his soul surely grew,
Split from one into two,
Understood only a few,
Of others that grew weak in love.
All alone among the rest,
Gracing at an empty chest,
Waiting for the next,
For heartless next of.
Any few that come to see,
His death of heart to be,
Rotting soul will soon bleed,
And then will be gone.

Jim Staszowski
Grant Community High School
Fox Lake
Grade 12

Love

Love has meaning to learn,
All fun and thoughtful memories
Love closes in on a heart,
True love that grows and remains,
And is cherished forever
Love is like a ray of golden sunshine.

Love has meaning to learn,
Lessons like a heart of gold,
Footprints of memories in the past,
People that care for you, hearts that hold,
Dreams that make the world.

Love all you can for self worth,
Try and never fail,
For one day of many
Count many a year of loving well done,
And for a lifetime
Love all you can, or never learn.

Christy Shotts
Marshall High School
Marshall
Grade 10

In the Woods...

In the woods there will be...
A meadow for you and me.
Dance and sing, laugh and play,
Having fun during the day.

In the woods there will be...
A gigantic climbing tree.
Swinging wide, climbing high,
Watching how the clouds go by.

In the woods there will be...
Many places to be free.
Thinking of things we give,
Thinking of the lives we live.

In the woods there will be...
More than one memory.
Of the times on our lives,
When we did not have any strives.

Susan Koch
Althoff Catholic High School
Belleville
Grade 12

A Crushed Crush

She's in love,
She's in love, but he left her behind.

She sits there waiting,
She sits there waiting, but he never comes by.

She tries to forget,
She tries to forget, but she can't get him out of her mind.

Katie Uhrich
Newark Community High School
Newark
Grade 10

Wrestling

Wrestling isn't just blood and gore.
If you really like it, it's something more.
It's a sport, a show, and a little fun.
Yes, it's all three, wrapped up into one.
A lot of people think it's only a fight.
But if you've watched it, it's a real sight.
50% actor, 50% athlete.
Yes, being a wrestler is quite a feat.
Now I'm not saying that I'd be one.
But I know that on TV it looks sort of fun.
The taunting and the cheering crowd.
I've never heard anyone clap so loud.
Now I ask that you watch it, before you dismiss it.
Who knows? You may like it and not want to miss it.

Justin Thibault
Newark Community High School
Newark
Grade 10

Wolf

In the night I come.
Howling to the sky.
But I am but a ghost.
I come and go as I please.
I do only what I am needed for.
I hunt in the stealth of my being.
But I am but a lost soul.

Wandering the land that I call home.
For I am alone.
I eat what is left behind.
A scavenger.
Surviving on what is weak and defenseless.
My brothers and sisters join me.
On my journey through life, time expands.
But our lives come to be a dead end.
And we are but ghosts left here to howl at the moon
from a distance.

Steffen Villarreal
Schurz High School
Chicago
Grade 11

Basketball

Basketball has skills to teach,
All enjoyable and fun things,
Coaches yell loud on a court,
Teaching plays that are fluid and exciting,
And water bottles sit aside waiting to have players take a drink,
Wet and cold like an ice rink.

Basketball has skills to teach,
Moves like the running of a car,
Passes of players on a court,
Coaches that tell you plays that make you run far,
And for their eyes with the end of practice insight,
A crusader that makes them cringe with delight.

Practice all you can for those plays,
Do it and never regret the running,
For on motion of an offense,
Remember many a time of practice well done,
And for benefit of a younger player,
Show all you have been taught or will learn as a player.

Robert Flinn
Marshall High School
Marshall
Grade 10

Paradise

I see your face in the kiss of a sunrise,
while bathing in the sunlight.
For I live each moment for that glow,
and fear the grip of night.

Will I ever know the thoughts within your mind,
or of the tears you cry.
For I will give all I shall ever have
to make those tears run dry.

I want to learn the dark mysteries
that sleep deep within your glance.
From eyes that so hypnotically,
place me under your consuming trance.

Through the seas of your mind and the depths of your soul,
do you strive for something more.
From the possible touch of his hand and the love he would give,
would you so secretly soar.

This journey to you may be fruitless
and you become my vice.
But for me I see no other way,
but to pursue your paradise.

Dale Sweetnam
Highland High School
Highland
Grade 12

Drunken Love

Breaking up, aching hearts,
Tears flow like rain with rage.
Embrace sorrows in my heart,
Eternity's togetherness fell apart.
Unsure forgiveness,
Complex haze,
Drunken love forever stays

Jazmin Melendez
Schurz High School
Chicago
Grade 10

My Private Room

If I would have
My own private room
It would be just for me
And I would need a code to enter it.

There would be a swimming pool
That was always warm,
A sauna with a water fountain in it,
And a driving range for my golf addiction.

There would be a pond
For me to fish in
On top of a mountain,
That is close to a restaurant.

Every once in a while when I get lonely,
God would invite me to dinner.

John Leonard
Marian Central Catholic High School
Woodstock
Grade 12

A Light of My Own

Floating on a sea of lies,
wearing a life jacket made of lace,
I can't remember his laugh or his smell,
and I can't picture his face.
I remember bits and pieces,
of a past that I can't find,
I wander around in a world,
that long ago left me behind.
I was born into darkness,
and found a light of my own,
I learned to take care of myself,
and I made it all alone.
Others have tried to help me,
in my fight along the way,
but I have to push myself forward,
just to get through each day.

Jesseca Spears
Vienna High School
Vienna
Grade 11

Time

Time has special moments to offer,
All both good and bad it brings,
Trying, testing, giving on a whim
It's a gift that shines and sings,
And shows all those that let it
A precious treasure like a jewel or gem...
You just can't forget it.

Time has bad times too, to show,
Grumbling like a storm of hate,
Mending hurts of times past in the darkest hour,
Showing truth that doth prevail, sharing stories that do quite compensate,
And for over all one can truly even say,
Time that is sacrificed is surely the best you see,
....for it has a rewarding way.

So, all you looking for a moment in time,
Give and never look behind,
For one who dwells in the past of sweet memories
Can share many a laugh of pleasures well in mind.
And for a single moment in givin'
Give all you can give, and show life's sweet livin'.

Morgan Medsker
Marshall High School
Marshall
Grade 10

Dark

Darkness has forgotten human life
Lost in his shadow
Become his own nightmare.
Black angel flies through the dream of darkness.
His shadow lost in the light
Flying, looking back
His own body crowned.
Gloomy in the dark night
Open eyes only – see a dark shadow
The black body becomes a dark angel,
Flying through the dreams of darkness.
A gloomy night
A man dressed in black following a man in the dismal night.
The world becomes so darkened.
With open eyes, he sees that he is the middle of the dark shadow.
Looking back, he sees his own body
But the body is dressed as a man in black.
The man in black says, "You are the black angel."

Angel Luis Rivera
Schurz High School
Chicago
Grade 12

upon writing poetry

sometimes, ideas—like vicious rapists
force themselves upon me.
they ruthlessly assault my hand
until i am forced to write them down on paper.

sometimes, ideas—like last month's garbage
sit in my brain and rot.
they fester for weeks until i convince myself
to think of something else, because it stinks.

sometimes, ideas—like summer rain
happily dance upon my subconscious,
pooling and puddling until eventually
i have enough to splash and play in.

sometimes, ideas—like mint meltaways
lovingly caress my senses,
but only remain for a short while
and leave me craving more.

sometimes, ideas—like fra gm en t ed sentences
make perfect sense to me
but appear incorrect to others
and don't offer a sense of closure...

Mary Scalero
Marian Central Catholic High School
Woodstock
Grade 12

Friendship

Friends have happiness to share,
All fun and young at heart,
Laughing together on a bright summer's day,
Never thinking that they will one day part,
And friends always love being together,
It feels like a dream going on forever.

Friends have happiness to share,
Fresh like a vase of flowers,
Filled with moments of laughter in the air,
Talking that lasts for hours,
And for all the days spent in the sun,
Friends that share all the fun.

Love all you can for true friends,
Live now and never regret the past,
For one lifetime of friendship,
Was meant to last,
And for being the best friend you could be,
Give all you can, and then they'll see.

Jamie Elledge
Marshall High School
Marshall
Grade 10

Dreams

Dreams are movies
Inside your head
Horror
Drama
Comedy
And romance
You pick the actors
You write the script
Your unconscious mind is the director
You are the audience
You are the critic
Your dreams are thoughts of your life and what you want
In it.

Emmy Gill
Schurz High School
Chicago
Grade 10

This Day

On this day the wind is cold,
Oh how I wish the sun was shining gold.
Nothing to do, nowhere to play,
I like to sleep on days like today.
I look at the sky and all I see is gloom,
All I want is roses to bloom.
The bees are gone, the birds have flown,
Spring, where are you, make yourself known.
It seems so far away,
I don't know if I can wait another day.
To see the sun and have some fun,
Would make my day bright.
I'd feel all right.
I don't like the rain, I don't like the snow,
On days like this there's nowhere to go.
I want some sun, I want some rays,
I want to smile, not wet days.
If I don't see that bright light,
I'll probably never be in sight.

Brook Schlueter
Beardstown Sr High School
Beardstown
Grade 12

Poems

Poems are a mysterious thing
Some are easily understood
And others are not
Some are quite lengthy
And others end rather quickly
Poems come in many shapes and sizes
But one thing is for sure,
Each has a meaning hidden somewhere inside it
It's just up to you to find it.

Jennifer Thompson
Althoff Catholic High School
Belleville
Grade 12

Tears

Tears flow like a waterfall
     hearts break like a twig
     emotions are crushed like cans
Sometimes LIFE is rough.

Liz McCarthy
Marian Central Catholic High School
Woodstock
Grade 12

Losing Him...

losing him
was hard for me.
losing him
was the worst thing
that could happen to me.
losing him
made me realize
that someone could
come and go.
losing him
was bad for me
but good too,
because it made me
realize that
losing him
meant how good
a friend could be.

Michelle K. Tobar
Bowen High School
Chicago
Grade 11

The Ocean

The sea
My heart
Is like an ocean
Full of things untold
It's full, it's big
There's hatred
There's love
It's a machine of feelings
That are being processed
To my soul
That remembers everything
It is kept in a compartment
I have harmed
But I will pay
My palm life tells me so
My heart
The sea
The ocean

Lyneth Romero
Schurz High School
Chicago
Grade 10

Observing Memory

I am the sentient mirror who once
Savored the taste of her fingerprints, the soft curves of her image,
Both of which now roll through warm candle-lit tunnels
On endless, incessant parade.
Sultry images emerge, dancing from the flame —
A crackling spark of emotion
Which rises on bright taper wings over the current of marble smoke swirls.
Then, like a thought, the ember maneuvers up
Through the tangled canopy and the insidious cul-de-sacs of apathy,
Its glow ebbing ... ultimately an ethereal gray carcass.

The remaining wisp of her body
Finally adjoins to ghost-heavy clouds
Endowed with all the common remedies:
Tears for joy, tears for pain,
But mostly, tears for pity, tears for gain —
And especially tears for blinding.
Celestial masses dim her rose petal lips, perfumed by sunlight,
But her laugh is as indelible as the first breeze inhaled,
Carrying crushed blossoms freshly plucked from the oblivion of drought.
Only she, buried in the poignant sap of each petal,
Still waits for those next tears to fall.

Adam Lavitt
Glenbrook North High School
Northbrook
Grade 12

My X–Files Poem That Really Isn't About The X–Files

At times I fight the future
Threatened by its coming horrors
I throw blind punches at a faceless enemy
But he has proven to be unbeatable

I feel threatened by its coming horrors
As I reach back for the ties with present and past
But failure is all I find
The future engulfs me at every moment

I cling to the comfort of my present and past
Desperately hiding from my life-long nemesis
But the future consumes me at every moment
Being aversely dragged into a place that has no answers

At times I fight the future
Desperately trying to escape its inevitable hold
But I am forced forward into this place that has no answers
As I throw blind punches at an adversary that will not be defeated

Adam Jennrich
Marian Central Catholic High School
Woodstock
Grade 12

It Isn't Fair

Why can't I see her?
Why can't I hug her?
Why can't I fight with her?
Why is she up there while I'm down here?
Why can't I share all of the new gossip with her?
Why can't I tell her I love her?
Why can't I be the innocent girl I used to be?
I can't, I can't, I can't!
So many restrictions and no good reason!
Why is my mommy dead?
...It isn't fair.

Erin Keefe
New Trier Township High School
Winnetka
Grade 10

The Powers of String

We hold and pull this wonderful thing
That binds things together, it is called string
A bunji jumper, a parasailer, a bit of hope
There is even soap on a rope
Yet we are so trusting in this powerful thing
To risk our lives for a thing called string
The fear, the rush, that leaves us a half of a breath
To trust this string that could cause our death
They are used for fun, like in a tug-of-war
A string of that power can be found in a store
They are stressed and tested not to give
So in a situation everyone can live
It is like a chain so powerful and strong
It resembles a snake so limp and so long
A noose that hangs can be cut with a knife
A string or rope can cause death or save a life

Peter Tronick
Morton High School
Morton
Grade 12

An Ageless Moment

There are no wrinkles here,
as I lay with the cool tickling
grass beneath my body.
An ant marches across my bare stomach,
in sync with the other that is marching across my heart.
Fingers of wind comb through my hair
and massage my toes.
Dead leaves crackle and
slip away from beneath me,
and I see the new ones reaching
towards the clouds.
I make an imprint of every ant,
every breeze, every leaf, and put it in my pocket.
There are no wrinkles here.

Robin Jordan
Libertyville Community High School
Libertyville
Grade 11

I Remember

I remember when the sun shone bright,
I remember when the stars twinkled in the night,
I remember the moon, full in the night's sky,
I remember the day, beautiful and majestic.

I remember Andrea, ebullient and energetic,
I remember her spirit, joyous and magnificent,
I remember her face, full of life,
I remember her smile, full of God's love.

I remember life, given to me by Jesus Christ,
I remember my mom, watchful of what I do,
I remember Señora, loving and patient,
I remember Bethany, caring and compassionate,
I remember death, taken by God.

I remember Ernie, touched by God's grace,
I remember his voice, used to sing for God,
I remember his love, full and unending to all,
I remember his spirit, kept alive by all.

I remember the grass, green as can be,
I remember the sky, blue as Baby's Breath flowers,
I remember the clouds, white and fluffy as feathers,
I remember me, sweet and full of love and His grace.

Nicole Berry
Waterloo High School
Waterloo
Grade 10

Peace

Nature has peace to offer,
All golden and mild days,
Brilliant butterfly landing on a lone blossom,
Ornery squirrel that jokes and plays,
And big, old trees standing tall
Protecting everything like a security guard in the mall.

Nature has peace to offer,
Warmth like a sweater of wool,
Shadows of animals in the grass,
Sun that nourishes, rain that cools,
And for the lonely one,
Acquaintances that make the fun.

Give all you have for peace,
Cherish it and never let it lay,
For one part of nature
Keep many a trouble of life well away,
And for a moment of harmony
Appreciate all you have, or accept a memory.

Leslie Sutton
Marshall High School
Marshall
Grade 10

Melt

I had friendship,
but when I left it
like the last drops of
bitter liquid
mingling with melted ice
in yesterday's tumbler,
I realized I never
had it to begin with.

Erin Reschke
Marian Central Catholic High School
Woodstock
Grade 12

Life

What is life for,
Is it for happiness,
Is it for hardship,
Or is it for confusion,

Life goes by,
We still don't know,
We don't know why we are here,
We don't know how we got here,

With all these questions,
We still live on,
We don't know what is ahead,
Yet we still move on,

What will become of us,
On that black endless day,
When we are gone from this life,
And where will we go.

James Han
Schaumburg High School
Schaumburg
Grade 11

That Special Someone

Was there when I was born;
Had two jobs to raise the family;
Came from the gutter and raised me well;
Played with me many games;
Taught me how to walk;
Taught me right from wrong;
Gave me advice on how to succeed;
Was always there for me;
Always had the answer to my question;
Will always be a great role model for me;

Is my father.

Anthony Brisuela
Morton East High School
Cicero
Grade 12

Happiest Day

You took me by surprise as you bent down on one knee
Looked me straight in the face and said, "Will you marry me?"
I smiled and cried as I said, "Yes, my dear."
You returned it with a kiss and wiped my tear.
"I love you, little girl, wholeheartedly;
I'm yours forever, even if you depart from me."

Shane P. Hood
Kankakee Trinity Academy
Kankakee
Grade 12

A Lovely Time of Year

I love the spring
All of Mother Nature's beauty, hidden during the winter, springs to sudden life,
The grass growing greener and the trees sprouting fresh leaves
The neighbors all walk their dogs outside and as they pass,
The dogs bark noisily at each other
Lawnmowers are heard as I come home from school,
And the smell of the recently cut grass brings a smile to my face
As I step outside to do my homework on the patio
The smaller kids have no work to do today,
And I am tempted to go play tag with them at the park
The warm breeze soaks into my legs, breathing now that I am wearing shorts
I lean my head back and close my eyes
My book still unopened at the table by my side
The sun is warm on my pale face, and I smile
Listening to the children in the distance and the birds behind them,
Singing their happy songs
I love spring

Anthony Altamore
Willowbrook High School
Villa Park
Grade 11

Misunderstood Love

You say it's for my own good but I don't understand,
If it's for my own good why do I hurt so bad.
Everyday I dreamed of the love from you I had,
Now that love I had has left me alone, bitter, and sad.
Everything I ever wanted I had, but it did not stay,
I really wish you would have stayed with me day after day.
You expected me to get what you meant when you ignored me,
But it was impossible because it was something I didn't want to see.
I don't believe I will ever understand why you did this,
At least the love that was left ended with a hug and not a kiss.
I am sorry I turned away so fast and didn't say goodbye,
But goodbye is so final and at that point I feel like I wanted to die.
I honestly don't believe you will ever understand how this made me feel inside,
But you did what you felt like you should and I am not gonna ask again why.
Maybe one day I will again have you to hold,
But until that day comes I will have to put on a fake smile and be bold.

Terra Lee West
Vienna High School
Vienna
Grade 11

Perfect World

Imagine a world full of happiness,
Sunny days,
Presence of loved ones,
Hope for tomorrow,
Understanding the unexplainable.

Imagine a world with no worries,
No violence,
No prejudice,
No poverty,
No depression

Is this possible?
Can it be done?

Close your eyes.
Dream of the times when you were young.
The world seemed perfect.
We are older now.
We see the world differently.
What happened?

Imagine a world where we can all join hands,
And maybe for one day we can live in a perfect world.

Jennifer Ziehm
Willowbrook High School
Villa Park
Grade 11

Searching

All of my unanswered questions,
Waiting for a reply.
Hoping to have some type of connection
Where my roots lie;
Who was my first mother?
Was she black or white?
Was her personality somber?
What was her weight, her height?
Am I who I think I am?
Or am I someone else?
Am I a black woman hoping to be damned?
Or am I a black woman with confidence in herself?
Who am I?
Am I really happy with the color of my skin?
But I can lie,
Because I'm happy with the color within.
Will I find answers to my experiment?
Will I find out my past roots?
Maybe I will and find excitement,
Or, maybe I won't and continue to stay in a non-achieving mood.

Lashunda Shelby
Schurz High School
Chicago
Grade 10

The Greatest Fan

My mom always said, "Gram's coming today!"
And I would always say, "I can't wait to play!"
I remember she was always there to cheer me on,
To say, "Good game," to let me know that someone cared.
As I played I could feel her there,
Giving me her lucky stare
That made me want it even more,
Hitting me right down to the core.
That's what made her the greatest fan.
She drove me to be the best,
To play my hardest, to never rest.
I took it for granted that she'd always be there,
But now I realize she still is here.
And after every game I always say,
"Gram, you came today—thanks."

Natalie Pedroza
Regina Dominican High School
Wilmette
Grade 10

You

She hypnotizes me with her brown eyes,
Her beautiful and smooth skin feels like silk.
Every time she smiles at me my heart cries,
I even see her image in white milk.
When she passes me by, my heart stops cold,
Her dark brown hair glistens in the bright light.
I feel her warm touch and turn to pure gold,
Sometimes I picture myself as her knight.
At last I have met the girl of my dreams,
I would kill any man for her sweet love.
Yet, I cannot have her and thus I scream.
The love I have for her flies like a dove,
Please don't leave me, when time runs out next year,
If you do my eyes will swell up with tears.

Danny Kim
Curie Metropolitan High School
Chicago
Grade 11

Don't Go Away

Somehow, some way, I will make it through this
Another challenge of life, I can't miss
The best time of my life they seem to say
I'll tell you if it's true another day
Because right now I just can't win
And I can't keep the rain from getting in
I don't want to try to speak
For fear that I might sound weak
Someone please help me, I do not want to fret
For I don't think I'm old enough to be grown up yet
So promise me that you will stay
By my side forever and a day

Justin Kraudel
Althoff Catholic High School
Belleville
Grade 12

The Single Strand

Am I a golden thread
Whose purpose is
To adorn
To shine
To inspire envy?
Or
Am I a practical suture
A tool meant for mending wounds
Inflicted on others
Existing for everyone but me?
No.
I am a single strand
Entwined with those around me
Clearly I am but a single brilliant strand
Of some unfathomable twisted line.

Emily Watson
Morton High School
Morton
Grade 12

Rising Above

Today I learned to walk on air,
I saw what all the others see.
Before I sunk beneath the soil,
Hiding from what may come of me.

Rachel L. Urquhart
Grant Community High School
Fox Lake
Grade 12

Tuesday Afternoon

The cypress tree has always stood
down by the black lagoon
I noticed it while walking
on a Tuesday afternoon
Its leaves of red
its branches thick upon the tree did grow
Its shadow came out and captured me
I stopped and said hello
the wind blew warm around the trunk
lazy, stiff, and dark
It whimpered for my affection
so I touched its aging bark
Its coldness from an isolation
growing everyday
pricked my senses wide awake
and so I ran away
but the cypress tree still stands alone
down by the black lagoon
and I will never forget that day
that Tuesday afternoon

Valerie Esrig
Willowbrook High School
Villa Park
Grade 11

Love for Today

The world of today has many troubles to face,
Such as violence, drugs, and separation of race.
Is there a way to overcome all these evils,
And transform our world so that we all are equal?
Is there something that we can be taught,
So we will not judge and just accept as we ought?
Yes, I say, and love is this thing,
Which will bring peace to our world and cause all men to sing.
Love can heal all the pain that we face,
It can be our salvation and our saving grace.
I say that love is the only sure way,
To bring back our hope for a brighter new day.

Rebecca McCorkle
Springfield Southeast High School
Springfield
Grade 12

Surviving Life

Triumphant dreams and classic memories,
Life
A wonderful song worth singing. Surviving the moments of awful destruction.
And celebrating the victories life brings.
People ... motivated, dramatic, witty and competitive.
The love of sweet success that turns in your stomach like a bad hunger.
Being determined
Being excited
Being emotional
Being free

Lorraine Johnson
Hubbard High School
Chicago
Grade 11

What Would Tomorrow Be Like?*

It's been just about a year, since the tragic accident.
I miss you just as great today as the day this sadness sent.
There hasn't been a day gone by, that I haven't thought of you.
What would tomorrow be like? It wouldn't be as blue.
My eyes swell up full with tears to think you were taken away,
All the time together we've lost, the thousand things we never got to say.
It's so hard to think of you as gone.
I want to know what happened, what really did go on?
I wonder what went through your head that very night.
I wish I could have been there to say it'd be alright.
I'd give anything to see you just one more time.
I hope you know I love you, and I'm proud that you are mine.
Now that you are gone, I'm not as scared to die.
I'll see you in Heaven when my time comes to say good-bye.

Alexis Beyer
Althoff Catholic High School
Belleville
Grade 12
In loving memory of my cousin, Jamie

The Color of My Skin

Does the color of my skin matter?
Why am I afraid?
Will you stop hitting me?
Or will tomorrow be the same?
Are you upset at me?
Will my dream ever come true?
Will I ever smell freedom?
Or will you corner me and beat me to death?

Juan Luevano
Schurz High School
Chicago
Grade 10

The Light

People come and people go, some are young and some are old
You have to believe you're going to win.
People live and people die, we are not to question why
To do so is thought to be a sin.

I think about the times we had, the easy, hard, the good and bad
I was never one for long good-byes.
This emptiness, it fills my heart, no one else could play your part
Every night the light, it slowly dies.

There's no fight left or so it seems, I live a life of broken dreams
I have nothing else to hope for now.
Life goes on and time goes by, I never win, why do I try?
I keep thinking it will come somehow.

Strength and courage must lead the way, if I expect another day
I have lived a lifetime full of lies.
I forget the times we shared, I forget the way you cared
Every night the light, it slowly dies.

Patrick Sheppard
Genoa-Kingston High School
Genoa
Grade 11

Macbeth

Ambition is the longingness to thrive
I am not the kind to lie sick in shame
For I want what is called strong will and drive
Bizarre as it may seem, I long for fame.
Action is the key to achieving praise
Expanding my realm of rule is a must.
The social ladder is not just a maze,
This passion hurts more than a simple lust.
The royal throne is my lone focal point
I have a cunning hunger in my eye.
The hierarchy will crumble at the joint
There is a horrid storm up in the sky.
 I will soon reign supreme across the land
 A hold on the great kingdom will be grand.

Andrew Michael Teel
Du Quoin High School
Du Quoin
Grade 12

My Voice

They force their ways upon me,
I have no choice.
They say what I can and cannot do,
I have no voice.

I am being shown the right thing to do,
I have no sight.
They are shaping my world for me,
I look at them with spite.

It is so wrong but what can I do,
They are so many, we so few,
Can I help what they do to me, oh do I try.
But so far what they tell me has been all a lie.

They force their ways upon me,
I have no choice,
All that I can do is speak up,
And try and make them hear my voice.

Matthew Musielak
Althoff Catholic High School
Belleville
Grade 12

Young Poets
Grades 7-8-9

I Learned From the Story

I'm opening this book
Not knowing what it will hold.
But I've decided to follow the reviews
And not my mind.

And the character I most relate to
Is full of sorrow and pain.
He learns how to love,
Even if he'll lose again.

And when I finish reading,
I may laugh
Or I may cry.
And it feels like I have to say goodbye forever
To a friend I know and love.

But then I remember
I can open the book
And read it again.
And my heart soars to the sky
Because I'm not following the reviews this time;
I'm following my own mind.

Alicia Bellis
St Colette School
Rolling Meadows
Grade 8

Empty

A house sits lonely and empty
waiting for a family to move in.

The walls are still white,
having never experienced the work of art
of an excited five-year-old with a new box of crayons.

The refrigerator is empty and bare
never before used as a showcase for a proud mother
to hang her children's high test scores.

Table tops are clear, lacking the priceless photographs
of beloved family members
who will never be forgotten.

A house sits lonely and empty
waiting for a family to move in...
waiting to be changed from a house to a home.

Amy Boysen
St Thomas Of Villanova School
Palatine
Grade 7

The Storm

The roaring water fell from above,
A monsoon of H2O
Winds pounded the sides
Of the great city

Floods arose, destroying passageways
And entire families
Tidal waves came up from the bodies of water
Roaring down, and drowning hundreds

Eventually the water stopped,
And so did the winds
The great city was quiet
For half of its inhabitants were dead

They set up to work, rebuilding their home
They brought dirt from the quarries
And turned it into walls

Much food had been lost, in the terrible storm,
So scouts went to find some more

The city has survived the storm
Its inhabitants have begun to recover
Until a 3-year-old above
Smashed their ant hill

Alex Herskovic
Fenwick High School
Oak Park
Grade 9

Top Poems Grades 7-8-9

Incessant Horizons

Gazing toward the sunset skies,
the heavens look like a wonder.
How could something so beautiful exist,
without a single blunder?
The painting spreads across the endless canvas,
like a magical work of art.
Something so beautiful the eyes cannot perceive,
but can only be seen through the heart.
The beautiful heaps of cotton candy appear,
scattered throughout the sky.
The pinks, oranges, blues, and purples,
glide over the mountains as they fly.
A scene so unique and so spectacular,
yet it happens every day,
but somehow every time it's seen,
it appears in a more picturesque way.
This beautiful sky, a wonderful canopy,
proves that splendor it cannot lack.
But just as swiftly as this work of art emerges,
it promptly turns into a sea of black.

Kara Kinzel
Mascoutah High School
Mascoutah
Grade 9

Jack Frost

He comes quietly across my windowsill.
With his brush, he paints frosted strokes of ice.
He leaves
The morning light shines within my window.
The frosty forest comes alive.
He leaves a gift of joy that lasts but a minute,
A different scene each winter's night.

Nicole Michalczyk
Stratford Jr High School
Bloomingdale
Grade 8

Do You Remember the Holocaust?

Do you remember the holocaust,
and all the lives that were taken?
Do you remember the souls that were lost,
and our world which was forever shaken?

Do you remember the war that was fought,
and all the men who died?
Do you remember the prize that was sought,
and all the children who cried?

Do you remember the Nazi troops,
and all the families they killed?
Do you remember the Jewish groups,
and the blood they all had spilled?

Do you remember the horrible screams,
and the endless Jewish cramps?
Do you remember the terrible dreams,
and the concentration camps?

Do you remember the holocaust,
and all the lives that were taken?
Do you remember the souls that were lost,
and our world which was forever shaken?

Joshua Patterson
Wauconda Middle School
Wauconda
Grade 8

Two in One

A mother in my heart, another in my life is what I guess you could say,
When you're adopted it usually turns out that way.

One gave me life, and to a different family,
One gives me love, and shows me the person inside of me.

One gave me a nationality, beauty, and race,
The other shows me beauty beyond the face.

One gave me faith, but not how to live it,
The other gives me the Bible and how to believe it.

One gave me form of how I shall look,
The other gives me an education of writing, and reading books.

One gave me to a mother, who looks out for my wellbeing,
The other shows me love and what truly are feelings.

One gave me talents of how to participate,
The other gives me the wisdom not to judge or hate.

This is for you mom, for all the times I yell and scream,
A thank you for always holding me up with your wings.

Even though I can be a "bear" like you say sometimes,
I want you to know I love you, and you're the best mom and always will you be mine.

One mother gave me life and to a different family,
My mom shows me what love really, truly can be.

Emily Reed
St Peter's Grade School
Rockford
Grade 8

Top Poems Grades 7-8-9

The Park Through the Window

The trees were stripped on the cool fall day,
As the sun streamed through exposed branches.
The leaves from the branches split, covering the ground.
The frantic squirrels hoard food for their winter stash.

At the far end of the playground three children play crouched in a sandbox
Laughing and pushing sand around to make roads for their cars.
The kids romp in the crisp stray leaves
Fanned along by a gentle current.

A small flock of geese travel overhead in a vee formation
Calling to each other as they go.
A few inexperienced geese break the linear flight pattern
As they struggle to keep up
On their journey to their winter destination.

As the light dims I realize it's time for bed
With one last glance around the park.
The rustling lullaby of the trees sings earth to sleep.

Adam Reich
Harrison Elementary School
Wonder Lake
Grade 7

Nature

Wind is a quiet sound,
Lifting weightless dancers off trees,
Calming the destruction.

The sun is a solitary piece of gold glitter,
Giving life to reaching plants,
Warming the Earth with its beaming rays.

Clouds are like cotton candy,
Sweetening the ground with sugary raindrops.
And relieving the brightness of the sky.

Rain is full of sculpted diamonds.
Replenishing the dry and cleaning the dirty.

The moon is a glowing cat's eye,
Taking away the fears of the dark,
And giving hope for a peaceful night.

Juanita Rodriguez
Taylor Elementary School
Chicago
Grade 8

Think Of

Think of –
Stepping on shore and finding it heaven.
Of taking hold of a hand and finding it God's hand.
Of breathing new air, and finding it celestial air.
Of feeling invigorated, and finding it immortality.
Of passing from storm to tempest to an unbroken calm.
Of waking up and finding it home.

Savannah Stachnik
Hubbard High School
Chicago
Grade 9

If I Were A......!

If I were a pen, you couldn't see my aggravation and frustration.
Being thrown in a case of pencils and shavings one minute
and being crushed by math, social studies, reading, science, and language arts books the next.
It is not my fault if I get broken and get my lovely ink all over your books.
Never a moment's rest. Being handed from person to person. Give me a rest!
Put me down I say! Let me get some rest! Soon, you will need a new pen for I am almost depleted.
Put me down, for I shall unleash my brothers and sisters upon you.
So, user of me.....

     beware!!!

Arthur Hartnett
Nichols Middle School
Evanston
Grade 7

Then and Now

As you grow up, things change.
You have to change with them.
Then you were babbling things,
And now you say real words.
Then you couldn't change into your own pajamas,
And now you wash your own clothes.
Then you had to be fed by someone,
And now you make meals by yourself.
Then when you did something wrong it was "cute,"
And now when you do something wrong you get grounded.
Then you weren't judged much because you couldn't communicate with your "peers,"
And now you are judged by how fat you are, how stylish your clothes are, what you look like,
How smart you are, and everything else.
I wish it was still then,
Not now.

Carrie Renee Townsend
Scales Mound Jr High School
Scales Mound
Grade 8

Shining Hope Upon the World

This crazy world we live in, filled with hatefulness and sin.
A place where dreams die, sometimes all we can do is cry.
So much pain and sadness is taking place; we need to realize there's a soul that comes with that face.
With tragedies and sorrow we need to cope, and fill the world with hope.
Bad memories of the past in spite, we need to make things right.
So many things are wrong, for love and peace we long.
Children are growing too fast, and love cannot seem to last.
Hatefulness strikes us like a spear, and our lives are lived in fear.
It's hard to express how we feel; our lives can seem so unreal.
Sometimes it doesn't seem fair, when our life turns into a nightmare.
The pain is hard to erase, with the problems we need to face.
For healing we pray, as our lives speed by from day to day.
Let's learn from the mistakes that were made, and let the sadness fade.
We have an obligation to spread love to God's creation, across every nation.
Let's put away the sorrow, and work towards a better tomorrow.

Kerri Cadwallader
Quincy Jr High School
Quincy
Grade 8

A Mother's Heartbreak

Little kids start to run;
off to Kindergarten to have fun.

Mommies left at the door;
go inside and cry some more.

Kids come home and mothers say;
"I missed you today."

But the kids say nothing more;
for they already left to go play more.

The mother's sad to see;
their kids leaving joyfully.

The kids stay out all day;
only stopping in for a dinner tray.

As time goes by and kids grow up;
the tears of moms dry up.

Mom's now happy to see;
kids going to school happily.

But a mother's heartbreak will start again;
when marriage is in the final plan.

Kari Parkinson
St Matthew School
Champaign
Grade 7

My Wish

My sister died eleven years ago.
She was only one year old.
I can't remember that day too well
because I was only two at the time.

I do remember that her little hands
wouldn't stay inside her coffin.
When my father closed the lid of the coffin,
her fragile bones creaked.

When we went to the cemetery,
I was only playing
because I couldn't understand what was happening.
But now that I understand,
I feel really sad
and wish my sister could be with me.

Susana Pineda
Logandale Middle School
Chicago
Grade 7

Butterfly

Butterfly
Strong and free
You remind me of the great beauty and simplicity
Fluttering inside everyone
I wish my butterfly could be freed.

Nicole Cudiamat
Stratford Jr High School
Bloomingdale
Grade 8

The Test

Life is a test,
Everything is fine until a problem comes up,
You do well in school until it's time for the exam.

A problem is given to you
The teacher is the friend that argues
"It's probably multiple choice
You have to choose the right answer,
If not, you could fail terribly."

There are chances at this,
And chances at that,
If you pick the correct answer,
You can go to that school, or be like that person.

You can stay with him or them,
You could just not go to school
Everything depends upon your choice,
Since everything is multiple choice,
Why not guess once in a while?

Lisa Perna
Fenwick High School
Oak Park
Grade 9

Basketball Game

I have a lot to say,
About a game I got for my birthday.
It's a game of basketball.
"In the Zone" is what it's called.
There are so many things to do,
Against a friend, or the computer and you.
You can play a game in a season.
Do what you want,
There is no reason.
You can have a three-point fest,
Or enter a player in a dunk contest.
I think it is a wonderful game.
I wouldn't make a single change.
It has awesome graphics.
This video game is fantastic.

Daniel Helie
St Mary of Czestochowa School
Cicero
Grade 8

Growing Up With Grandpa

When I was young with grandpa
we always had a good time.
When I was young with grandpa
we always went to play ball with
my dad's dog Shotgun.
When I was young with grandpa
I always sat next to him when
we rode in the car.
When I was young with grandpa
we always went to McDonalds.
I always had a Happy Meal.
Guess what? I still do.
When I was young with grandpa
he would always rub my back
and then he would always start
tickling me and I would start laughing.

Erin Louise Hesselbacher
Scales Mound Jr High School
Scales Mound
Grade 8

A Winter's Day

Winter is fun.
I like it when the sun
Reflects off the snow.
I like it when we go
To the park.
It's such a lark.
Snowball fights
And the beautiful sights.
It's best with family and friends.
I wish this day would never end.

Josh Hansen
St Mary-Dixon School
Dixon
Grade 7

I Wish

I wish I were a bird,
flying high above the trees.
Choosing my own destiny.

I wish I were a fortune-teller,
knowing life's surprises.

I wish I were a tree,
watching the world pass me by.

I wish I were the sun,
shining bright for everyone.

I wish...I'm glad I'm me.

Mike Kelly
Queen of Martyrs School
Chicago
Grade 8

Day/Night

Day
bright, sunny
lighted, radiated, scintillated
the sky is growing inky
darkening, dimming, evening
fading, ending
Night

Abbie Armbruster
Holy Angels School
Aurora
Grade 7

Best Friends

I have some best friends
who will be until the end
through good times and bad
through happiness and sad
they will be there for me
can't you see
when I look into their eyes
I see they tell no lies
through smiles and tears
they've been there through the years
I have to say
that they always make my day
I recommend
that you get a best friend
they treat you like gold
no matter if you are young or old

Megan Leahy
St Irene School
Warrenville
Grade 7

Monkey

Funky!
Monkey!
Listen to him sing, ooo-ooo.
Spring!
Swing!
The monkey swings towards a tree.
Boom!
He hit the tree.
He falls into some bushes.
Rustle!
Rustle!
He makes it out of the bushes.
Thump!
He tripped over a rock!
Bang!
Bang!
Two coconuts fall on his head.

Cyndi Saari
Shirland C C Elementary School
Shirland
Grade 7

Farm Boys

Work 'til dark;
make their mark.
Sleep 'til dawn;
mow the lawn.

Mike Todd
Quincy Jr High School
Quincy
Grade 8

H

You are the actor
whose fur is white
and cape is black.
You are young;
you are old,
then young again
though you have never changed.
He who is calm,
presiding over his pride.
It's as a lion over its den.
He who bears the scars
from battles fought
to keep his gains.

Sarah Grigg
Lanphier High School
Springfield
Grade 9

Happy

Marked by pleasure, showing good.
Being lucky. Something to do
to cheer up while sad.

Also, a piece of your personality.
Something that comes and goes,
but should always be with you.

When getting a present,
getting what I want,
winning the lotto.

Being with your friends.
Cruising around,
never letting it go away.

Taking it and sharing it.
Playing around and having fun,
trying not to hurt someone.

Talking on the phone.
Getting your license,
just having plain old fun.

Lesly Guzman
Hubbard High School
Chicago
Grade 9

The Poison in the Bottle
Do not drink the poison in the bottle.
It destroys.
It kills.
It distorts the vision of life.
It deceives and conceals.
Victims are involved:
Elders,
Children,
Babies,
Adults.
It brings a dark cloud that some never escape.
It burns lives.
It causes hurt.
The forms are many:
Shots,
Cans,
Bottles.
Steer clear of the poison in the bottle,
Alcohol.

Alicia Corso
St Matthew School
Champaign
Grade 8

Chester
Chester waddles about his territory
His fat belly shows his love for food.
He screams a high pitched wail
Such as a baby would for its mother.
Chester wants broccoli!

I come, with offerings of sacrificial vegetables
And delicacies of all kinds,
To serve him as would squires to a noble king.
I'm merely a jester in his court of straw.
Awaiting his commands.

Smooth, silky whiskers twitch
As the moonlight glows gently on them.
His large, beady eyes sparkle
With delight as I enter the room.
"Welcome," he says.

Chester squeals with delight
As I lift his large mass
And embrace him with my arms.
Not only does he crave food,
But my love.

Alex Gilman-Smith
Highland Middle School
Libertyville
Grade 7

Summer
Summer is fun when you are out of school
When you spend all day at the pool
Go to the park and play around
Or jump off the swing and hit the ground
When you go back to school it is not fun at all
When you have to walk down that scary hall

Kyle Klostermann
Beckemeyer Elementary School
Beckemeyer
Grade 7

As I Watch
As I watch my guiding light
I watch the sun go down at night
The moonlight is the only light I see
I know the angels are watching me

I watch the stars blink on and off
Feeling the clouds that are so soft
Wanting to hold your precious one
Just thinking that they are done

I hear the angels sing so sweet
Their voices are such a lovely treat
You think they are far but are close as can be
Now the angels are watching you and me

I know it's hard to believe, but it's true
I know the angels are watching you
You pray to the Lord – the Angels too
The Lord and the Angels say I love you!

Lauren Muellner
St Celestine School
Elmwood Park
Grade 8

Out of the Darkness
The moon, in its splendor, lighting the sky
And I, his companion, only and one
He listens to me and watches me cry,
About troubles I face when day is done.
'Cause not even the stars, can comprehend
Sadness that lies in the depths of the dark
But the moon is my light, he is my friend
Until it is heard; the song of the lark.

The past still haunts me, it won't go away,
Darkness surrounds me, but I won't give in.
Soon sun will be rising, it will be day,
And I'll try to forget my God-awful sin.
The future looks brighter, of this I'm sure
Than the darkness and pain I've had to endure.

Tanya Noronha
Fenwick High School
Oak Park
Grade 9

Wind

Strong and powerful.
Lifting the birds to new heights.
Cooling the summer air.
Propelling boats to explore.
Festering forest fires.

Jim McAnelly
Holy Angels School
Aurora
Grade 7

Dreams

The night is dark
The room is black,
Your dreams embark
On their journey back.

The bed is waiting
Your head is numb,
Your thoughts are debating
On dreams to come.

Big dreams or small
It's all up to you,
Don't let a wall
Block anything you do.

Your dreams are finding
More nights for peaceful sleep.
But be sure to keep on climbing
Your next dream is just a small leap.

The night is dark
The room is black,
Don't let your dreams park
On the journey back.

Chrissy Cane
Quincy Jr High School
Quincy
Grade 9

The Beach

The sweet smell of sunflowers
Sailed through the air.
The waves crashed against the mountain.
Like lightning hitting the ground.
The sun was beating down
Like a warm blanket.
The summer sand seemed so soft.
The people played at the park
While having a picnic.
At the beach,
Memories are bound to last forever.

Amanda Marshall
Francis Granger Middle School
Aurora
Grade 7

Me

If my hands could talk they would speak of:
A child falling off his bike, but who always got back up
A boy who has nursed a wounded rabbit back to full health
A young man crying himself to sleep every night, hoping for better days
If my ears could talk they would speak of:
A child who heard of far-off lands but never got to see them
A boy who heard other children mock him
A young man who listened to his mother scream out in pain
If my eyes could talk they would speak of:
A child who feared everything that was new to him
A boy who gave his all to fit in but never succeeded
A young man who watched his mother slowly die, but could never help
I can talk and when I do I speak of a person
Who has been through a lot, but has much to go through

Brian McNees
Stratford Jr High School
Bloomingdale
Grade 8

Melissa

My life used to be a piece of cake
Yesterday I didn't know what would become of these four years
Inside my head there is now a constant war
Today people see my life easy but in reality I live in a fast paced world
I have never been happy with second best which has given me nothing but success
Tomorrow when I walk across the stage I will carry in my hand a piece of history
That important piece of history will not be easy achieving

Melissa Gonzalez
Hubbard High School
Chicago
Grade 9

What Happened to That Man?*

What happened to that man everyone knew, loved, and cared about?

What happened to that man named Robert (Bobby/Babyface) Lee Bensen?
He came into this world on Feb. 20, 1939, and was taken on Dec.13, 1998.

What happened to that man who dedicated his life, for 36 years,
in the Chicago Public School System, as a Physical Education teacher.

What happened to that man, who was always there for his students,
he never let them down. If there was a problem, he would try and help.

At Charles N. Holden Elementary School, he might have been 59 years old,
but he had the heart of a 12 year old.

Oh, how the time has passed, but still there is pain.
Will this pain ever go away?

What happened to that special man?

Vanessa Gracia
Holden Elementary School
Chicago
Grade 8
*Dedicated to Mr. Robert Lee Benson. We all miss you!

My Trip to Devil's Tower

My trip to Devil's Tower was fun,
We met some friends who had a son,
Who almost died when he was only one.

We didn't stay with them for very long,
My dad said that we needed to get moving along.
After we left, it wasn't long to get to Devil's Tower,
I unpacked my stuff, then went to take a shower.

Around Devil's Tower we did hike,
For as long as it took; I wish I had my bike.
Near Devil's Tower was a prairie dog town,
I've never seen a prairie dog that was so darn brown!

We saw a lot of motorcyclists there,
A bit of tension was growing in the air.
At last it was about time to depart,
I wish that is was just going to start.

Jonathan Gish
L J Stevens Middle School
Wilmington
Grade 7

The End?

You see nothing but black and white.
You close your eyes,
A serene mountain in a green, lush valley is seen.
Without warning it erupts.
A *burning, scalding, black* lava
Shoots like a shock wave after a nuclear bomb.
The serene picture turns to the cynical underworld.
You're enveloped by flames of apprehension.
You open your eyes in terror,
Then close them in courage and curiosity.
The peaceful utopia is back.

You are nervous
Twisting, turning and *throbbing* over and over,
A searing sensation encases your stomach
You shriek in pain and trepidation.

You *feel* a flash of blinding light.
As if you're in a state of nirvana,
Surrounded by white.
You feel calm, mellow, and no pain.

Is it the end? Is it the beginning?
Is there an answer?

Brett Thompson
Thompson Jr High School
Oswego
Grade 8

Back in the Day

I wish I could go back to the time when I could
Just do nothing but watch TV without a care in the world.
Not worry about having a girlfriend or getting good grades.
Wanting to go and wait for my mom and dad to come home.
Not having to pay for anything.
I wish I could do what I want.
Little kids have all the fun.

Michael Hesselbacher
Scales Mound Jr High School
Scales Mound
Grade 8

A Time for Destruction, A Time for Rejuvenation

A light drizzle starts to fall from the sky,
the whistle from a faraway train rolls through,
the sun descends lower and lower below the horizon,
wafting through comes a cool, misty breeze.
All of the beasts are still in an unconscious state.
A leaf crackles across the blackened ground, alone.
This environment is now in utter stillness,
as it slowly drifts away in the breeze.
Branches scratch and snarl at one another,
they creak and twist in the heat.
The drizzle had stopped,
until a violent gust of wind brought it back up,
only to leave as quickly as it came.
Through the branches of the old maple tree,
a keyhole of scarlet light shines through,
as if inviting you in but not too close.
Trees are left standing bare,
after the red blaze shown through.
Now everything is charred and blackened,
the trees that were bathed and coated in redness wave farewell.
The fire has passed.

Kendyl Wyman
Albright Middle School
Villa Park
Grade 8

The Goalie

Here I stand in the net.
Throughout the game I work up a sweat.
Stopping pucks left, stopping pucks right,
Up and down, back and forth—Oh what a night!
I hear the crowd chanting my name,
I've got to keep my head in the game,
The game is tied two to two,
With time running out one more goal will do,
As long as I do my job right,
I know we will win this game tonight,
It's over—We've won!
I'm tired—but I had fun.

Eric Bragagnolo
St Ferdinand School
Chicago
Grade 8

A Spring Day

A Spring day is a warm, joyful day.
You see little children playing all around,
and birds flying through the sky.
And the flowers are blooming.
And that is "A Spring Day."

Kim Kerr
Queen of Martyrs School
Chicago
Grade 8

Freedom, Justice, and Liberty

Freedom, Justice, and Liberty
Are very important to me.

Justice means to put things right,
Such as breaking up a fight.

Freedom means that you can choose
Whether you want to win or lose.

And liberty is the freedom to
Do what you really want to do.

Thomas Haine
St Mary School
Alton
Grade 8

Billy's Box

Billy was a nice boy
he loved to run and play
no one ever figured
that his life would end this way.

Billy graduated Jr. high
and moved up a new school
all the older kids smoked there
and Billy thought that was cool.

All his friends would tempt him
and Billy said he was straight
he said he'd try one later
but his friends, they wouldn't wait.

He figured he'd try just one puff
but one puff led to two
if only Billy would have known
that his life would soon be through.

Billy became addicted
and threw his life away
little did Billy know that
he'd be in a box soon that day.

Mandy Wilkening
Grant Park Middle School
Grant Park
Grade 7

On the Playground

People talk about racism all over the world,
but no one ever talks about where it starts,
the playground.

Kids won't talk to other kids because they aren't cool enough.
Why?

Why should little kids be put in tears because they are different,
this is not the way God wants us to treat others,
and yet it goes on,
Why?
Kids make fun of others just to fit in, but they don't know the pain it causes,
When will people learn that words can hurt others so much.

Matt Biszewski
Queen of Martyrs School
Chicago
Grade 8

This Ship Has Sailed

This ship has sailed from port to port with many lessons learned.
Leaving no sea untraveled, and not one stone unturned.

This roving vessel hath encountered many a trial in time
And it also had those moments, when completely sublime.

And now its sailing days are done, it's old and torn apart
But if you look closely at this ragged ship it seems to have a heart.

Krissy Witt
Fenwick High School
Oak Park
Grade 9

The Rush of Day and Calm of Night

Light shines on iridescent flowers
as the brightness displays the morning.
People awake to see the splendor,
never growing to appreciate it.

Rushing to work, rushing home,
never looking at life.
Rushing in, rushing out,
yelling, crying, laughing themselves into a superficial cycle.

Night falls,
and darkness floats in like clouds on a sunny day.
People relaxing, stretching, breathing,
calmly driving home,
fully appreciating the night.
Sleeping peacefully in a dreamy haze
as the soft darkness illuminates the pink brightness of the sunrise.
Dreams submerging into a sea of sub-consciousness,
restarting the vicious rush of day.

Chelsea Murphy
Blessed Sacrament School
Belleville
Grade 8

Twin Brothers

I cannot say my life was always a beautiful song,
With twin brothers I felt I did not belong.
I know you both will be home very soon,
I will get to see you two sitting there in your room.

We used to be so close and strong,
Can you guys tell me what went wrong?
I don't know what to say,
All I can do is sit and pray.

I cannot recall telling you both that, "I love you,"
Without you what would I do?
I can only tell you both what I feel in a letter,
How I really feel, and that things will only get better.

I will be here when you walk through that door,
I will be your little sister that's heart once was sore.
When you both get home my heart won't be sore at last,
I pray for you two to come back safely and fast.

I only shed a few tears,
But it seems like you've both been gone for years.
The man up above knows what went wrong and why,
He is God and he knows why you two said goodbye.

Kayla Hall
Hardin County Jr High School
Elizabethtown
Grade 8

Feelings Not Yet Known

All around there is pain,
Pain caused by former friends.
A lonely girl walks the halls,
Where she once smiled happily.
Every person taunts and teases,
Pokes fun until it has to stop.
She calls for help and lets it out,
All that has been kept inside.
"I can't handle it," she says,
Then cries tears of hurt.
There has been a crime committed,
The crime of mental abuse.
It's hard to let it blow over,
To keep your feelings hidden.
Only the victim knows what it feels like,
The others just don't understand.
It hurts feelings and kills self-esteem,
Until the girl finds her strength and conquers all.

Amy Jordan
Garvy Elementary School
Chicago
Grade 8

A Heavenly Battle

A large confrontation,
Driven by forces uncontrolled by man or nature,
Going into battle,
In the sky,
A collision of fronts,
Release their fury
Hail, rain, wind,
Throwing bolts of lightning,
The deafening battle cry of thunder,
Pillaging, raging, terrorizing,
A path of destruction is all that is left,
Of the great battle in the sky.

David Milender
Prince of Peace School
Lake Villa
Grade 8

Deafening

Everything was silent; no one made a sound
Not even the animals
It was dead quiet everywhere
So quiet
So deafening

Now came a sound
A loud rumbling
The sky turned yellow, then orange, then red
As the rock came closer, as everyone stared in horror
The sound became even louder
So loud
So deafening

And then when the damage had been done
Everything was still and quiet for seeming eternity
DEAD quiet
Until a blade of grass emerged from the rubble

And life continued its path.

CJ Arellano
St George School
Tinley Park
Grade 8

My Special Place

I have a special place.
My special place is down by the lake.
I go there when I'm down and have a frown.
Do you have a special place?
I found my special place one day when I was sad.
My special place is somewhere I don't go with my dad.
It's a very special place.
My special place turns my frown upside down.

Albert Flores
Owen Scholastic Academy
Chicago
Grade 7

Homework Rules!
Whenever I hand it in,
My teacher always gives me a grin.

When it's time to take a test,
I always try to do my best.

Homework is a lot of fun,
Especially when I get it done.
Homework Rules!

Kurtis Kunath
St Irene School
Warrenville
Grade 7

The Sun
The sun so bright,
It gives off heavenly light.

Heating the earth,
And giving it birth.

It will soon rise,
Above the blue skies.

Fotis Perizes
Fremont Elementary School
Mundelein
Grade 7

The Perfect Friend
The perfect friend is the
one who is there;

The perfect friend always
does care;

The perfect friend grows
never apart;

The perfect friend is always
in your heart;

The perfect friend is
always loved;

The perfect friend seems
like a gift from above;

The perfect friend means
the world to me;

The perfect friend will always
be with me.

Caitlin Balsam
Owen Scholastic Academy
Chicago
Grade 7

Friends
You are the light,
if the sun goes down.
You are the path
when I am lost.
You are the answer
when I am confused.
You were my voice
when I could not talk.

Megan Webb
St John The Baptist School
West Frankfort
Grade 7

Chicago
Luminous lamps
shining all around
could spot anyone
but can't catch a sound.

One lamp holds a candle
which under it has a sign
for all who are attending
to be here at nine.

When they are here and seated
the play will start
can you guess where we are
the Theater of Music and Fine Arts.

The play is at an interlude
everyone is walking around
admiring the architecture
up and down.

Now the play is over
the audience is standing
clapping and cheering
you could even hear it on the landing.

Emily Pendse
St Cyprian School
River Grove
Grade 8

Music
Hip hop, jazz, rap, alternative, rock—
just to name a few.
Emotions—happy, sad, angry, forlorn.
Can bring people together;
Music is universal.
Different people, different tastes.
At the top of the chart one day,
but the bottom the next.

Karen Bachmeyer
Pope John XXIII School
Evanston
Grade 8

Lullaby
Close your eyes,
Fall to sleep;
Dream many dreams
Of me and you.

Close your eyes,
Fall to sleep;
Sail a ship
On an ocean blue.

Close your eyes,
Fall to sleep;
Dream of satin gowns
And a beautiful dress.

Close your eyes,
Fall to sleep;
My sweet little
Princess....

John Lence
Cisne Middle School
Cisne
Grade 8

Friend
Friend
Kind and caring
Talking happily
Like a shadow
If only we could spend
All of our time together.

Jennifer Reszke
River Trails Middle School
Mount Prospect
Grade 7

Injure
Physical pain
wounds victims as it strikes
afraid to feel the wrath of this...
torment.

Courtney Ward
Francis Granger Middle School
Aurora
Grade 7

I Remember
I remember when I got my first dog.
I remember my first 4 wheeler.
I remember my first bike.
I remember my first tool box.
I remember.

Nick Nolte
White Oak Academy
East St Louis
Grade 8

It's Winter

When I feel the wind rush against my face
It seems as though it's a race.

It's Winter

When I hear the bells chime
I want to scream it's Christmas time.

It's Winter

When I see the snowflakes fall
I remember playing basketball.

It's Winter

If winter weren't here I would miss it.
But I'm happy that it's winter.

Enedelia Marquez
St Joseph Catholic School
Harvard
Grade 7

Sisters*

They're here to make you crazy,
And make your life feel hazy.
But, even if you're mad
You'll always be glad
When you see each other.

They could maybe let you borrow
Something that takes away your sorrow.
And the friendship will always last,
No matter how far away you're cast.

Your parents will be glad to see
Not screaming at her like a banshee.
When their friend calls to talk,
Why not take a walk?

They prefer to be left alone,
When they are talking on the phone.
If they kick you out of the room to see
What is playing on TV.
Act as if you do not care, for it is always best to share.

So whether there are 1, 2, or 3,
Take care, and love them to the drying up of the sea.

Liz Nosek
St Jude The Apostle School
South Holland
Grade 7
*To my own two sisters whom I love and cherish.

Lost Thoughts

An eclipse of ideas,
Only to be forgotten.
Lost thoughts return to haunt you,
Vagabond ideas become confused with one another,
The main idea vaguely remembered,
The details escape like wisps of eerie smoke.
Lost ideas, the failure of remembrance.

Joseph Stull
St Matthew School
Champaign
Grade 7

Moving On

Today is the day to be moving on,
One more precious day gone.
Today is the day, I find,
I will not be left behind.

And I make a vow, though it will be hard,
I'll go on with a smile and play every card.
I try and strive to do my best,
But still can't keep up with the rest.

As we grow older, things must change;
Places in time can rearrange.
We try to keep in touch, but we don't,
You think they'll call, but they won't.

Although life has many setbacks,
We will give whatever it lacks.
And you will always find,
I will not be left behind.

Megan Robinson
Hardin County Jr High School
Elizabethtown
Grade 8

Angels

Angels are fun.
Angels are cool.
Whenever you want to see them,
they are there, waiting for you.
Angels are pretty.
Angels are smart.
They help you whenever they can,
whether you like it or not.
They're always behind you.
They're always around you.
Waiting for the right moment,
to talk to you.
So always remember to thank God,
for giving you such a wonderful angel that's fun.

Isis Avila
Armstrong Elementary School
Chicago
Grade 7

Window to the World (Television)

It connects us to the outside world
Other countries' customs are unfurled,
It provides us entertainment too,
When we have nothing else to do.

Andrew J. Cardella
River Trails Middle School
Mount Prospect
Grade 7

Untitled

The day will come
When you cease to
Grab onto your life.
Everything as we know it
Become those eerie memories
We dread to think about.
The lives of the loved
We once held so dear,
Now despised
Because we let it happen.
We let others
Take our lives
And twist them
Into manipulative lies.
Then let them laugh
As you fall further and further
Away from the world.
The life you once knew,
Gone.

Linda Casey
Conrady Jr High School
Hickory Hills
Grade 8

A White Rose

A white rose I'll never give.
A white rose I'll never receive
As I think about the day,
The heavens took you from me,
I remember the white rose,
By your casket it did lie,
As I stood by your side,
I begin to cry,
You were so young,
But again you were so sick,
When I think of it now,
It all happened a little quick,
With your heart with mine,
I'll leave each day,
Remembering your sweet memory,
My little sister I'll love you forever,
I know someday again we'll be together.

Tanishia M. Jones
Owen Scholastic Academy
Chicago
Grade 7

Traces of You

I was taught to love You with all my heart, for being with You is my desire,
From a babe I was given to be a part of Your wondrous holy fire.

You saw me through the good and bad, and when I thought no one cared
Traces of You shined through, You gazed at me and stared.

Why do I love You as many do? I can't see and can't hear You.
I only feel Your presence here deep inside I hold You dear.

Faces come and faces go friendships never last,
It's You alone, I truly know, who will always hold me fast.

I've been led to blackened pits of hid'ous human error
Disasters come and strike me down, but I don't feel the terror.

For You are with me, I believe though skeptics mock faith I conceive
Out of dust you made us all, back to dust we all will fall.

The noblest saint falls short of Your glory. The greatest thought of man,
Doesn't compare to Your weakest moment.

When I die, I know You'll be there. You'll take me home, into Your care.

Rachel Halfpap
Quincy Jr High School
Quincy
Grade 8

The Marathon

In all their minds, the outcome is feared.
Yet all race with many different goals.
The gun bangs and it all starts there.
Many will see that the race is filled with different turns and curves.

It begins with people in many groups.
But as time goes by, they drift away.
Some give up and quit on what they set for themselves.
Some are strong and don't stop fighting until the end.

Dropping out and giving up,
One by one they fade away.
While some are still strong and still running.
Following a goal they set ages ago.

Those who faint trying are unfortunate winners.
Those who stop trying are cowards.
Those who finish are great!
All who race learn valuable lessons.

It doesn't matter whether they finish first.
And it doesn't matter whether they finish last.
All that matters is that they have finished,
And that they won the battle.

Sean Dacanay
St Colette School
Rolling Meadows
Grade 8

Earth

The planet Earth,
Is what all the people deserve,
This grass, this sun,
Is where you play and run.
The ground you walk on,
The air you breathe,
That's the payback
That people receive
All the people who care,
Don't hurt one another as a dare,
The people who brought themselves in the world of fame,
Should not get their hopes up, it's only a game
The life you live, is chosen by you,
The progress, commitments, and loses are too
To live and to love, is a gift that you got,
Is what most people nowadays forgot
To realize that you are happy,
Is very hard to do, so wish and dream
And all you do is wait and wait, to see if they'll come true.

Ally Spivak
Aptakisic Jr High School
Buffalo Grove
Grade 8

A Book

A book is a story
Full of many thoughts,
Thoughts for everyone to share.

A book is a treasure
Hidden in the sand,
And in the sand is where I'll find that special book for me.

That book tells a strange tale
About a strange place,
And to that place I will be taken, where I've never been before.

It will be of kings and queens
All dressed in funny clothes,
Clothes that no one could have ever dreamed of.

I will fly on a magic carpet
A carpet made of silk,
Silk that only princesses use because they are so special.

That book I'm going to read
Is the book I like,
And that book I like is very special.

That book holds a story
Full of many thoughts,
Thoughts for everyone to share.

Ana Golchert
Clifford Crone Middle School
Naperville
Grade 7

Types of Moms

Some moms listen well
While with others it's hard to tell.
Others are caring,
But there are some who just hate sharing.
But thankfully,
There are some who are quite right.

Amber Morris
Harrison Elementary School
Wonder Lake
Grade 7

Just Because

Just because I am a girl
I should still be treated like a human being
I want to have the same rights as boys
Just because I am a girl
I am not weak
I am not punk
I am not going to let any boy or girl control me
Just because I am a girl
I can be athletic
I can like sports
I can do anything a boy can do, if not better
Just because I am a girl
Expect the best from me...that's what you'll get

Romonica Smith
Forest Trail Jr High School
Park Forest
Grade 8

All I Ask

There are many things people ask in life
Some come true but yet some don't
But when you ask for something important
You'll think it will come true, it won't
All I asked is for one last day
To spend my life with you
I pray all day and all night
But my wish just won't pull through
All I asked is just to have you,
To hold and to share my love with
But more and more I think about it
You become more and more a myth
All I asked was for one last minute
To see you laugh and smile
Because I know you want to
And I haven't seen it in awhile
All I asked was for one last moment
To let you know you are in my heart
And if my wish would come true
It would be easier to part
I want you back is that such a task? That is all I ask.

Angel Martin
Finley Jr High School
Chicago Ridge
Grade 8

Friends

F un to be around
R eliable
I nspiring
E njoyable
N ever tells secrets
D oes everything to make you happy
S tays together forever

Ashley Wesselmann
Beckemeyer Elementary School
Beckemeyer
Grade 7

Broken Heart

You made me hate you
for reasons I cannot stand.
You said you loved her
and wanted to hold her hand.
I can't take all of your lying
I can't help but start crying.
We were headed on a track
but I guess you wanted to go back.
You have something to say
that is to go our separate way.
I never thought we'd have to part
or ever mend a broken heart.

Stephanie Cummings
Holden Elementary School
Chicago
Grade 8

A Man Who Has Nothing

A man who has nothing
Cannot have his possessions
Taken away.

A man who has no goals
Cannot be let down.

A man who has no wife
Does not have to answer
To anyone.

A man who has no
Imagination has no life
Worth living for.

A man who has no love
Is a man that cannot
Have a broken heart.

It's just too bad a lot of men
Don't have these things.

David Erickson
Beckemeyer Elementary School
Beckemeyer
Grade 8

Night

Click. The light goes out. The terrors of the night arise,
Every shadow, every shift of the tree.
The moonlight casts an eerie glow to the room through the window.
As you try to go to sleep, the floor creaks.
The imagination runs wild. What could it be?
Nothing. Just the house shifting and groaning with the wind outside.
Calm.
As your eyes begin to close, your mind wanders.
Your mind goes blank as sleep envelopes you.
Letting your imagination take over your sleeping conscience.
Finally sleep comes.
The next morning, fears are forgotten in the dawning of a new day.
Life goes on until night falls and the hallucinations of the dark begin again.

Erin Smith
St Paul School
Danville
Grade 8

My Dream

I have this dream that one-day I will be great.
People everywhere will know my name and cheer when they hear it.
I will do my best to achieve my dream and I will not stop until I'm done.
It doesn't matter what people say or think about me
because they cannot live my life for me.
It is funny how people try to put you down when you are trying to be on top.
It is funny how they try to stop you or even slow you down.
Well they will not stop me or slow me down. I will not
Stop until my work on this earth is done.
I will be great; I will achieve my goal.
People will remember me when I am here and when I am gone.
I will make my parents proud and when they see me they will say that is my daughter.
I just hope while I'm doing this you will be with me and not against me.

Tasheka Cook-Banks
Marya Yates Elementary School
Matteson
Grade 8

Walkway to the River

A twisting, turning path gives an extraordinary view of nature's beauty.
The lush vegetation glistens in the sun from the morning dew.
The birds return with breakfast.
The dirty, cracked stepping stones are worn
By the many feet that have sauntered along them on a cool spring day.
I smell the fragrant and vibrant flowers we planted last spring.
As I near the river, I can hear the trickle of the water flowing over the rocks.
It's the song of nature—peaceful and calm.
When I need to clear my head, I walk down this path.
This walkway to the river.

Curran Duffey
St Thomas Of Villanova School
Palatine
Grade 7

Deceptions

Shadows dissolve like tears in the eyes,
As if scared of the dark, a new kind of shy.
An escalator goes on forever but where does it go?
A fish swims in the sea so cadent and slow.
Believe in yourself and all things are possible,
Believe in something else and the effects will be colossal.
We all will lie to one another,
And when it comes around we know how to cover.
Look at the sun is it actually there?
If you look it up it's actually a ball of air.
So who will decide what's an optical illusion?
Why do all of these fill us with confusion?
Believe in yourself and all things are possible,
Believe in something else and the effects are colossal.
Does a dog really think, does it know what we say?
When we ask it to fetch, does it know how to play?
Life goes on but to how long we don't exactly know,
These deceptions, like our life, will go so cadent and slow.

Melissa Woodley
St Paul School
Danville
Grade 8

The Boy

As I saw him walking down the street,
In my head I pondered.
Why would he be doing this?
And he still wandered and wandered.

It seemed like he was looking for something.
Something of which I do not know.
But as he came closer I realized
He was searching for his soul.

The eight-year-old boy walked right on by,
With a cigarette in hand.
I froze, I couldn't think,
All I could do was stand.

He was probably homeless
And probably poor,
But my emotions ran wild
As he collapsed to the floor.

He taught me a lesson
That I will through my life know.
To never do drugs,
Or I will have nowhere to go.

Erica M. Zuniga
John F Eberhart Elementary School
Chicago
Grade 7

My Shield

I put my shield up wherever I may go
I'm afraid of what you'll think, so the "real" me doesn't show
I'm tough, I'm hard, I have no trust
I've been through trials, unfair and unjust
I see the world as a complete lie
I hurt, I ache, then I die
I am on an endless pursuit to find my "dreams"
Life to me is what you make of it, so it seems
Once in awhile Ill put my guard down, just a bit
In return, I'm crushed, torn, and hit
I see no one to confide in
So I stay silent, like I've always been
I'd like to be happy and carefree,
For someone to love the "real" me
I need to find a friend if I can
Who will accept me just the way I am

Danielle Snider
Tri-City Jr-Sr High School
Buffalo
Grade 8

Memories

Memories we think of,
Memories we see in the past,
Memories we think of that will soon become rewards,
in our minds and in our souls,
the people we think of
the places we've been,
the things we did wrong and the things we did good,
the times we spent with the ones we love,
and the love that we give to each other
the things we will do for love
the things we do to gain love from others
will all someday become a memory.

Brittany Pickens
Mayer Elementary School
Chicago
Grade 7

A Moment in Time

Have you ever experienced the perfect moment,
When everything in time seems to wait
As you watch a waterfall tumble slowly down,
Or see a wild horse jump over a gate?
Or see the seeds of a dandelion float slowly away
On the gentle fingers of an evening breeze?
Or watch a boat's sail venture ever closer
On the horizon of one of the seven seas?
Or it could be as simple as spending spare time
Along side of a person you like keeping company with.
And it could be a week, or a thousand years later,
But your moment in time seems never to drift.

Adrienne Dudlo
Conrady Jr High School
Hickory Hills
Grade 8

Sweat Shop
School is a sweat shop
Where little kids are
Put to work.

Mike Scianna
River Trails Middle School
Mount Prospect
Grade 7

Snow
Snow
Glimmer bright
Airy as daylight
Falling down at night
Snow

Himadri Shah
East Prairie Elementary School
Skokie
Grade 8

The Dog
There was a dog on the floor,
like a old pile of wood,
when the dog heard the door open,
he jumped up like a bell that just rung.

David Edwards
Pleasant Hill Elementary School
Peoria
Grade 8

The Ones They Left Behind
It's a sad sad thing
a heartbroken teen
brought down by the grip of reality
sitting alone, curled in a chair
she cries as she brushes her hair

Why do boys show off?
Why do they risk a life
to be part of a club
they drink too much
then drive too fast
they speed through life
with a slip of the hand

They live for flashing lights
sky high highs, living in lies
they steal to live, and live to steal
they cannot stop, they're over the hill
they've done too much
they cannot stop, they cannot slow
they cannot think or remember
the ones they left behind.

Samantha Murphy
Tri-City Jr-Sr High School
Buffalo
Grade 8

Crystal Water
I see a gloomy light
Shining upon three men.
It is crystal clear
Like a magic glass.
It reflects the surface
Like a gigantic mirror.
Inside the water I also see
Bright, white angels coming down
From the sky towards the wind.

Fernando Virgen
Hubbard High School
Chicago
Grade 9

Why?
I wiped her eyes
When she would cry
I made her laugh
When she was mad
I made her happy
When she was sad
I was there when she needed me
Why isn't she here when I need her
Why did she have to go?

Fallon Feazel
Hardin County Jr High School
Elizabethtown
Grade 8

Music Is Life*
Music is
Wind blowing soft love sounds
  Putting feeling in what is believed.
Happiness
Joy
Love
  But never pain.
Music is
  Your brain being fondled.
Music is so strong you can do no wrong.
Music is
  Butterflies
  Spring
  Hummingbird wings.
Music is sharing with
  Friends
  Family
  Teachers
Because of Mr. Cook
  I say
  Music Is Life.

Ashley Lindsey
St Jude The Apostle School
South Holland
Grade 8
*In memory of Mr. Cook

Spring
Spring is nice and cool.
Breezy flowers blow in the wind.
Sunshine fills the sky.

Flowers are pretty.
They are different colors.
They bloom all spring long.

The sky is very blue.
It is starry in the night.
Becomes black at night.

Stacy Zeller
Shirland C C Elementary School
Shirland
Grade 7

Dinner
Dinner is ready
I rush to the table,
and there's a feast waiting for me.

My parents told me
when I went for the food
you have to wait for your brothers,
I'd rather do others.

My brother is here
and I am so dear
because we can start eating.

The food was so great
as I ate,
and I almost started to drool.

But then I was done,
and I had to run
because I had to finish my homework.

Greg Lazarus
Nichols Middle School
Evanston
Grade 8

Wishing for a Picture
A long time ago, I made a wish.
A wish for a girl so beautiful and sweet.
That every time I looked at her,
She makes my heart skip a beat.
A few days ago I was looking at a picture.
Realizing my wish finally came true.
And the picture I was looking at,
Was a picture of you.

Andrew Vega
St George School
Tinley Park
Grade 8

Jack

Aunt Stacy was gonna have a baby.
Is it a boy? I dunno, maybe.

She had to go on bed rest.
It was a heavy burden on her chest.

He was born 10-10-99
Perfect and fine.
Two arms, two legs, ten fingers, ten toes,
Blue eyes like mine and his grandma's nose.

His name is Jack; and he has little hair,
But my Aunt Stacy and Uncle Tim don't care.

They asked me to be the godfather,
I said yes, that'd be no bother.

So Jack's my godson and it's all fun,
Because I really love the little one.

Ryan Fogerty
St Vincent De Paul School
Peoria
Grade 8

Window

I'm a window away from the world of unknown:

Where enemies strive along the roads,
    trying to break through the locker codes.
Where friends cry and laugh on each other's shoulders,
    soon to be pushed by a gang full of boulders.
Where rumors get spread quicker than e-mail,
    which are about either male or female.
Where people say things without a thought,
    and hardly any of them get caught.
Where feelings are hurt ten out of ten,
    and their not only hurt by the men.
Where several groups are made of different kinds,
    but only a few include the minds.
Where force is used instead of words,
    and it's usually used on the so-called "nerds."
Where people are judged by their looks,
    and the bad looking ones are put in the "ugly books."
Where the sun doesn't shine,
    and kids drink wine.

This is the place so called high school,
    where everyone wants to be cool.

Nikhila Loomba
Clifford Crone Middle School
Naperville
Grade 7

Loneliness

Loneliness is the color of a blank white page.
It tastes like warm distilled water.
It smells like a musty forgotten wine cellar.
It feels like a bitter cold draft coming in from a broken window.
Loneliness sounds like a fading echo.

Greg Swiss
St Bede School
Ingleside
Grade 7

Why Science?

What's up with Einstein and his E=mc2?
Why did he do it?
It's not like I care!
Why do we need to know the Theory of Relativity!
What does it do for me?
Who cares about the speed of light?
It never helps me in a fight!
There's no need for science for me at all.
Just having fun with friends is a ball.
Wait a sec! This isn't fair!
Without science I would care!
Science gives us a lot to do.
I'm so surprised I didn't' catch this clue.
Without science there would be no games or TV.
Now that would make my life so sleazy.
Science gives us light and stuff.
And a lot of things that are really pleasing.
So thank you Einstein and Mr. Franklin
Because of you and many others,
Our world is really changin'!

Blake Wolfenbarger
White Oak Academy
East St Louis
Grade 8

The Rebirth of a Friendship

I feel grief and sorrow for a loss,
Forgotten and so distant memories.
Independent minds, each wants to be boss,
Distrust and betrayal are some of these,
Obstacles that have upset our friendship.
Our hearts have been stressed, while anger resides.
Pride allows no kind words out of our lips,
But there will be a time when one decides.

I remember the times when she was there.
Why did we act with such hostility?
Since life began we have had so much care,
We work as one with much ability.
Treasured always will be my special friend,
With her I will never have to pretend.

Susan Sweeney
Fenwick High School
Oak Park
Grade 9

Winter Reflections

Winter reflections
Bare trees, white snow, stillness, cold
All signs of winter

John Buhle
St Mary of Czestochowa School
Cicero
Grade 8

The Invisible Enemy

Spring!
Flowers blooming, trees budding,
Everything turning green,
Vegetables growing, the sun is shining,
It creates quite a scene.

But once I go outside,
To admire what I see,
I get a strange feeling,
And something comes over me.

Hack! Cough!
I suddenly have no air,
Something bad has hit me,
It's coming from everywhere!

Itch! Scratch!
Hives are starting to appear,
I've had this since I was little,
This happens every year.

I know why this is happening,
There can only be one reason,
Since it is the beginning of spring,
It must be allergy season.

Jacob Nitzberg
New Trier Township High School
Winnetka
Grade 9

The Waters That Once Ran

The waters once ran,
But not now,
We killed them,
The fish once swam,
But they are gone,
The birds once flew,
But they have flown away,
The bears used to hunt,
But their prey is gone,
The waters once ran,
But not now,
We killed them.

Gerald Meyers
Nichols Middle School
Evanston
Grade 8

My Dream

I go to sleep and dream I was a pigeon, so I could fly.
Swift, swift, swift.
I would fly really high and pass up all the mean people in the world.
They would laugh at me, but I don't care.
I am too high to hear them anyway.
I am higher than any other bird because now I am a hawk.
Then I dive down.
Deep, deep, deep into the ocean.
I am a dolphin.
The crisp cold water splashes my face.
I drink some.
It's so pure and so cold, it feels as if I cut my mouth every time I take a sip.
It is delicious.
But, not as delicious as the fruit in the highest trees in the Amazon.
For now, I am a bird again.
A beautiful macaw.
Everyone who sees me will smile, because they know I bring happiness.
Then, I will sleep for my wings have grown weary.
When I awake, I am me again.
Happy as can be after my long night's trip.

Rogelio Garcia
Taylor Elementary School
Chicago
Grade 8

Unconditional Love

Your love is my light; you brighten up my day
Like the sun coming out on a rainy day,
Or another summer day to run, laugh, and play.

You're my love and there's no other, you love me like my own sweet mother.
When I'm around you I'm never blue, you say you love me, I love you, too.

You are my guiding light when I'm lost.
Your love is as peaceful as a river,
You hold the key to my soul,
You're peaceful and loving as I can see,
The light of my heart is here with thee.
Smooth skin and lovely eyes, you are the center of my pride.
Remember me and this one thing, "We are in love and always will be."

My love is stronger than my fear
Because when I'm alone your image appears,
Then it seems very clear, somehow I feel that you are here.

When you sleep it feels like heaven.
I reminisced about the time I said my first prayer,
And when I was little and often scared,
An image of you as an angel was there.

As you sleep I quietly pray,
"God, please let us see another day."

Tiffany Johnson
Children of Peace-St Callistus School
Chicago
Grade 7

Black Tears

Black tears are falling from the sky
no one wonders why;
these are the tears of black people crying
with jealousy and race destruction;
my people are killing each other
from gang and drug corruption.
Black tears are falling from the sky;
no one seems to wonder, or care why.
we came from a great nation,
brought here to work on racist plantations.
With these years our forefathers craved
equal rights and the end of slavery;
and here we are, cleared the rope
and running to the dope.
My people, is there any hope?
black tears are falling
can you, my brother or sister, hear our calling,
black tears are falling from the sky;
isn't it time we care and wonder why?

Christopher Adams
Albright Middle School
Villa Park
Grade 8

I'm Different, Yes, I Know

I'm different,
But isn't everyone,
Different from someone?

I'm different, yes, I know.
Do you have to show me
By doing hurtful things?

What do you want me to say?
I think I look okay.
Anyway, I'm not able to change.

I might be small for my age,
But don't forget,
My emotions and feelings are just the same.

No matter what you say
I will always be this way,
So your hurtful words can stop!

You don't bring me any pain.
No, not anymore,
I stay strong,
And stand tall; in my own special way.

Lauren Harvey
Owen Scholastic Academy
Chicago
Grade 7

Sunset

A sunset is so pretty to watch on a beach,
You watch as the sun comes down and meets the sea,
As it moves down inch by inch,
The moon moves up gracefully,
And when the sun has finally gone down,
You know it is time to go,
But, the memories will stay with you forever.

Austin Ducey
St Matthew School
Champaign
Grade 7

God's Calling

God has a calling that we will find.
It may not be what we had in mind.
But if you answer His calling to you.
You will be happy in whatever you do.

His little voice whispers in your ear.
Listen closely and you will hear.
He may not come right out and say.
But He knows what's best and He'll show you the way.

When you were born angels stood by your side.
Guiding you always, never letting you slide.
They are there to protect you and help you in need.
They are there to save you and help you succeed.

And now as we finish this season of Lent.
Let's remember the message He's sent.
God has His plans for us all.
Listen carefully and fulfill your call.

Jessica Parrish
St Vincent De Paul School
Peoria
Grade 8

The Night Camping

Gather the tent, the tools, the food, the poles,
Camping season is almost here this year,
Spread the tent on the ground and dig the holes,
The view is awesome of wild life and deer,
Collect the wood and build a big bon fire,
Place the fish over the big open pit,
Watch the flames as they get hot and higher,
We eat fish and watch the stars as we sit,
Night moves in and the moon glows in the sky,
Pull out the sleeping bags and climb inside,
We can't fall asleep even though we try,
The tent falls down and crushes everyone's pride,
Morning breaks and it is time to go home,
The city is busy and we can't roam.

Brock Peters
Sullivan High School
Sullivan
Grade 9

True Friends

When I am sad and I feel alone
And I think no one cares.
But then that's when my
friends come along.
I can always count on my
friends to cheer me up
They always lift me up
When I am down.
When something's wrong I
Know they will always stand
Aside me.
Thanks friends

Trevor Castro
St Barbara School
Chicago
Grade 8

Mother Nature

As the gust goes
the trees blow

the flowers bloom
the plants grow
the rain comes
the rain goes
All as Mother Nature
has planned

the roots pursue water
the roots require soil
the leaves produce
and some plants oil
All as Mother Nature
has planned

Amanda Meier
Francis Granger Middle School
Aurora
Grade 7

What Freedom Means to Me

Freedom is doing what's right
Just like staying out of a fight.

Freedom is how we spend our day.
that is why it is OK.

Freedom means being free,
but some people take advantage of it,
unlike people who are not free.

We all should jump for glee,
because we are free.

Billy Sloan
St Mary School
Alton
Grade 8

Searching Higher

There is a flame inside our hearts although it only glows
There is a light inside our souls that no human being knows

We're searching for some truth
We've had stomachaches of lies
We're searching for a mouthful
Of something deeper in our lives.

We're searching higher.

A soul is like a candle, burning clear and bright
Bringing cheer, comfort, aid; casting guiding light

Sometimes a soul can flicker – it never is blown out
And the way that God has it planned; these candles can't burn down

We're searching for some comfort
An ending to our grief
We're searching for that bridge
To where these two roads will meet.

We're searching higher.

We're searching deep within
To find the good inside
We're searching for the meaning
Of what it means to be alive

We're searching higher.

Kimberly Davis
Driscoll Catholic High School
Addison
Grade 9

Wrong Choices

On that dark, rainy night,
why did you choose not to do what was right?

Late that night you were on a joy ride,
you were only thinking of your pride.

You were going ninety-five in a fifty-five zone,
and because of that you changed many others' lives, not just your own.

Why didn't you slow down when you saw that hill?
I guess you thought you were in for a thrill.

You ran right into an oncoming car,
the driver of that was thrown pretty far.

You cared about nothing that night, except having fun,
and now because of that the other driver's life is done.

Amber Holtgrave
Beckemeyer Elementary School
Beckemeyer
Grade 8

Nothing

There is nothing left for me to do
nothing I can say
to prove my love for you
each and every single day
I tried to show you truthfully
until the very last
then you went and cheated on me
and now you are the past
so I know you could not be
the one that's always there for me
if I could have known before
the things that you would do
I would never let you know my love's for sure
and now my love will start brand new.

Brittany Eck
Lanphier High School
Springfield
Grade 9

Life Is Short

You have grown older, and much more mature.
Your mind is bright and your heart is stronger.
Your soul is clean, you've reached a new stature.
Life was so easy, now it's much harder.

You will soon be leaving graduating.
Your friends are moving to many places.
Your life is changing, it's rearranging.
You will meet new people, see new faces.

You'll soon be alone no one to help you.
Be responsible more reliable.
Be smart and trusting, and go get a clue.
Have self respect, be indefinable.

The near future holds many surprises.
Your life can change just like the sun rises.

Adam Dola
St Ferdinand School
Chicago
Grade 8

Easter Egg

I am an egg just white,
colored and decorated very bright,
colors pink, light purple and blue,
I am ready for the season and so are you.

I am an egg just white,
just painted bright,
decorated with glitter and designs,
and ready to be placed in your Easter basket all nice and right.

Brittany Szaflarski
Francis Xavier Warde School
Chicago
Grade 7

Christmas

You start to see red holiday bows,
Then there's that frostbite on your toes.

The stockings are not all in a case,
They're hanging over the fireplace.

The toy stores are filling up,
Your mother takes out her favorite Christmas cup.

Snowflakes fall from the sky,
People hang lights way up high.

You say "hello" to the people you miss,
Green and red wrappers are on the Hershey's Kiss.

Now we know it is Christmas time of year,
Hooray, hooray, we're going to cheer!

For all of the fun in Christmas I found,
Next year I can't wait till it comes around.

Torrey-Paige Szofer
St Michael School
Orland Park
Grade 7

Friends Forever

On the very day we met I knew
That I was meant to be friends with you

We said we would be friends forever
No matter what we must endeavor

But suddenly our conversations are growing short
At school b-ball games I can only stare at the court

The time that we spent together went way too fast
I see our friendship may be a thing of the past

At night I lay awake and cry
Constantly asking myself why

Why you treat me that way at school
Why you make me feel like a fool

For sticking around and waiting to see
If you really want to be friends with me

I guess I do not want us to part
For it would truly break my heart

But I guess that this is the time that I went
Because friends forever was not what you meant.

Nichole Goedeke
Beckemeyer Elementary School
Beckemeyer
Grade 8

Faded Stripes

The red, white and blue
Emblem of the USA
Hangs limp, unnoticed.

Rebecca Allen
Nichols Middle School
Evanston
Grade 8

The Rose

The rose grows on a vast plain,
The scarlet color grows bright,
It gets refreshed by the noon rain,
And rests through the night.

It wakes up before dawn,
Yearning for the sun's bright light,
The moist dew on the fresh lawn,
Helps the rose grow after the night.

The rose sat there where it was meant,
Before the dropping rain,
It sat there in the cold silent,
On the vast open plain.

Aaron Ianno
Immaculate Conception School
Morris
Grade 7

Winter

Snow
white
polar bear
North Pole
Santa Claus
Christmas
presents
decorations outside
cold
winter

Jessica Gaeta
River Trails Middle School
Mount Prospect
Grade 7

Sadness

It's upsetting
when you see a man
with no money
and no job
and nobody to help him.
It's sad
when you see him not eating.

Jonathan Campos
Logandale Middle School
Chicago
Grade 7

Splitting Up

My dad has gone away
I want him to come back to me
And forever stay

I love my dad
And I know that he loves me
I want them back together

But I guess it's not my choice!

Jessica Marler
Meridian Elementary School
Mounds
Grade 7

A Life in a Day...

What I've done...
What I'll do...
Just a thought to kill today.
Today is so long...
Wish I could sleep it away.
How many days will I allow
Myself to succumb to the prison within.
It's up to me. What will I do about me?
Think...Hope...
Make tomorrow better,
Make today better.
Sleep, think about all this tomorrow.

Synimin L. Blickhan
Quincy Jr High School
Quincy
Grade 7

My Dog Chewed Up My Homework

I'm glad to say my homework's done.
I finished it last night.
I've got it right here in this box.
It's not a pretty sight.

My dog chewed up my homework.
He slobbered on it, too.
so now my homework's ripped to shreds
and full of slimy goo.

It isn't much to look at,
but I brought it anyway.
I'm going to dump it on your desk
Even if...I don't get an A.

Give me the grade you think I deserve.
I'll take it no matter what.
But please be kind and gentle
cuz I gotta keep the mutt.

Jacob Ritzheimer
Beckemeyer Elementary School
Beckemeyer
Grade 7

Lion

Silent predator,
the lion watches and waits,
and then, it pounces.

Anya Helsel
Forest Trail Jr High School
Park Forest
Grade 8

My Heritage

I am Irish – I help my grandma
make her Irish soda bread.

I am German – I help my grandpa
make his German beer.

I am Bohemian – I like making
Bohemian bread with my mom
for Thanksgiving.

I am English – I like going
horseback riding English style
with my aunt.

I am French Canadian – I like to
watch my dad set up trap lines
like our early ancestors did.

Finally, I am American – I like eating
apple pie and watching baseball games.

I am very proud of my heritage.
They make me, me.

Sarah Richards
Owen Scholastic Academy
Chicago
Grade 8

Words

So many words left to be said,
Yet so many words are wasted.
So many words floating in our heads,
There, but yet to be tasted.

One word, so small, so easy to say,
That is said without a thought,
Can brighten up a person's day,
Or make their spirit rot.

Like birds they fly on a summer breeze,
Singing their songs for all.
But they are forgotten with relative ease,
Whether they are big or small.

Michelle Johnson
St Matthew School
Champaign
Grade 7

My Secret

I have this one secret
That I cannot share,
If I tell anyone, I know that they
Will look at me and stare.

I keep this secret
Deep inside,
So that I won't
Have to run and hide.

I also hide
My feelings deep inside,
I don't want to talk
To them and confide.

I think that I soon
Will be free,
I will tell everyone
What I feel and see.

My feelings are my secret,
The most terrified part of me.
I hope I will be free
So I can be me.

Lauren Strong
Clifford Crone Middle School
Naperville
Grade 7

Mañana

The tears of an unwed maiden,
Fin of a mermaid,
Sand from the deepest sea,
Wing of a fairy,
A golden lock of hair from a curly headed angel,
Innocence of a child,
Presence of a unicorn,
Stardust,
New life in spring,
Love in summer,
Tranquility of autumn,
Beauty of winter,
Memories,
The air around a waterfall,
Majesty of the mountain,
Love of God,
The shadow of a weeping willow,
A petal from a single flower amidst boundless trees,
Magic.

Sarah Grandt
Murphysboro Middle School
Murphysboro
Grade 7

Water with Love

People are like tiny flowers,
starting out as just a seed.
When stepped upon they wither,
just shrivel up and hide.
But when showered with love they bloom,
and open up inside.
Showing us their beauty,
their fragrance from within.
Isn't each one of us beautiful,
so beautiful and unique.
But only when we're watered with care,
and given the love we need,
do we open up and show the world,
how special we are inside.

Amy Wenerski
Southwest Chicago Christian School
Tinley Park
Grade 8

Things of Life

When I look high into the sky
I think of God watching us.
When I look low into the ground
I think of the devil trying to destroy us.

When I see the wind blowing,
It makes me think God is sweeping me off my feet,
And taking me to Him forever.

When my eyes look all around,
It makes me think of what God gave us.
If you take the time to look,
You will see the real things of life.

Shalisa Rembert
Children of Peace-St Callistus School
Chicago
Grade 7

The Game

Dribbling, dribbling down the court,
Never wanting to abort.
Basketball is what I love to play,
On the court is where I want to stay.
Running, jumping, shooting, scoring
The game is never ever boring.

Under the basket is where I stand,
As the ball just falls into my hand.
But wait, I'm not alone, I'm part of a team,
We work together and that's what makes the fans scream.
On the court is where I will always be,
Basketball is definitely the game for me!

Jennifer Carroll
Owen Scholastic Academy
Chicago
Grade 7

Sonnet of the Sky

At night there is a moon above so high,
Diana guides it by her faith and love,
Her light is shot across the star lit sky,
Embracing beauty like a pair of doves.

The stars are there to guide the ships at sea,
The reflection is a glimmer of hope,
To rise and become eternally free,
They give us courage when we need to cope.

The sun shines bright and gives us warm feelings,
Guided by Apollo one of the Kings,
Turning us closer to our hearts and minds,
The sun gives us an outer reach of kinds.

The sky has many features to observe,
Which all of us at one point do deserve.

Lana Stenger
Sullivan High School
Sullivan
Grade 9

My Cat

Sammy is my kitten and only three weeks old.
I found her in my shed, hiding from the cold.
When I saw her trembling body, I didn't know what to do.
So I opened up my arms, and up to them she flew.

I brought her to my parents and asked if she could stay.
They took one look at her body, and quickly said, "OK."
She is my favorite kitten, and we'll never be apart.
Sammy is the best, and I love her with all my heart.

Mallory Hubbard
St Mary School
Belleville
Grade 8

Dreams

Though days are long and time stands still,
There is a weapon against idleness.
Dreams.
They are elusive, leaving as quickly as they come.
They are inevitable, our doorway to endless mortality.
Whether conscious or sleeping,
We leave our fears, inhibitions, and regrets.
We travel to a world where nothing can go wrong, because
We lead perfect lives.
Dreams are a way to escape, a way to return to sanity.
They are an infinite vastness, waiting to be tapped into;
A cache of wealth, unique to each individual.
Dreams are a perpetual Fountain of Youth.
Dreams.

Megan McMillen
St Matthew School
Champaign
Grade 8

It's Simple

When I feel alone
And there's no one round to play
What I do is simple
What I do is simple.
I pray:

I pray to my God for strength
And I pray to my God for love
And I pray to my God to keep me away from sin.

What I do is simple.
I pray:

I pray to my God for mercy.
I pray to my God for peace.
I pray to my God every night and day.

What I do is simple.
I pray.

Jessica Conlin
Holy Angels School
Aurora
Grade 7

Vehicles

There are many different kinds of vehicles.
Slow ones fast ones and classic ones too.
Cars can be many different colors,
And different shapes and sizes.

I like the ones that are big and powerful.
The ones that can climb almost anything.
It would have to be a truck or RV.
I would prefer a truck.

Trucks, cars, vans, roadsters, or station wagons.
There are many kinds of vehicles.
I just told you the cars that I like.
You might like the same ones I do.

Philip Buhl
Beckemeyer Elementary School
Beckemeyer
Grade 7

The Winter Season

Winter is my favorite season...
The snow falling to the ground,
Building snowmen outside in the cold,
Hiding in snow forts from the freezing wind,
Skiing down the snowy mountain,
Sledding in different paths down the hill,
I just love the winter season!

Dan Griffin
Queen of Martyrs School
Chicago
Grade 8

Rain Outside My Window

The rain falls down, departed from clouds of innocence.
In a sense, I feel it's only falling on my building.

I listen to the sound of cleansing,
Washing, reviving, purity, creation,
As it hits the pavement;
And the hate and ugliness on the sidewalks disappear.

And people with umbrellas run by,
Without looking up from their boots;
The sound of their galoshes
Echo throughout the cold, dull air.

The green comes back to the tree below.
Renews its leaves, and the thin branches
Shiver, quake, wave, shudder,
Tremble, quiver, sway, lean,
Shake, move,
To the sound of the rain.

So pure, unfiltered,
Faltered not by sun's gloss,
With eyes glazed over,
The fog, the veil pulled from the eyes,
An awakening! A rebirth! A calling!

Brittany Bellgardt
Peacock Jr High School
Itasca
Grade 8

In the Pitch-black Night

When the dark night creeps up on me,
I never believe what I see.
There are creatures with untold danger,
For there are no rangers.
They start to creep from the closet and behind the door,
I've tried to let out a roar.
But there was no sound to be heard,
Not even the chirp of a bird.
Then the sun starts to rise,
And catches the creatures by surprise.
They started to disappear,
Faster than they had appeared.
I survived last night,
But that is not the end of the fight.
They seem to get closer every night.
And I try to fight,
But what weapon should I use,
Because in the end I probably will lose.
Every night I must try,
Or else I probably will die.
Or is it just my imagination.

William Gosewehr
St Irene School
Warrenville
Grade 7

Swimming

Swimming is such a rush
Freestyle, butterfly, breaststroke, backstroke
Goggles, swim caps
Moving fast
Effortlessly

Emily Krystof
St Gerald School
Oak Lawn
Grade 7

Love Is...

Love is sent from the heavens and above,
and looks like a pretty white dove.

Although some may not see love but know it's there,
because of the people that show that they care.

Love is something that sometimes may be expressed in words,
or seen like the cute little birds.

Some say love will never last forever,
but some say love is happily ever after.

Love is like the love I have for my family,
'cause they keep food in my little belly.

God loves everyone in the world equally,
even the ones that may seem geeky.

Love sometimes may seem fake,
and also lets you know that you have made a mistake.

Mercedes Russell
Dunbar Vocational Career Academy
Chicago
Grade 9

Why Did God Have to Take Her Away So Soon?

Why did God have to take her away so soon?
I guess her duty was done
And now she's gone to the heaven above.
It is hard to accept her death
When I didn't even get to say one last good-bye
Knowing that I will not hear her voice
And see the smile on her face she always had
When I saw her lying there so still and stiff
I could not help but shed tears
Realizing she was dead
Her death was so sudden and unexpected
It felt like a nightmare that I could not awake from
But I know that she has gone to a better place
Where she will be waiting for her loved ones
To welcome them to the heaven above

Mirna Villarreal
Norman Bridge School
Chicago
Grade 8

A Mother Is a Gift

A mother is a special person that consoles you when you are not feeling well or have a problem.
She knows when something is wrong with you, so you can't obscure anything from her.
It is needed to have a mother because she is a treasure that you won't have all your life.

Theresa Alvarez
Francis Granger Middle School
Aurora
Grade 7

Heavenly Sister

You may think it's funny, although it's not
It's quite serious, is it not
For I once had a heavenly sister, but now I don't
For God took her away, I know it was so she could run, laugh, and play
Right now I know she's fine, in a life so sublime
For now she can run, even if she had a bad heart
I know she died young, but she taught me a great deal in life
She made me look deep within, she made me realize who I was
Is it selfish of me to want her back, for the one who made her, took her back
Now she's gone, even though I want her back
I know I'm blessed to have a friend like her, for she is what I call a gift from God above
I just ponder sometimes, that's all, if she was really my friend or a heavenly gift from above

Katie Mullins
Hamilton County Jr High School
Mc Leansboro
Grade 7

From Fall to Winter

The red, orange, lavender, and golden colored leaves practically leapt from the trees, now bare and dead,
Leaving the lonesome plants grasping for love and support during the long winter months ahead.
The wind picks up the objects, and throws them around,
Spins them in circles, and drops them back to the ground.
And soon enough, the winter snows will come and cover them away,
Letting the crispy leaves disappear forevermore, following that day.
But soon enough the summer sun will blossom the plants and flowers,
Allowing children and their loved ones to play outside for hours.

Liz Hutchison
St Mary School
Buffalo Grove
Grade 7

Three Angelic Boys

I don't understand, and I don't know why, you people love to make others cry.
I ask myself, Hey what's the big deal? I can like who I like, and feel how I feel.
What you call stupid and annoying noise, I call heavens music, made by 3 angelic boys.
Is it really my fault that I got caught in the wave? I was in way too deep, and could never be saved.
You call them girls because they have high voices, well it's called puberty and it wasn't their choices.
Tell me what harm did they ever cause you, yet you sit there and rag on them but nothing's true.
They make me feel happy and warm inside, but because of you, my feelings I hide.
You say that everything about them is wrong, just because their hair is too long.
Well I disagree but I can't stand up, because in the past you made my life tough.
So next time you trash them and make them look bad, please think of the people whom you have made mad.
Cause you can make fun of them and tear them apart, but that won't erase their place in my heart.

Lauren Dixon
Francis Granger Middle School
Aurora
Grade 7

Fear

Did you ever think of all the little noises you have heard?

They may be loud.
They may be quiet.

You mostly hear them when you're at home,
but most of all when you're home alone.

The noises may scare you.
they may frighten you at night,
but most of all when there's no light.

When there's no light,
There's definitely no sight.

So you may be scared if you are dared.

So when you're alone
and no one is on the phone

Beware

Because I'm sure that someone's there.

Gladys Rojas
Hamlin Upper Grade Center
Alsip
Grade 7

Spirit in the Night

He doesn't need the sunlight to beat on his face;
To show all of his beauty, all of his grace.

He showed us all the way;
To live, think, and love every day.

He comes to his creation in every way;
Spirit, body, and soul.

Many people forget what is most important in life;
The spirit that watches us during the night.

He isn't something you see or touch
But in your heart, he means so much.

He carries you when you fall;
You just don't remember, you think you know it all.

Many people forget what is most important in life;
The spirit that watches us during the night.

Nicole Prokopec
Leland Elementary School
Leland
Grade 9

Houston: We Have a Problem!

Holy moly! This is not my day,
I've got a poem to write, but nothing to say.
So many subjects, but I can't decide,
Should I pick music, school, or playing outside?
My brain hurts from making rhymes,
Oh my gosh! Look at the time!
I can't think clearly, my thoughts are overflowing,
I don't know what to write! I'd better get going!
Sweat rolling down both of my cheeks,
Come on! I've been planning this for weeks!
I'm down to my last seconds; I've got to finish this,
Everyone can see I'm nervous, even my baby sis.
I'm nearing the end of this poem, I think I'll be just fine.
Looks like I *will* be able to finish this on time!
I'm not sure they'll like it, I don't know if it will win,
At least I can stop worrying...
NOOOO!!! I forgot to turn it in!

Amy Dettmann
St George School
Tinley Park
Grade 7

Spring

Trees are changing into green giants,
Flowers are blooming with brilliant colors,
Showers bring beautiful rainbows,
The snow disappears,
Grass becomes green again,
Birds return from their vacation in the south,
Kites fly through the air,
Breezes weave through the trees,
These are the beautiful signs of spring.

Ricky Bailey
St Joseph Catholic School
Harvard
Grade 8

Mother

I pray for my mother, and every day that passes by,
I wonder what would happen, if one day she should die.
I wish the day would never come, although I know it will.
Just like I know the flowers will decay, upon the windowsill.
Oh Lord, you know I love her so, please just keep her here.
I promise, Lord; I love her, Lord. I always will be near.
It hurts my soul, to see her cry. It tears apart my heart.
Just like an old, neglected book, the pages fall apart.
So when I pray, I pray for many things,
For summer, winter, autumn, and spring,
For my friends who are always there, whenever I'm in need,
And so we never cross in life, I pray for my enemies.
I thank you Lord, for those I love, for family and other.
So Lord, for Christmas, all I want, is good health for my mother.

Vincent Icalia
Nathan Hale Middle School
Crestwood
Grade 7

Jake

Brother
Screaming, yelling
Hitting, kicking
Sweaty, dirty
Doing homework, playing video games
Loving me
Brother

Stefanie Bradley
River Trails Middle School
Mount Prospect
Grade 7

Sharks

Sharks swim searchingly,
Under the cool blue water,
Hunting their small prey.

Geoff Desillier
St Vincent De Paul School
Peoria
Grade 8

The Rain

When the rain comes,
the day gets sad.
The people are locked
up in their house,
the children are bored,
bored as a mouse.
But when the rain leaves,
the people are happy,
the sun shines,
and a rainbow appears.

Ashley Pearce
River Trails Middle School
Mount Prospect
Grade 7

What's a Mother?

A Mother is someone who...
—takes care of you when you're sick
—reads you bedtime stories
—is always there for you no matter what
—loves you very much
—always lends a helping hand
—makes you happy when you're sad
—gives you good advice
—prepares you for your life ahead
—will do anything and everything for you
—always cares about you

Now, that's a wonderful Mother!
I love you, Mom!

Emily Pospiech
Fremont Middle School
Mundelein
Grade 7

White Christmas

Snow was falling all day long all night long
With children playing in the snow.
You could see stars above,
All of a sudden beautiful it looks with all the snow falling on the houses
And the trees.
With all the houses decorated so nicely.
You couldn't ask for a more beautiful white Christmas.

Cecilia Martin
Harrison Elementary School
Wonder Lake
Grade 7

Life

Life's no fair anyway you stare
Birds can soar high up in the sky
All we can do is wave good-bye.

Fish swim in the deep, beautiful sea
We can swim, we just can't breathe.

Cats and dogs pampered pets, they don't worry about their debt.
There's something life gives us that is fair, there's love and someday clean air,
There's music and flowers and pure green grass,
There are animals and friends and pictures that let you get a view into the past.
Now I guess that life is fair in some ways, but now it's crystal clear:
Life is great!!!

Belinda Brouette
Nathan Hale Middle School
Crestwood
Grade 7

I Am

I am a dancer and music lover
I wonder what goes through celebrities' minds, oh I wonder
I hear the music playing joyfully through my mind
I see me on stage singing cheerfully and gracefully all the time
I want to sing just like my grandmother
I am a dancer and a music lover

I pretend I'm moving freely, gliding on two feet
I feel that dancer on TV could be me
I reach and pull towards all of my goals
I worry if I become a dancer who would all know
I cry in search of being discovered
I am a dancer and a music lover

I understand not all dreams may come true
I say, "Girl, don't be afraid, just be you!"
I dream that everyone will see my talent, and see me as I am
I try to be the best I can be and have at least one fan
I hope that everyone will be proud of me like my sisters and brothers
I am a dancer and music lover

Brittany Hare
Francis Granger Middle School
Aurora
Grade 7

Drifting From the Holocaust

A tear fills my eye
why, I can't let you die
just the thought of you gone
well I couldn't go on
after all we've been through
just me and you
alone in the camp
so cold, dark, and damp
with strangers around
while mass graves fill the ground
holding your head
my hands turn red
those Nazi soldiers, I want them dead
people gather around
your eyes fall down
drifting
drifting
oh so deep
I know at last you're now asleep

Kristina M. Berry
Pleasant Hill Elementary School
Peoria
Grade 7

The Movie

I walked into the theater
Where I had planned to be
I bought candy that was
Sweetly satisfying to me.

I placed myself in a seat.
It wasn't too close.
I thought it was comfortable,
And it was the place I wanted to be the most.

The movie had started,
That I came to see.
And I ate candy,
That was satisfying to me.

When the movie had ended,
I couldn't believe
That the movie was over
And I had to leave.

When I walked out into the gloomy street light,
I felt funny leaving my favorite place to be
Because I had to leave,
The movie I came to see.

Mark Niewolik
St Colette School
Rolling Meadows
Grade 8

You

You are the sunshine that lights my way.
You show me the path to a better and brighter day.
You are very special to me and greatly loved.
I am thankful you are a part of my life.
We've had our ups, and we've had our downs.
And through it all, you have been by my side.
You mean the world to me,
And I hope our friendship will never end.
And that is why you are my best friend.

Jennifer Kelm
Leland High School
Leland
Grade 9

It Happened Almost a Year Ago

The one thing that would never happen, happened.
It was an ordinary night,
then one simple movement I made changed my life forever!
My arm bumped it, and it fell to the floor.
In seconds the bed was in flames
I ran to get help, by the time they got back to my room,
it was too late. 911 was called!
All I could do was watch my home go up in flames.
Not all was lost, but all was ruined and not livable anymore.
After the firemen, friends, and neighbors left
we went to a small trailer.
The night passed as we talked and cried.
I finally went to bed
and counted the seconds until I fell asleep.
I woke up praying it was all a bad dream.
I ran to my home, and as I entered,
I smelled the smoke and my room was a burned out shell.
It was no dream!
As I look on it now, I realize
that one simple movement can change everything.

Tanya Lowe
Harrisburg High School
Harrisburg
Grade 9

Raindrops in the Ocean

My dreams are like ice, my dreams no one can break.
Every dream I dream makes the ocean bigger.
In a dream, I run to Pegasus,
he turns to face me and looks into my eyes.
I see his fear as he walks to a waterfall and drinks.
He runs and jumps as high as he can.
landing beside me:
I jump on his back and we fly to the painted sky,
while music plays in my head.
Behind the waterfall is a cave that is only in my dreams,
My dreams of Raindrops in the Ocean.

Tanya Aldridge
Lewis & Clark Jr High School
Wood River
Grade 8

A Win and a Defeat

A win is something very sweet,
A loss is very sour.
Some losers cannot accept defeat,
All want to be men of the hour.

Losers learn valuable lessons,
Some of pain and loss.
They experience bad feelings,
Which we would never have come across.

Winners experience sweetness
Each time they win.
Especially if the winner
Defeats a certain kin.

Elizabeth Reising
St Vincent De Paul School
Peoria
Grade 8

You Look Like a Million Bucks

Feeling good about myself
Smiling
Look like a million bucks
Sun shining
Look like a million bucks
I
Am
A
Walking
Talking
Green piece of paper
Lots of zeros

Claire Thomas
Sacred Heart School
Lombard
Grade 7

Forgive and Live

I had another bad day today,
Again, I was beaten and bruised.
I tried to get away,
I had been abused.

They tore my clothes,
They slapped my face.
I'll never go back,
To that horrid place.

Yes, they have hurt me bad,
But, with the scars, I can live.
What they did I'll never forget,
But, thank God, I can forgive.

Ashley Dawn Brooks
Hardin County Jr High School
Elizabethtown
Grade 8

Baseball

Baseball is cool
Baseball is fun
If you get lucky you'll hit a homerun

Even if you sit on the bench
And don't like it
Deal with it and like it

So pick up a bat
And go "WHAM"
You could have hit a grand slam

Dave Bowers
St Irene School
Warrenville
Grade 7

Weekends and Weekdays

Weekends are so short,
so small,
and so little.

Weekdays are so long,
so big,
and so huge.

We all ask,
"Why are they so different?"

We all wish
it could be
the other
way around.

Margaret Genge
St Mary's of Kickapoo School
Edwards
Grade 8

The Great Charade

Every day's a trial
A case you cannot win
Like a man at a masquerade
We hide, behind our clothes and hair
The personality and characteristics
Of our great selves.
While we gab the night away
With our contemporary companions,
We should be coming out of our masks,
Maturing all the while.
But the masks are glued to our faces,
In this war we are all guilty.
No one can escape
The Great Charade.

Jacqui Pycz
St Paul School
Danville
Grade 8

Contented

It floated along
Like an afternoon daydream;
A child blows bubbles.

Tree sways in breeze,
Afternoon sun in its branches;
I sigh, contented.

Sun is on his back
While planting, growing more lives
On this summer day.

Grass on his wet legs
Children laughing in the backyard,
Leaping through sprinkler.

Brendan McGurk
Fenwick High School
Oak Park
Grade 9

Desk

Desk
you put stuff in it
you take stuff out of it
you sit at it
you look at it
you work at it
and you stare at it

Cody Hand
Jonesboro Elementary School
Jonesboro
Grade 7

I Don't Understand

I don't understand
why people hate,
and why dogs chase me,
and why people want to fight me.

I don't understand
why people hate
my rights and my color.

I don't understand
why people have guns
to hurt other people,
and why they want
to kill and destroy.

But I do understand
that I love myself, trust myself,
and will stay myself.

Markeisia Jones
Forest Trail Jr High School
Park Forest
Grade 8

The Seasons

Winter is a torture chamber for the warm lovers,
Summer is a dungeon for the cool lovers,
Spring and fall are just in between and just right for me.

Melissa Tyrcha
River Trails Middle School
Mount Prospect
Grade 7

The Power of Words

Life without language would be quite a bore.
How would you talk to your friend at the store?
How could you express what you really think?
When you are mad how can you say "You stink?!"
People could not see a certain natural beauty.
When a baby is born you can not say "What a cutie."
You wouldn't know up from down.
That could give some one a major frown.
How could you explore certain wonders of life?
How can a husband say he loves his wife?
The power of words is very strong.
One thing is you can't go wrong.
To have words is a gift.
You would be able to ask your friend for a lift
to school. Words help the world go round.
You would be able to say "What pretty flowers in the ground."
Life without language can be a pain.
Without language the world wouldn't be the same.

Nini Castle
Hanna Sacks Girls High School
Chicago
Grade 9

Friends

We all have friends through thick and thin.
Don't matter what color of skin.
I feel really safe when they're near.
When friends stick together they win.

When they're around you never fear.
They will always bring you good cheer.
They always help you when in need.
They mean so much and are so dear.

Friends never have the need for greed.
They never try to take the lead.
Friends are people we need to keep.
So friends should never be deceived.

Friends should keep promises very deep.
My friends never try to take a leap.
Good night my friends for now I sleep.
Good night my friends for now I sleep.

Kim Thole
Beckemeyer Elementary School
Beckemeyer
Grade 7

Summer Fun

Summertime is a time to relax,
Chewing bubble gum by the packs.
Ice cream is a cool treat,
In the hot summer heat.
You can take a swim in the pool,
Or not and be a fool.
Go outside and ride your bike,
That's what I really like!
You can go on a nice vacation,
Or even do some multiplication!
Curl up and read a book,
Or surprise your mom and be a cook!
These are some ideas for the summer,
Because when it's over it'll be a bummer!!

Cara Condon
St George School
Tinley Park
Grade 7

As I Walk

As I walk alone in the streets,
I ask myself,
What's going to happen to me?
I walk fast when I see a scary man,
Thinking he might do something to me.
When I walk by the alley,
I ask myself,
Is someone going to grab me from the back,
And beat me up or rape me?
Or what if someone in a car or walking,
Has a gun and starts to shoot at me,
What am I going to do????

Guadalupe Ceja
St Procopius School
Chicago
Grade 7

You and Me

As I think of you and me
I still can't see why we can't be.

I still don't know why we can't be
Because you were meant for me.

I still can't see why you fear to be with me
Even though you were meant for me.

You were meant for me,
And I was meant for you.

Even if we are rich or poor,
I still love you more and more.

Chris Nagelli
Children of Peace-St Callistus School
Chicago
Grade 7

Basketball

Round, orange
Shooting, passing, traveling
Swoosh attack
Miniature earth

Jeff Rowe
River Trails Middle School
Mount Prospect
Grade 7

Sun

Here comes the sun,
Shining down on the earth,
It's our sunshine,
It's our light,
They're the bright rays,
Shooting down.

Mrs. Chambers,
Has some flowers,
They're purple,
Or are they violet,
I can't tell the difference,
I'm over excited.

How will I say this,
I don't know,
But I'm finished,
With all my poems,
Well Good-bye
Here I go!

Diana Soriano
Trumbull Elementary School
Chicago
Grade 7

As I See You

As I lay here thinking
about you

I'm hoping you're thinking
of me too.

I can't figure out why
others can't see,
how wonderful you are,
and how much you mean to me.

As I watch you very closely now
with every step you take

Every time I dream about you,
I hope I never wake.

Miranda Snyder
Dieterich Jr-Sr High School
Dieterich
Grade 8

School — Go With the Flow

Adults may not remember,
Children say they'll never forget,
Anyone would describe it,
As one big fishing net.

Constantly you fight your way upstream,
With fisherman everywhere,
Trying to keep you from moving on,
Tossing nets here and there.

If you're small you can wind your way through each net,
If you're big you're gonna get stuck,
If you're weak and give up fighting, you're stuck down in the muck.

Then there's always a dam to fight past, when success rests just above it,
Pay big expenses to fight you're way through,
And you now know just what to do.

School prepares you for life,
Pressure practice for deadlines, family, and peers,
It prepares you for the world each day,
Teaches you how to go through life each day.

So don't fluff it off, it's crucial,
And don't let it frustrate you so,
Why? I'm sure you all know!!

Jackie Fontanetta
L J Stevens Middle School
Wilmington
Grade 7

Things in Life

Some things I hear, some things I see
Some things I learn, some things I want to be

I want to hear silence, I want to see the air
I want to learn how to teach, I want to be one that cares

I want to hear the moon sing a song, I want to see the stars above
I want to learn how to see clear, I want to be loved

These are things I want to hear, to see
To learn, and things I want to be

But there are things that I cannot hear, things that I cannot see,
Things that I cannot be taught, and things that I cannot be

You see some things are easy, some are tough
Some are smooth, others rough

These things I know, and that is okay
If there's something I want, I'll just keep on trying, hard as it may

Angela Black
St Vincent De Paul School
Peoria
Grade 8

Stars

Stars shine like a big bright light.
They look so pretty at night.
Sometimes they even make shapes like a kite.
While I'm looking at the stars nothing seems wrong.
It just seems all right.
That is why I love looking at the stars,
In the big blue night.

Ashley Jansen
Beckemeyer Elementary School
Beckemeyer
Grade 7

Eladio

I had a brother I never met.
He would have been older than me.
It would have been cool having him around,
But he died three months after he was born.
My mom told me that when he died,
He waved goodbye,
Like he knew he was going to die.

Every time I look at one of his pictures,
I see a shadow.
It's not my mom's shadow, or his.
Instead, it's a shadow of a grown man...
My brother's name was Eladio.

Samuel Ortiz
Logandale Middle School
Chicago
Grade 7

Camping Tasks

When I am camping, there are many things to be done.
They are not always fun.
They have to be finished.
Putting the tent up is the hardest thing to be completed
It is like a maze of poles.
It requires real art.
After the tent is set up, we still can't have fun.
It is as much fun as a rainy day.
Sometimes I don't want to stay.
Next, we go into the woods to gather wood.
It is always a big strain.
It is always a big pain.
We are oxen working to gather the wood.
When the wood is gathered it's time for fun.
I go and play.
My mom and my dad stay at the campground.
During the night is the most fun.
We sit by the fire and roast marshmallows.
When I'm done, I go to sleep.
The fun is done for the day.

Kevin Herrington
Blessed Sacrament School
Belleville
Grade 7

Sun

It is very bright
It makes some light
Sometimes it can hurt your sight.
It makes things grow and it melts the snow
And that's all you need to know.

Nathan Wenger
Jonesboro Elementary School
Jonesboro
Grade 8

Fell Head Over Heals into Love

Megan and Justin are good friends
Then high school comes
They grow apart
But Megan likes Justin
School play is starting
It's *Rapunzel*
Auditions are taking place
Megan is Rapunzel
Justin is the prince
Practice begins
Thinking of a way to get up Rapunzel's *hair*.
Has an idea
Puts holes in the tower to climb
Idea works
All goes well
Night of play comes
Everyone's nervous
Play begins
It goes smoothly
Until Justin trips off the tower
Megan falls head over heals into love

Moira Flood
Sacred Heart School
Lombard
Grade 7

What a Friend Means to Me

A friend is someone like a sister to me.
She is someone who will be my eyes
when I need her help to see.
A friend is someone who you can trust,
and won't leave you all alone in the dust.
She is someone who will call you on
the phone just to say Hi.
A friend is someone who will hold your hand
when you're about to cry.
She is someone who will stand by your side
in good times or in bad.
So ask yourself,
is your friend there for you
when you're down and sad?

Kayla Wollenzien
L J Stevens Middle School
Wilmington
Grade 7

Me

I don't feel right today,
I don't feel like myself,
I feel like you but yet I don't know how you feel,
I don't think that I'm me today,
At least I don't feel so!

Matt Lee Miller
Scales Mound Jr High School
Scales Mound
Grade 8

Leaves

Leaves
colorful
bright
yellow
red
orange
and
green
Different shapes and sizes
Colors of the wind
Which will someday fall off their perch so high
and float with the breeze

Michela Bonadonna
River Trails Middle School
Mount Prospect
Grade 7

Life in the Park

People pass me every day,
Sometimes they sit and stay.

I have a very lovely view,
Of big oak trees and flowers too.

I have been here many years,
I've seen happiness along with tears.

Throughout the seasons things fall on me,
I've held broken branches, snow, and leaves.

The rain has battered my coat of paint,
The wind has cracked my weathered back.

Some people rest on my comfortable lap,
They sit down in peace, their dogs lay by my feet.

And this is life, day after day,
I especially love watching children play.

So the next time you see a bench in the park,
Remember it has a life like you, through the daylight and dark.

Julie Conner
St Matthew School
Champaign
Grade 7

Seasons

Winter makes me want to curl up and sleep,
Spring makes me want to jump up and shout,
Summer makes me want to jump in a pool,
Fall makes me think of school.

Natalie Young
River Trails Middle School
Mount Prospect
Grade 7

My Human Body

As I walk I see my shadow.
The shadow that no one else can copy.
The shadow that belongs to me.

As I look in the mirror I see my face.
The face that no one else has.
The face that belongs to me.

As I look at my hands I see my fingers.
The fingers that help me at all times.
The fingers that only belong to me.

As I look down at my feet I see my toes.
These are the toes that help me walk.
These toes belong to me.

No one has the same physical body like me.
No one can do all I do.
I'm proud of my physics.

Osvaldo Mendez
Pablo Casals Elementary School
Chicago
Grade 7

Showers

Rain, rain go away,
I would like to play in April and May,
But with this rain I cannot play,
But it's okay
Soon you will have to go away,
And the sun will dry up all the rain.
No, the rain has not gone away.

I might as well go outside and play in the rain,
Rain, rain I never knew,
It could be so fun,
To play in the rain.

Oh, here comes the sun up to dry the rain,
So I have to say good-bye to the rain,
Bye, bye rain,
Come back another day!

Yvonne Hernandez
St Procopius School
Chicago
Grade 7

My Heart

My heart is heavy, torn, and worn.
It hurts to talk, walk, and run.
If only I could be loved by you,
My heart would be as good as new.

My heart is green, blue, and black.
Every color but not intact.
If only I could be loved by you,
My heart would be as good as new.

My heart is broken in two.
I can't seem to find a way to believe in you.
If only I could *repent* and ask for forgiveness.
God I know I'll be loved by you.

Danielle Brown
Cairo Jr High School
Cairo
Grade 8

Sports

Football is such a great game
Basketball is about the same
Each of these have four quarters
Plus they have some boundary borders
Offense or defense I don't care at all
All I want is the ball
I shoot, throw, or run with to score
Neither of these are a bore
I run, I stumble, I jump, I fall
But at least when I do it, I don't lose the ball
Every quarter has 12 min.
And the only thing on my mind is to win.

Cory Grathler
Harrisburg High School
Harrisburg
Grade 9

Rhythm, Rap, and Rhyme

Rhythm, rap, and rhyme,
We do it all the time.

It has the tendency of flowing,
Without us ever knowing.

The rhythm part is easy, that's how the poem flows.
The rap part I'm unsure of, and the rhyme is how it goes.

How can something be so fun,
That sounds so cool when we're done?

We do it all the time,
It's called rhythm, rap, and rhyme.

Heidi Hannon
Clifford Crone Middle School
Naperville
Grade 7

Slow but Steady

I walked around the unidentifiable terrain
Looking for any trace of life
Walking dignified and proud.

I see a stigma of a flower in the harsh wind
As I come closer, I ponder about what kind of flower this is.
Marigold? Rose? Lilac?

When I reach the site of the beautiful display,
A mum bursts out of a beautiful green bulb.
Weak but determined, defenseless yet dedicated.

As I watch the phenomenon,
I contrast it with my own life,
Slow but steady.

Chris Hoffmann
Lake Bluff Middle School
Lake Bluff
Grade 7

Daydreaming

Daydreaming is fun,
You can be anyone.

You can go to the moon,
And be back before noon.

You can put on tanning lotion,
And walk across the ocean.

You can go to the sun,
And bring along anyone.

You can be on TV,
For everyone to see.

If ever you want to have some fun,
Just sit down and let your imagination run.

Kelly Shinnick
St Gerald School
Oak Lawn
Grade 8

Florida

Palm trees gently swaying in the wind,
Swimming in the ocean or the hotel pool,
Laying on a warm beach getting tan,
Searching for seashells in the sand,
Building giant sand castles with flowing moats,
Children running around in swim suits,
Sitting on a beach sipping a cool drink,
Take me to Florida, it's the place to be.

Ashley Howerton
St Matthew School
Champaign
Grade 8

Dark and Stormy Nights

Dark and stormy nights,
Are the best for cozy rests,
Next to a warm fire.

Michael Q. Matias
River Trails Middle School
Mount Prospect
Grade 7

Football

Smashing hits,
Running everywhere.
Coaches yelling,
When you are sweating.

You run to get
The play.
The quarterback
Says hike.
The ball is snapped,
He throws deep,
It is caught.

He runs into
The end zone and they go
To overtime.

The coin is flipped,
They won the toss,
It's their ball first.

The first play
Is a touchdown
The game is over,
They win!

Jimmy Spebn
Clifford Crone Middle School
Naperville
Grade 7

Gracefully Aging

Wrinkled hands
Full of stories
Gracefully aging
Wisdom comes with age
Some say
Gracefully aging
Hardships come and go
As the years pass
Gracefully aging
With each breath
Cheating death
Gracefully aging.

Katie Fine
Nichols Middle School
Evanston
Grade 7

My Computer

The computer is a friend of mine
He helps me in the nick of time

He sits there with his mouse nearby
Ever waiting for my next reply

When I forget and fail to spell
He quickly helps and doesn't tell

If I don't know the meaning yet
He takes me to the internet

As my task becomes a sight
He'll use another megabyte

And if I can't keep things straight
My computer has Windows 98

What kind of friend would be so loyal
But never let his temper boil

He teaches me the things I know
and never tries to steal the show

If only all my teachers guessed
That my computer is really blessed

Danny Jackson
Beckemeyer Elementary School
Beckemeyer
Grade 7

Poem for Rynder

My teacher says
That I must write
Some kind of poem
By tonight.
I've thought and thought
But cannot think
Of any words
To put in ink.
My mind has flown
To far off places
And has considered
A lot of faces.
I've touched upon
A hundred topics
Like polar bears
And distant tropics.
But, now at last
I think I've said
All I can
In ink or lead.

Devin Conlon
Parkview Jr High School
Lawrenceville
Grade 7

Ghosts

Ghosts are scary fellows,
They're never in the sun.
You can hear them bellow,
When they're having fun.

Some wear greenish shoes,
And some are very fat.
Some are navy blue,
And some have twenty cats.

Rachel Ruppel
Parkview Jr High School
Lawrenceville
Grade 7

Spring

In spring it's fun to be a kid
While on my bike I like to skid
In spring I like to ride my bike
My brother and I played and hid

My dad and I go on a hike
So then I will not ride my bike
I also like to climb big trees
I will not ride my bike but hike

I hope I do not catch any fleas
I hope I do not cut my knees
My dad and I go to the park
I think I had just lost our keys

Well I will stay until it's dark
Then I will see my best friend Mark
I really had fun at the park
I really had fun at the park

Nathan McCrary
Beckemeyer Elementary School
Beckemeyer
Grade 7

Spring

Spring is here.
Summer is near.
There's nothing to
fear it's all filled
with cheer.
In the forests the animals
are starting to come out.
While in the gardens the
tulips are starting to sprout.
There's not a doubt about spring
it's filled with
a lot of wonderful things.

Nicole Johnson
St Barbara School
Chicago
Grade 7

Afraid

Sometimes I get so mad
I think that everyone is out to get me
When they really just want to help
I know the truth behind the wall
But I act that way anyway
I want to say what I feel
But can't because I'm too afraid
I want to yell and throw things at a wall
But don't because I'm afraid of what they'd do
So I keep my feelings bottled up
I wonder if that's good
Why can't I say what I want?
Guess I'm too afraid.

Anthony Siegert
Forest Trail Jr High School
Park Forest
Grade 8

What's the Dif?

Racism, racism I hate so dear
Something that I always fear
Just because people look different in the mirror
There is so much hating going on
Something that happens year after year

Racism, racism should be a crime
And you go to jail for a long time
I wish the subject would drop
And someday maybe it will stop

Michael Zera
St Joan Of Arc School
Evanston
Grade 7

Trapped

People closing in around me,
Walls closing in around me,
Life trapping me,
Trapping me in a world,
A world full of rushing crowds,
Rushing crowds coming at me,
Trying to knock me over,
Trying to keep me down,
Trying to suppress individuality,
Trying to make an international blob of commerce,
Taking over the world,
Suppressing individuality,
Knocking people down,
Keeping people down,
Never lending a hand to any other race,
Never seeing,
For they never care

Ezra Hilton
Nichols Middle School
Evanston
Grade 7

Homework

Dear homework, I despise you.
You take up my time!
I don't understand you.
I could rip you and stomp on you,
And even throw you out.
You're mind boggling and uncompromising
Without a doubt!

Laura Voaden
Francis Granger Middle School
Aurora
Grade 7

Christmas Morning

The reflection of sun on the snow,
Shined brightly in my window.
I opened my eyes,
To a huge surprise,
Christmas has finally come!

I breathed in and out,
Ready to shout,
This day is gonna be fun!
The turkey was cooking and smelled so good,
The fire was burning bright with plenty of wood.
Christmas has finally come!

I ran to the tree.
My face filled with glee,
And ripped open a present or two or three.
I heard Christmas music playing prettily,
And Jingle Bells jingling all over the city.
Christmas has finally come!

Pop! Cracked the fire in the fireplace.
Heat was blowing like a hair dryer on my face.
Thank you Christmas for visiting me,
Come back next year, please, please, please.

Jill Bollinger
Blessed Sacrament School
Belleville
Grade 7

Summer Nights!!

On a hot summer night, I swim around in my pool
watching the stars.
As I dive under water my body is refreshed
by the cool water.
As I come up for air, I open my eyes and see fireflies
buzzing around me.
They are twinkling like the beautiful stars up above.
They make the meadow light up like diamonds.
As I sit and watch them, I feel like I live in a golden temple.

Kathryn Hollis
Beckemeyer Elementary School
Beckemeyer
Grade 7

The Big Race

Our lives are Indy cars,
And we're behind the wheel.
Starting off slow,
To prepare for what follows.
All of the fast stretches,
Loaded with turns,
Lead to crucial choices,
Made in split seconds.
Some leading to success —
Others to disaster.
Mistakes make us pit,
To repair confidence and wounds.
Then back out we go,
In the treacherous world.
Vying against all others,
To first reach the finish.
The weak end in failure,
While the strong triumph.

Steven Kurtz
Fenwick High School
Oak Park
Grade 9

This Little Lightning Bug

There was a little lightning bug
as small as the eye could see,
it liked to fly around small dogs
and even likes to fly on me.
This little lightning bug
lives in a willow tree
it seems very lonely
so, that's why it plays with me.
He flies around in my tiny room
around the goldfish bowl
because it was so small
my goldfish ate it whole.

Brian Lang
St Celestine School
Elmwood Park
Grade 7

Cat

When my cat gets hungry
It does
Meow, meow
When she gets cold
She says
Purr, purr
What do you hear?
Squeak, squeak
Pounce, pounce
My cat just captured a mouse!

Dhruva Patel
River Trails Middle School
Mount Prospect
Grade 7

Neglected

Life is full of challenges, despair, and excitement.
Life is wonderful. Life is great.
There are people who like it, and people who don't.
Those who don't, are stuck in a black hole filled with hate.
They think no one loves or cares about them.
Even though everyone around them cares and prays for them.
It doesn't matter how much you love or care for someone.
Because you never know what is going on in their mind at that time.
Until it is too late.

Karissa Stoltz
St Irene School
Warrenville
Grade 8

My Tree

If I could have one thing in the world, I would have a tree.
It'd have leaves and branches, and it would grow just like me.

"What would you do with a tree?" they ask me very gently.
"But of course, I will climb it and play on the wooden swing."

"And where will you put this tree of yours?" I say, "Well naturally in the yard...
We'll plant it and water it, it won't be very hard."

To grow a tree takes a lot of patience, but I don't mind that much.
I'll give it sunlight and water...and care for it and such.

And when I finally get my wish, I will be so filled with glee...
That I'll be with it all the time, and not want another thing.

For now I have to wait. It won't be as long as it seems.
I'll just sit here and think, and dream about my tree.

Karen Furkert
St Vincent De Paul School
Peoria
Grade 8

Sitting Under the Tropical Tree

Sitting under the tropical tree
I look at the sky, the birds, and the bees
And ask myself why life couldn't be so peaceful, so quiet, so blissful.
Not a sound of yelling could be found.
I sit under the tropical tree.

Sitting under the tropical tree,
I listen to music, but nothing you can hear.
It's the beat of a drum, the soul that can sing,
The wind is the backup singer so you know that it's there,
While the trees make you stand up tall and be proud of your performance.
This is what happens while you are sitting.
There is nothing to think of when you are there.
While sitting under the tropical tree.

Jessica Exposito
Pope John XXIII School
Evanston
Grade 8

What Is Love

Love has different meanings.
Love is a word that comes from the man above.
You can love someone or be in love with someone.
Some people don't know the true meaning of love,
Maybe because they feel that they haven't been loved,
Or that they have never been in love.
You can't see it nor touch it but you can feel it.
It is a good feeling.
You can sometimes hurt from it, but you can learn from it.
So if you never knew love the day will come sooner or later.

Candice Veasey
Dunbar Vocational Career Academy
Chicago
Grade 9

The Wolf

The wolf is a sleek sly creature,
Who runs way faster than you can
His colors are a feature,
Brown, silver, black, or tan

People try to catch him in the trees,
But he's as quick as lightning
They thump and bump, stopping for a breeze,
And are starting to think that these woods are frightening

But the wolf could care less
Because this is his home
He knows these woods,
And is not alone

People think that wolves are frightening,
Just because they move like lightning
But they are simple, peaceful dogs,
Who enjoy sitting contently on their favorite logs

Shannon McAlpine
John F Eberhart Elementary School
Chicago
Grade 7

Dream Car

A 1967, blue Corvette is the car for me.
The Corvette smiles at me with his silver bumper.
He hates Porches though.
His ears are silver.
His body has no dents.
He eats engines and drinks gas.
He only needs eyes at night or rainy days.
Because he senses where he drives me in my dreams.
But in real life he taunts me.
Because I won't make enough money in my life,
To pay one year's insurance.

Ryan Ballard
Holy Cross Lutheran School
Collinsville
Grade 7

Weather

It is April tenth,
And it is snowing.
Snowing!
In April!
I swear, I will never get used to the weather here.
In February,
for nearly a week on end,
it was seventy-five degrees outside.
The startled remnants of snow
had not yet left the ground,
but people were in their shorts.
Shorts!
In February!
People nodded their heads wisely.
Global warming, they said
Polar ice caps, they explained.
Hurricanes in the Pacific, they laughed.
Pacific! This is the Midwest!
I swear, I wouldn't be at all surprised,
If, when I wake up tomorrow,
It is raining hot dogs.

Molly Hales
Nichols Middle School
Evanston
Grade 8

Dying*

Not ready to give up
Knowing you won't win
The battle of life
The battle of sin.

Slowly your body surrenders
Seeing the life beyond
You struggle to keep your legacy going
And the eternal bond.

You've traveled for the last time
But you haven't made the last trip.
You've not seen the last of the glorious places
You have not seen this clip.

With the shed of a tear
You surrender with grace.
A labored last breath
You catch a glimpse of her face.

You no longer are sick
You no longer feel pain.
You have nothing to lose,
Only to gain.

Jackie Durgin
Roselle Middle School
Roselle
Grade 7
*Dedicated to Grandpa Durgin

Bumblebee

The bee,
Stings very hard,
It's little but deadly,
Flies around in search of honey,
Buzzes.

Kathleen E. Essenberg
River Trails Middle School
Mount Prospect
Grade 7

Feelings

Inside of me are feelings,
The feelings that I hide,
All the feelings never said,
When you are by my side.

Some of them are good,
Some of them are bad.
Some of them are feelings,
That I have never had.

I really want to tell you,
All the feelings that I feel,
If I said what I want to say,
Your wounds would never heal.

I am really sorry
For what I'm about to say
Our love wasn't meant to last–
So I'm letting go today.

Ashley Hall
Parkview Jr High School
Lawrenceville
Grade 7

My One and Only Angel

You are my angel.
You keep me safe,
and unharmed.
You are my angel.

You have wings of gold,
and hair as golden as the sun.
You have eyes as clear,
and blue as the deep blue sea.
You are my angel,
Perfect as can be.
You are always there for me,
guiding me in the right direction,
Keeping me from any danger.

You are my one and only angel.

Tiffany Vanick
Queen of Martyrs School
Chicago
Grade 8

Missing You

My love for you is incomparable, you are better than the rest.
Living without you would be unbearable, my love for you is the best.

So much love for one person, but so little time to show.
I want to be with you forever, but the time has come for me to go.

Leaving my life, friends, and you behind, and starting over again.
Trying hard to keep in touch, hoping us will never end.

Now school is starting, and I'm making new friends.
But something in my heart is missing, it feels like I'm losing a best friend.

I miss you so much, because we are so far apart.
Just not being able to see you tears a hole in my heart.

Not a second goes by, that you're not on my mind.
I just wanted you to know, you will always be mine.

Amanda Adcock
St Ferdinand School
Chicago
Grade 8

Somewhere to Run

No matter where I've been, no matter where I go,
I can always run to you, for this I know.

As long as I'm here on an earth full of sorrow,
I will run to you today and tomorrow.

And when I think no one cares,
I remember that you and me are great pairs.

I will remember that when my days are dark and there isn't any sun,
That to you I can always, always run.

Amber Young
Chester Community Elementary School
Chester
Grade 7

The Sky's End

Where does the sky end?
Can we comprehend how high and far it goes?
Does outer space count as being part of the unknown called the sky?

The clouds tell us we are high up,
But they are not the end.
Even the area between the sky and outer space is not the end.

The end of the sky could just be more land.
After the planets it goes beyond into what is not known to us.
When we get as far as we can go,
How much farther is it to the end?

Drew Hauffe
St Matthew School
Champaign
Grade 7

It's Fall!

Old, dead, and brown all around
It's fall!
Leaves on the streets
winds in the air
It's fall!
Kids running and playing
playing in the leaves
It's fall!
Bags of leaves
and not a pinch of grass to see
It's fall!
Rakes all around
and trees turning colors to show that it's fall
It's fall!
It's fall!
It's fall!

Alex Leamen
Wethersfield High School
Kewanee
Grade 8

Trust

There are many different types of friends.
There are friends who are there for you
until things go wrong.
And there are friends who are there for you
through the bad things to keep you strong.
Some friends claim they care,
and some friends you know will always be there.
But in the end, only some friends are a must.
The only friends you need are the ones you truly trust.

Christine Berg
Pope John XXIII School
Evanston
Grade 8

Alone with Silence

I was walking home
All alone with silence.
No one to talk to, no one to listen to,
All alone with silence.
Everywhere I look was all still, silent,
All alone with silence.
Only the wind blowing through the trees,
All alone with silence.
As the fog rose into the light, I see a shadow,
All alone with silence.
Hoping it was a creature to talk to, instead a figment...
All alone with silence.
A figment of my imagination,
All alone,
I walk home...all alone with my friend silence.

Heather Vershay
Chaney-Monge Elementary School
Crest Hill
Grade 8

The Way It Is

Every day Clean digs a hole
And gets dirt on her pretty dress,
And goes home and gets yelled at for being dirty.

And every day Dirt takes a bath
And washes off all his grit
And goes home and gets yelled at for being clean.

And every day Clean's parents
Throw white wishes into the wash.
That wish for Clean to stay in her place and be clean.

And every day Dirt's parents
Draw dark desires on the door.
That desire Dirt to stay in his place and be dirty.

Until one day Clean meets Dirt,
And he teaches her to take a bath,
And she teaches him to dig a hole,
And they both go home, and are happy.

And their parents ask their children where they went wrong,
And they yell at their kids for granting their requests.

And the next day Clean gets dirty.
And Dirt gets clean
And both children get in trouble.

Mary Beth Grady
Fenwick High School
Oak Park
Grade 9

The Lonely Chair

Everyday is like the next,
I just sit here bored as can be.
Friends you say I have none,
it's just lonely me.

People come and they go,
some even give me abuse.
I am at the end of my years,
just like a caboose.

Kids jump on me,
this gives me great pain;
it feels like a hundred bullets
straight into my chair brain.

One day come and visit me,
you may think I am boring, yes, that's what you assume.
I'll be sitting here,
in the lonesome living room.

Fred Walz
Frances Xavier Warde School
Chicago
Grade 7

Thumbelina

Thumbelina is a friend of mine
She is my little princess
Sometimes when we go out to dine
She gives me hugs and kisses

Thumbelina has an odd perfume
Even though she is well groomed

Thumbelina likes to eat a bit of carrot
She is my pet ferret
Gabriel M. Gruba
St Joseph Catholic School
Harvard
Grade 8

America

America is beautiful
Yet we mistreat
WHY?
America tries to help others
Yet they don't accept
WHY?
Walter Droba
Queen of Martyrs School
Chicago
Grade 8

Water

Moving cold and still
Waves are whirling and swirling
Liquid is so cool
Grant Lo Destro
Holy Angels School
Aurora
Grade 7

The Balls Are Flying

You can play anytime,
Morning, noon, or night.
All you need is a racket and might.
The huge, rectangular, green court,
With its white boundaries,
And a treacherous black net,
Which the player must avoid.
The swinging of rackets,
The strings strung tight,
The balls being hit,
Faster than light.
The opponent returns the ball,
You miss,
The game is lost.
Maybe next time.
Andy Koester
Dieterich Jr-Sr High School
Dieterich
Grade 8

Larry

I saw a flower, pretty and yellow
and when the wind blew
It wiggled like Jello

Its leaves were short
but its stem was long
with a bulging bud
tall and strong

A fragrant smell
just like a berry
and inside these sacred walls
Lived a fairy named, Larry

Larry flew in and out
Flapping his wings
Flitting all about

Then one day as Larry flew
a cat came by and looked
Larry straight in the eye

Flying as fast as he could
Larry flew as a fairy should

The cat got lost and Larry was glad
But in the end the cat was mad.
Kelly Stempinski
St Barbara School
Chicago
Grade 7

Leaves, Leaves, Leaves

Leaves, leaves, leaves
The snowflakes of fall
And in the winter
You won't see them at all

So get out those jackets
Zip them right up
For the cold air is in
And that is enough

Crunching the leaves
As kids walk along
Or play in the leaves
All day long

Whoosh, whoosh
Came the wind
And all I can wait for
Is summer again!
A.J. Vasseur
Francis Granger Middle School
Aurora
Grade 7

Life Without a Sister

No sharing
No fighting
No messes
No teasing
No arguing
No baby sitting
Just privacy, peace and quiet
Doraliz Reynoso
Mayer Elementary School
Chicago
Grade 7

I Hate You

You say you've swam the lake,
Yet you have never felt the chill,
Bathed in its dirty water,
Or watched the fisher kill.

You say you've flown the sky,
Yet you've never seen the stars,
Welcomed yourself to the heavens,
With your outstretched arms.

You say you've walked the forest,
Yet you've never taken a step,
Crawled in the brush and weeds,
Or fulfilled nature's needs.

You say you know your daughter,
Yet you have never heard her cries,
Held her for many hours,
Or looked beyond her lies.

You say you know the poetry,
Yet you've never heard a rhyme,
Bothered to realize what you do
No, not even one single time.
Karena Johnson
Quincy Jr High School
Quincy
Grade 8

She Said

She said the trees talked to her,
And the wind whispered in her ear,
And flowers stood up for sure,
And the leaves stroked her hair.

She said she heard the sea speak,
And heard the mountain cry,
And listened to the secret creek,
And heard the ocean die.
Vanessa Salvato
St John the Evangelist School
Streamwood
Grade 8

Sister

I have always kept you in my heart
So many years have passed
And today is the thirteenth anniversary of your death
Every day I wish I had you
Right next to me

America Campos
Holden Elementary School
Chicago
Grade 8

Obstacles

Just for today, I will face obstacles with a smile,
Just for today, I will go the extra mile.
Just for today, I will be your friend if you are in need,
I would be glad to do a good deed.

There will always be something in our way,
Then we will realize, it is only for today.
The road for today, let's you and me lead,
And don't worry, you have a friend forever in me.

Kurt Nicholas Hohenberger
Leland Elementary School
Leland
Grade 9

Flowers

The sun rises, and they shake the dew off.
The field is filled with colors, some loud, some soft.

The flowers swing and sway, in the wind.
They all wonder, when will it rain again?
They live a carefree day,
They have no worries, none at all.

Sunflowers always love to play,
And daisies love to have a ball.

Yet, some flowers must worry,
When little children come,
Always in a hurry.
They are like giants to the tiny flowers.

Pluck, pluck, pluck, one by one they come up.
Children carry them home to their mothers.

When night comes, she tiptoes slowly.
Coming carefully and quietly,
Watching the flowers fall asleep,
She doesn't intend to make a peep.
She blankets the flowers in their earth-made beds,
And then moves on her way,
Soon to come another day.

Sara Wagner
Blessed Sacrament School
Belleville
Grade 8

A Meadow

In a meadow far away,
There hop little bunnies out at play.
They run all day and they run all night,
When you get near them they run with fright.
They sit there all quiet and nimble,
You sit as still as a thimble.
They are so soft and warm,
They are so afraid to go through a storm.

Elizabeth Hennessy
Parkview Jr High School
Lawrenceville
Grade 7

I Love You, Ed

You will never be a teenager
You will never experience prom
You will never graduate 8th grade
You will never say bye to your mom
You will never see your brother again
You will never again play soccer
You will never see your friends as men
You will never cause any more laughter
I haven't seen you since that sad day
Hoping this bad dream would go away, I held my friends tight
But there in the casket you lay
Without your glasses, without your sight
I hope never again to see anyone in that case
Every now and then, for you, I pray
You were never different because you were another race
I wish you could come back some day

Lauren Topol
Hinsdale Middle School
Hinsdale
Grade 8

Bloom

Art thou a spring flower blooming yet wilting
One petal falls, still another—now it grows—
Giving up too soon, it reaches new lows

Starting over, no more falling—stronger—
Facing the troubles of the world that form
The weeds of evil are growing farther
Trying now to choke from the wicked born

Evil is gone, uprooted and trampled
Breathing once again, stretching once again
Growing away from earth—being untamed—
Being fresh and free like a flying wren

Life is too short, to not have a dream
Bloom—no time for wilting or being mean

Laurie Kania
St Ferdinand School
Chicago
Grade 8

Oak Tree

The Oak Tree is tall and strong
With its beauty its life is long
Dropping acorns for squirrels,
Holding swings for boys and girls
On a hot summers day,
    I wouldn't trade
The gift it gives of nice cool shade
I only wish that I could live,
As long as that strong Oak Tree did.

Lauren Borst
Fremont Elementary School
Mundelein
Grade 7

I Really Love You

The other side,
All alone.
I fight for acceptance,
Yet I'm still unknown.

I want to go home.
I want to be loved.
I'm sick and tired,
Of being shoved.

The world doesn't like me.
It's nothing new.
I just want to go home,
To be loved by you.

I talk to you rarely.
When do I see you? – Never
You say you care.
And I feel much better.

Every girl needs an aunt like you,
I'm not afraid to admit that it's true.
You're there for me,
And I really love you.

Stacey Woolford
Sandburg Jr High School
Elmhurst
Grade 7

Friends

F acing tough times together
R especting each other's decisions
I nspires you to do good
E xpects you to be there for them
N ever lets you down
D oesn't make you do bad things
S omeone who cares about you

Leticia Moran
Holden Elementary School
Chicago
Grade 8

Spencer

...can recognize and verbalize the letters of the alphabet.
...can run, jump, crawl, and drop-kick a soccer ball.
...comes to church every Sunday and pulls me into the room to play.
...greets me with a smile and a hug, which I most certainly love.
...can communicate in sign, and watches Veggie Tales all the time.
...is very special and sweet, Spencer, my Down-syndrome friend.
I know he may be different from you or me, but in my heart he is part of my family.

Connie Ribley
Virden Middle-High School
Virden
Grade 7

My Friend*

I see the winds blow the leaves, and here I lay.
Remembering when you went on that journey far away.
I sit here now and think of the fun times we had,
Playing games, jumping fences, the good times and bad.
There are many times I ask myself, why did you have to go?
Away from your loving family, and friends that cared for you so.
I lay at night and think, of how it would be,
If I was there for you, and you still here for me.
But I know that it can't happen, that you can't come back.
Why did you have to die so young, nothing did you lack.
I still remember your bright eyes and your smiling face.
When you left there was something missing, something I could not replace.
I would give up anything, just to have you here.
No matter where you are you will always be, my friend so true and dear.

Alison Gosewehr
St Irene School
Warrenville
Grade 8
*In memory of Bradley Kang Price

Graduation Day

Today a whole new life will start,
With our childhoods we will part.
We must not forget our past,
Or grow up too fast.
Today is a happy time,
A time to be proud of what we have done,
And remembering while we did it we had a lot of fun.
On this special day we will remember
Good and bad times.
Happy and sad times.
We remember:
When we began school,
How hard we tried to obey every rule,
And how when we got older how hard we tried to get around every rule.
Before we were aware the years have passed,
It seems like the past nine years have gone so fast.
As we accept our diplomas we realize what's ahead.
And that we have accomplished a lot.

Katie Foat
Harrison Elementary School
Wonder Lake
Grade 8

Basketball

The whistle sounds,
You enter the hardwood floor for the last time,
The last 10 seconds,
The play starts.
The ball comes to your hands,
Dribble, drive, step back.
The ball leaves your hands and floats in slow motion.
The buzzer sounds,
Swish!
You feel invincible.

Matt Goelz
St Paul School
Danville
Grade 8

My Religious Melody

When I am down
When I am sad
When I think I have no one to turn to
I think of my best friend

When life is hard
Illness is in
And my family is having problems
I look to my best friend

When people are dying
From violence and different types of diseases
I turn to my best friend

Who is this?

This best friend of mine
No one but God
My best friend all the time.

Brittany Gail Thomas
Owen Scholastic Academy
Chicago
Grade 8

The Dream

I close my eyes and fall asleep,
I see a girl, who begins to weep.

Everything looks distorted to me,
Is this a dream, could it possibly be?

The different shapes put me in a trance,
I even see little prairie dogs dance.

I finally awake, feeling battered and sore,
Tossing and turning, I'd fallen to the floor.

Alex Cimino
St John the Evangelist School
Streamwood
Grade 8

The Girl that Was Forgotten

There once was a girl who was loved by all,
  All people big and small.
Everyone asked her to come and play,
  Man! Those were the good old days.
For one day, she went to school, but when she came,
  No one was exactly the same.
No one would talk to her, not even a little.
  She became so quiet and acted so brittle.
For everyday this went on.
  Until the day she went somewhere new.
But she would only talk to a few,
  They would ask her questions
But she would say nothing.
  Until the day she said something.
But it was too late, no one would listen,
  She cried, cried, and cried until the morning came.
When she went to school, something wasn't the same.
  She walked and talked to the people she called her friends.
She was happy again!

Katey Mitchell
St George School
Tinley Park
Grade 8

Kate's Bait

There once was a girl named Kate.
She went fishing, but forgot her bait.
She dropped her pole
Down the hole
But, she didn't care because that's the one food she hates!

Nikki Pearson
River Trails Middle School
Mount Prospect
Grade 7

Love

Love is special Love is kind
Love is always on our mind
Love is free
Just like you and me
Love is humanity Love is grace
Love is found in the most uncommon place
Love is priceless
Love is niceness
You can buy gifts and flowers
They can grow within the hours
You cannot find or buy Love
But you can give Love
If you Love me
You'll do what is best for me
If I Love you
I will do what is best for you!

Emily D. Allen
Hamilton County Jr High School
Mc Leansboro
Grade 7

Can You Imagine?

Room without a mess
School without a test

Christmas without presents
Pet store without pheasants

Easter without a bunny
A joke that is not funny

Floor without tiles
People without smiles

Book without words
Sky without birds

Pond without toads
City without roads

Emily Klein
Jonesboro Elementary School
Jonesboro
Grade 7

My Friend

I have a friend
Who is more than a friend
He's my life
He's my soul
I don't know why
He can be so mean
But that doesn't matter
As summer comes
He will be sent off
Far, far away
When will I see him again
It could be a month
Or even more, a year
I don't know who knows
When I'll see my friend again
Please God say it'll be soon
Don't take my friend away from me.

Bree Paris
Parkview Jr High School
Lawrenceville
Grade 7

Kill the Lights

Room with a light
Yell too bright
Kill the lights
BOOM!
The fire has spread
It's on my head

Pat Kelly
Sacred Heart School
Lombard
Grade 7

A Prayer from Mom

A mother lies in her bed at night.
As she prays to God,
her pillow she holds tight.
She prays for the kids,
she prays for the dog,
and she prays, "Dear God please bring my man home."
She lets out one more prayer,
and with this, tears stream down her face,
her prayer is, "God please bless us with food in this old shack place."
Amen

Jessica Willis
Finley Jr High School
Chicago Ridge
Grade 8

The Unthinkable

For several years they tortured us, with blood, with whips, with pain.
They took away our clothes and families, and left us here with shame.
They starved us and beat us. the diseases spread by day,
and now I sit here waiting, waiting for the day.
The day this cage will open, and I can run away,
but run to where, I ask myself, and then my sky turns gray.
Where would I go, I have no family, they all were sent away.
So now I sit here waiting, just waiting for that day.
The day this cage will open, and all these awful memories will fade away.
The memories of all the pain my friends and I went through,
and now I sit here writing, and sharing them with you.
Hoping no one will forget what happened those many years ago.
What happened was the unthinkable, the Holocaust,
and all the unthinkable things, have left me all alone.

Melissa Willey
Quincy Jr High School
Quincy
Grade 8

I'm Sorry

I'm sorry for getting mad at you.
I'm sorry for yelling at you.
I'm sorry for giving you disrespectful looks.

I'm sorry for bugging you.
I'm sorry I won't leave you alone.

I'm sorry we can't be together.
I'm sorry you're so distant.
I'm sorry you don't love me.

I'm sorry I put you through this.
I'm sorry it turned out this way.

But there's one thing I can't ever be sorry for...
And I'm sorry I'm not sorry for it, but I can't ever be sorry for loving you.

Jaimie Hasten
Harrison Elementary School
Wonder Lake
Grade 7

Clouds

Clouds are in the sky
Where you see kites flying high.

Clouds are funny things.
They can morph into things such as diamond rings.

Clouds can also look like a tree such as a willow.
And isn't it funny that they look like a big, fluffy pillow.

Clouds can come during wind, rain or sun.
Looking at them is fun for everyone.

I think I shall go look at clouds outside.
This secret, in you, I will confide.

Amanda Wilson
St Gerald School
Oak Lawn
Grade 8

The Sweet Summer Sonnet

The midnight sky in one's sweet dream lives on
The summer breeze that blows love through the air
The flowers with sweet fragrances near dawn
The sound of doves and owls cannot compare
The moonlight glares upon the peaceful stream
The stars appear and show their strong beauty
The clouds soon disappear in the moonbeam
The stars' shine in the stream run out to sea
The burning beat of the heart's desire
The icy breath of a cold one's whisper
The flames everlasting, maintain their fire
The morning comes again and brings sun blurs
The flowers open once more all the way
And the summer lives on in us each day.

April Hicks
Sullivan High School
Sullivan
Grade 9

Love?

Just what is love?
Can it be defined?
Love is something all inclusive of heart and soul and mind.

Love is something special,
It doesn't happen every day
Love cannot be categorized for it's felt in different ways.

Love is just a feeling.
Or is it something more?
Will it come right to Me?
Or do I open up the door?

Kristin Nisbet
Leland High School
Leland
Grade 9

My Only Wish

I once again would like to taste my grandpa's fish
It's my one and only wish
I can see him right before me
I can feel his arm across my back
He always had a special knack
He always smelled of fish and pine
That was his one design
If only I could hear once more
His deep voice coming through the door
If I could only see my grandpa before me

Heath Caufield
Virden Middle-High School
Virden
Grade 7

Sonnet of Faces

All the faces that we see in a day
From black to white they never look the same
They all look different in their own way
All mixed together in this life, a game.
So many are quick to judge what they see
Faces can cover up the hurt inside
'Cause they are different from you and me
They only look at the figure outside
From every country and from every land
Faces can tell what someone is thinking
They speak of feelings or tell of the plans
When happy or sad, yelling or singing.
Some faces bring fortune, or some bring fame
Some may show sadness, or some may show pain.

Meghan Parrish
Sullivan High School
Sullivan
Grade 9

August

We sat on the edge,
You with me, I with you.
Seeing our destinies nowhere before us.
But suddenly you slipped.
You fell and you reached, and grasped for my hand
Why I couldn't hold on,
I don't understand.
You fell,
Leaving me alone.
Sitting at the top of the cliff,
In the cold world.
There's no love,
No beauty anymore.
Please someday come back to me,
And fate will weave
Our destinies.

Carmen Aiken
Quest Academy
Palatine
Grade 7

Revenge

I'm falling apart,
Deteriorating more than ever before.
This doesn't let me feel cool inside,
So instead, I feel sad, gloomy and so lonely.
This happened months ago, how can I still feel this way?
All those songs replay us every day.
I'm a tragedy. . . it has to be true.
I'm a tragedy because. . . I fell in love with you.

Trying to keep my cool and keep my distance,
But in a mere instance you're there.
I'm breaking down about what's to build up.
I feel like I'm corroding,
And will soon be left to corrupt.
What's happening to me,
I hope happens to you,
Then maybe you can tell me what I should do.

Abby Rodriguez
Colona Grade School
Colona
Grade 8

The Sunflower

Sunflower, sunflower what are thee to me?
With the mane of a lion and a meal for a bee,
Your long tail for a kite that could sail o'er the sea,
You are many, many things – yes, many things to me.

Sunflower, sunflower what are thee to me?
You form a blanket that is golden
Stretching far as eye can see,
Or a servant to a king as you bow upon your knee,
You are many, many things — yes, many things to me.

Bridget Fagan
St Mary School
Buffalo Grove
Grade 7

Clouds

When I was young, I thought God was a cloud.
I thought angels lived on clouds.
I thought rain was God's bath water splashing.
I thought love was the sky.
I thought thunder was him dropping things.
I thought grass was his royal green rug.
I thought flowers were his smell.
I thought the wind was his breath.
I thought we were his toys.

As I got older I learned the truth.
Every day I see him as a cloud,
I remember what it means to believe.

Briana Chelsi Cheatom
St Irene School
Warrenville
Grade 8

Colors

The color of my hair is the color of licorice.
The color of my skin is the color of a butter pecan cookie.
The color of my eyes is the color of a grizzly bear.
The colors of my friends are like a crayon box.

Noe Torres
Thomas J Kellar Middle School
Robbins
Grade 7

Friendship

Nothing more beautiful than a friendship
a strong,
good friendship

The talking
the late night calls
asking
"What do you wanna
do tomorrow?"

When it's time to go
and you're not there
I'm sad, I'm lonely
    I'm weak!

And when I lose you forever
I fear for what I'd do
I'll cry until my eyes are red...
Please don't leave me here to waste away!

Jenna Mashak
Queen of Martyrs School
Chicago
Grade 8

My Diary

My diary is very special to me.
I write my secrets and thoughts
For no one to see.

My deepest secret I dare not show,
For it is far too embarrassing
To let anyone know.

I write in here my hopes and dreams,
If anyone were to find it
I think I might scream.

A little book of thoughts of mind
Better memories, I will not find.

It's time to put an end to my diary of fun,
Now I know this is my favorite one.

Clare Mucker
St Gerald School
Oak Lawn
Grade 8

Spring

I like spring because it makes me sing
With the birds who bring cheer to my heart.
I like the scent of spring rain,
Pelting against my windowpane.
I like the sunshine in the morning,
When it lifts me out of bed
And I wonder what lies ahead.

Elvis Garcia
St Mary of Czestochowa School
Cicero
Grade 7

School

My alarm clock went off,
I went to my mom and pretended to cough.
My mom said not to fake,
She didn't care what measures I had to take.
I said I was sick all night,
She said yeah right.
The truth was I had a test,
and I didn't get enough rest.
My math wasn't done,
because yesterday I was having fun.
So here I am in school,
I really feel like a fool.
By the way I failed the test,
And I still didn't get enough rest.

Michelle Sus
St Barbara School
Chicago
Grade 7

The Unbeliever

You act as if the world is full of sorrow
That it will only bring you endless pain
If I could only show you a brighter tomorrow
With sunshine rather than rain

Because then you would be able to see
What's waiting outside for you
How no matter how bad it gets, there's always me
And believe it or not, it's true

But all you want to do is block everything out
And hide yourself away
Yet nobody else would ever think to doubt
The trials and tribulations of your day

I can't start to fathom your ignorance
Your feelings bring me no relief
I hope you understand your worldly importance
And finally stop your unbelief.

Erin Ball
Triad Middle School
St Jacob
Grade 8

Dreamer's Sonnet

While running through so dark a night alone,
So deep a fearful cold seclusion felt,
For crowded streets I run but still unknown;
I wished a new illusion might be dealt.
At first the night was full of warmth and love,
I spent my time so close to maiden, yet,
The skies so dark did shed their rains above,
I slowly tossing, turning, start to sweat.

Begin the nightly dark, I need escape,
To rid my mind and dreams from thoughts untrue,
I needed brighter scenes, and sweeter grapes.
Another chance I need I think I do,
To live my life a better way and take,
The life I have so great, with joy I wake!

Matt Drago
Fenwick High School
Oak Park
Grade 9

The Outside and the Inside

I'm starting to realize
That you can't judge
A book by its cover,
Although it took me awhile to discover.

It's not the outside, it's the inside.
It's not about the looks, it's the person.
It's not the cover, it's the pages.
It's the person and not the ages.

It's not the clothes, it's the person.
It's not the cup, it's the content.
It's not the telephone, it's the call.
It's not the paint, it's the wall.

The outside died today,
And the inside was born.
I guess the old saying was right.
It's not about the looks, it's the inner light.

Crystal Kantor
Parker Jr High School
Flossmoor
Grade 7

The Lion Within Me

Everybody has a lion within them,
sometimes they release it during emergencies,
and sometimes just for them to get through something.
When I release the lion it strengthens my whole body,
and I can do things I usually can't do.
The lion gives me strength, courage, and numbs me from pain.

Seth Gutierrez
Stratford Jr High School
Bloomingdale
Grade 8

Snow

Is winter really here?
We really do not know.
There is nothing more to fear
Except the falling of the snow.

The snowman is on guard outside
With the snowflakes slowly drifting down
There is no more reason to hide
So let a smile replace your frown.

Lauren Seber
Parkview Jr High School
Lawrenceville
Grade 7

Minstrels

Sing your song in gentle tone;
Words carried on subtle breeze;
Borne through air, soft voices lone;
Whispers passed among the trees.

The Minstrel's voice outdoes the lyre,
Far surpasses nightingales,
Weaves words well beside the fire,
Citing verse and old loved tales.

Turn your words to sound and sight,
Let them see your stories told,
Trill light tunes into the night
To warm the bitter winter's cold.

Poem, prose, or pretty piece,
The Minstrel's heart bears no surcease

Nicole Huiras
Pope John XXIII School
Evanston
Grade 8

Little Sisters

L oud and very bratty
I ndecent around my friends
T otally disturbing
T otally interrupting
L osing her mind
E nergetic

S o ignorant
I nto everything
S assy
T oo weird
E nthusiastic
R ude
S pecial in her own way.

Lauren Voss
Beckemeyer Elementary School
Beckemeyer
Grade 7

Memories

A memory–
Something that cannot be
Picked up or touched.
Something that will never
Break or rip.
Something that exists
Between you and yourself

Brianne Swan
Francis Granger Middle School
Aurora
Grade 7

Teddy Bears

They may not be alive
Or have anything to say,
But they are very special
In their own little way.

You may get one on your birthday
Or win one as a prize,
They are something you will cherish
And keep by your side.

They will make you smile
When you're feeling blue,
They will always be your friend
And always be true.

Who are these special creatures
You ask me very clear,
All I can tell you
Teddy bears my dear.

Lisa Perrone
Prince of Peace School
Lake Villa
Grade 8

Candy Land

All the children laugh and play
in a candy bowl, one sweet day.
Sliding down a row of mints
all possible colors, shades and tints.

Tasting all the lollipops,
smelling the sweet scent of gumdrops,
jumping on the gummy bears,
and bouncing just about everywhere.

Chocolate truffles lying on the ground,
stop and take a look around.
All the children smiling with delight,
until their tummies ache tonight.

Rose Rubino
St John the Evangelist School
Streamwood
Grade 8

My Parakeet

I have a yellow parakeet.
I hardly ever see him sleep.
He bobbed his head as if he'd bowed.
My parakeet is very sweet.

My parakeet is never loud.
Sometimes his head is in the clouds.
He has a toy that gives him joy.
His singing makes him very proud.

There is no one that he annoys.
My parakeet is never coy.
He is messy but that is fine.
His ladder also gives him joy.

His yellow feathers seem to shine.
This parakeet is so divine.
I'm so delighted he is mine.
I'm so delighted he is mine.

Deanna Gnaedinger
Beckemeyer Elementary School
Beckemeyer
Grade 7

Life

Life is a gift
given from God.
Life is a blessing
we don't always want.
Life is at times
hectic and hard
but it's worth all the joy
and happiness that you get out of it.
Life is something
you don't take for granted;
it won't last forever.
So, live each day to the fullest
and make the best of your life!

Colleen Orth
St Philip The Apostle School
Northfield
Grade 8

New Tomorrow

No end,
always at the beginning.
Each new day
starts over again.
Wait to see
what will come
because every day
is a new tomorrow.

Gina Chimino
Queen of Martyrs School
Chicago
Grade 8

The Garden of Joy

When dew sets into cold grass,
Flowers bloom, buds begin to grow.
What I do changes
A cold colorless world
Into a world of joy and harmony.
Worlds away, I become a wonder of happiness;
Here on earth they could not lead a life without me.
I am a garden;
I show feeling, joy, and color in my seasonal moments.
The flowers within me bring slowness in growing,
wisdom and standing,
and sadness withholding the dying and wilting of my presence.

Shannon Foster
North Park Elementary School
Chicago
Grade 7

The Life of a Flame

Peeking up from logs at night,
Cinders start to give off light.
Flames start licking up the air,
Without a worry or a care.

Fire, nature's bright red bloom,
Glowing in an evening gloom.
Dancing, crackling, smiling bright,
Lighting up the velvet night.

Smaller and smaller it gives less heat.
It has been such a good treat.
It's gone and everyone says with a tremor,
"We wish that it could last forever!"

Cyrus Vandrevala
Highland Middle School
Libertyville
Grade 7

Outdoors Sonnet

The stars look like diamonds in the bright sky
The clouds hang over the old willow tree
When the sun comes out the moon will soon die
The sounds of the ocean reach out from the sea
The flowers sway in the gentle air breeze
The plants near the sea reach down by the shores
The ocean surrounds the tiny, small keys
The world is a peaceful place out of doors
The stars, the sun, and the moon all shine bright
The grass is so green and looks so pretty
When it rains the ocean fills up a lot
The outdoors is better than the city
The sun is beautiful all the time now
The great outdoors was built by our great God

Wesley Davis
Sullivan High School
Sullivan
Grade 9

Dear Boy

Dear Boy, here comes the dream.
On its way, where the moon shines.

You could hear his crystal horses galloping.

The dream crosses between sleepy lands,
and suddenly it turns toward your house.

In your avenue,
you could see his little paper made chariot.

Dear Boy, the dream goes on,
and it stops in front of your house.

He lifts the house with his hand of cotton.

You could hear the cricket.
With his key, he opens your door to pass in.

The passenger comes to you,
with his step of happiness.

Alejandro Saez
Taylor Elementary School
Chicago
Grade 8

Star

Star
shining bright
in the clear sky at night.
A symbol of guidance.
Lighting our path. A glowing omen of
good fortune. A vivid object that has guided lost
civilizations, and is shining on us now.
The glory and light blind one's
eyes in great amazement:
reminder of our wishes
That   always
come   true.

Amy E. Power
Holy Angels School
Aurora
Grade 7

Spring Time

Spring time, spring time a time to share,
Where all children forget all cares.
They run out and play.

Where April showers bring May flowers.
Where school homework bring a time to play.
Spring time, spring time

Omari Frazier
Dirksen Middle School
Calumet City
Grade 7

One Single Drop

I can feel it build up inside of me, but it just won't come out. It feels like I can cry a river but all that comes out is one single drop. They always said that they were here for me, but when I need them the most they just pushed me away. Then that feeling of tears comes back, but nothing comes out except for one single drop. All of a sudden this feeling of pain and grief takes over my life. It feels like I am the only one here, here on earth. Yet I see all of these faces, but no one seems to help me. When I am alone my vision gets all blurred and my body gets all hot, but all that comes out is just one single drop.

Amy J. Trickie
Harlem Jr High School
Loves Park
Grade 9

I Wonder

I wonder what's going through their minds when they hurt someone;
Or when one makes fun of another with comments that should be left unsaid.

I wonder what the world is coming to when I see another get hurt.
Knowing that the people behind all the criticism now feel more powerful somehow.

I wonder if I can be strong enough to stand up for myself even though it is very hard.
I might surprise myself and others will start to stand up for themselves, too.

I wonder why these people think they can walk all over others the way they do.
I can't imagine what they will think when we are all grown up and people start to look up to us.

I wonder if they will know that they should have paid more attention to school other than popularity.
Maybe I don't have to wonder anymore. I could ignore them and see what they think now that I've gotten stronger.

Now I know that in the end it will all work out.

Khristen Rasmussen
Leland Elementary School
Leland
Grade 7

Anything Is Possible

She told me I will make it, he also told me so; but my reaction was, it will be impossible.
They said that once they, too, had felt the same; but I said to take this seriously, this is not the same game.
I said I would miss his warm body when I am cold; they said it is his time, for he is too old.
I said I can't take this, I want to leave; they said he must be free from his pain and misery.
I said this is not fair, it is not his time; they said to say goodbye, for in my heart he will always be mine.
So I held him in my arms, with his head beneath my chin; he looked back at me confused, yet grim.
I told him it's okay, don't be scared; just close your eyes and let God take you there.
I said I can't stand this anymore, this is all I can take; he then lifted his head, for he felt my tears upon his face.
I said my final goodbye, my parents did, too; and my last words to him were "you brought me such happiness,
And don't forget that I'll always love you."
Just that same second, for eternity, he closed his eyes; with great despair I started to cry.
They took my hand and walked me away; but I said, "Don't touch me, it is you who I blame."
They both turned away, I could tell they were sad; but I didn't care, for they've never felt this bad.
I went to sleep that night feeling angry, no furious; but they said, "Don't be mad, you will get through this."
My parents stood by my side, giving me all the support I could need; they said, "Think positive, for now he is free."
I told them thank you for being there giving me your love and your care; they said, "No problem, it's our job, my dear."
As I looked through the window and the thick fog, I knew they were still watching over me, the eyes of my dog.
They could see the pain in my glance and said "Making it through such a hard struggle and once not thinking you
Were capable, makes us believe that for you, anything is possible."

Lauren A. Olszewski
Tobin Elementary School
Burbank
Grade 8

Princess Diana

Princess Diana was one of a kind.
She was caring, sharing, and full of life.
Her beauty and grace left us in awe,
her dedication and spirit have helped us all.
She inspired us in different ways
and continues to do so today.

Mirjana Biljan
St Michael School
Orland Park
Grade 7

You

I'm sending you my heart and soul
This is what I'll say
I dream of you coming home
I dream of you being here
Without you, I can't go on
Without you, I'm too weak to bear
I want for you to be okay
I want for you to understand
Say our love will never die
Say our love will stay alive
I can see you in my mind
I can see you walking through that door
And opening the letter that I've sent 100 times
It's been hours, seems like days
Since you went away
I'm sorry, so sorry
Can't you give me one more chance
To make it all up to you
I'm sending you my heart and soul
And that is what I'll say

Briana Reynolds
Francis Granger Middle School
Aurora
Grade 7

Ocean

To me the ocean is like a person:
Some days they're both furious.
Some days they're both calm;
Some days they're both warm.
Some days they're both cold;
Some days they're both merciless.
Some days they're both delightful;
Some days they're both beautiful.
Some days they're both hideous;
Some days their fragrance is nice.
Some days their fragrance just stinks;
Some days they're both festive.
Some days they're both somber:
Some days there is hardly any difference at all.

Dan Blake
Owen Scholastic Academy
Chicago
Grade 7

A Funny Sonnet

I like to eat cheese pizza and ding dongs
But my mom won't buy me any more food
I dance to weird Al Yankovicks "fat" song
I found out that Jenny Craig's food ain't good

My ten ton tank won't fit in normal pants
Instead, I have to shop at "Just my Size"
When I walk all things shake not just the ants
The Richter scale's needle bounces and jives

When I swim, I look like a fat blue whale
Maybe I shouldn't have worn a blue suit
When I check my weight, I destroy the scale
'Cuz I'm fat the state pays me lots of loot

When I bathe, I go through ten bars of soap
Even Richard Simmons gave up on hope

Jame Cole
Sullivan High School
Sullivan
Grade 9

Graduation

At the end of the year, we had no fear.
But in August we will begin freshman year.
On May 27th we will be dressed in our caps and gowns.
We will be full of tears and frowns.

When we started we were small
And now we have grown to be very tall.
We remember the friends that we have had;
And we remember the times, both good and bad.

As we say good-bye, we try not to cry.
The eighth grade class of 2000 is something we will never forget.

Jenny Twomey
St Gerald School
Oak Lawn
Grade 8

How Noble a Man

How noble a man who's true to his heart.
How noble a man who finishes something he starts.
How noble a man who's kind to others.
How noble a man who loves one another.

How noble a man who cares for others.
How noble a man who helps each other.
How noble a man who loves only one.
How noble a man who has lots of fun.

How noble a man.

Stephanie Perry
St John The Baptist School
West Frankfort
Grade 7

Rainforest

Canopy so tall
Animals as loud as cars
It's the rainforest

Ryan Helmerichs
Virden Middle-High School
Virden
Grade 7

Motocross

Starting the race
I feel tension in my face.
The gates drop down.
Who's watching? The whole town
We're rounding the first turn.
Some racers crash and burn.
The dirt was flying all around
I thought I was going to hit the ground.
I'm in third place.
I'm doing my best.
To win this race
I cannot rest.
One more jump.
One lap to go.
Will I win this race?
I don't know.
I'm thinking of a prize.
It was right before my eyes.
I cross the finish line
And realize the trophy is mine.

Justin Roy
Parkview Jr High School
Lawrenceville
Grade 7

Dream a Little With Faith

Up in the air, oh so high,
Oh look at me mom,
Look at me fly.
I feel like a bird,
An angel in heaven.
My dream has come true.
No longer do I feel blue.
But I can't stay up,
My time is almost up.
So down I come,
My time is done.
I never gave up
Now my dream is fulfilled.
So listen my son
To what I have done.
And please learn don't give in,
'Cause in the end you'll always win.

Jeremy Larson
L J Stevens Middle School
Wilmington
Grade 7

At Night

You crawl under the covers waiting for your dreams to come,
your eyes close slowly and they have begun.
You see a mountain with trees,
the flowers with bees,
and you think nothing could be more fun.
As you sit there relaxing in the valley below,
it seems as though everything moves so slow.
Abruptly you are awaken from your little wonderland,
Your eyes open slowly and you remember the glorious dream you just had.

Marin McCabe
St Matthew School
Champaign
Grade 8

For Now

As I sit here and daydream, it makes me wanna cry, cry out for you,
You, the one I love so much, so much it hurts.
Hurts to breathe as my mind wonders,
Wonders what it would be like to be,
Be with you and know you care, care for me,
Me being the one that wants you so bad,
Bad enough it makes me wanna die,
Die because I love you so.
So I'll never know,
Know for sure if this could work—work the way,
The way I'd like it to be.
I just want you to be aware,
Aware of how much I love you.
You, the one that's so fresh in my mind.
Mind games are what you play with me continually.
Just let me tell you,
I love you, I need you, I want you, and I care for you
Give me a chance, the chance to be with you.
Cuz, for now, that's all I ever daydream about.

Rachel Snyder
Stratford Jr High School
Bloomingdale
Grade 8

First Impressions Only Last a While

What are your thoughts about me when you turn toward me?
What do your eyes see standing there?
What untrue life have you given to me?
Who do you really think I am?
When I turn toward you I try to see past, the looks to what must be.
I try to peer through your sweet eyes,
break through what seems clear and cut my way through others' lies.
What do you see looking at me?
A little girl with broken dreams?
A bag full of tired emotions, and bursting seams with dark brown oval eyes.
To all who say they know me, and especially to you,
You'll never really know me because first impressions only last with you . . .

Jennifer Alatorre
Children of Peace-St Callistus School
Chicago
Grade 7

Ocean

Listen to the ocean on a summer's day,
For waves as they trickle and play.
Spraying crystal beads,
Filling one's joyful needs.

Calling children to cool down,
Floating kelp flowing as a gown.
Surrounding ankles, feet and toes,
Encountering all – friends and foes.

On the shore smooth and black as a hearse,
Lies what's known as a mermaid's purse.
Carried by gently moving waves,
This is what a child craves.

A treasure!

Terrence Hanlon
Highland Middle School
Libertyville
Grade 7

Summer

Summer is the season with lots of sun.
And that makes it so much more fun.
People play in water all day long
While birds sit in the trees singing their song.
Going out with your friends
And coming back when the day ends.
You can also go and play sports
Plus activities of all sorts.
Going outside with a friend to play
While listening to what they say.
That is why it is so much fun
To go out in the sun.
Summer is a season you should never fear
Because it is the very best time of year.

Matt McLaughlin
St Michael School
Orland Park
Grade 7

Reach for the Stars

As the dark clouds rumbled across the sky,
the old oak tree seemed to open his branches
to quench his thirst.

Hit by lightning from a previous vicious storm,
life lives within its bark.

The old oak tree stands proud,
weathering many sunrises and sunsets,
yet still reaches for the sky.

Lauren Donahue
Queen of Martyrs School
Chicago
Grade 8

Friends

Friends should be friends.
Friends should stay friends forever
Friends should tell friends secrets
Secrets should never ever be told
Under any circumstances
Friends should share almost everything
Not just anything
They should share feelings
And things in common.
Friends should be friends.

Sade McDonald
Laraway Elementary School
Joliet
Grade 8

I Am

I am strong and I am proud
I wonder if my sun will be ambushed by angry rain cloud
I hear exaggerated roars of thunder
I see things and often contemplate or rather wonder
I want my pride and strength to be heard out loud
That is how I know that I am strong and I am proud

I often visualize myself as an honorable hero
I never picture myself as much of a zero
I touch my mind to see what's there
I worry and ask myself "to what extent do I care?"
I cry in my mind, but not too loud
But still, I'm strong and I am proud

I understand that things don't always go my way
So I say "okay" and I'm happy as I walk away
I dream one day that I'll become a famous musician
To do so, I must maintain my first trumpet position
I hope that my sun isn't halted by that menace of a cloud
And as always, I am strong and I am proud

George Douglas Jackson III
Forest Trail Jr High School
Park Forest
Grade 8

Basketball!

Basketball is a great quality I have
It builds up my strength, confidence, and courage
You win, you lose, but know never to give up
I practice hard every day and I know it's paying off
It's a great feeling to know I have this tremendous skill
I know if I stop playing hard or give up in what I'm doing
My talents will quickly start to fade
But I know, to do these things I have to believe in myself
If I believe I know I will succeed
Play hard, practice hard, and your goals will come true

Mark Sinodinos
Queen of Martyrs School
Chicago
Grade 8

Night and Day

The darkness of night
Evaporating into
The brightness of day.

Veronica Tello
Forest Trail Jr High School
Park Forest
Grade 8

Shopping's Too Easy!

S tores
H oliday sales
O nly entertainment here!
P urses
P ennies
I n and out the doors!
N ature has found its way to me!
G ap

A merican Eagle
N o
D etours to...

S top me.
P lenty to spend
E mpty the wallet
N ow borrow from mom
D ebt paid off
I n the car
N ow it's time
G o home!

Amanda Lampert
Francis Granger Middle School
Aurora
Grade 7

A Year of Haiku

Flowers bloom in spring,
Raindrops fall down everyday,
Time to play outside.

Rays hit like fire,
Going to the beach to swim,
The summer is here.

Yellow and orange,
Many leaves fall beautifully,
Autumn has arrived.

Snow falls gently down,
Like soft cotton on the ground,
White and beautiful.

Bridget K. Comiskey
Fenwick High School
Oak Park
Grade 9

Break a Leg

Olympics
The chance to go
The excitement
You're favored to win
You know the best jump
It's finally your turn
The excitement builds up
You hear break a leg
Then stiffen up
You go out on the ice
Get ready to jump
One twist
Two
Three
Your foot gets caught
You land and it cracks
You think to yourself,
"I've broken a leg."

Ryan Knoll
Sacred Heart School
Lombard
Grade 7

Fear

Guns are what I fear.
I can feel them near.

I hear the shots
Once.

Twice.

Then I hear people
Yell, scream, run.

They are not at all fun.
I run, run and run.
To my house I go.

Fear is what I show.

Then I hear ambulances come.
Then the siren fades in the sun.

I go to bed.

Tomorrow I just might
Go back to the shack
That held that horrible attack.

Fear I still hold about guns.
Just remember they are not fun.

Nicole Yost
Hamlin Upper Grade Center
Alsip
Grade 7

Diploma

I'm cherished for one day
and one day only.
After that I'm put away
sad and lonely.

You jump and cheer
when you get me,
but the thing for me to do
is to leave and be free.

I get you into college.
I get you a job.
When I think of how you use me,
I want to sob.

Twenty years later,
your parents find me
and smile, then put me back
where I can't be seen.

I'm just a diploma,
nothing more.
Please think of me
when you're on that graduation floor.

Cassie McLaughlin
Francis Granger Middle School
Aurora
Grade 7

An Extraordinary Place

A dynamic place of wonders,
A mysterious land of shudders.
A petrified place of exotic dreams,
A wondrous place of purified dreams.

What a glorious land of freedom,
What an exciting land of secrets.
No one dares to determine the truth,
Who dares to behold the knowledge?

At moments it's magical,
But can keep you hysterical!
No more worries to be found,
All is left; way behind!

All that is left to be
You and me.
What holds the future is evolution,
What is present is the ocean.
It is extraordinary, what we
All are meant to be.

Brittany Johnson
Armstrong Elementary School
Chicago
Grade 7

Life

You are born,
Slowly but rapidly you're growing,
Growing so fast you hit your prime.
You figure life is great,
And life is going so fast, before you know it you're old
And all you have left are your memories.
The memories that you bring to your grave,
Death.

Adrian Saldana
River Trails Middle School
Mount Prospect
Grade 7

Sports

There are many different kinds
Football, basketball, and baseball
They are all fun and involve different things
Hitting, running, shooting, kicking, and jumping
I think they are lots of fun

Most people play sports
Some like fishing, bowling, or golf
While others like contact sports like football and hockey
I like fishing, baseball, and basketball
I don't know how to skate so I can't play hockey
But I do play it on foot or on roller blades.
I also enjoy watching them on TV
Going to watch them is even better

Well now I am done
Saying what I have to say
So why don't you go play?
A sport today

Cal Hefner
Clifford Crone Middle School
Naperville
Grade 7

Cars

Cars are really unique and luxurious.
There are many different models, structures, and colors.
Cars, cars, they go really fast
When you ride in one you'll have a blast.
Some cars have V8's or they have V10's,
But I prefer the Mercedes-Benz.
The best car in the world is the Dodge Viper.
When I look at it, it makes me hyper!
The easiest way to burn rubber is to push the gas pedal
All the way until it hits the metal.
The greatest thing to do is to watch cars race,
To see them dash at their lightening-quick pace.
I love cars and I always will!

Chris Drag
St Gerald School
Oak Lawn
Grade 8

Old Love

Silently separating, because of "a new job"
Calling, visiting, but never staying.
Fewer calls, fewer visits, more excuses
Soon, everything split, property, possessions, love.
New love breaks all hope of old love.
Everyone knows, but doesn't understand,
Everyone comforts, but doesn't help.
Trapped, alone, insignificant thoughts of the past.
Those who understand leave,
Never talking to me about how I should feel.
I feel confused about the old love.

Rachel Pollock
Pope John XXIII School
Evanston
Grade 8

Aghast Dreams

I am a nightmare.
When you shut your eyes, I appear.
I disturb your precious dreams.
I'm that horrendous thing that makes you scream!
I'm a stimulation of your worst fears.
Sometimes, I can be a twist of reality.
I destroy your peace.
There's nothing anyone can do to stop me from coming.
So sleepers, *BEWARE!*

Jina Kadakia
Francis Granger Middle School
Aurora
Grade 7

When Winter Comes

As I walked down to the lodge.
I stopped to check the view.
What winter can make,
What winter has done.

Its appearance is beautiful yet deceiving.
The perfectly coated slope
Will break at a ski's touch.
The wonderfully placid, frozen lake
Will crack under the weight of a child.

Staring back and taking a breath,
"I love winter" repeated in my head.
This is the truest season,
Making even the strongest show fear.

Knowing that experiencing winter is a constant challenge,
Feeling lucky that I survived this day,
Being unable to comprehend what else awaits me,
I can only love it and live by its rules.

Margaret Knap
Fenwick High School
Oak Park
Grade 9

Sledding

I just bought a new sled,
It is fast, sleek, and swift.
As I rush down the steep hill,
I can feel the wind in my face.
It is quite an exciting experience,
Going so fast,
It makes me feel like I am flying.
The wind in my hair,
The sharpness of my mind,
Dodging bumps to go as fast as I can,
Spinning, turning, and a few other stunts,
Add to the experience
As a million snowflakes rush toward me,
It makes me feel like I am in outer space amongst all the stars.

You should try it some time.

Brian Donovan
Queen of Martyrs School
Chicago
Grade 8

Growing Up

No one ever told me growing up would be so bad.
No one ever told me, seeing the years pass would be so sad.
I never thought things would change.
Though now, everything seems strange.
All of a sudden you realize Santa Claus isn't real.
Christmas no longer has the same happy feel.
You find out, the tooth fairy is nothing but a myth.
They're all just stories to fill your mind with.
You begin to see everything in a different color and shade.
Your little kid spirit begins to fade.
You wish you could turn back the hands of time.
To when everything in your life was fine.

Karina Diaz
John F Eberhart Elementary School
Chicago
Grade 8

Grief

Grief is something that is hard to live with.
We all do things that we regret, or feel guilty about.
Some things that we do, do not seem wrong
at the time of the crime,
but in the long run it hurts someone
physically or emotionally.
When you are filled with grief
all you want to do is get rid of it,
it is like a cold that you can't wait to recover from.
And sometimes, when you think it is gone,
it comes back to visit you again; reminding you of what
you did and causing you to feel horrible all over again.

Brooke Rowland
Frances Xavier Warde School
Chicago
Grade 8

The Dance

There once was a young man from France,
Whose favorite thing was to dance.
He first danced the polka,
Then drank some mocha,
And fell into a deep, deep trance

Konstantinos Papadopoulos
River Trails Middle School
Mount Prospect
Grade 7

Sonnet of Time

As I look back upon the growing years
And remember the events of my life,
My eyes relieve themselves of silent tears
Recalling sad things that caused so much strife.
Unhappiness consumes the world today
So much pain and suffering we do see,
Relations torn apart day after day
This constant struggle revolves around me.
But amidst all the challenges we face
Friends and family are still standing true,
Ready to comfort with a warm embrace
Their unconditional love strengthens you.
Though change, as a whole, will always abide
Time cannot change the love we have inside.

Kristen McGhghy
Sullivan High School
Sullivan
Grade 9

Good-bye*

Some may mourn
this great day.
We all endure it
in our own special way.

Some may laugh
and some may cry,
but most just remember
the really great times.

When mournful times
like this arise,
we think of her
and her loving eyes.

So now's our time
to say good-bye,
a very sad one
with tears in our eyes.

Angela Hill
Quincy Jr High School
Quincy
Grade 8
*Dedicated to my loving grandma, Mildred Dee Straube:
November 8, 1937 to March 27, 1999.

Mall

I like to go to the mall,
'Cause when I go I have a ball.
Shopping is really fun for me,
Go, and soon you'll see.
Shopping with friends and buying some clothes;
Take a picture and strike a pose.

Vicki Dzura
River Trails Middle School
Mount Prospect
Grade 7

I Am

I am a dancer.
I wonder if the world will ever set me free.
I hear the sound of leaves rustling in the distance.
I see the ground slipping from beneath my feet.
I want to fly and glide across the sky.
I am a dancer.

I pretend I'm in the mud, in the grass.
I feel the breeze sweep by my face.
I reach for the moon, yet yearn for the ground.
I worry I will never be set free.
I cry for the innocence of the world.
I am a dancer.

I understand that I can't reach all impossible.
I say, I can.
I dream I will dance across the mud with the ball.
I try to breathe for the world.
I hope I learn how to understand.
I am a dancer.

Ariel Fortune
Francis Granger Middle School
Aurora
Grade 7

Under the Stars

Under the stars we lie,
My brothers Justin, Michael, and I
Eating popcorn in the moonlight,
We hear the wolves howl; it's almost midnight.

The campfire is going out,
It's getting cold without a doubt,
We get into our sleeping bags,
We're done for the night with all our gags.

We stare at the sky to see the big dipper,
As I snuggle in and zip my sleeping bag zipper.
It's quiet now we hear no cars,
Here we lie under the stars.

Danny Kindgren
St Joseph Catholic School
Harvard
Grade 7

Beautiful Pride

This is the way I am,
the way I want to be

And when I look in the mirror
I'm glad that it's still me

I'm glad that I don't see the reflection
of someone working at her best,

Trying to be someone she's not,
just to look like all the rest

I'm looking back at someone pure,
who's showing what is true,

And not giving what she doesn't have,
just to do what she can't do.

My beauty is a special one
because I was naturally this way.

And I learned that personality
can make your beauty stronger each and every day.

I have my own sense of compassion
because my beliefs are so divine.

I'll hold my pride within me
to keep my beauty mine.

Diahann Bayan
Clifford Crone Middle School
Naperville
Grade 7

Children

Children laughing,
Children crying.

Children healing,
Children hurting.

Children living,
Children dying.

Children eating,
Children starving.

Children loving,
Children hating.

Why should children cry, hurt, die, starve, or hate,
If they could laugh, heal, live, eat, or love?

Alyssa Bechtel
St Matthew School
Champaign
Grade 7

Teddy Bear

Cute little teddy bear,
All warm,
All fuzzy,
Always loyal,
Silly silly little teddy bear,
Soft just for me.
Kind and fluffy at the same time.
Always loving, loving, loving teddy bear.

Mike Barker
Stratford Jr High School
Bloomingdale
Grade 8

Friends

There are friends to be there for
Friends to watch out for
Friends to laugh with
Friends to cry with
Friends that are serious
Friends that are crazy
Friends to share secrets with
Friends you'll fight with
Friends you'll make up with
Friends you've grown up with
Friends you'll grow old with
Friends that you'll never forget
Friends that will come and go
And friends you'll be friends with forever

Brittny Allbee
Francis Granger Middle School
Aurora
Grade 7

Peace in the World

P ortrait of love
E verlasting
A wesome
C omforting
E nd of prejudice

I nfinite
N ecessary

T rust
H appiness
E veryone

W arm
O pen to all
R ainbow
L ife
D ancing

Art Vilutis
St George School
Tinley Park
Grade 8

Family

Grandparents–They start the family tradition
They are always there when you need them
They believe in you even if you don't believe in yourself.

Mom–She helps me with some projects
She is always there when I need her
She takes care of me.
She reminds me to do my responsibilities
She takes me shopping (which I like sometimes)

Step-Dad–He helps me with my homework (sometimes)
He too takes care of me,
We don't get to see him much cause he travels.

Brother–He is in first grade
Sometimes we play games
But we really like to aggravate each other.

4 Aunts and 1 Uncle–They let you stay with them when you need to
They are supportive and supply your needs
And you can talk to them whenever you feel the need

10 Cousins–You have fun with them
They're also a form of recreation, surprises,
And just plain friends to you within the family.

Kristin Bonds
Clifford Crone Middle School
Naperville
Grade 7

The Sunset

I am awed in beauty at the majestic sight
Of the setting sun that disperses light.
That light that lives and the light that stays
Is now about to perish away
Its colors are mangled like a blur
Of orange, yellow, and a light amber
The darkness vanquishes the colors faster than a cat's blink
As our setting sun begins to sink.
That sun is a radiant fireball in the sky,
And it has just fallen over and begun to die.

The sky is now an endless sea of black, but I still stare.
I wonder how so many people can be amazed, but then don't care.
That exquisite sun that will come and go
Thinks that nobody knows.
But, I know why the sun dressed so elegantly tonight.
It was helped by the polluted air that reflected the light.
So maybe this majestic sunset isn't so majestic after all,
And maybe it was our pollution that caused it to fall.
Then the sun will fall for its last time,
And then we will know we have committed a serious crime.

Tim Heafner
Blessed Sacrament School
Belleville
Grade 7

Contact Sports

Contact sports may hurt your head,
Which will have you lying on a bed,
Or maybe it won't hurt at all,
Or most of the year anyway, because they start in the Fall

Thomas C. Santora
River Trails Middle School
Mount Prospect
Grade 7

Light in Me

Way deep inside of me,
There is something others can't see.
It is a light that shines, brightly glows,
And consists of things no one knows.

Caught inside this gleaming light,
Are things I've learned or tried to fight.
It grows as experiences come and go,
And shows the best of me, I know.

Memories are found here to help the gleam,
It spotlights on the future's hope and dreams.
Others will try to make it dim and hurt me,
But I'll always be sure to keep it radiant with glee.

So I hope this light will begin to shine through,
To show others someone shiny and new.
Because this light shows the best of me,
I just wish others would see.

Liz Prebish
Clifford Crone Middle School
Naperville
Grade 7

Lacy

You went to the park as a normal day.
But it didn't seem to be that way.
Beautiful butterflies in your hair.
I felt you would always be near.
You are so beautiful and tall.
I would catch you before you'd fall.
Lacy gave me the privilege to be her friend.
Since then I knew this friendship
would never end.
Along came Randy
and his three sweet sweet daughters.
They gave Lacy and me so much to offer.
Lacy wanted to grow up
to be a singer, a dancer, and even a model.
Always since then Lacy has been my idol.
Lacy I hope you thought I was your big sis.
Lacy B. Zefo I sure would love to hug and kiss.

Angela Brownless
Alexis Jr High School
Alexis
Grade 7

His Child

I dreamt last night of you and me together,
only it wasn't meant for us to last forever.
We started out as one,
but soon after came our son.
You didn't take the news very well,
but you tried to hide it I could tell.
You decided to leave your son and me,
said you wanted to be free.
There was nothing I could say or do to change your mind.
You were convinced and I was in a bind.
But now I realize
that it wasn't a dream last night.
And now I find myself all alone
without the one man I loved,
left with only one thing to remind me of him,
his child.

Charlene Arroyo
St Ferdinand School
Chicago
Grade 8

A Calm Walk

The quiet, rhythmic rushing in and out of waves,
Sends a calm feeling through my body.
Cool colors streak the sky
Leaving a brilliance to reflect behind the clouds.
Hot sand warms my feet as I walk.
A seagull's cry fills my ears and breaks the silence.
Who, I ask, could have created such a beautiful moment?
A response comes immediately as the artist signs his work
With two jets crossing high in the atmosphere
Leaving an "X" made of clouds.

Betsy Giblin
Pope John XXIII School
Evanston
Grade 8

The Eagle

To heaven the eagle soars
Flapping its wings as it flies
Over majestic seashores
high in the bright blue skies

The eagle is a dominant bird
Because he is King of the sky
Not being dominant is absurd
Because he can really fly

Hunting is what the eagle does best
Swooping down to snatch its prey
With this fact people should be impressed
Because he does this every day

Brian Yatco
Immaculate Conception School
Morris
Grade 7

Little Girl

Little girl riding her bike
Thinking of the things she likes
Barking at the birds
And chirping at the dogs
Croaking at the cats
And purring at the frogs
These are the things she likes
As she rides her bike

Amanda Logsdon
Parkview Jr High School
Lawrenceville
Grade 7

Looking Out the Window

I sit in the classroom
Waiting for the bell to ring.
Looking out the window
Wishing to be outside.
Looking at the birds
Wanting to be like them.
Wanting to be a bird
So free to fly anywhere.

Sarah Gard
Parkview Jr High School
Lawrenceville
Grade 7

Immigrating

Crowded people cry,
Over the endless sea.
Smile, they are here.

Samantha Raddatz
Francis Xavier Warde School
Chicago
Grade 7

Championship Game

The team was near
As many can hear.

With the help of fate
We went to state.

The crowd cheered
As the other team feared.

That they might lose
It just may make the news.

But, we won the game
As next year we'll do the same.

Kim Behrns
Smithton Elementary School
Smithton
Grade 8

Fall

A time for apples
Find, pick, wash, cut, slice, bake, eat
A delicious feast

Amy Leahy
River Trails Middle School
Mount Prospect
Grade 7

The Streets of Evanston

Drugs, activity, people
Feeling good
Frustration with girls
Hazy day
Surrounded by friends
Having fun
All found on the streets

Gunshots heard
People fleeing
Feeling scared
Screams of fear
"OUCH"
I bumped my head
When I fell out of bed.

It was just a dream.

Dameon Graves
Evanston Township High School
Evanston
Grade 9

A Dream

Being a kid and
having a dream,
which sometimes
rips at the seams.

Is hard for me
and others, too
because sometimes
it makes you feel so blue.

And trying it over
again and again
sometimes puts you
right back where you began.

But dreams are good
for kids like me
they open the world
for us to see.

Mandie Curia
St Mary-Dixon School
Dixon
Grade 7

Autumn

Autumn leaves fall to the ground,
raking them up all around.
Some blow away in the breeze,
away from their home in the trees.

Halloween comes to celebrate,
people have options to decorate.
"Trick or Treat" door to door,
candy will add up more and more.

Thanksgiving is almost here,
giving thanks while it comes near.
Cooking a big meal for all,
every person big and small.

The breeze grows colder,
autumn is also growing older.
Take out winter coats today,
while autumn slowly fades away.

Mary Eck
St Tarcissius School
Chicago
Grade 7

Class of 2000

We've walked the halls,
Received our grades.
Made new friends,
And now time fades.

So much fun,
So many laughs.
Now the time has come.
I can't believe we're done.

Congratulations to my friends,
The St. Matthew 8th Grade class of 2000.

John Minneci
St Matthew School
Champaign
Grade 8

Home Run

The bases are in place,
The fields are groomed,
The chalk is put down,
The game will start soon,
The players are ready
To catch a high fly,
Their mitts in the air
And the ball zooms by.

Erik Borczon
St Mary of Czestochowa School
Cicero
Grade 7

Grams

Dear Grams,
I miss you
I wish you'd still be here
I see you in my dreams
You're such a glory with your wings
And your beautiful smile
That cleans out my soul with gold
It has been one year but I remember it like yesterday
When you gave me my birthday present
A kiss and hug
I will never throw away what you have given me
Because it means so much to me
And that is all I have from you
I miss you and I love you

Ulysses Diaz
Francis Granger Middle School
Aurora
Grade 7

The Bout

W inning is everything
R est after you pin him
E veryone's eyes on you
S hoot and finish it off
T he only time to quit is when the official raises your hand
L osing is for the other man not you
I f you want to win you have to give it your all
N ever give up
G et the trophy

Danny Dolan
St Vincent De Paul School
Peoria
Grade 8

Loneliness

She was so sad.
No one knew what the problem was.
She was very quiet and kept to herself,
Talking to no one, obviously deep in thought.
She looked as if she could collapse at any moment,
But not knowing when.
No one could prevent it
If no one knew the problem.
She had no support
From anyone in the world.
She was alone,
Left alone by herself.
She was even ridiculed,
By someone with no idea
Of what she was going through.
For now she is alone,
By herself, and alone.

Linus Coy
North Park Elementary School
Chicago
Grade 7

Flaws

Tell me why you can't be happy with me.
You always find something disappointing to see.
Whether it's what I do or what you see,
There is always something disappointing in me.
I do my best, but you just can't see,
How much I try to make you proud of me.
I am not perfect, as you can see,
When I tell you this you don't agree.
You say, yes you can, you can be,
Even more perfect than anyone, even me.
Perfect! Perfect! Nobody's perfect, not even me.
Perfect is something I choose not to be.
Perfect is flawless, I need my flaws.
They define me, they are my laws.

Nicole Springer
Grant Community High School
Fox Lake
Grade 9

Peer Pressure

Living with peer pressure it is hard to say no.
Even if it's the right way to go.
Sometimes it has to do with smoking,
Other times just plain joking.
Sometimes it may seem funny,
But it is not worth the money.
So be your own self.
Not someone's personal elf.

Toni Paxson
St Joan Of Arc School
Evanston
Grade 7

Sometimes I Wonder

Sometimes I wonder

Why my grandfather says
We only live for a period of time.
But now I know.
We live like flowers.

I wonder why

Every season a flower dies,
A person dies, too.
Every time a leaf falls,
A person does, too.

It's like the world gets larger every minute,
And gets shorter every second.

I wonder why?

Ashlee Osbourne
Thomas J Kellar Middle School
Robbins
Grade 7

I Want a Snow Day

I was playing outside in the snow.
Oh no, where did it go?
It's turning warm, what can I do?
I love snow I'm sure you do, too.
Snow is bright, snow is white.
We can have many a snowball fight.
All I want is a simple day.
A simple day to have a snow day.

Brittany Buttle
Grant Park Middle School
Grant Park
Grade 7

Storm

The clouds roll in like gentle waves,
Slowly crashing into one another,
Making a sound startling to the ears.
The clouds cover the golden sun.
The sky grows dark.
Rain starts to fall.
Calmly at first then it is a wall
Of falling water.
The rain comes to a stop.
The sky is clearer.
The air is fresher,
So much fresher than before.

Jessica Milligan
Parkview Jr High School
Lawrenceville
Grade 7

Zelda's the Name

Hi, my name is Zelda
I am a bird.
A cockatiel to be exact.
You hear my beautiful song
When I wake you up.
When I am let out
You see me fly around
Your house with grace.
I land on the highest perch.
I have good taste in seed.
I am that wonderful bird
In that cage.
I love to stretch
My wings with glory.
When my top knot is straight up
I am ready to move with action.
When it is flat
I am calm and relaxed.
I am a very active bird.
I hope I find a mate.

Megan Lupsha
Francis Granger Middle School
Aurora
Grade 7

I Am

I am a sister and friend to many
I wonder if crime will ever end
I hear the sound of my dad's parents
(even though they're no longer here)
I see my dog when she is not here
I want to have a good education
I am a sister and friend to many

I pretend to know what I'm doing but sometimes I don't
I feel the pain of when I hurt myself or when I am sick
I reach for my friends and family when I have problems
I worry about my cousin who has a tumor
I cry when I think of the crime and diseases
I am a sister and friend to many

I understand that I will have to do certain things that I don't want to
I say NEVER give up!
I dream one day world peace will be a cure
I try to satisfy everyone I can
I hope the world becomes a better place
I am a sister and friend to many

Angela Pifer
Francis Granger Middle School
Aurora
Grade 7

Remember Us

We are the ones that make a difference in this world.
We are the future, the present, and whom you will depend on.
We need love, care, compassion, kindness, and most of all trust and truth!

Children are God's gifts from up above,
Filled with laughter and with love.
We are scared and unsure.
How do we live and learn?
Who do we go to when we are hurt?
We have loved since our birth.

We cry, laugh, smile, get hurt and feel pain.
So don't leave us in the rain.
Pay attention to us. We need your love.
The love of two parents, not just one.
We want to grow and play with our friends.
Go fishing and make amends.
So many times we have had many memories of sadness, joy, and humor.
Spend some time with us, we are humorous.

We can be so easily crushed, we are so fragile and meek.
There are secrets that we cannot keep.

So love us to death, and enjoy our company.
We are kids, we love life and to be funny!

Jenny Louise Bedeker
Leland High School
Leland
Grade 9

From My Room

I love watching that big beautiful sun
But when the moon comes, I run
I love watching the beautiful baby blue sky
But when it turns black, I want to die
I love that early morning smell
But at night, it makes me ill
I love waking up, and hearing the birds sing
But at night, all I hear is that hooting thing
I love seeing all the pretty flowers bloom
But at night, it feels like doom
I love the morning
But I hate the night
Because at night
All I see is blackness
Blackness..............
From my room

Richard Maggio
Clay Elementary School
Chicago
Grade 8

What Liberty Means to Me

What Liberty means to me,
It's about being free.
Our forefathers came here because of unrest
and here in America they were put to the test.

In that test it made them strong.
It showed them the difference between right and wrong.
It's wrong to make people live in great strife,
but it's right to let them live a free life.

Freedom's a gift, a God-given right,
guard it and cherish it with all of your might.

Ben Hawkins
St Mary School
Alton
Grade 8

Grapevine

A little boy had heard his mom say
Something about the neighbors
Dad replies,
"Honey you probably heard that through the grapevine."
The little boy
Got on his bike
Rode to Grapevine Park
And sat
And sat
The little boy came back home and said,
"Dad, I have been to the Grapevine Park every day,
But, still I have not heard anything about the neighbors."

Cassie Tanner
Sacred Heart School
Lombard
Grade 7

Dreaded School

As I sit here in this school,
They're treating me like I'm a fool.
The classmates are the prisoners,
Your identity is no longer yours.

They keep us in rooms of stone,
Making us feel all alone.
The doors and windows suddenly have bars,
And our identity is no longer ours.

The teachers are the guards and police,
They never want to create peace.
We left this place with bruises and scars,
Once our own identity was no longer ours.

Messina Truttman
Smithton Elementary School
Smithton
Grade 8

I Am

I am an unstoppable athlete
I wonder what my life will bring
I hear the earsplitting bellow of the crowd
I see the 300-pound monsters coming for me
I want to carry the pigskin across the emerald meadow
I am an unstoppable athlete

I pretend to receive the burnt-brown ball
I feel the burning in my legs
I reach toward the goal line
I worry I will not succeed
I cry for the losers
I am an unstoppable athlete

I understand everyone is not a perfectionist
I say the season is too short
I dream of being on top
I try to rise up above the others
I hope to be the best
I am an unstoppable athlete

Dana Wright
Frances Granger Middle School
Aurora
Grade 7

Day Goes By

I see the clouds passing by
And as I see them passing by it turns to night.
Now I see the bright starry sky.
I see the moon's reflection fluttering in the sea.
As I see the blanket of stars fading away
I see the sun rising in the east.

Ashley McCarty
Shirland C C Elementary School
Shirland
Grade 7

Wolves

Wolves are cunning.
Swift as the night.
Bright as day.
Hunting their prey.
Through the meadows
They wait for their prey.
Trying to survive.
In the lonely night
Where danger lurks about
But they are smart
For they know how to hunt.
They wait and wait.
All alone waiting for their supper.
Endless waiting.
The prey's judgment awaits
For its last day in the wilderness.

Andrew Castillo
Lansing Christian School
Lansing
Grade 7

Splat

You can do it, cat
Cats live from nine story jumps
Splat! Guess I was wrong

Dane Christensen
Stratford Jr High School
Bloomingdale
Grade 8

A Rule Against Running

A man one day was running,
He ran into an old lady strolling,
She broke many bones and went rolling.
Run, run, run, run.
She took him to court to sue
She wanted a no running zone,
Judge decided in her favor,
And called for a run free area.
Run, run, run.
So he couldn't run there anymore,
But he could run anywhere else,
So, it didn't matter at all—Or did it?
Run, run.
The areas in which he could run,
Began to shrink and disappear,
Until all he had was the track,
And he didn't like to use that.
Run.
In the beginning it was a run free zone,
The zone grew larger as time went on,
And now the running track is gone.

Alex Voitik
Kennedy Elementary School
Spring Valley
Grade 8

The Mouse and the Bug

A little mouse went out one day to catch a bug or seed,
He ran around to the barn where the chickens have their feed.

The little mouse saw a bug who was only four seeds high,
And gave a smile big enough to almost touch the sky.

The tiny little bug, not knowing what to do,
Hopped a little further, the length of a seed or two.

The little mouse sharpened his claws just like an alley cat,
And swung his paw right past the bug, just like a baseball bat.

The tiny bug looked up to the sky; He then turned to the mouse and began to cry.

The little mouse stepped back, and looked down at the bug,
Soon the mouse began to cry and gave the bug a hug.

"Sorry," said the little mouse, now knowing his bad deed,
How could he compare a precious bug to a tiny, no good seed?

The tiny little bug hopped back to his home,
And the little hungry mouse, believed his heart had grown.

The little hungry mouse did find a seed to chew,
And the bug lived long and healthy, and grew and grew and grew.

One day the two met up at the barn where the chickens feed,
And the bug showed the mouse his family, and they had some cookies and tea.

Which shows that two enemies, two very different kinds,
Can be the very best of friends, for all of eternity's time.

Nyssa Graff
Richmond Consolidated Grade School
Richmond
Grade 7

I Am What I Am

I am a flower when it blooms
I am a dew drop full of mist
I am a child filled with care
I am but a gentle kiss

I am a blown out candle but I'm still lit
I am a written out pen but I still have penmanship
I am a wagon with only three wheels but still am able to roll

I am but a broken clock but I still go tick tock
I am a tree with no branches but when the wind blows I still manage to sway.
I am a whisper with not one secret to hide
I am a ribbon, not a bow, but I look just as nice
I am a smile turned upside down when things tend not to go my way.
I am me, and that is all I could be.

Ellenia Izzo
Joan F Arai Middle School
Chicago
Grade 8

Choices

Here we go around again
Wondering if the road will ever end.
Twisting and turning every which way.
Moving faster and faster every day.
Will it stop? I'll never know.
Will I ever know which way to go?
Before my eyes I see a path of never-ending choices.
As I listen in my head to all the convincing voices.
I finally stop and think to myself,
"Will there ever be a time I can choose without anyone else?"
I am so confused and very upset.
Will a conclusion ever be met?
So many ways to go
Will I ever be able to say no?
Do I choose this one
Or do I choose that one?
I don't think I'll ever know
Which way I should go.
So many choices
And so many voices.

Jennifer Fitzgerald
St Mary of Czestochowa School
Cicero
Grade 8

Board Wild

Going off all the huge ramps,
Doing all the sickest moves.

Wondering how high you can go,
Winning the competition or stealing the show.

Going to the skate park and seein' all your friends
And having the best time ever.

Going everywhere you can see,
And seeing how good you can be.

Britt Arlen
St Michael School
Orland Park
Grade 7

My Family

My family is great
it's made of eight:
six boys one woman and a man.

All my brothers play basketball
while my little brother plays bittyball.

Even though there are seven boys and a mother
we all get along and love each other.

Patrick Bruno
Pope John XXIII School
Evanston
Grade 8

The Painting

A painting stood there on the wall,
No one said anything, nothing at all.

The figures merged with beautiful color,
Yes, indeed this painting was like no other.

Then one man said that it represents life,
But there he sat in complete strife.

Another man said it represents love,
"Clearly," he said, "the picture's a dove!"

A woman appeared and asked what the artist left out,
"He left out the feeling, so don't sit there and pout."

A painting stood there on the wall,
No one said anything, nothing at all.

Becky Murphy
St Matthew School
Champaign
Grade 7

Ocean

The ocean is like paradise.
It relaxes your body.
It helps you sleep.
When the sun rises over the ocean it's so pretty.
A stream of yellow and orange.
The sky behind it changes to pink, orange, purple,
Green, light blue, and blue.
You can also swim and build sandcastles.

Brittany Leach
River Trails Middle School
Mount Prospect
Grade 7

Do You Believe?

Do you believe in angels?
The ones that swing and sway;
The ones that bring happiness all through the night and day.

Do you believe in miracles?
The ones that do come true;
The ones that bring happiness when you are sad and blue.

Do you believe in God?
The one that's only true;
The one that brings you happiness the whole day through.

The 3 things above represent hope and love

Do you believe?

Alkedis E. Allen
Pablo Casals Elementary School
Chicago
Grade 7

Lighthouse

Silent, alone
Brightens, helps, points
Poetic, helpful, lonely, quiet
Beacon

Nick Cicciarelli
St Vincent De Paul School
Peoria
Grade 8

Pseudo Inspiration

No way to prove it,
but you can't deny it,
so you believe it
because you need it.
Hail Mary, Sweet Jesus,
and with that,
all sins are washed away.
Little black book
in a filthy motel room
solves all the problems,
solves all the puzzles.
Tragedies happen,
so blame it on fate.
"As I lay me down"
every night before bed.
I suppose now you're holy,
pure and innocent,
just like a newborn
from only one prayer.

Rita Koganzon
Niles West High School
Skokie
Grade 9

Fish

I wish, I wish
I was a fish.
To swim
in the
deep blue
sea eating
worms and algae.
I want to run away
from man so they
can't put me in a can.
The only bad part
of being a fish
is having to
live in a
school
!

Anne L. Wendel
River Trails Middle School
Mount Prospect
Grade 7

No Break

I hate housework,
My Grandma does too
Dusting, sweeping, cleaning,
It never seems to end.

My brother's room is a mess
With toys and clothes galore.
I have to straighten his stuff
But detest doing it.

If I win the lottery
The thing I plan is
To hire a maid.
No questions asked!

Jake Warner
Parkview Jr High School
Lawrenceville
Grade 7

Mother Nature

Nature, nature it has a glacier.
it is pretty and dirty.

Its nickname is Mother.
It isn't just one color.

There are snakes
and lakes

You may find thrills
on one of its many hills

Many people seek
the highest mountain peak

Her snow is white.
It is a sight.

Life comes and goes
being watched by crows.

For her king is the
grass that is green.

there are seas
and buzzing bees.

The trees stand high
enough to make you sigh.

Nature, nature will probably die.

Brian Sheridan
Hamlin Upper Grade Center
Alsip
Grade 7

Dog

Dog
Loyal, obedient
Greets, begs, obeys
Loving, peaceful, caring, cheerful
Friend

Peter Myers
St Vincent De Paul School
Peoria
Grade 8

Clara Barton

The fire is after fire,
The death is after death.
To stop this violence is my desire,
And stop making my life a guess!

There is no way to live
In any of this place,
I know, I might not see
Even one alive face!

If I was just a man,
I will be at front lines.
I will do what I can
And I won't change my mind!

I want to be a soldier,
But I know that I can't.
And now I'll help the soldiers,
And I will do my best!

Kira Malycheva
Francis Xavier Warde School
Chicago
Grade 8

The Intruder

Why won't you believe me?
It's not all in my head.
Something wants to get me
And it's underneath my bed.
There's something out the window,
And it wants to get inside.
This is one intruder I simply won't abide.
I'm hiding in the closet,
Curled up like a ball.
I just want to be left alone,
That's all.
Then all of a sudden,
I hear a scream.
"Get up, Get up!"
I woke up to realize, it was just a dream.

Laura Rediger
Harrison Elementary School
Wonder Lake
Grade 7

Graduation

Soon it will be graduation day
There are so many things I want to say.

Graduation's a time to laugh and cry
It's hard to say one last good bye.

The years flew by, one by one
There are many fun things we have done.

Now that we have to say good bye
All of our memories just fly.

We look back at the good times and the bad
Some of these things make us sad.

We'll all go our own separate ways
Maybe do sports or be in plays.

We'll have to walk down different halls
With different people and different walls.

All new teachers and lots of new faces
Who will take us to all different places.

No one knows what the future will hold
So sit back and let it all unfold.

Everyone listen, I really mean this
All of you I will truly miss.

Molly Cosgrove
St Irene School
Warrenville
Grade 8

The Titanic

A cold clear night, all was quiet and calm.
Graceful and majestic the Titanic sailed on.
From old England to New York bound.
Until fate at hand turned plans around.

The blare of alarms pierced the dead of night,
Awaking passengers with panic and fright.
One by one they lined up to hear,
Their ship of dreams was sinking, the end was near.

The flares lit the sky with a bright white light,
But no help appeared, none came to sight.
All hands on deck as orders were declared.
All women and children on lifeboats as men waited, scared.

The ship rose high, then broke in two,
As they clung to their hopes of life anew.

Olivia Sabatini
St Matthew School
Champaign
Grade 7

Shooting Star

Stallions across the starry night
Hover above the clouds so bright
Over the moon's crest you lay
Oblivious to dawn's golden ray
Tempting to the eye you are
Imperial, always the best by far
Night is the time you come out
Gorgeous as you go round about
Silent as you fall and die
Tame, to call you, would be a lie
Alas your flame is burning low
Rays of sun burst through, I'll miss you so

Eva Lezith Tellez
Francis Xavier Warde School
Chicago
Grade 7

Mom

I'm sorry I never really appreciated you
I figured you'd always be there.
You'd always take care of me.
I never once thought that you wouldn't be there for me.
You taught me right and wrong
Left and right
And now to see you in pain makes me think
How much I really appreciated you
Now it's my turn to take care of you
Would you like some soup?
A sandwich?
No?
Would you like a hug?
Just to let you know I appreciate ya?

Ashley Mars
Francis Granger Middle School
Aurora
Grade 7

The Forest

This morning it is really cold.
I wish I would have worn a coat.
I will not freeze until I die.
I will stay warm enough inside.

This afternoon the sun came out.
Then the animals played about.
The rain will come and end the drought.
When the rain comes out I'll start to pout.

Later on I start to cry.
Because it's time to say goodbye.
I hate to leave this place I love.
Because this is a place I love.

Robby Riggs
Beckemeyer Elementary School
Beckemeyer
Grade 7

Going Fishing

going fishing
can be fun and
relaxing
sitting in the sun
thinking of tales to tell
watching the bobbers
bob up and down
with the flick of
a wrist
the fish is brought
to shore
taking a picture
and letting it go
is all about
going fishing

Daniel J. Dembkowski
River Trails Middle School
Mount Prospect
Grade 7

Future Road

I look down the road, hoping to see,
A road to my future, waiting for me.
I look to the left.
Then turn to the right.
But I go neither way,
Frozen with fright.
Because I see you standing in the road.
My guess is you are the key to it all.
I smile at you,
But you turn away.
Now I'm back at the start.
Lost in my heart.
Knowing you'll never be a part,
Of my road to the future.
So I look to the left,
And I turn to the right,
And follow the path guided by light.

Katharine Wertman
West Middle School
Rockford
Grade 8

Love

Love is comforting,
Love is warm,
Love is people taking care of each other,
Love is a heart full of happiness,
Love is thinking of the ones you love,
Love is helping loved ones,
Love is friendship,
Love is being with the one you love.

Amanda Rose Brant
Scales Mound Jr High School
Scales Mound
Grade 8

Eagle

Mist on the grass energizes me as I carry my pack across it.
I don't mind it, I even enjoy the weight I bear.
Out of the strapped bag I pull a dimpled sphere and a shafted club.
As I bludgeon the white ball my friends cheer.
Again I shoulder the weight as I wander toward the ball.
The greenery and trees around me will pose a problem
But at the same time they give me confidence.
A magnificent curve out of the wooded area and on to the bent grass.
Enthusiasm builds in me.
My first Eagle.

Mark Chmura
Fenwick High School
Oak Park
Grade 9

Take the Baby Steps

Living life is very difficult
You have to take baby steps
If you rush things you'll miss out on the good things
And go through life with the bad things

If you live life to the most complete you'll have a good life
Living life gives you the experience to learn, to discover, to communicate with others
You probably have already done this
But there is still so much you didn't achieve

Life is an award, but you have to figure out how to use it to get there
It takes a lifetime to get there but when you do you know you found the right place

You are this little thing and surrounding you are billions of different lives
They may have problems or they may have the best lives in the world
We are all different
The people that live their life to the fullest are the people we should look up to
Take the baby steps
It helps

Francesca Cuzzone
St Philip The Apostle School
Winnerka
Grade 7

Alonso

From glory to pain, and from pain to glory,
I'll never forget, this is my life story.
It all happened one day,
We were playing in the park
Knowing we shouldn't have been there it was already after dark.
For just five minutes I decided to take a walk.
Not knowing a minute later you would be laying surrounded by chalk.
My memories of you still pop up in my head.
I still think to this day it could have been me instead.
So when fate comes to get me, I know it will be true
Together again we'll be friends, me and you.

Jason Howard
Schurz High School
Chicago
Grade 9

Life

Life for me ain't been no straight flat road
there's been bumps and potholes
stop signs and traffic jams
u-turns and accidents
construction and drunk drivers
but don't give up!
life can get better,
but life for me
ain't been no straight flat road.

Brian Theriault
Stratford Jr High School
Bloomingdale
Grade 8

Winter Wonderland

Looking out the window on Christmas morning,
The ground covered with fresh fallen snow
Covering the ground with a sheet of white paper
Kids throwing snowballs to and fro
Wind howling like a blustery blow
Going outside is like sitting in the freezer
It couldn't get breezier
As the wind whipped at my face
I lowered my pace
Wishing winter would end
The only thing keeping me going
Were the warm thoughts entering my head

Michelle Green
Francis Granger Middle School
Aurora
Grade 7

You Are There

You are there when I am sad.
You are there when I am mad.
You are the greatest friend I have ever had.

You are there when I am having a bad day.
You always know the right things to say.
You are always prepared, if I have a bad hair day.

There isn't anyone in the world that could take your place.
I have never met anyone with such grace.
You make my world a peaceful place.

You are always there for me.
When I'm sick, you bring me tea.
I can talk to you about things that others just don't see.

Although we sometimes disagree,
I know you will be there for me,
Especially when I really need you to be.

Lauren Kopitke
Finley Jr High School
Chicago Ridge
Grade 8

Roxanne

Roxanne is a chocolate Labrador.
She belongs to my oldest brother Mike.
She lives with him, but is at our house more.
Roxanne loves to follow me on a bike.
Roxanne is a very lovable dog
She sometimes gets locked up in a small cell.
She likes to play joyfully in the fog.
To get her attention we right a bell.
Roxanne is a dog that likes to give hugs.
She always goes to venture but comes back.
She hates late nights because of the pest bugs.
She often likes to dig in paper-sacks.
Our life with Roxanne is never a bore.
But dad thinks she should have to stay outdoors.

Chad Yoder
Sullivan High School
Sullivan
Grade 9

Brothers and Sisters

Brothers and sisters
Or
Like we call them
Pests
Some can be nice
Some can be weird
Some can be your slaves
Some can be your siblings or can be aliens
But we'll all learn to love
Our brothers and sisters
Or
Like we call them
Pests

Amara Hussain
River Trails Middle School
Mount Prospect
Grade 7

The Baseball Game

As we loaded the bus,
Loud cheering came from us.
But as we approached Marrisa,
the bus broke down.
Everyone on it began to frown.
So for the last game in State,
we thought we came too late.
The game hadn't started.
So off we all darted to the best seat we could find.
As the seventh inning rolled around, we were up by five;
we could hardly sit down.
Strike tree yelled the ump, it was easy to see,
that the Cougars had a great victory.

Sara Randle
Smithton Elementary School
Smithton
Grade 8

Sweetness

With 34 upon his back,
This one great man would never slack.
He'd run with grace, he'd run with might,
For that one extra yard, he'd always fight.
Sweetness was this great man's name,
When his team was down he'd show no shame.
This one great man would always try,
Right down to the day when he'd lay down and die.
Sweetness was a legend, and a hero in his own time,
His strength, his pride, and glory, those will always shine.

Dominic Piriano
Francis Granger Middle School
Aurora
Grade 7

I Am a Dancer and Dreamer

I am a dancer and dreamer
I wonder how the world flies upside down
I hear special sounds, though they may not be there
I see pigs floating in the air
I want to be heard
I am a dancer and dreamer.

I pretend to be a famous dancer, actress, and singer
I feel some things that don't exist, really do
I reach toward the STARS
I worry when people fight
I cry when people yell
I am a dancer and dreamer.

I understand people make wrong choices
I say you should go toward your goals, not away
I dream about accomplishing my dream
I try at making an effort towards something I may not like
I hope to believe in myself, which I know I can do
I am a dancer and dreamer.

Stacey Cohen
Francis Granger Middle School
Aurora
Grade 7

Eight Ball

A tunnel of depression,
a bottomless abyss.
Delusion, not knowing reality from anything else.
High and giddy, then depressed again.
An emotional roller coaster day and night.
Tension and anxiety,
afraid that you'll get caught.
Raging tempers,
snapping at anyone that confronts you.
Illness.

Elizabeth Fitzgerald
North Park Elementary School
Chicago
Grade 7

Falling Leaves

I watched as the leaves started to wither and die,
they just keep going to their deaths.
As the wind blows, I think to myself, one of them will fall soon.
Why must they all die?

Where will they go when their stem eventually snaps,
but to the ground in the dirt.
For they will never be seen again in this world,
not by any living things.

When the spring comes new leaves pop out of the tree and
I ask myself when will they die?
The answer is when God had his reasons.

John Lehner
Queen of Martyrs School
Chicago
Grade 8

Homework

I am a force no one can take
I am a thing all kids hate
I am HOMEWORK

I know you don't like me but that's good for me
Because you get more frustrated
I make you mad
I make you sigh
I even sometimes make you cry
Well that's just what I do

You even created excuses just to get away from me
Like my dog ate it
Or my little brother ripped it to shreds
So get used to me or you'll always be frustrated

Julian Marquez
Francis Granger Middle School
Aurora
Grade 7

Fear

Fear is when two friends start to fight
Fear is when you hear things, go bump in the night
Fear is when you hear big dogs bark
Fear is when you see strange shadows in the dark
Fear is when someone holds up a gun
Fear is when you watch a scary movie and it's not fun
Fear is when a friend is stabbed and loses his life
Fear is when a little kid plays with a knife
You can deal with your fears, you just have to face them.
You just can't find anywhere to place them but your mind
If this doesn't work, there are solutions you can find

Elizabeth Fouts
Virden Middle-High School
Virden
Grade 7

I Understand

I understand when you are feeling down.
I understand how you feel.
I understand when you're not around.
I understand how you don't understand me.
I understand that you don't like me.
I understand that you hate me.
I understand everything that you tell me.
I understand when you're not around.
I understand when you cry.
I understand when you're bad.
And I understand what you're trying to say to me.
I understand you.

Desiree Ceja
Washington Irving Elementary School
Chicago
Grade 7

Teacher

As the teacher stands before me my eyelids start to droop.
But suddenly they open wide
  my teacher looks at me with burning eyes
just like a devil in disguise.

  She screams and yells at me
until she is red.
  She has told me many times before,
but I can't help it.
  I just sit there in a daze
while my mind is running wild
  feeling like I'm trapped inside a
never ending twisting winding maze.

Ariel Lembeck
Nichols Middle School
Evanston
Grade 7

A Wonderful Friend*

Thank you so much
You're a wonderful friend
You've been there for me till the end
We cried together in thoughtful times and bad
You held me back when I was mad
We've been in fights
That have been difficult and dumb
Sometimes we lounge around like big bums.
Together we have achieved more than one person alone
We've worn disgusting makeup that wasn't our skin tone.
We have laughed and cried
And to each other we have lied
But I know deep inside
You're a wonderful friend.

Kristen McKinley
Francis Granger Middle School
Aurora
Grade 7
*Dedicated to Monica

This Thing Between Us

This thing between us is a cloud
  spitting nasty floods on a dark day
floating peacefully when things go its way

  Others bump it, make it kind of angry
so it thrashes out, pouring down madly

  We must keep our clouds content
  for however long need be
for if they get upset you'll have to deal with me

Valentina Lisa Flores
Saucedo School Academy
Chicago
Grade 8

Sonnet of Spring

The smell of colorful flowers in bloom.
Green leaves cover the limbs of trees once bare.
Away with the cold and dark winter gloom.
Sweet wonderful smells fill the cool, clean air.
Life in the world is prevalent once more.
The birds are back from their winter trip south.
This is the time of year I most adore.
A robin flies by with a worm in its mouth.
The streams and rivers are flowing again.
Falling outside are steady spring showers.
Baby coyotes play outside their den.
Just walking outside I could do for hours.
Now after the long winter, spring is here.
I wish it could be like this all the year.

Dane White
Sullivan High School
Sullivan
Grade 9

Self Defense

Flying, soaring, floating,
As I move my leg over my head.
My foot makes an impact on his chest.
I see his face.
The grimace, the agony, the fear.
A touch of sympathy runs through my blood.
Then I remember the attack.
I remember how he came after me.
My fear
And now I see his fear.
We float down to the ground.
He on his back,
I feet first.
I won, I am strong.
All in two seconds.
All in self defense.

Margaret Emmons
St Matthew School
Champaign
Grade 8

Military Man

There he stands,
    tall and proud.
Beneath our nation's flag.
He is wearing his Dress Blues,
    covered with medals.
His hat tucked neatly under his arm.
He has big, brown eyes,
    that are gleaming.
His hair is sandy brown,
    and perfectly done.
He does not smile or frown.
His expression is serious.
You can see in his eyes,
    his pride and joy.
He has defended his country well,
    and gone where he is needed.
He is now retired.
He forever will be proud of the country,
    he has loved and served.

Tricia Smith
Nathan Hale Middle School
Crestwood
Grade 7

Nature

Boating in the lake
While the cool breeze hits your face
The sun smiling down

Shannon A. Delaney
River Trails Middle School
Mount Prospect
Grade 7

Scuba Is . . .

Scuba is an unknown world for most.
Scuba is extravagant.
Scuba is exciting.
Scuba is dangerous.
Scuba is majestic.
Scuba is my passion and my life.
Scuba is fun!

Sean Judy
St Matthew School
Champaign
Grade 7

The Mask

There once was a mask that giggled
only until the strings began to wiggle
Then the mask began to cry
for new strings was what he had to buy

Michala Atkinson
Pleasant Hill Elementary School
Peoria
Grade 7

All Alone

I feel all alone,
All alone at home,
Is where I sit on my own.

For I sit there at home,
I sit and waste my wealth,
It does no good for my health.
So I know I won't be very well.

I am here,
I am there,
But I'm with sadness everywhere.

Peggy J. Weakley
Thompson Jr High School
Oswego
Grade 8

Rain

Rain falls very soft
To the ground that welcomes it
Will it go away?

Adam Yoder
St Vincent De Paul School
Peoria
Grade 8

Unforgettable

That perfect red dress
On the lovely little lady,
Who for months and months
Had been anxiously awaiting.

The black suit and tie
Before laid across the bed.
Now on the nervous young fellow
Off to see his lady in red.

The rosebud on his jacket,
The flowers in her hair,
The countless pictures taken,
She glances, back he stares.

Remembering that night,
As if it were yesterday.
When the lovely lady in red
Had taken his breath away.

Hold close to your memories
In your heart they always stay.
Forever yours, those memories
That can never be taken away.

Amanda Ofiara
Fenwick High School
Oak Park
Grade 9

Running

Racing down the road
Now my worries drift behind
Never will I stop.

Katy Bock
St Michael School
Orland Park
Grade 7

The Earth

The sky is blue
The clouds are so very white
The grass is so green

Ross E. Feighery
River Trails Middle School
Mount Prospect
Grade 7

Death of a Nation

As the leader of
    the newly
restored union
sat in peace in
Ford's Theatre
a very crazed actor
    had decided
to kill our fearless
leader on the holy day
    of Good Friday
in an instant his
    dreams for this
    fair land were
shattered forever

Michael Gillott
Francis Xavier Warde School
Chicago
Grade 8

Love

Did he really love me?
I'll never really know.
He seemed to be the best,
But it never really showed.
He broke my heart
And now I'm falling apart.
Did he really love me?
I'll never really know.
I would look into his eyes...
And all I saw were the lies he told.
I'll never forget how he made me feel.
Now I know that I was stupid to
Think that this was real.

Kristie Pagan
Norman Bridge School
Chicago
Grade 8

Valentine

It's amazing how you do everything with ease
You are nice and gentle like morning cool breeze
There are things I want to know
But when I'm with you time goes like a blow
You are sweet, kind, but most importantly
YOU ARE MY VALENTINE!

Jessica Almanza
John F Eberhart Elementary School
Chicago
Grade 7

Sonnet of Daydreams

I sit to work, but my thoughts are not there
The themes may change some, but not the people
They float from scene to scene, without a care
It is he and I, perhaps, a steeple
Through it all we stay so close, like we should
He's there and so am I, we're together
From the bright day's sun to the dark night's hood
He always makes me feel like a feather
Hand in hand it matters not when or where
Anything could happen; a stolen kiss
I can say it all; my secrets I share
Everywhere we go it is complete bliss
As I come out of my dream I smile some
I start my work 'till the next dream will come

Marci Beals
Sullivan High School
Sullivan
Grade 9

Rider of Anarchy

In a dark forest, on a rocky path
A fearless horseman sends his wrath
His sword like fire, his spear flies straight
Whoever steps forward receives an untimely fate
Slayer of dragons, Killer of beasts
When the hunt is over, a marvelous feast
Once in a great while, he strolls into town
With his sword on his back, on his face, a dark frown
As soon as he gets there, he turns and walks back
In monarchy domination, he plans his attack
A raid on the king, the greatest hunt of all
He'll track him down through the Royal Hall
Cross bow in hand, hounds at his feet
The strong scent of blood, the craving of meat
This is his plan, but it is not at its end
Malicious as it is, it has another sick bend
He plans to rule this kingdom so fair
Forever and ever, he'll sit in the king's chair
It's almost time, a day of reckoning is here
Into hearts of many, he'll spread menacing fear

Ian McIntosh
Bement High School
Bement
Grade 9

A Sonnet of the Seasons

The flowers are so beautiful in spring
Yellow daffodils, tulips red and blue
And the birds, the happiness their songs bring
In the spring the world is so fresh and new.
There are things I like in the summer time too
I enjoy the smell of freshly mown grass
There are always so many things to do
And the taste of fried fish, crappie and bass
In the fall I love the crisp morning air
Also the beautiful rustling leaves
And the warm sunshine on my face and hair
I am so unhappy when autumn leaves
Winter is so dreary and very cold
But spring will come back soon so I am told.

Melissa Palmer
Sullivan High School
Sullivan
Grade 9

Chechnya

A barren circle of space,
Stripped to the bare essential roots,
Through the smoke, you can see their shadows,
Here they live, this is their home.
They were one, and are one,
Connected by an unseen force,
Bruised and beaten, they do stand,
Murdered and maimed, they do stand.

Four steel crosses, reflecting the glow,
The stones fall, no one notices,
The ones who are left will testify,
Branding their words like fire.
The ones who leave are the dead,
The ones who stay are among the bones,
The right of thought and life is denied,
The act of death is forced.

Andrew Ozga
Fenwick High School
Oak Park
Grade 9

My Fishing Experience

I threw the bobber into the water
and watched it go down farther
I thought it was a bass
because it was a great cast
After I caught it
we laid it on the ground
and it looked like it was ten pounds
It wasn't a bass, it was the least of my wish
It had been a catfish.

Travis Fuzak
Holy Family Catholic School
Rockford
Grade 7

Dancer

An image of beauty that flourishes and grows before you in colorful arrays

A beauty in a rose is of the same kind, but   never   dies

It is graceful as a swan and as elegant as a queen

It is able to soar like a bird—forever
it keeps itself up by its horsepower strength

The image of perfection is so harsh   harsh
it pushes you to practice practice practice
even though you practice you don't reach perfection but you grow more in   beauty

You feel the stuffiness in the room as sweat trickles down your back
sticky slimy smelly sweat that no one likes. You leave trails of it behind you like a bird

throbbing   throbbing muscles   shaking
as your feet *SCREAM*   in pain
you have to bear it like a wall bears nails

Sighs that hang about the walls
sighs that walls can hear
sighs for perfection that you will never reach even though you try

wanting to soar like a bird through the air
defying the gravity that pulls you down with omnipotent strength

This is what a dancer   is. A dancer perseveres. A dancer is a swan in the air, a rose on land
A dancer you may not know   but this is what a dancer is

Karissa Brown
Naperville North High School
Naperville
Grade 9

My Great-Grandma

I once had a great-grandma who meant everything to me.
She had a grand pond in her backyard full of ducks for me to see.
I loved going to her house – I could hardly wait to get there,
and when I did, she would tell me I was special and stroke her fingers through my long brown hair.
Well, I grew up and she got old.
We found out she'd had cancer and had been very bold.
Then a chill went down my spine – it was evil and cold.
She was sent to the hospital, it was horrible and bad,
and at the same time it was terrible and sad.
She said, "Where is my Krista?" when we finally got there,
and for the last time, she told me I was special and stroked her fingers through my long brown hair.
Well, years have passed by since my great-grandma passed away,
but in my own mind I can still hear her say,
"Krista, you're special in your own special way."
I still remember when I was hopeless and didn't know what to do,
so Great-Grandma, if you're listening,
I love you, and this poem's for you!

Krista Branson
Metamora Elementary School
Metamora
Grade 7

Nature

Nature never was so deep—
to look further into it
you'd be surprised what you'd find
the shine of the ocean is like that of diamonds
the birds and fish help make harmony,
the natural greenness of trees
is something so great,
Nature's intent is to help humans
which it has done,
but what people take for granted
is what makes them blind
to things so great, they should see...

Danny Lopez
St Ferdinand School
Chicago
Grade 8

A Sonnet for Change

I often wonder when the day will come,
For peace in the streets and life without fears.
The homeless who live their lives so lonesome,
And runaways who have shed many tears.
No guns on the streets in a young one's hand,
And the drug dealers in every home town,
The fear for your life has spread through our land
There's no reason to smile, only to frown.
There must be a way to stop this madness,
Life is too short to waste on these reasons
The news is filled with way too much sadness.
We need a change and not just of seasons,
I wish more people were concerned like me
Then the answers may be easy to see.

Dennis Loy
Sullivan High School
Sullivan
Grade 9

Summer

Summer is when the wind softly whispers in your ear,
Warm and clear.
The weeping willows are swaying,
While the small children are playing.
The lake water is warm,
The tiny gnats swarm.
Mother Earth is alive,
The bees are making honey in their hives.
The summer nights are sweet,
You can run free with bare feet.
The sky is a gorgeous blue,
Your free life feels brand new.
The robins will fly high in the sky,
Summer will never die.

Carmen Meier
St Irene School
Warrenville
Grade 7

Snow

S now is white, snow is cold.
N obody can resist the beauty of snow.
O n a blistery day, snow will fall.
W hen winter is here, snow is in the air.

Kory Blumenstein
Beckemeyer Elementary School
Beckemeyer
Grade 7

Friend + Ship

Together every moment going everywhere together
Just spending precious time What a wonderful world
it was having everything in common, both knowing that
nobody can break this perfect relationship
Then once others come into the picture it's a whole
'nother story People try their hardest to interfere with
this so–called FRIENDSHIP He said She said stuff
shouldn't really matter if you know the friendship you
have is a true one But the question for most is what is a
TRUE FRIENDSHIP well it all lies in your heart So
always remember what a friend is and choose your friends
wisely and make sure they're someone you really trust

Danielle Edmonson
Laraway Elementary School
Joliet
Grade 8

School

We sit in our cold chairs as we try to stay awake,
And wonder how much more of this we can take.
It's hard to pay attention to the teacher up in front,
When all that we can think about is what we're having for lunch.

The day keeps dragging on and on,
And everyone is starting to yawn.
It's easy to see why we're snoring,
'cause some of our classes are pretty boring.

My fingers hurt now and then,
From having to hold a small, black pen.
My stock of paper wears away,
From taking notes throughout the day.

The teacher in front stands like a tree,
When we wait for the clock to strike three.
School seems to go on forever,
When we'll leave, maybe never.

We watch the birds laugh from the trees,
And wish that we could be just as free.
Soon school will be out for the day,
Then we will hear a big hooray.

Gabe Toennies
Blessed Sacrament School
Belleville
Grade 8

One Dry Leaf

A soft wind at dawn
lifts one dry leaf
and lays it upon another.

Marquis Jackson
Forest Trail Jr High School
Park Forest
Grade 8

Outside

The sky goes dark
The clouds take over
The rain pours down
The thunder rolls and lighting flashes
A tree gets struck and burns to ashes
But the rain puts out the blazing fires
And the rolling thunder never tires
The rain splatters everywhere
Pitter-patter on the window
On the houses, on the sidewalk,
As it spills out of the air
Like tea pouring out of a kettle
All while I stay inside and warm
Listening to the soothing sounds
Of a thunderstorm

Amanda Piell
Stratford Jr High School
Bloomingdale
Grade 8

Six Flags

The people love the rides
Especially the ones with tides.

They got the American Eagle.
This ride is very legal.

They have the Viper.
It is very hyper.

They got the Shock Wave.
This ride is like a crave.

They got the Giant Drop.
It is like a very big top.

They got the Batman.
It's like getting hit by a fat man.

They got the Iron Wolf.
It's like getting hit by a horse's hoof.

Six Flags is the best place.

Joe Nowinski
Hamlin Upper Grade Center
Alsip
Grade 7

We Are . . .

We are the past, the present, the future.
We are the celebrated, the studied, and the dreams of many.
Like an undated coming, many knew we would be here, but when, how.
We are like a prophet, explaining the past and foretelling the future.
Millions have marveled about our time and existence,
When it would come and how.
Millions will marvel at our survival with inferior tools
And wonder what we were thinking when we got dressed.
We are what is, what was, and what will be.
We are like astronauts, going into the great beyond
With only what mission control taught us.
Who knew we would be here, who knows where we will go.
As an infant is born unto this earth without a clue what they will do . . .
That's who we are.

Kim Weisensee
St Philip The Apostle School
Addison
Grade 8

Friendship

Friendship is like a never-ending bond

According to "society" a friendship is a relationship that exists out of love
Real friendships have ups and downs all the time
The differences between each individual
is what makes each person unique in their own special way

Friendships are like flowers,
they grow when they are fertilized
and die when they are neglected

When your flower freezes over and dies
one must find peace and love from within
to cope with the loss

I will always have my friends
whether fat, thin, black, white, poor or rich
they will always be there for me
I will always be there for them

Crystal Gaines
Nathan Hale Middle School
Crestwood
Grade 7

Untitled

The repercussion of my work landing on the same note again and again.
For the unreachable knowledge to know if it is a great poem or just another doggerel.
I am told my work is good, but fear my work is nothing, for I am just an observer.
God is the true poet, but of words his poems are not.
Just look up at the sky or down upon the earth and see the poetic genius.
For I have not truly seen a poem until I have seen God's everlasting sonnet.

Erik Woolbright
St Peter's Grade School
Rockford
Grade 8

Someone Too Good to Be True

Have you ever fallen in love
With someone who seemed too good to be true?
At the moment you first saw him,
Did it seem like he was meant for you?

These thoughts occurred not too long ago.
I thought how could this be.
For you see I fell in love with someone before,
But I found out he did not love me.

I tried with all my heart to move on.
It was the hardest thing for me to do.
I was left with a broken heart,
But soon in my life came somebody new.

Have you ever fallen in love
With someone who seemed too good to be true?
At the moment you first saw him,
Did it seem like he was meant for you?

The answer to this question
All depends on you.
For you see, I've found my prince charming
And learned that wishes do come true.

Joy Hernaez
St Philip The Apostle School
Addison
Grade 8

Babysitting

Babysitting is neat,
Kids can get hurt in a heartbeat,
They can be a lot of fun,
But they do make you run,
And after you read to them,
You put them to bed,
And when you leave they color the wall all red!
So you clean their room and the house,
But then the little one begins to fuss,
(His name is Gus.)
Then the two other ones come down and want to play,
So we do!
When the game is over....
The short one shows good sport,
And the tall one begins to bawl,
The little one is fast asleep!
So you take them up to bed,
And say good night!
And when the parents get home,
The washer begins to foam,
And when you get paid,
You waste it on a maid!

Sarah Kurt
St Mary-Dixon School
Dixon
Grade 7

Ocean

The ocean is an underwater garden
The tides are a deep blue mystery
The shore is a flat sapphire, newly polished

Sarah Chamness
St John The Baptist School
West Frankfort
Grade 8

Saying "Yes"

Have you ever been afraid
To say "yes?"
To commit, to go forth
To fulfill the test?

Have you ever had something
Standing in your way
Of achieving your goal
Perhaps a question or delay?

Have you ever been so confused
You didn't know where to turn?
Have you ever had a brain block
That teaches you not to learn?

If you have been in any of these positions
You'll find you can't do it yourself
You need something stronger
A push, some desperate help.

If you're lost and seem to stray
Do you always do it your own way?
Or do you find that strength inside
To help your senses come alive?

The answer: God

Carla Sell
St Vincent De Paul School
Peoria
Grade 8

Snow

Snow is white and flaky
Its cold makes me feel shaky
It's soft and fluffy
Like a pillow, it's puffy
It glistens beautifully
Falling to the ground slowly
Its wonderful shapes are mesmerizing
So many kinds, there is no need for sizing
It's a sign of winter
The soft prevents a splinter
I love snow!

Christina Mihaljevic
St Philip The Apostle School
Northfield
Grade 7

Sun

The sun shining bright
Glistening in the clear blue sky
Warms the earth below

Mary Ekstrom
Holy Angels School
Aurora
Grade 7

The Long Kiss

I kiss you, I hug you,
but never get a response from you
I understand you want to take it slow,
I don't think this is the way to go
I serenade you with love songs,
fill your heart with laughter
You'll smile at me,
nothing ever happens after
One day I finally get the courage,
to melt your heart with a long kiss
For a few moments you treated me,
like you weren't my sis
It's been two whole weeks,
we're happily going steady
I think it's time to move on
Do you think we're ready?

Maggie Marcinkowska
Norman Bridge School
Chicago
Grade 8

Where Have You Been?

Where have you been,
Oh where have you been,
These last two years of my life?
I know you died, but can't you see?
I'm missing you dearly,
Like you never would believe.
Can't you come down just once,
To make all my dreams come true?
I would give anything,
To see your beautiful smiling face.
People say I act and look like you,
But if I could only be like you,
My life would be complete.
I wish there was no cancer,
Or at least 100% cure.
Then you would be here.
But you are not.
Cancer killed you.
And now I am left wondering,
Where have you been?

Erika Russell
Quincy Jr High School
Quincy
Grade 8

My Love for You

My love for you
is as happy as can be,
My love for you,
is as far as the eye can see,
My love for you,
as far as space will go,
My love for you,
will not stop or slow,
My love for you,
will set with you in the horizon,
My love for you,
is as sweet as my temptation,
My love for you,
as perfect as a fallen snowflake,
My love for you,
not even a spell could break,
My love for you,
is a smile that never fades,
My love for you,
goes day to day and forever,
and forever as happy as children play.

Anthony Zagajewski
Stratford Jr High School
Bloomingdale
Grade 8

Dream

I had a dream last night
I dreamt you were mine . . .
I dreamt I was happy
but it passed with time.

I dreamt we had each other
and nothing else mattered
but as the sky began to brighten
the dream I dreamt was shattered.

I long for the crescent moon
and fear the sun's light
for the day is full of empty promises
that are only fulfilled at night.

So if my mind seems somewhere else
and my eyes drift into space
please do not disturb me . . .
. . .I'm longing for the dream I chase.

And if my heart seems weary
and I'm lost in a different place
I'm only searching for the night
and the warmth of your embrace.

James Mellon
Morgan Park High School
Chicago
Grade 8

Baseball

Baseball is a great sport.
You do not play it on a court.
It is played at a park.
I do not suggest play after dark.

Go to the park on a summer's day,
Hoping you will be able to play;.
I find the game a lot of fun.
A game like it, there is none.

The skills you need to learn are many;.
But there should be no concern of any.
Some may think it is rather lame,
Yet I believe it is the best game.

Joseph D'Antonio
Immaculate Conception School
Morris
Grade 7

All About the Sea

The sea is a calm place
A place full of grace
The waves, the sun, the sand
Makes me want to get tanned
Watching how peaceful this place is
Makes me wonder of other things in life.

Earl Rogers
Armstrong Elementary School
Chicago
Grade 7

The Agony

I have a long wait,
'Till my parents let me date.
Strict they are too much,
My friends' parents aren't such.
Sixteen is so far away,
But I will just take it day by day.

Megan Leach
St Matthew School
Champaign
Grade 8

Farming

F resh air
A lways open spaces
R ich fertile soil
M achinery
I ndustry of hard work
N ever a dull moment
G rowing crops

John Luebbers
Beckemeyer Elementary School
Beckemeyer
Grade 7

Sectionals

We started out strong,
We had the lead.

They soon caught up though,
And oh too soon.

Time was winding down,
And we were tied.

This was the championship,
If we win we go on!

It seemed like the game had just begun,
But as I looked up there were nine tenths of a second left.

They had the ball,
Some way, somehow, they made a shot.

We gave it our all.
But it was over.

A few shed tears,
Some kept their grief to themselves.

It was over.
Everything we had worked so hard for was over.

All we can do now is try harder,
And I know we will.

Megan Clarkson
St Matthew School
Champaign
Grade 7

Children

They love to play and hate to stay.
They can't stand still and never will.
They do what they want and do what they may.
They drink from their bottle but always spill.
They often make their mother mad.

When their hearts cry sadly, they can become mad.
Their unremitting cries are very much despised.
They throw many fits and then become bad.
Their languished countenance then starts its cries.
They often make their mother mad.

Children can be a nuisance and pain.
They may not listen and don't understand.
Their heart is gigantic and is filled with no shame,
But in the end, they will become a helping hand.
Children give their parents much JOY.

Kevin Lisch
Blessed Sacrament School
Belleville
Grade 7

Untitled

During autumn the sky looks like a rainbow.
It has colors like yellow, red, and brown.
The tree leaves start to fall and turn into these wonderful colors.
The ground looks like the sky had fallen down on the leaves
and made them into these wonderful colors.

Jeanette Flores
Taylor Elementary School
Chicago
Grade 8

Everlasting Love

We argue, we fight,
But we always make it right.
Because our love is everlasting.

You tell me lies and ignore my cries.
But we'll be together after all the good-byes.
Because my love is everlasting.

No matter what happens, we'll be together.
You and me—in love forever.
Because love is everlasting.

Candace Brown
Cairo Jr High School
Cairo
Grade 8

Chester and His Hat

Chester was a little old man,
who needed nothing other than a hat.
He hinted his wife about one for his birthday,
but instead, she got him a baseball bat.

He then went to his son Dan,
who always got him what he needed.
This time, though, was an exception,
for Dan got him a shirt that was pleated!

"Well!" thought the little old man,
'These people don't catch on quick.
If they keep giving me the wrong gifts,
I am sure I will become sick!"

Next, Chester tried his intelligent niece,
he was sure that she would get his gift.
Again, he was wrong for the third time,
because he received weights that he couldn't even lift!

One day, Chester found a good hat,
just lying in the street.
"Nobody's ever going to get me one," said the old man,
"So I might as well take this one for keeps."

Raj Patel
Highland Middle School
Libertyville
Grade 7

More Friends Than Before

Walking down at night
I thought of how happy we were
And thinking of you made me cry
Of pure joy instead of sadness.
I am happy that I share a
Piece of life with you.
And now that we can't share our lives
Together I am happy to split apart.
It doesn't hurt at all
Cause we've become friends
We don't hurt each other anymore
We seem to get along pretty well,
More than before.

Daisy Carrillo
Trumbull Elementary School
Chicago
Grade 8

Sleep, Sleep

Laying out
underneath a tree
You hear the wind
in your ear
saying softly
shhhhhh
sleep my baby
you listen
to the green river above
and you dream
you are on a raft
floating on a never-ending river
being peaceful and calm

Matthew Robinson
Rockridge Junior High School
Taylor Ridge
Grade 7

What I Think

I think of life
I think of death
I think of you
I think of me
I think of all the jealous people
I think of all the good people
I think of sadness
I think of goodness
I think of what he said
I think of what she said

But when I'm all done thinking
I know that only what
I think is what matters

John Henry Robinson III
Owen Scholastic Academy
Chicago
Grade 7

Through My Eyes I See

To be trapped inside walls,
and no way to break through,
your mind filled with thoughts that you can't escape.
To be sheltered and closed up,
with just you.
Wanting to be free from the shallow and emptiness that surrounds you.
To be on the inside looking out,
on all you cannot have.

To feel free and alive,
but no one to share it with.
To feel like an outcast, because you are alone.
No one understands you as you wish they would.
You yearn to have the sheltered life with all the luxury.
To be on the outside looking in,
at all you cannot have.

To break through the barriers,
and come together as a whole,
we will truly be able to see what we are missing
and see things as one.

Jemia Cunningham
Francis Xavier Warde School
Chicago
Grade 7

Monday Mornings

I hate the morning.
Especially Monday mornings.
It's the most dreaded time of the day.
The sunlight burns my eyes and I feel like a vampire.
The singing of the birds feel like nails on the chalkboard of my mind.
There is no other time I hate as much as mornings.
There's a bad taste in my mouth and my joints are stiff.
I would love nothing more than to go back to sleep.
There is nothing worse than mornings.

Kellye Fleming
Nichols Middle School
Evanston
Grade 8

Day at the Beach

Lying on the beach as wind wisps by my face.
Soft sand soothes my burning feet.
Watching birds dive for the fish that live under the blue green water of the Gulf.
Sitting and thinking in the pleasant shade of a cloud passing overhead.
Watching dolphins fly through the crowded ocean of the Gulf.
Lizards scamper over my feet and tickle my toes.
The breeze blows swiftly through the soft plants and palms.
Howling winds crash waves against the helpless sand shore.
Birds run in and out with the tide avoiding the waters at their feet.
Drifting into sleep listening to the sea as it bounces off the seashore.

Adam Rehage
Nichols Middle School
Evanston
Grade 7

Stars

The stars shine so high above,
Shining on me and the world below.
There is a star out there just for me.
When I will find it the world will be free.
I know someone will find it someday.
Won't they?

Once they find this special star,
Everyone will know where they are.
The world will be happy you wait and see,
And I know everyone will look out for me.

Laura Swantish
Tobin Elementary School
Burbank
Grade 7

8th Grade Year

I have many memories from 8th grade year,
When I graduate I'll shed many tears.
Washington D.C. was the best,
While we were there we could never rest.
Confirmation will be great,
I can't wait 'til we graduate.
High school will bring great memories too,
Classmates, friends, and teachers too.
I hope I keep in touch with friends,
'Til the very very end.

Amy Hall
St George School
Tinley Park
Grade 8

Pilgrim

Trotting in the wind
Faster and faster gaining speed
Heading over mountains
Higher than I can see.
The wind blowing in my face
Leaving all my thoughts behind
Cause it is just Pilgrim my horse and me.
Riding somewhere we are not sure
Just felt like riding till we couldn't anymore.
Walking through a stream
Splashing water every which way
Refreshing ourselves for the long day that lies ahead of us.
Pilgrim's mane blowing with the wind
Her tail swatting at the flies
Long braids woven in her tail.
A white stripe down her nose like she got in a bucket of paint
Her golden brown coat glistening in the sun
Making her the best horse ever!

Chelsea Shawen
Clifford Crone Middle School
Naperville
Grade 7

Stanford's Food

Have you ever eaten at Stanford Middle School?
Their school lunches are gross if you take a lick,
Take a bite and you'll start to feel ill,
If the mashed potatoes don't get you sick,
The vegetables sure will!

Please never eat at Stanford Middle School.
Their salads really taste like putty,
The milk is hot and sour,
Their fish is really cruddy,
Their food is really hard to devour!

Faren Viehman
Parkview Jr High School
Lawrenceville
Grade 7

Moving

Some say it is the best thing that ever happened to them.
Some say it ruins their lives,
But I am here to say neither of them.
I believe it is a new experience, a challenge for me.
It will change my life, but I am hoping for the better.
Even though I leave everything behind,
I get to start over and become a new person.
This is something I will always remember doing,
Moving.

Michelle Shanahan
St Matthew School
Champaign
Grade 8

I Love Baseball

It's springtime in the air
Baseball is near
I just can't wait for opening day
I love baseball

My jersey's been hanging since the end of last year
My pants need replacement
From sliding here and there
I love baseball

I've been training since January
To hit that ball hard
Maybe someday I'll play in Camden Yards
I love baseball

I hope to be the man that the team will cheer
I'll be the hero by the end of the year
I can hear the umpire now, "Play ball"
I love baseball

Colin Dolan
St George School
Tinley Park
Grade 7

The Blanket

It covers you. Your lies, your truth.
It all gets covered.
The blanket covers your face, your body.
The real you gets covered.
You can hide behind the blanket.
You can cover your problems, but they shall not die.
They shall come back.
To cover them is not to dispose of them.
The blanket. What does it really do?
Can lies become truth? Never.
Nothing really ever dies.
It lives, whether in spirit or reality.
Will the blanket help you? You decide.
But think of this, it can cover you,
But can it really help you?

Aly Collins
John T Magee Middle School
Round Lake
Grade 7

a grain of sand

a grain of sand sitting in the ocean
just waiting to be pulled onto the beach
flowing with the waves
being pushed and pulled by water

a white, round grain of sand
on a route to the desirable beach

it is brought up by the waves to a happier place

but land is not always happier than the sea
feet stepping on you, the hot summer sun baking you up
being in a sand castle, you're only one grain of many

as i squished my feet onto the hot sand
i thought that being sand is like life
you always want something you don't have

Katy McShane
Lake Bluff Middle School
Lake Bluff
Grade 7

Our Destinies

Once we didn't control our destiny.
Now we can control and shape our future.
Nothing can stop us now but our own restrictions.
If we could end hatred and racism
And all fears and oppressions
But our minds are too weak and scared to let us go
For now we control our single and only destiny.

Ricardo Flores
St Mary of Czestochowa School
Cicero
Grade 7

Through My Window

Through my window I see the night
and the moon that smiles at me.

Through my window I see the day
and the sun that shines on me.

Through my window I see the spring
and the flowers that bloom for me.

Through my window I see the summer
and the birds that sing to me.

Through my window I see life
and the world around me.

But the question is
can you see what I see through my window?

Chris Davila
St Mary of Czestochowa School
Cicero
Grade 7

Love at First Sight

At first everything is so new,
You're always looking for things together to do,
When looking into each other's eyes,
To be together makes me feel so happy, I could cry.
When you take me out all we do is talk,
Then afterwards we go for a romantic beach walk,
When you call and you have to cancel a date,
Who do you really appreciate?
Even when we get in a fight,
I knew it was love at first sight.

Sara Perry
River Trails Middle School
Mount Prospect
Grade 7

Snow

Falling from the sky all cold and white
Landing on the ground after a long, long flight
Providing a good surface for sledding downhill
If you don't wear a hat it will make you ill
Covering houses and trees everywhere
Forming big mounds, here and there
Melting into puddles when it gets warm
With it, round snowmen you are able to form
Cloaking the land like a white sheet
Sometimes piling up to many feet
Weaving a maze through it when it's piled up tall
A snowfall is the best of all!

Margaret Kaiser
St Philip the Apostle School
Northfield
Grade 7

Matthew

Whenever I kiss Matthew,
I get a feeling that can't be true.
Whenever I see his smile,
I start to imagine a little while.
It's hard to believe that he is finally mine,
The man I have loved for the longest time.
One day he was Ashley's one day he was not,
The day he was mine, I was in total shock.
When people ask, "Are you single or not?"
I say "Hell no, I got a man who is hot!"
The love I have for him is very strong,
Hopefully it lasts very long.
A lot of girls have done him wrong,
With me, however, that will not go on.
Now I know what heaven is like,
He is heaven to me both day and night.
What more could a girl possibly need,
From a guy who is there down on both knees?
I don't know the answer, how could I want more?
All that I know, is he is worth dying for.

Mary Mocodeanu
Schurz High School
Chicago
Grade 9

Native Hope

The land was dusty, crops dry
Irrigation was needed.
Bodies were frail, dried to the bone;
The sun beat down upon the people.
The rays braided among the desert,
Creating a glowing weave of heat
The women cried, but no tears fell.
The men stayed brave but doubted.
The elders came and lifted their arms
Toward the golden sky.
The chanting began, all through the night;
In the morn, the rain had come.

Colleen Cullen
Fenwick High School
Oak Park
Grade 9

Memories

As I sit here alone with nothing to do
My mind becomes filled with thoughts of you
Things I should have said
Things I should have done
These expressions of words that make two become one
Thoughts of good times that we had together
Memories of love that will last forever

Kristal Cabanas
Holden Elementary School
Chicago
Grade 8

Beach

Sometimes when it's really hot,
We migrate to a huge sandlot.
To the left of the lot is a puddle,
That is large enough to hold a space shuttle.
People are everywhere running around,
Making all sorts of loud sounds.
With lots of happiness everywhere,
I run around to dry my hair.
Then I stop and think to myself,
I love this sandlot with a puddle to the left.

Gregory Jones
Owen Scholastic Academy
Chicago
Grade 7

Hollywood

Take away all the makeup,
Take away all the name brands,
Take away all the perfect smiles,
Take away all the millions of dollars,
Take away all the headlines,
Take away all the plastic wrapping,
Shielding them from the rest of society.
And now all you have is an ordinary person,
Like you and like me.
But is this what we live for?
The glamour, the fame, the money,
The makeup, the perfect skin,
And especially the gossip...
Is this really what we live for?
There's got to be something better...

Katie Roberts
St Matthew School
Champaign
Grade 8

My Best Friend

I have a best friend,
I hope our friendship will never end
Her name is Amber, and she is kind
She has so many ideas, it blows my mind

She always gives me needed advice,
And she is really, super nice
She once went to a concert with me,
We had so much fun, we felt like we were free

I love hangin' with her
With her, all my worries are just a blur
When we're together, we have so much fun
She's my best friend, my only one.

Angie Hutchings
Beckemeyer Elementary School
Beckemeyer
Grade 8

Clouds

White, puffy, drifting
Soaring to who knows where
Weightless as the air

Giant bumper-cars
Racing around in the sky
Crashing playfully

Plip, plop, plip, plop, plip
Tears fall from the sky
The clouds are crying

Jean Hosty
Fenwick High School
Oak Park
Grade 9

Me

Friends think I'm funny,
with a personality that's sunny.
I love to give hugs,
but don't like bugs.
I like to help people with things,
and to make people laugh
I'll go ahead and sing.
I can get mad,
and I will get sad.
I'm not trying to be anyone but me.
You should be you.

Nicole Maldonado
West Middle School
Rockford
Grade 8

The Newsletter

Hanging on the wall,
Saying, "Look at me!"
Knowing more than most things.
Telling what's going on,
Shouting, "Schools Out!"
Yelling loudly, "Spring Break!"

Kasey Boeger
Holy Cross Lutheran School
Collinsville
Grade 7

Pen

I pick up my pen,
And watch its ink trace,
As it records information,
My name, my answer.
So insignificant yet so important.

Blake Chamness
Parkview Jr High School
Lawrenceville
Grade 7

One Life Instead of Two

The light fades
Over the horizon
As the night draws near
Stars overhead
Speak to me for once
Telling me there's nothing to fear
My hands are cold
The hair on my arms stands straight
As I see the ghost come near
Its pale outline
Hardly fits its beauty
My feet won't move from where I stand
Time freezes at this interaction
Between me and the angel
I feel myself go white
The feeling in my limbs fades
I see myself fall
Broken dreams
Turn to cruel reality
My only regret is that I only had one life
Instead of two

Meg Walla
Lake Bluff Middle School
Lake Bluff
Grade 8

A Death of a Friend

As she lays there, really sleepy
I look at her, my eyes get weepy
She is dying really slowly.
I get real sad and start to worry.

She used to love food a lot,
But now she hardly eats a drop.
As she reaches her dying days. . .
It's really sad because she's only eight.

We had to bring her to the vet.
12 p.m., the appointment is set.
My dad brings her in, I can't go.
The time seems to go by really slow.

My stomach turns into a knot
And I begin to cry a lot.
I cried and cried and could not stop.
I lost a friend at 12 o'clock.

Life is different without her
And she's always in my heart.
I'll always love and think of her,
Though we are apart.

Amanda Pumpera
Hamlin Upper Grade Center
Alsip
Grade 7

Dreams

Dreams
Starry, imaginary
Flying, falling, floating
Magical wishes
Mysterious adventures

Jackie Kellett
River Trails Middle School
Mount Prospect
Grade 7

If We Look for the Good

If we look for the good in people,
Every day and everywhere,
We will surely find it there.
It may be hidden beneath the skin,
Under the diversity, prejudice, and sin.
It is His will to seek the just,
To earn His favor this we must.
This may be hard at all our tries,
But watching us are the Maker's eyes.
He'll help us always still,
As we try to live His will.
Because through it all,
Good overrules.
To live this,
We must become the Maker's tools.

Nicole Blackburn
St Mary's of Kickapoo School
Edwards
Grade 8

Life

In the beginning
You are born
If you die
Some are forlorn

You could be rich
You could be poor
Born during peace
Or born during war

Life can be good
Life can be bad
Life can be happy
Life can be sad

If you live your life
The way that you should
Then I tell you my friend
Your life will be good

Greston Dorney
Parkview Jr High School
Lawrenceville
Grade 7

Untitled

Have you ever gotten that feeling
Deep inside your heart
When the one you love
Starts tearing things apart
When they don't know exactly what they're doing
And all you can do is sit and listen
When you don't want to hear
When you don't want to see
When all you want to do is be held gently
It's the feeling of loss
It's the feeling of sorrow
It's the feeling that there will be no tomorrow
It's the feeling I've got inside of me now
And I want it to go away
If only God would send an angel
Maybe I could find somewhere to lay
Somewhere safe, in someone's arms
Where I can't be hurt
Where I can't be found
Where there is no pain or sorrow
Then maybe I can find my tomorrow

Katy Atwell
Norwood Elementary School
Peoria
Grade 8

Locked by a Key

I wanted to be free
exactly like a bee
but there was this key
that used to lock me

I wanted to fly
just like a butterfly
that spread its wings wide and flew
and became better and new

I wanted to be like others that time
to be nice and fine
but if I wanted to find who was "me"
I had to unlock the key.

I am now independent free as a bird
new as a letter or word
I opened my wings and heart
and do my own thing and my own part

Like a chick that comes out of its shell
my heart rang out with independence like a bell
at last I was free
and I learned how to unlock the key!

Estera Ciomag
John F Eberhart Elementary School
Chicago
Grade 7

The Beach

The feel of the sand between my toes,
the taste of the cool ice cream in my mouth,
the sounds of the kids splashing in the water,
the touch of a starfish buried deep in the sand,
the look of the sunset after a long day at the beach.

Poonam Sura
Stratford Jr High School
Bloomingdale
Grade 8

I Am

I am a speaker and a leader, not a follower
I wonder where my life will lead me
I hear a song even when I am alone
I see the world's utopia
I want hatred to end
I am a speaker and a leader, not a follower

I pretend to follow in Martin Luther King Jr.'s footsteps
I feel special in my own ways
I reach out to others
I worry about my future
I cry when people put down others
I am a speaker and a leader, not a follower

I understand no one is perfect
I say it will turn out all right
I dream for peace and justice
I try to make a difference
I hope to be all that I can be
I am a speaker and a leader, not a follower

Kathryn White
Francis Granger Middle School
Aurora
Grade 7

I Can't See

I can't see skin I can't see light
for I am a man that has no sight
we are all the same from my point of view
I can't judge but from what's inside of you

character counts not what's outside but in
I don't see color, I don't see skin
and if everyone had my point of view
I could be me and you could be you

I guess I am blessed because I cannot see
when I think of the world that could be
if there was no black and there was no white
there would be no prejudice, no need to fight

Chelsea Deitz
West Chicago Middle School
West Chicago
Grade 7

Baby Blue

Baby blue giggles when tickled.
Baby blue babbles about gossip.
Baby blue hiccups while singing.
Baby blue whispers at night!

Rebekah Young
Shirland C C Elementary School
Shirland
Grade 7

Spring Time

The frost departs,
The buds appear,
I awake and spring is here.

As the sun arises,
Birds honor spring's appearance
With a tweet, twitter, chitter, and chirp.

Children playing in their yards
Neighbors begin to garden
Making my life a paradise of Eden.

As I peer out my window
Glimpsing the adventure of spring,
I realize I am a fall, not spring.

Dreaming not living,
Reaching out to join the others
But unable to touch the season.

Philip Martin
New Trier Township High School
Winnetka
Grade 9

One Spring Morning

One spring morning
As I lie on the ground

The birds were chirping
In the trees all around

The incense of flowers
Spread through the air

With nature's sweet powers
I could have not a care

These are the mornings
I love the most

With Mother Nature
As the host!

Trina White
Clifford Crone Middle School
Naperville
Grade 7

Shani

...a speed skater that glides gracefully on the ice.
...a senior that looks forward to going to college and having a career.
...a boy that is always looking for adventure and fun.
...a loving person that understands and comprehends
when you have a problem.
...a confident and powerful person who fights for what he thinks is right.
...a comforting father figure that consoles you.

Alexandra Papillon
Nichols Middle School
Evanston
Grade 8

Life Is too Long Love Is too Short

Life is too long, a love is too short
He has her heart like she has his love
She is his like he is hers
They are together for a moment's time
Is life too long or is love too short
If love is forever will time always be life
She reproduced love like it was time
But shall we not understand that love is time love is time
Like time is love
She never understood like he understood
But who can understand by the soul being restored and no one at hand
Love was once her life like the rigid story untold
Her heart beats slowly like life's not there anymore
She moves on as slowly as possible
Life is what we all have
But love is what many will never have.

Candice Lovrant
Paxton-Buckley-Loda Jr High School
Paxton
Grade 8

So Shall Our Love Be

Like the river rushes into the sea,
so shall our love be.
Like the warmth of summer never cease,
so shall our love be.
Like the north force of you and the south force of me,
so shall our love be.
Like a prize without a cost and a ride without a fee,
so shall our love be.
Like mending with glue or opening a door with a key,
so shall our love be.
Like those who are healed to walk and those who are blind to see,
so shall our love be.
Like an offering to the highest or the bending of a knee,
so shall our love be.
Like her and him and he and she but you and I are we,
so shall our love be.

Brandyss Adams
Laraway Elementary School
Joliet
Grade 7

Summary

Every summer I like to play.
I don't come home until the end of the day.
I go to the park, I go to the mall,
Or I go to the court and play some ball.
Then the summer comes to an end
And I say, "Good-bye, my friend."

George Rangel
St Mary of Czestochowa School
Cicero
Grade 8

The Storm

The rain pours over the land.
Its merciless beating creates a song.
The drops pummel my outstretched hand.
The thunder's sound vibrates like a gong.

A flash of lightning lights the sky.
The sudden flash irritates the sea,
And in its anger, its waves rise so high.
I can also feel the anger rising in me.

Then the rain begins to soften,
And the thunder begins to cease.
Flashes of lightning occur less often.
My rage and gloom begin to decrease.

The sun peeks through the heavy cloud.
The storm puts up a violent fight,
But the sun destroys the mist-like shroud,
And the land is flooded in light.

Samantha Blank
North Park Elementary School
Chicago
Grade 7

Spring Is Here

The time has come for flowers to bloom
Gazing out of my beautiful room
Everything is so very bright
Glistening in the warm sunlight

Suddenly a robin catches my eye
Flying quickly through the sky
He is here for a special reason
And that is to announce the brand new season.

New beginnings all around
Green, green grass from the ground
Butterflies, bees and ladybugs
Flying through the air, buzz, buzz, buzz

Laura Kilbride
Immaculate Conception School
Morris
Grade 7

The Gateway

Once when the light was so bright,
The heavens shone upon me a light,
It was a message from the sky,
In where the angels sat so high.

As many people knew,
Such a thing only happened to a few,
For one entire day,
I drifted far, far away.

But when I had landed,
A gate to me they handed
The angels said I had died
For they knew many cried.

Not wanting to go on,
I sat morning till dawn
Was I meant to go below?
An answer in which I needed to know.

Is heaven not for me?
The wonders of it, will I ever see?
Please thy lords show a sign
Tell about the destiny in which is truly mine.

Swati Patel
Stratford Jr High School
Bloomingdale
Grade 8

Life

Life is a wonder
You never know what to expect
You can be born one day
But gone the next

Everyone is afraid
But afraid of what
Is it death
Or could it be loneliness

There are those who hate life
For what they have gotten
But you have to think
You should be happy to get the chance to live

No one truly has a perfect life
People seem happier than they really are
But no one knows what they really feel
Because they can't always show it

Life is a wonder...

Doug Grandsart
St Ferdinand School
Chicago
Grade 8

Waves

The striking waves
are cold and dark and shimmering
in the deep depths

Sean McCann
Holy Angels School
Aurora
Grade 7

Hiding

My life takes a path of its own,
never knowing why it goes so slow.
Many times I fall away.
Many times I even let go.

Everyone taking me for granted;
pushing me to do my best.
My mom always yelling at me,
for getting an F on my test.

Sometimes I just can't handle it.
I run away and cry
thinking no one ever cares for me;
no one even thinks to try.

I hope one day these visions
will pass away and die.
But until that moment comes
beneath these shadows I'll hide.

Amy Fujinaka
East Prairie Elementary School
Skokie
Grade 8

The Game

I feel the adrenaline pumping,
The ball in my hand,
The sweat running down my face.
I'm in the game

We're ready to hit,
we're warmed up,
we're pumped up.
let's play

I get the ball,
I take off,
The 10, 5, 1.
we score

we won
we won
we did our best.

Patrick Hogg
Beckemeyer Elementary School
Beckemeyer
Grade 7

The Sun Will Rise Again

Soft flakes slowly fell upon the trodding masses,
a sign of lost hope, and lost life.
One foot after another, they slip and slide
the bottom of social status and rank.

Heads once held up high now stare at the ground,
bodies that once never had done work are now callused and worn.
Stomachs once filled with delicacies of every kind,
now hunger and growl each hour of every day.

Here, the proud are made humble, the many made few,
the loss of life greater than ever before.
The sun is kept hidden from every eye,
all brightness is gone, dark now rules the world.

Days drag on, as do weeks and years,
an ongoing nightmare that never seems to end.
The world has shrunk to just this one place,
where it is impossible to escape.

But the nightmare will end, the sleeping will awake,
when the cruel disappear and the kind take their place.
The gray flakes of ashes from burnt bodies stop falling,
and the darkness disappears.

And reminds all that the sun will rise again.

Theresa Luebbers
Carlyle High School
Carlyle
Grade 9

The Beach

On the way to the beach, I hear the neighbor's kids screaming
and those crazy kids skateboarding down the hill,
Anyway once I got down to the stairs, I feel the wood creek beneath my feet,
and then I finally get down to the hot sand,
and because of this hot sand
you would burn as fast as you could to get the water.
As you run towards the water
you feel the sand move slowly beneath your feet
and stepping on rocks that would also be burning hot,
quickly you throw down your towel onto the sand
and then you realize that the water was freezing cold
so you would jump out of the freezing water.
And then onto your feet burning sand
so again you quickly jump right back into that freezing water
but this time you stay in there because you realize
that it was so peaceful and happy having the sun shine on you.
Then you realize that you forgot to put some sunscreen on your face,
but then you didn't really care on that nice day at the beach
feeling so peaceful and happy.

Jamie Patterson
Pope John XXIII School
Evanston
Grade 8

I Know

The place where I live
I feel snug and warm
Safe and secure endured from harm.

The place where I live
I feel and see me growing up
Such fond memories.

The place where I live
Times have been good and bad.
Getting through tough times, happy and sad.

The place where I live,
Stands by me in the hour of need
Also chases away my doubts and fears.

So where I live is always there
Without a doubt when I return
"I know" I can call it my home.

Marie Sell
Owen Scholastic Academy
Chicago
Grade 8

Memories of Grandpa

Memories of Grandpa,
Are cherished more than anyone could ever know.

Memories in the garden,
Where flowers bloom majestically with bits of every hue.
Where the wind rustles through the sweet corn,
Straight, and true.

Memories in the barn,
Each time a new lamb is born.
With the sweet, sweet smell of hay,
In the hayloft, tucked away.

Memories of trains,
Train rides and model trains.
Trains of every shape and size.

My Grandpa was a special person,
To me he will always be that way.
Even though it has been years since that cruel day,
When cancer took his life away.

Now you can see just why these memories,
Are so precious and special to me.
My memories will forever stay with me,
In my heart.

Carrie Francis
L J Stevens Middle School
Wilmington
Grade 7

Secrets

If I could put things in a box,
I'd make it so it never unlocks.
To fill one's heart with good things I could,
I'd do it for them, I know I would.
Beautiful lakes, wonderful willow trees,
Little itsy, bitsy buzzing bees.
Now favorite birds, birds like a dove.
These are things I'll always love.

Stephanie L. Williams
River Trails Middle School
Mount Prospect
Grade 7

Angel on Earth

Most people's angels are up in the sky,
But mine is quite nearby.
Angels are usually thought of dressed in all white
But mine...no, not quite.
My angel is the strongest person I know
With a face that has a beautiful glow.
She may not know what an impact she's had on me,
But trust me, she's changed my life dramatically.
She made my eyes open and aware
And made me realize I should show others I care.
Even if it's a simple "hello" with a smile,
She said it could make one's life worthwhile.
Whenever I see her,
All of my problems go to a blur.
She's helped me see all the things that are important,
And not so much on my misfortune.
She has given my life a new sense of worth,
And that is why she is my angel on Earth.

Marybel Carpio
Stratford Jr High School
Bloomingdale
Grade 8

Keep Watch Over Me

Keep watch over me,
Keep me in your sight,
The road I'm on is dark,
So extend your hand and lead me into the light.
Keep watch over me,
Keep me in your sight,
Losing you was the hardest thing to go through.
I took our love for granted,
Never thought the day I'd lose you would come,
But it did, and now you're gone.
So I ask you,
Keep watch over me,
Keep me in your sight.

Jennifer Giza
Norman Bridge School
Chicago
Grade 8

My Cat

Quietly sleeping
Purring on the windowsill
Stretching and yawning
She awakes to my footsteps
And excitingly greets me
Chantal Villain
Clifford Crone Middle School
Naperville
Grade 7

Love

Love is a special thing
That every person has.
We use it every day
Whether happy or sad.

Love is not bad
But good all around.
It is what I felt
When you were around.

Even though it is there
I don't really notice.
'Cause ever since you left us
Everything has been bad.

We cried and cried
Till our eyes were red.
I am still horrified
When I go to bed.
That another loved one
Will soon be dead.
Becky Springborn
Holy Angels School
Aurora
Grade 7

Sick

I could have ended the world
Crashed computers
Cost you money
Spoiled your food
Could've stopped the world
In a blink of an eye
I was thought to be a media-hype
Then I got sick
On December the 30th
And missed my New Year's bash
So I'll name myself Y2K+1 bug
And have a bigger bash
In New Year's 2001
Lisa Cassista
Francis Granger Middle School
Aurora
Grade 7

Bowling

Every day I wake up at eight,
and I go to start the car.
I put it in drive and quickly speed off,
because I have to go very far.

When I get to the bowling alley,
I go to get a lane.
When I see my friend behind the desk,
I ask him for a game.

I step up to the lane to bowl,
and launch my first ball.
It hits the pocket really hard,
And so all the pins fall.

This continues for frames to come,
strikes now till the last.
I could have a three-hundred game,
but soon that's the past.

Today it happened all at once,
I bowled a three-hundred game.
I worked for this forever,
a strike in every frame.
Jon Pesek and Anthony Razza
Albright Middle School
Villa Park
Grade 8

Fate

Some call it destiny.
Others think of it as chance.

Most say it's unchangeable.
Others try to predict it.

Some know how it feels.
Others dream of when it comes.

Most can find happiness.
Others face disaster.

Some can pinpoint its location.
Others never know it's there.

Most discover true love.
Others meet with their demise.

But ...

They all know it exists.
Jerry Gomez
Nathan Hale Middle School
Crestwood
Grade 7

God's Creations

Butterflies flying free,
Dolphins swimming in the sea.

Peacock feathers oh so bright,
Wolves howling in the night.

Ants are so tiny and small,
But no matter what, God loves us all.

God created all these things,
In this world, me he brings.
Elissa Pfeiffer
St. Mary School
Belleville
Grade 8

Writer's Block

I cannot think of what to write,
Being a poet is just not easy.
I wish I were smart and bright,
And writing was simple and breezy.

I have been thinking for hours and hours,
But still don't know what to write.
I wish I had magical writing powers,
So my poem would be happy and bright.
Erica Harmony
St Matthew School
Champaign
Grade 8

Colors

Will I ever see colors?
People say the grass is green.
People say the sky is blue.

I hear cars drive back and forth.
Children laughing having fun.
Are these children laughing at me?

I want children to think that I'm normal.
I'm not different from anyone else.
My only friend is myself.

I pray every night that I can see.
Then thinking to myself why me?

Someday I'll see.
I'll see all colors.
Then laugh at people,
Who laughed at me.
Bora Grujic
Taylor Elementary School
Chicago
Grade 8

Rockets

I like rockets and the way they fly,
As they slice through the bright blue sky.

I wait for the count-down, three, two, one,
Now here comes the real fun.

You can hear the thunder, and the big loud boom,
Before you know it in the air it will zoom.

They come big, little, and small.
Despite the size, I love them all.

Tim Philbin
St Gerald School
Oak Lawn
Grade 7

My Confession

Playing basketball is the best
I've been holding something in so I must confess
As I hold the ball in my hands I feel a power
Especially while my game lasts for an hour

Shooting hoops takes good aim
But being on the bench stops my game
Running, shooting, scoring points
Sometimes gives me sore joints

Basketball is my favorite sport
I love the feeling when I'm on the court
Now that I've told my confession
I am the lead of the parade procession

Olivia White
St Joan Of Arc School
Evanston
Grade 7

I Know a Girl

I know of a girl,
More valuable than a pearl.

She's skinny and tall,
If you need advice, just give her a call.

She's into music and boys,
But has outgrown playing with toys.

If you tell her a secret, don't worry
She won't tell anyone your embarrassing story.

She likes to eat candy,
She's my best friend Mandy.

Gena Alvarez
St Joseph Catholic School
Harvard
Grade 7

Sometimes

Sometimes I feel that if I were to fly,
Then maybe I would touch the sky.
Sometimes I think that I am being ignored,
Then I think of the things that I have, and I thank the Lord.

The worst of all is when I sometimes sigh,
As if I were about to cry.
I think of all the bad things in life,
All the pain and all the strife.

Of course I am thankful that all the agony is not for me.
I have plenty of happiness and glee.
When the pain does come, keep in mind,
All the positive things in life.

Tara Varndell
St Matthew School
Champaign
Grade 7

Waterfalls

Waterfalls are so free
Free to go any which way they want
They are so rapid

They give me time to let my thoughts out
They give me many ideas to write
They are so calm and peaceful

Even if I'm just looking at a picture of a waterfall
I can imagine it actually flowing and then hearing
The water flow down the fall

Rebecca Ruiz
Taylor Elementary School
Chicago
Grade 8

The All-Knowing Fan

Is there anyone who likes Star Wars more than I do?
If you know one, please tell me who.
I'd love to talk about how the fighter pilots battled,
And how the notorious Rogue Squadron never got rattled.
About Han Solo and the history of his checkered past,
And his beloved Millennium Falcon, being so incredibly fast.
The big furry Wookie named Chewie,
And the first Death Star going kablooey
How Luke and Darth dueled,
Luke's hope for his father, how he was fueled.
I've got over thirty good books,
About Imperial villains and crooks.
I know everything there is to know about Star Wars,
But everyone around here says who cares.

Greg Wetzel
St Matthew School
Champaign
Grade 8

M&M's

When I think of something sweet
Of something that I love to eat
Yellow, green, red, and blue
Only just to name a few

Crispy, plain, small, and round
Always known to bring a crowd
What's sweet and rich that I love to eat?
Only I will know the treat!

Sarah McCall
Parkview Jr High School
Lawrenceville
Grade 7

Earth/Sky

Earth
hard, colorful
playing, swinging, jumping,
grass that grows, water that flows
shining, soothing, glistening
beautiful, bright
Sky

Michelle Wright
Holy Angels School
Aurora
Grade 7

Courage

When trouble comes your way,
Do you run or do you stay?
But whatever you do, be brave,
Then you will be saved.

Then it draws near.
But don't worry, have no fear,
For God is near.
So don't shed a tear.

When it's all over and done,
You know He watches everyone.
Now you're through, the game you won
Now you walk home in the sun.

If you trust in God, you'll never be alone.
But with the courage that you've shown
Your life has a new seed sown,
While you walk your hair is blown.

Sunlight dims into the night
But you know there is no fright.
Because the street lights shine bright,
And God watches from your right.

Mark Hopkins
St John The Baptist School
West Frankfort
Grade 7

You Could

Who could make us laugh when we were down?
You could.

Who could be the only one to help us through tough times?
You could.

Who could always love and care for everyone and anyone?
You could.

Who could tell us what was wrong and what was right?
You could.

But most of all, who could always make us laugh?
You could.

Now you're gone, we've learned from you
you thought you were a failure, but you did all you could.

We'll never forget the good times we had,
and all the jokes you made.

We wish you were here but now you're gone
and we don't know what to do.

We don't understand why you had to leave, but only you will know.

We wish we had more memories,
but I guess we'll have to remember the past.

From everyone that ever knew you,
we wished we could have said goodbye.

Kristi Ervin
Huntley Middle School
Huntley
Grade 7

Grandpas

Grandpa, have you ever thought about what Grandpa could mean?
Sometimes my grandpa even eats a bean.
My grandpa stands for...let's see...
G is for great, which is one thing that my grandpa is.
R is for reliable, because my grandpa is always there, he passes the test.
A is for appreciative, because my grandpa appreciates the little things we do.
N is for nifty, because my grandpa is up to date and has a clue.
D is for devilish trickster, because my grandpa likes to pull tricks.
P is for pen, because my grandpa likes to write with the famous pen, Bics.
A is for apprehension because my grandpa is able to understand.
S is for senior, because my grandpa has lived a while on this land.
That is what my grandpa means to me.
Think for yourself and find out what your Grandpa means to you.
It will be fun, just wait and see.

Jessica House
Rockridge Junior High School
Taylor Ridge
Grade 7

Opening Day

I am nervous for the time.
I have waited for this all year long.
I listen to it every time I can reach my locker.
I wish I could be there, but I never can.
I cheer when the Cubs get a run on the base.
I can smell the popcorn when I picture being there.
It is opening day.

T.J. Wysocki
Francis Xavier Warde School
Chicago
Grade 7

I Am

I am small and sweet
I wonder what will happen to me
I hear my friends all laughing together
I want to meet my grandpa in heaven
I am small and sweet

I pretend sometimes to be someone I'm not
I feel excited about what I have done with myself
I touch the stars when I dream
I worry about losing everyone I know
I cry about losing my grandma
I am small and sweet

I understand that all people have to die
I say that respecting others is the way to go
I dream about helping the helpless
I try to make the best of life
I hope I will succeed at whatever I do
I am small and sweet

Molly Gudewicz
Finley Jr High School
Chicago Ridge
Grade 8

My First Love

Did you ever really care?
It never was really clear.
You claimed you loved me or was that a lie?
I question it now because you said goodbye.
For you I'd do almost anything,
I'd even give up a diamond ring.
I thought our love was really strong,
With you I thought I could do no wrong.
I miss the way you said my name.
And the way we thought the same.
I understand you and me, again will never be.
But till the day we're truly sure,
I'll keep our love in my heart pure.

Amanda Scully
Tobin Elementary School
Burbank
Grade 7

Reminiscing

I remember that scary Halloween night
We were at the park.
Me and you, us alone.
The two of us with no one around.
The night was young and very dark.
It was a full moon out, and also your last day.
You were leaving to Mexico and I didn't have the words
To say how much I really loved you.
I wanted to tell you, really I did.
But nothing came out, it stayed in my head.
The time had come, for us to be on our way.
You walked me home and said good-bye with a kiss.
A kiss on my cheek, that I will never forget.
That night was special, and I will forever treasure
The precious time we spent.
I will remember it always and I'll remember you as well.
Even though nothing happened between you and me,
I loved you once and I always will.
I have your picture carved in my heart, and forever it will stay.
Wouldn't it be perfect if you hadn't passed away?

Sophia Velazquez
Schurz High School
Chicago
Grade 9

The Part of Me I Never Knew *

We came into the world together
I thought we would leave too
He was very sick and he was
The part of me I never knew

A year passed it was our 1st birthday
He wasn't there
I looked and looked he wasn't there he was
The part of me I never knew

Five years passed it was our 5th birthday
He still wasn't there
I wished and wished it didn't come true he was
The part of me I never knew

Ten years passed it was our 10th birthday
He wasn't there again
I hoped and hoped it didn't happen he was
The part of me I never knew

Now we are 13 teenagers I am having a tough time without you
I so wish, hope, and dream that you are here
You aren't I am crushed I love you, you are
The part of me I never knew

Robin Spector
Aptakisic Jr High School
Buffalo Grove
Grade 8
**Dedicated in the memory of Steven Michael Spector*

Over You

You and me can never be,
So why is it so hard to see,
That our love's just a fantasy,
Without a trace of reality.

The time we shared seemed like an eternity,
You made me happy,
Brought me ecstasy,
You were my one infirmity.

But now out time has got to end,
And I don't want to be your friend,
I just want you to go away,
So I may see a brighter day.

Sarah Yarrito
St Ferdinand School
Chicago
Grade 8

I Wonder?

I wonder about my future.
What will I grow up to be?
A teacher, a doctor, a lawyer
I just cannot wait to see.

I wonder about my future.
Where will I be in ten years?
Will I be in Asia, Africa, or Alaska?
I have so many fears.

I wonder about my future.
What college will I attend?
Penn State, UCLA, or the University of Illinois.
Will this wondering ever end?

Brittany Ince
Visitation School
Kewanee
Grade 8

The Sea

The sea is for the whales to live,
But for us it's just a place to swim

The sea is of many colors, on the top blue or green,
But on the bottom, yellow, red, orange for the coral reef

The sea has many animals that are alike,
Some bigger than others that depend on each other's life

The sea is like the land at night,
Almost everyone is sleeping and off go the lights.

Savanah Albert
Pope John XXIII School
Evanston
Grade 8

Stars

Stars, stars
In the night
We can't see them in the light

Floating, gleaming
Are their jobs
But why in the night, not the daylight?

We wish every night
To see them in the bright light

Stars are always made of dust
So ... that's why they come out at dusk

To put dust in your eyes
So we can float through the night
But never in the daylight

Sometimes in our special nights
They float in our eyes to make them very bright

They're always shooting, flying, and floating
One day we might even see them boating

Well for now they go on floating in the night
While we are daydreaming in the daylight

Sam Manus
Jonesboro Elementary School
Jonesboro
Grade 7

I Am

I am a mixture of love and hate
I wonder if pigs could fly
I hear voices even when no one is with me
I see a world where even the worst criminals can be forgiven
I am a mixture of love and hate

I pretend to be the ruler of a massive colony
I feel that no one can overpower me or underestimate me
I reach to my highest ability of skill
I worry of the thought of death
I cry for the safety of my family
I am a mixture of love and hate

I understand that sometimes I will fail
I say that everyone is unique
I dream to be accepted
I try to always do my best
I hope to one day succeed
I am a mixture of love and hate

Jordan Trutman
Francis Granger Middle School
Aurora
Grade 7

Friends

Friends are caring people,
They listen to you when you have problems.

Friends are there for you when you are scared,
They comfort you and tell you that it is O.K.

Friends tell you secrets and laugh at your jokes,
They do not make fun of you.

Friends respect your decisions,
They do not force you to do something wrong.

Friends share things with you,
They are not greedy and they do not steal your stuff.

Friends are great to have,
They make every day bright.

Jenny Fitzpatrick
Queen of Martyrs School
Chicago
Grade 8

Mom

You are the sun in my day.
You are the moon in my night.
You are my mentor. You are my keeper.

You are the radiant light,
which guides me through the darkness.

I look to the east, you are there.
I look to the west, you are there.

I look to the north, you are there.
I look to the south, you are there.

You are there to clothe me.
You are there to give me food and drink.
You are there to give me warmth and shelter.

Your cheery disposition leaves a wonderful impression
to those near and far.
The way you display your love and good will
is an inspiration to us all.

So, Mom, I just wanted to say
throughout the ages and years to come,
I will remember the things you did and
the things you have said.

I love you, Mom.

Troy Kerber
St Irene School
Warrenville
Grade 8

Scared Straight

Scared and cold,
first night on the streets,
Your body hurts,
from your head to your feet,
You miss school,
not the work but your friends,
You are wondering what to say when they ask,
"Where have you been?"

Got a dollar-fifty,
every penny you gotta spend,
Make a wrong move and—BOOM—
your life comes to an end.

Heather Williamson
St Mary's of Kickapoo School
Edwards
Grade 8

The Strong Heart

I agree
That our love is stronger than a tree
But then why do you cry so many tears
If in your heart deep down you have only two fears
The fear of me and you dying
And the fear of me to stop loving and trying
The love I have for you is much more than a race
It is true love trying to take its place
I know right now, my heart is glowing
Glowing in the same way that the wind is blowing
If I had a tear for each year I have lived in pain
It would drive me crazy, no just completely insane
Because I have put all thought and love into it very deep
Even when I lay to rest and go to sleep
I will give you two choices
So they will sound like two voices
Either you can take my love so it shall never be broken
Or you can take my broken heart so it shall never be spoken

Mitch Berens
St Augustine School
Belleville
Grade 8

Eagles

Eagles, phantoms of the dark night sky.
Their feathers are armor as a knight's armor would shine.
An eagle's eyes are as the eyes of a fox.
Whey are they so special, look at the grace.
The beauty in their face. Wow!
Their sleek beak is the spear of a warrior in battle.
The eagle encourages us all, as a knight, as a warrior as an
EAGLE!

Marvin Collier
Beckemeyer Elementary School
Beckemeyer
Grade 7

The Picture

Does Jack make the frost?
Frost makes designs
Then the morning is lost
And frost resigns

Does Jack make the frost?
I think so
The lines are crossed
But I don't know

Does frost make a picture?
It looks nice
Or is it just a mixture
Of snow and ice

Does frost make a picture?
Pretty lines and stars
It's a winter fixture
And it's all over cars

Lisa Kersey
Parkview Jr High School
Lawrenceville
Grade 7

I'm Not

I'm not odd
I'm not normal
I'm not the coolest
I'm not the best
I'm not the funniest
I'm not the smartest
I'm not the best looking
I'm not the greatest
But I'm original and myself

Mark Bryant
Harrisburg High School
Harrisburg
Grade 9

My Cat

My cat sits in the window,
Wondering where we go.

My cat sits in the window,
Just to see the snow.

My cat sits in the window,
Staring into space.

My cat sits in the window,
To see a smile on my face.

Megan Roberts
Prince of Peace School
Lake Villa
Grade 8

The Girl with the Sun-Kissed Hair

Of all the days and through the week
I write the name I dare not speak.
The girl with the sun-kissed hair.
When she passes, I do nothing but stare.
I can't work up the nerve to speak
Of all the days and through the week.

Julian Watkins
Cairo Jr High School
Cairo
Grade 8

Remember

Some times are happy.
Some times are sad.
But grandpa I'll always remember
All the good times we had.
I remember the jig.
I remember it all.
I remember all the time
We spent together in the fall.
I remember the summers
We spent working in the garage.
I remember all the time
We spent working on the lawn.
These are the times
I'll treasure forever.
Then sometimes I'll go back
And then I'll remember.

Andrea Stiles
Parkview Jr High School
Lawrenceville
Grade 7

Books

Books are good
Books are nice
Books can tell you
About mice.

Books have lots of
Good stories that could
Fill you up with glory.

So if you don't know
How to do beading,
Then you better start reading,
Because books can teach you things
Like how to tie strings.

So take my suggestion to read
And you'll be in the lead.

Kulsum Javid
Armstrong Elementary School
Chicago
Grade 7

The Day You Were Born

On the day you were born,
stories were told
by music and stars.
Everywhere soft music
played in the background.
Animals told each other
you were coming.
Everything came
to greet you.
Sun lighting your way,
moon glowing in the dark,
so you wouldn't get lost in the dark.

Elizabeth Corzine-Migdow
North Park Elementary School
Chicago
Grade 7

Life

Life is filled with many different things
Both great and small
Happy and sad
Difficult and easy
Live it to the fullest and be happy

Patrick McHugh
St Philip The Apostle School
Northfield
Grade 7

Shyness

Living in her silence
Afraid to speak,
Afraid of being rejected.

Someone speaks to her.
Her heart pounds,
She breaks into a sweat,
Thinking of a response,
Any response,
But none come.

Feeling like a deer,
Avoiding humans,
Tiptoeing around,
Hoping no one speaks to her.

After the day ends,
She thinks, "I've made it!"
Made it through another day,
Another battle.
But tomorrow,
Another minefield to cross.

Priscilla Lizasuain
Logandale Middle School
Chicago
Grade 7

Every Christmas

To my dear mom and dad,
Even though I'm sometimes bad.
I wake up every Christmas morn,
And hear in my ear, a little French horn.

It tells me that my parents care,
And I know they'll always be there.
I'm not the only one who knows this,
But sometimes they just have to say, "tisk tisk!"

I sit at the top of that blue staircase,
And wait and wait with a smile on my face.
For I may not be there in another six years,
But I promise, at college, I'll have no fears.

For then, I run down those wide, winding stairs,
To see all the presents wrapped up by the pairs!
I have a tiny twinkle in my eye,
As I hear my family say, "my, my, my!"

And when I look up at our beautiful tree,
I know for a fact, this family belongs to me!

Jessa Becker
Illini Central Middle School
Easton
Grade 7

Nature

Nature is a wonderful place
Where animals live and grow,
Where plants live and blossom,
Where leaves change colors in the fall,
And where trees grow and grow.

Nature is a place where
Streams connect to rivers,
Where waterfalls drain into the sparkling rivers,
Where valleys are just a plain of grass,
And where mountains tower over the valleys.

Nature is where
Spring blooms every April,
Where summer comes every June,
Where leaves fall every October,
And where snow sprinkles the ground every December.

Nature is where we play every day,
Where joy fills the Earth,
What we watch every year blooming
And growing,
Just like us

Kristen Nowdomski
L J Stevens Middle School
Wilmington
Grade 7

Life Goes On

Day by day time passes on
without knowing what to ask.
All we have to do is ask and pray
and God will lead your way.
Life changes so quickly in time
you just don't know what the future may hold.
It's hard to say but you have to be bold
like the seasons that keep changing.
That's how life goes on.

Candace Houpy
St George School
Tinley Park
Grade 8

All Aboard

We're all leaving our comfortable surroundings,
We're not all boarding the same ships.

I wish we would all board the same ship,
But now I know that is not possible.

Our emotions are like the weather;
We go from gladness to sadness and back again.
We're all kind of frightened where we're going;
None of us have been there before.
All of us will be tasting new experiences.

Some of our journeys will be smooth;
Others will be rough.
We will be meeting new and different experiences
Throughout our journey.
We will be going to new lands.

I hope someday our ships shall meet again.
We can share what has happened on our journeys.
That way I will never forget any of you.

Alexandrea O'Connor
St Colette School
Rolling Meadows
Grade 8

Remember When

Remember when any Holiday was
to be spent with family and friends.
And when on a Sunday morning
your bed and pillow was your only care.
When food was your major priority
when you get home from school.
Remember when love was your only care in the world
along with sports.
And those were your only thoughts and nothing else.

Travis Bauman
White Oak Academy
East St Louis
Grade 8

Summer Night

Some nights,
I like to sit outside. I sit on the old picnic table in my backyard. The linden leaves rustle in the cool breeze, which ruffles my hair. The pine needles shake, playing with the breeze. I faintly hear a basketball dribbling on someone's driveway. There is another faint rustling noise, and a squirrel springs onto the maple tree. It continues on its way, noiselessly. Maybe it too will sit outside and enjoy the cool night air.
Some nights,
I like to sit outside. I sit on the old picnic table in my backyard. The garden is bathed in moonlight. My neighbor's trees are tall and mysterious, a dark grove of shadows. A light glows from a window across the street, a beacon of warmth. The gray clouds fly rapidly by, casting pale shadows over the grass and bushes. The maple leaves sway, they also enjoy the sights and sounds of a crisp summer night.
Some nights,
I like to sit outside. I sit on the old picnic table in my backyard. The air is fresh and clean. The light breeze carries with it the scent of a barbecue down the street. The grass has a sweet smell, like that of pure rainwater. The bush with its little red berries emits a fragrant odor. I taste the pure, crisp evening breeze. With my bare feet, I feel the grassy ground, still basking from the midday heat. The delightful scents of a summer night mingle in the aromatic breeze.
Then, my mother beckons for me to come in, and I leave the yard to the peaceful summer night.

Molly F. Moore
River Trails Middle School
Mount Prospect
Grade 7

Summer Events!

In the summer so many things happen!
The children are all laughing, swimming, and playing.
As summer approaches and the days grow longer
The intense heat grows stronger.
The parks, grass, and streets are filled with summer events.
As you work the day, you realize it's time to relax, sit back and enjoy this long summer day!
When you see the kids all having a good time,
You jump in the pool and it feels so cool!
When the birds fly over me I know it's time to party!
The girls jump rope, and the boys are playing in the dirt.
As you sit on the front lawn chair and stare, you realize that summer is taking place
And you will be part of these wonderful summer EVENTS!

Loren Baltimore
Francis Granger Middle School
Aurora
Grade 7

Sixth Grade

In sixth grade we were good friends,
We thought we would be there for each other through thick and thin.
We'd go everywhere together, and act the same in every way,
We always believed we'd be friends for forever and a day.
When we started to get older, we began to drift apart,
I knew that something was wrong and I felt that change in my heart.
By the time we were in high school, we had changed so dramatically,
But if you put our friendship in perspective, we were just hiding reality.
We had developed other friendships, and chosen those over ours,
Which resulted in a confrontation that released the feelings we've had buried inside our hearts.
This is just a reminder that life is not always as it may seem, that even though things change,
You will grow stronger from your mental and physical defeats.

Angela Murrell
Coal City High School
Coal City
Grade 9

Why

As I sit staring out my window at the snow,
  That blankets the ground below.
I wonder why I have so much,
  That some only dream to touch.

I wonder why me?
  Why I get almost anything without plea?
I have so much at my fingertips.
  Why do the sweetest foods touch my lips?

Any day it could all go away.
  And we would have no place to stay.
Why don't we help others?
  Instead of just watching with our sisters and brothers.

We travel all over the place.
  So many we couldn't even trace.
I see little and big countries in poverty.
  Why do there have to be so many?

So, as I sit and stare out my window,
  At the snow below.
I wonder why we don't care?
  Why we act like it's not even there.

Callie Palmer
Holy Angels School
Aurora
Grade 8

Oxygen

The very thing that we can not live without.
It keeps up going.
It fills our lungs and energizes our brain.
It feeds our muscles.
It helps us live.
It's oxygen.

It feeds our fires,
Which keeps us warm.
It is a critical element that we need to breathe.
If we didn't have it,
We would all die.
We take it for granted.
Yet, we pollute it and waste it.
Why?
We need it to live.
It keeps us alive and well.
It's oxygen.

The very thing that we can not live without.
It's oxygen.

Kevin Grentz
St Matthew School
Champaign
Grade 8

Thrown to the Ground

There are so many feelings
That are built up inside
Too many things that I can't define

I'm losing my mind just thinking of you
Now that you're gone, I don't know what to do

You took my heart and threw it to the ground
You left me lost—never to be found

Erin Blackburn
St George School
Tinley Park
Grade 7

Aim High

Aim high and reach for the sky
Make your dreams come true
Life is a precious gift given to you

Some may complain and like to place blame
They don't want to face
It's up to them to find their place

What you have to do
Is to yourself be true
Know who you are and then find your own star

Hold on tight and aim high to the sky
You will enjoy the flight
So fly, fly, fly!

Ari Fulton
Francis Xavier Warde School
Chicago
Grade 7

Sonnet

From the farthest lands and the deep blue seas,
I sit contemplating: does she love me?
From the snow-capped mountains to greenest trees,
I lie wondering: will she stay with me?
Feelings pouring forth from my heart and soul,
When I'm in her presence, I know for sure
The love I savor is past my control;
Every day passed, I love her even more.

How to tell if another loves you true;
Dreams of lying in your arms forever?
All I can know is I truly love you;
Our separation I hope comes never.
But through your kiss, your warm, enchanting eyes,
I feel between us loving compromise.

Michael Jewell
Fenwick High School
Oak Park
Grade 9

Spring Breezes

I can be
Like a tree
Feel the breeze
Through my leaves

My roots are deep
I like to keep
My branches high
Toward the sky

Trees can bend
But in the end
I will be
A stronger tree

Laura Redmond
Immaculate Conception School
Morris
Grade 7

Day and Night

Day
bright, sunny
playing, working, running,
warm, outdoors, resting, dinner,
darker, stars, moon,
cloudy, sleep
Night

Julie Rothman
Fremont Middle School
Mundelein
Grade 7

In the Darkness

Oh the darkness is all I see,
And all the shadows hide and flee.
The owl keeps his watch, keen and sleek.
He flies from the branch in the tree.

Out from his hole the mouse will peek,
Hiding from the owl, shy and meek.
The owl perches back on the limb,
Until he sees another streak.

He goes for it, the creature slim,
It dives for a bush on a whim.
Scared but safe it hides in the weeds,
The owl circling above him.

With his widened eyes he does plead,
He crawls to the top of the reed,
Wondering where this path will lead.
Wondering where this path will lead.

Kelli Schulte
Beckemeyer Elementary School
Beckemeyer
Grade 7

Seasonal Life

The rotation of the earth does not currently appear to us as daily,
But days pass so fast no one can.
The summer breeze soon turns to fall
And the falling leaves turn winter
Remorse for life after frost comes spring
Then life starts over with summer
We count the days but truly it is the days
Counting us closer, closer to heaven.
Death is not failure yet a place to look forward to instead.

Dena Andriopoulos
Francis Granger Middle School
Aurora
Grade 7

The Unicorn

As I walked through the woods late one night,
A strange beast came into my sight,
It was a unicorn yes indeed,
A unicorn with angel's wings,
He told me to ride on his back,
As I got on I heard his bones crack,
For he was still too young and weak,
And hardly knew how to speak,
We flew by past many stars,
And I was able to see the red planet Mars,
Then I felt a strong cold breeze,
That forced us to crash into the trees,
We landed on hard ground,
And I let out a painful sound,
I saw the unicorn in great pain,
And sweat began to flow from his silver mane,
Then I woke up from my dream,
And let out a frightful scream,
I looked outside my window and noticed that nothing was wrong,
'Cause there was the unicorn flying brave and strong.

Adrian Garcia
St Mary of Czestochowa School
Cicero
Grade 7

Cure

If I could I would find a cure
A cure to leukemia
A cure to cancer
A cure to any disease in this awful world
It is awful totally awful the way people think
It is the way people think that makes people sick
And I for one am sick of people being sick because of other people
I am sure there are people sick right now on this cold January afternoon
It is the eighth day of 1999 and no cure is found
Not for one single person

Collene Hughes
Westfield Jr High School
Bloomingdale
Grade 8

Nightmares

My name gives children chills
To parents I am discomforting
I stalk children at nocturnal hours
Searching for the unfortunate

I am the thing that swallows your dreams
And what I do is unruly
So if you're one out of many of my select victims,
Remember to set the alarm before...

It's too late....

Vivek Thayalan
Francis Granger Middle School
Aurora
Grade 7

Nothing to Do

Some days there's nothing to do
No one to talk to
No one to listen to me
No one to keep my company
No one to have fun with
No one to play with
No one to go to the mall with
No one to go with to a show
No one to eat lunch with
Just some days you have nothing to do
So I do what I do best
Lay down on the cozy couch, with a big bowl of popcorn
All crumpled in a blanket
And watch a movie

Peter Opalacz
St George School
Tinley Park
Grade 8

Sam

If only they knew how hard it was for me
I'm becoming an adult and the world I begin to see.
It is so different from the one I once saw
Changes are all around me they all seem to fall.

My friends have all changed right before my eyes.
They speak a different language and tell all sorts of lies.
Some laugh at me and some even make me cry,
But one sticks beside me she never says goodbye.

We're the same in every way right down to the very last thought.
She always knows what to say it all comes from her heart.
She is my gift from the man in the sky
I know our friendship will never die.

Jessica Harl
Hardin County Jr High School
Elizabethtown
Grade 8

A Mother's Wish

A mother's wish is for her children to grow strong
Strong enough to need her, strong enough not to
A mother's wish is for her children to grow up and have a family
A family of loving parents and wonderful children
A mother's wish is to see her grandchildren as much as she can
And to spoil them rotten
A mother's wish is for her children to be smart
Smart in the way of love, smart in the way of life
A mother's wish is for her children to be kind
Kind and respectful
Kind to all they come in contact with
As much as possible
Kind enough to walk away from trouble
Respectful to everything and anything
Even if not showing respect
To know when to go and to know when to come
A mother's wish is for her children to love her
A mother's wish is for her to be the best mother possible
Guess what
My mother's wish came true

Whitney Syverson
Still Middle School
Aurora
Grade 7

Piano Pauses

The big day finally came
I've been waiting for months,
Practicing every day
I knew it by heart.

Now here I am
Sitting on the back row,
Waiting to go up
And play my song in front of 100 people.

It's my turn now
And I walk up to the stage,
Adjust the bench, then sit down
Take a deep breath and put my fingers on the keys.

I start the piece
Softer and gradually getting louder,
I'm halfway done, almost there
And I end the piece beautifully.

I stand up and let the crowd applaud
I walk back to my seat and sit down,
My friends tell me how good I did
Even though I did mess up a couple of times,
But nobody's perfect...we all mess up sometimes.

Jessica Hoffman
Stratford Jr High School
Bloomingdale
Grade 8

Red, White and Blue

Our flag is red, white, and blue
and this is all so true.
We love it here,
here comes a tear.
Our flag is red, white, and blue.

Josh Pate
Beckemeyer Elementary School
Beckemeyer
Grade 7

The Scar

When we were young,
We had fun,
Climbing up a patriarchal tree.
One day the branch snapped,
To the ground I collapsed,
Landing vigorously on my knee.

A scar on my skin.

As the years passed,
We grew close,
Promising to stay together till the end.
Until one day I found,
You were nowhere around,
You had dumped me for another friend.

A scar on my heart.

When we grew older,
You went astray,
And partied until dawn.
You drove from the bar,
And crashed into my car,
In a second my life was gone.

A scar on my life.

Molly Maloy
St Matthew School
Champaign
Grade 7

Dream

I see you in my dream.
I wait for you,
that place I wish to be.
When I, with you, see that world I love.
Of dream, I long to be.
For I'd love to get away from this cold
world of consciousness,
and leave this abstract place.

Brent Don
Pope John XXIII School
Evanston
Grade 8

Toad Heaven?

Two toads were hopping in my yard;
They saw my big inviting pool,
Without me watching as lifeguard
It looked like a glimmering jewel.

Up the deck they took a hop
Across the wood; splat, splat, splat.
Down they jumped, they could not stop,
Into the water just like that.

Soothing, smooth, wet, and clear water,
Toads floating in heaven no doubt.
Zach was feeling so much hotter,
In he jumped, two toads flew out.

Along mowed Dad cutting the grass
Not seeing the toads on the ground.
He did not miss a single pass,
The mower made a horrible sound.

Anne Osterholz
Nativity of B V M School
East Dubuque
Grade 7

In the Air

Looking at the rocks,
the rolling rocks,

The danger,
in the air

Falling, falling,
to the ground,

Rip the cord,
fast,

How dangerous
it is

Be careful,
don't hit the mountain,

For see
The rolling rocks

Don't let one
hit you on your head

How dangerous it is
in the air

Rebecca Dyas
Tri-City Jr-Sr High School
Buffalo
Grade 7

Frogs

F avorite amphibians
R ed eyed tree frog
O h, so unique
G reen in color
S limy little creatures

Amber Caswell
Beckemeyer Elementary School
Beckemeyer
Grade 7

Colors

I love colors.
Bright ones, dark ones, any color.
Colors bring life to any object,
they make anything stand out.

My favorite color is yellow.
It is very bright and sunny.
Every time I see it I feel cheerful.
It brightens my day!

Without colors our lives would be dull.
All we would have is black and white.
Those are no fun!
Colors make up our world!!

Molly Dunne
Queen of Martyrs School
Chicago
Grade 8

Cannot

I wake up in the morning,
To hear the birds sing.
Even though, I cannot hear them.

After my mother cooks me breakfast,
Even though, I cannot smell it.

Later, I have a delicious sandwich,
Even though, I cannot taste it.

In the evening,
I lay on the silky grass.
Even though, I cannot feel it.

At night, I say good night to my mother.
Even though, I cannot see her.

Even though, I do not have any senses.
I'm me and always will be.

Danny Cacho
Taylor Elementary School
Chicago
Grade 8

Fate

Devoted to him for seven long years,
Divulging this conceit to only one —
But that one told others — her greatest fears.
She worried, could he have been told by some?
Her love unrevealed would become news too.
Forever told, the bittersweet treasure,
She-shattered, he-hiding, trouble for two.
Why does He do this — the Lord Creator?

He did know, she knew, everyone knew too —
But there it was lying softly — the rose.
Bright red on a background. It read, "For you."
Her face — smiling and colored a rose
"I loved you more than you ever knew —
Unreturned love — distraught without you."

Natasha Krol
Fenwick High School
Oak Park
Grade 9

The Sea

Walking along the white sandy beach,
with the sun bursting down like a ripe juicy peach.
Children playing in the sand,
leaving prints of their hands.
Seagulls come swooping to the ground,
while the huge salty waves are rolling around.
So peaceful and relaxing is the sea,
this is the place where I'd like to be.

Courtney Thoele
Beckemeyer Elementary School
Beckemeyer
Grade 7

Little Brother

There he is, my little brother,
Banging his toys on the bed,
While he's giving me a big pain in my head.
He has this habit of rolling small pieces of toilet paper together,
And then letting them fly away like a feather.
My brother also has this habit of watching this show,
Called Fox Kids and laziness.
I also forgot that his favorite hobby,
Is watching wrestling,
Every time it's on,
He's an angel.
But on commercials he acts,
Like Gangreal (wrestler.)
Sometimes I wish,
Wrestling was on all the time,
Just without commercials!

Stephanie Guizar
St Procopius School
Chicago
Grade 7

This Blood Is for You

They gathered in the upper room,
for 'twas the time of unleavened bread.
Jesus took the bread and broke it,
then He took the cup and said,
"This is my blood of the new covenant,
in remembrance of me this shall you do.
When you partake tonight of these things,
remember, this blood is for you."

He carried His cross to Golgotha.
He was beaten and whipped through and through.
Christ stumbled and His blood fell on the feet of Simon,
and as he bent to wipe his shoe,
Simon looked in the eyes of that spotless lamb as He said,
"This blood is for you."

Christ suffered and died for your sins and mine,
so we can be with Him in heaven some day.
Still need convincing?
Don't know what to say?
You need a fact or two?
Just remember salvation is totally free,
and Christ's blood was shed for you.

Dessa Mae Guyer
Hutsonville High School
Hutsonville
Grade 9

A Golden Road

Well, child, I'll tell you
Life for me hasn't been a golden road
It's had potholes
And roadblocks and detours
Sometime it's slippery
Sometimes my car goes off the road
But I always get back on
Sometime I reach rest stops
But not the final destinations
Sometimes there's a washed out bridge
Sometimes it's too dark to see
Sometimes I get caught in traffic
But I keep on pushing
I keep on going
Sometimes I get a flat tire
Or bad oil
Or engine trouble
But I always get it fixed up
And keep on going
Even when the going's tough
Because life for me hasn't been a golden road

Jonathan Wolf
Stratford Jr High School
Bloomingdale
Grade 8

Thank You

For sunshine warm and kind,
For flowers that I find,
For pretty stones lying around,
And for birds that sing,
For the trees so tall
Making a home to all,
For the cool, refreshing water,
And for the friends
I talk, laugh, and learn with,
I thank You, Lord.

Meaghan Brady
St Mary's of Kickapoo School
Edwards
Grade 8

Sun

The sun is like a giant orange
That brightens up your day,
And warms your weary heart
As you travel along your way

Your journey may be a long one
As you drift and roam.
But remember how good it feels
When you finally make it home.

Larry Ketterman
Parkview Jr High School
Lawrenceville
Grade 7

I Went on a Journey

I went on a journey,
to places far away
I went to different planets,
a different one each day
I went to Venus,
I went to Mars
I went to many planets,
and ended at the stars

Tiffany Robertson
Pleasant Hill Elementary School
Peoria
Grade 8

I Wonder

This may be a poem about songs.
This may be a song about poems.
If this was a poem about songs
Would I have to sing the poem?
If I have to sing my poem about songs
Would that make it a song about poems?
I wonder.

Matt Konow
St George School
Tinley Park
Grade 8

To Play and Win—Isn't That the Dream

Basketball is the best sport ever—to play it you have to be rather clever
Basketball is so much fun—I could play it 'till the day is done
But basketball is harder than you expect—you have to give everyone the proper respect
Did you do your best—did you pass the test
The day is done—but have you won
Basketball is a competitive sport—you have to be of the tough sort
Are you going to win—how much are you willing to put in
Will you practice hard and play tough—it's a fact the games will get rough
The refs will pick their favorite team—everyone will holler and scream
These are just obstacles to your dream
Coaches will tell you what to do—but it's up to you
Will you listen—will you hear—or would you rather be on the bench to cheer
We all know some refs are blind—but you won't change their mind
So no matter what—keep your mouth shut
Dive and fall for a loose ball—be willing to do anything—even slam into a wall
Keep playing your game—don't try to find someone to blame
Always do your best—hopefully you'll pass the test
Be prepared and practice the same—as if it was a real game
Play with teamwork and sportsmanship—and have a nice trip
To your dream

Talisa Franciscovich
Visitation School
Kewanee
Grade 8

The Power of Words

Words can scare, hurt, and kill you.
Words can captivate and entice you.
Words can describe you.
Words can heal you.
Words can reflect upon you.
Words can ruin your job.
Words can hurt your feelings.
Words can make you laugh or cry.
Words can make you successful.
Words can make you feel smart or stupid.
Words can make you happy or angry.

Words can make you do things you don't want to do.
Words can make you do a lot of things that we don't even realize.
Words are powerful things that make up each and every day.

You see, the choice is up to you.
Choose your words carefully,
You never know what they may do to someone.

You can take back toys.
You can take back dolls.
You can take back books.

You can *never* take back the words you speak.

Penina Sharp
Hanna Sacks Girls High School
Chicago
Grade 9

The Day it Rained Cats and Dogs

I'll never forget that day,
It was wet and rainy in mid-May.
There was pounding on my roof,
And the only noise I heard was, "WOOF!"
I rose when I heard the clatter,
And went to see what was the matter.
To my surprise, what did I see?
"It's my dog, Sparky!"
They hit the ground like wooden logs.
Why, it was raining cats and dogs!
Just when I dreaded, "We'd soon be dead!"
A light bulb went on in my head.
I raced to the house,
And, as quiet as a mouse,
I grabbed the 4th of July rockets,
Tied them to some tasty treats, and stuffed them in my pockets.
I shot them upward, very high,
As the animals chased their treats into the sky.
I had saved the town in time for lunch,
And everyone was as pleased as punch!

Hannah Hines
Sacred Heart School
Lombard
Grade 7

The Man in the Glass

You're judged every day
In every which way
You may pass every test
But does that make you best?

For there is a man, a Man in the Glass
His inspection is the one that you must pass
He'll tell you the truth, he'll never lie
He's like your best friend, but he'll never die

Everyone says what a great person you are and will be
But is there more of you for them to see?
Your friends may tell you what a grand person you are
Leave the door to your soul open ajar

The Man in the Glass decides who is the best
He is the one that gives the most difficult test
He can be your friend, your fellow, or foe
But what secrets of yours does he know?

So you're the perfect, smart, and innocent kid
Don't lie to yourself! You know the bad things that you did
Get on the good side of the Man in the Glass
That's the only way you'll really get to the head of the class

Amelia Kusar
Oliver McCracken Middle School
Skokie
Grade 8

Sleep

After day and all through night,
And when the world slips out of sight,
Into a dream all tucked inside
My head so clear it never died.
I know it well, indeed I do;
And when I see it, it's always new.
And in this time that I don't make a peep,
I slip into a thing called sleep.

Casey Orr
Cisne Middle School
Cisne
Grade 8

Mom's Song

In little words I can't express
The beauty of my happiness
To others you are a woman full of wisdom
To me you're the woman with charisma
I love you with all my heart
And because of you I was born smart
You've shown me how to love and care
That is why I'll always be there
Moms all around the world
Deserve a star pulled from the sky
Because on them their children can rely
So mom I want you to know
How much you've helped me grow
Into a lovely young lady
Who is still crazy to be called your baby!

Allyson Reboyras
St Ferdinand School
Chicago
Grade 8

The Masquerade

You are the focus of curious stares,
Your mystery intrigues the minds of all.
Everyone admires you but no one really cares,
Atop that pedestal; you're bound to fall
For when your mysteries come to light,
As your power begins to fade away,
You dread the day with yourself you will fight,
Because of your actions of yesterday.

Your thoughts once hidden, now are seen clearly,
By revealing yourself you show weakness
Resist the urge of popularity
Who knows the way you are beaming with kindness,
Who was your first true friend, who was always there,
Still, here I am, the one who always cared.

Christie LaMountain
Fenwick High School
Oak Park
Grade 9

Holidays Are...

Holidays are a time for sharing
And also a time for caring.
Like many people say
"You should be merry on these days."
It is a time when the whole family is around
And that is like we are forever bound.
Everybody is filled with joy
Just like a child who got a new toy.
Holidays are the best time of year
And on these days there is nothing to fear.

Sam Sebastian
Stratford Jr High School
Bloomingdale
Grade 8

The Song of Life

The song of life is something we all must face
The hurdles, the triumph and all the disgrace
The lyrics are special and always touch your heart
And as soon as you feel like your world will fall apart
The song is there to soothe your pain
And keep you sane in the heavy rain
So when you hear the sweet birds sing
Don't get mad and holler and scream
But thank the Lord you saw that sight
Because you've just witnessed the song of life

Semaja Haney
St George School
Tinley Park
Grade 7

Bright Shining Star

Be like a star that shines on me
Guide me through all the snares the day might call
Near or far, be the one to catch me when I fall
Because you are there for me
You always care for me
You will guide me through it all

Let me show you just how much you mean to me
Let me tell you how wonderful you really are
You let me see the beauty of everything
And you take me higher than I've ever been
You are the light of my day
You see me every step of the way
From the heavens like a bright shining star

Sylvie Rollason-Cass
St Joseph Catholic School
Harvard
Grade 8

I Play Music

When I'm alone
I can show my emotions.
I can express my feelings without words,
I just play music.
I forget my problems
and escape from my life.
I can show my anger
without using violence,
instead I play music.
I've got one thing that drug addicts don't,
they say when they're stoned they get away from their problems,
but when they aren't their problems are still there.
Well I've got it better than them,
I can escape my life without being high
and without creating more problems,
it's easy, I play music.

Matt Fries
St Paul School
Danville
Grade 8

A Sonnet of Rainbows

A rainbow shines through a prism of light
Colors to candy from a color wheel
All of the stars shine bright through the midnight
You want to taste it, but you'd rather feel
Colors of red, orange, yellow, green and blue
All of the colors unite and form one
And the sky turns to the colors of you
Your face is a smile that can't be undone
The rain starts to pour like a thunderstorm
The rain turns to skittles then to showers
As a pot of gold comes and then reforms
The rain's ending, and it's full of flowers
And when there's sun and rain there's a rainbow
When you see rainbows in colors they glow.

Ashley Cole
Sullivan High School
Sullivan
Grade 9

The Storm

BOOM BANG a flash of light
A raging storm in the night
See the lightning, hear the thunder,
There's no table to hide under.
The windows creak, the trees sway
And everything gets blown away.
A torrential downpour in the dark
Things washed away just like the Ark
Then comes a clearing in the sky
The sun comes out and starts to dry.
For damage the storm is the one to blame,
But soon things will be just the same.

Andrea Meade
St Gerald School
Oak Lawn
Grade 8

Changing of the Seasons

When winter begins
People shiver with a chill
"Let's have some hot cocoa
And scope out the best hill."

Snow is falling outside
To me this is not a surprise
"I'm waiting and waiting,"
For the sun to rise

For when the sun rises
All of the snow will melt away
Making me happy for,
"No more cold and dreary days!"

But when winter is over
People will cry, "There will be no more sled rides."
The sleighs will be put away
And people will take long walks outside

Summer is coming
For me it will be so much fun
For all the children around
To laugh, play, and run in the sun.

Anna O'Neill
Visitation School
Kewanee
Grade 8

Friendship and Movies

I am an appropriate friend and thespian.
I wonder if there is the perfect acting career.
I hear friends chattering to me.
I see me at a movie premiere.
I want my friends to stay close.
I am an appropriate friend and thespian.

I pretend to be in a movie in front of the camera.
I feel my friends' emotions when needed.
I reach for that movie opportunity.
I worry that I will be a failure.
I cry when I say goodbye to all my friends for the last time.
I am an appropriate friend and thespian.

I understand that I will be rejected.
I say, you scratch my back and I'll scratch yours.
I dream that I will walk on that red carpet.
I try to be the greatest friend and actor there could be.
I hope my career and my friends stay close.
I am an appropriate friend and thespian.

Justin Austin
Francis Granger Middle School
Aurora
Grade 7

Hockey

Hockey is my favorite sport,
On Saturdays, I play it on the court,
Always trying to go real fast,
Most of the time it is a blast,

I glaze across the floor with speed,
Trying to keep the puck with me,
Of course we all try to get the goal we need,
Our goalie is a great asset and his name is Reed,

Speeding down the court so fast,
Keeping the opponents in last,
Fighting for the hockey puck,
Hoping to get it with all my luck.

Jeremy Stock
Beckemeyer Elementary School
Beckemeyer
Grade 7

Nature

The wind blows through the leaves,
They roll across the ground.
The wind stops.
It is as still as can be.
Then it starts back up again, blowing through the sky.
The sweet smell of water drifts through the air
As the tides come in
And washes everything away.
And the birds gather around the water to feed.
The fish swim under the tide to seek what is up above.
The clouds fly in the sky
And the sun peers down on the land.

Raechal Cunningham
Jonesboro Elementary School
Jonesboro
Grade 7

Nothing at All

When you look in the mirror and see me
You wonder who you will turn out to be
You try to talk, but nothing comes out
All you see is a blank stare and empty pout.
What is going on with you inside?
The soul in you is trying to hide
The other side of the mirror sees the same thing
Just a plain old girl with nothing to bring
To give into the world, nothing at all
Just a little girl that you pass in the hall
Do you remember what it used to be like
To be seen alone? It felt like a cutting knife.

Andrea Kaplan
North Park Elementary School
Chicago
Grade 7

Candy

Sweet smells fill the air,
For the candy is so near.
Kids run in delight.

Jon Henry
River Trails Middle School
Mount Prospect
Grade 7

Break a Leg

Friend gets the lead role of the play
Opening night comes
Break a leg I exclaim
Smiles and waves back at me
THUNK!
CRACK!
OUCH!
She tripped over the prop ladder
Actually broke her leg
Director shoves me onto the stage
Silence
Eyes staring
Laughs
Embarrassment
Ring, Ring, Ring
Woke up!

Christina Zessemos
Sacred Heart School
Lombard
Grade 7

Dr. Seuss

There is a guy named Dr. Seuss.
He lives in book land with a moose.
He makes a bunch of silly books.
One story includes a fat goose.

He has too many books that rhyme.
He also has books that tell time.
In some of his books he has cooks.
He has books with people that climb.

He has a book on Sam-I-Am.
Who does not like green eggs and ham.
He has fish books with colored hooks.
And he won't eat them with a lamb.

All of his books are pretty neat.
His books are sold on many streets.
Oh, how I love to read his books.
Oh, how I love to read his books.

Ashley Hayes
Beckemeyer Elementary School
Beckemeyer
Grade 7

Old Man

Dreaming back to the day
When he went out to play,
And children respected their elders.
The people united,
And summer fireworks were lighted,
On a merry fourth of July.

But most of all, one thing he misses,
To be able to bite an apple he wishes,
For that red fruit he yearns.
His gums cannot tear it,
With his dentures he won't dare it,
He must find another way.

So he dreams of the crunch,
Of the fruit he loved to munch,
Remembering his mother's admonition.
"Of your teeth take good care,
So they'll always be there,
When you're old, you'll never regret it."

Jamie Ward
Pope John XXIII School
Evanston
Grade 8

I Love You

When I look in your eyes
I know it's true,
My heart never lies
I'm in love with you.

As you stood there
Just looking around,
My whole body melted
Into the ground.

I remember the day
I remember the time,
I remember the place
You are always on my mind.

You look so hot
In your shirt and jeans,
I see you every night
You are in my dreams.

I wish I could be with you
Every second of the day,
'Cause I love you so much more
Than words can say.

Veronica Windom
Lombard Jr High School
Galesburg
Grade 7

Keep Your Eye on the Ball

Keep your eye on the ball
Swing strike one
Keep your eye on the ball
Swing strike two
Keep your eye on the ball
Not that close — pow!
Keep your eye off the ball

Logan Greentree
Parkview Jr High School
Lawrenceville
Grade 7

Spring

As the trees get leaves
As the tulips are blooming
It has become spring

Tessa Aiossa
Highland Middle School
Libertyville
Grade 7

Dreams

I walked through a forest
Where everything was red.
Not a blood red,
But the red of passion.
There were hearts,
And the smell was unique,
Kind of sweet.
It was like paradise.

I felt I belonged there.
Then I opened my eyes
And I was back to the real world.

Karen Morales
Logandale Middle School
Chicago
Grade 7

The Real Me

I ask of you a little task
To give me strength to take off my mask
I need the world to see the real me.
I need you to give me some time though
I know I should show the world
Who I really am.
But when I think about it,
I wish it weren't so hard.
But I guess I should discover me first,
Then when I'm done I'll show you.

Ishally Vera
St Ferdinand School
Chicago
Grade 8

Dreams

Is there such a thing
As dreams coming true?
Some say no, yet some say yes.
They'll come true if you try your best.

Never let people get you down;
You'll find out you'll be the one to frown.
Follow your dreams and believe in you,
You'll see your life has changed into something new.

Accent the positives;
Eliminate the negatives.
Let people bring your self-esteem up.
Let compliments fill your cup.

Do you answer no or yes?
If you say no, your life will be a mess.
Follow your dreams; you'll be in good health,
If you don't believe me, find out for yourself.

Jennafer Kinney
Quincy Jr High School
Quincy
Grade 8

The Cat

Long and velvety
Sleek and slim
Wild and dark
It moves around
Quieter than the mouse
That isn't there any more
Because *it* was there first.

Leela Laxpati
North Park Elementary School
Chicago
Grade 7

The Holocaust

This world we live in may be rough
With the people beside us who **H**ave to be tough
The screams, the yells **O**n holocaust day
Running and bombing, come what may
The innocent mother who bore her chi**L**d
Will have t**O** act calm, as the bodies they pile
We hide **C**linged, under the bed
Afraid that the Devil will find us inste**A**d
The taking of children, the smells of the b**U**rn
A normal life I long to yearn
A normal life I **S**eek and find
And a way to leave **T**his world behind...

Jared Yates
St Paul School
Danville
Grade 7

Born Again

Rising like a ball of fire,
You warm us and light up the sky,
Like a candle in the dark.
Floating high as the clouds,
Your rays, like slender arms, reach down
And awaken the flowers.
They greet you.
The dew is done and gone.
We wake to go to school and work.

Your journey moves you along
To your place in the center of the sky.
You watch over us like an angel, high above.

As you slowly descend,
We gather back
In the warmth of our homes.

Then slowly you disappear
Into the night
As darkness consumes you.
She turns the world black and cold.
At day's end you sleep
Waiting to be born again.

Victoria Lewis
Blessed Sacrament School
Belleville
Grade 8

My Mother

She is a rose waiting to bloom,
A young flower flourishing in June.

Her eyes sparkle in the sun,
Her angelic rapture just wants to have fun.

She challenges our minds,
Into mystical wonders of all kinds.

Her power is obvious to all.
She knows when we're hurting,
She knows when we fall.

She secretly shows us the way,
She teaches us what we should do,
And what we should say.

She makes her way in the world,
With our everlasting love,
And the Spirit from up above.

Amanda Goetz
St Michael School
Orland Park
Grade 8

Jesus

Jesus,
Witness the shepherds gazing upon him,
Witness the kings offering gifts,
Witness the mother acclaiming the Lord,
Witness him sleeping in the manger,
Hear the angels singing for joy,

Jesus,
Watch the nine tails scar his back,
Watch the thorns pierce the skull,
Watch the soldiers pound three nails,
Watch him cry out in pain,
Hear him forgiving with love for all.

Andy Hackley
St Matthew School
Champaign
Grade 8

Spot

I have a dog named Spot.
Who has a black dot.

He once chewed up my shoe.
And drank all the Mountain Dew.

Spot chews stuff all the time.
He once even ate a lime.

Luz Valdovinos
St Mary of Czestochowa School
Cicero
Grade 7

Darling

Hello my darling
I'm doing okay
Wish you were here
But you are away

Hello my darling
I'm doing just fine
Say hi to your father
I'll see you in time

Hello my darling
I'm doing all right
You're 77
You put up a good fight

Hello my darling
I miss your lovin'
Say hi to my friends
How is it in Heaven?

Kelsey Michelle Polson
Quincy Jr High School
Quincy
Grade 8

I'm Forgotten

It is 8:30 in the morning, and I'm feeling extremely glad.
This is the weekend I get to spend with my dad.

I told the court I loved him, and they believed me so.
That's why on some weekends I gladly get to go.

I just looked at my watch and it's a little after ten.
You forgot to pick me up again, where oh where, have you been?

If you do not want me, then have the guts to tell me so.
My little OLE heart has been broken many times before, you know.

If mom didn't want me, what a mess I would be in.
I'd end up in some orphan's home, I guess I cannot win.

But mom *does* want me, and my grandparents too.
I still have someone to love me, I'm certainly not so blue.

Any man can father a child,
From an old man to a lad.

It takes one special man,
To be a loving and caring dad.

Christina Robertson
Illini Central Middle School
Easton
Grade 7

Bonnie

The best kind of friendships are the lasting, warm and wonderful kind,
That you and I have always shared.
Friendships like ours are the kind where the caring never goes away.
The understanding is deep, sweet, and sincere.
And the two friends are so near in their hearts, that they'll stay close forever.

I really cherish having you as a friend.
You're the best kind there is.
And it's a privilege to know you as well as I do.
But there's something more I need to tell you:
You and I have a trust, an honesty,
And a whole history together that makes me think of you so much more than a friend.

You're someone who is at the center of the circle of my life.
Someone essential to me.
And I know you'll always stay that way.
Because when a friend is as close as you are, they're just like family.
I can barely even begin to tell you how much you touch my soul,
Raise my hopes, and inspire my smiles.
Maybe the best way to convey it is to lovingly try and say
That you've always been, and always will be,
Just like a sister to me.

Emily Johnston
Clifford Crone Middle School
Naperville
Grade 7

Wine

Well there's Zinfandel, Champagne, and Merlot
Each one of these will make you feel very good.
It could even make you unwillingly propose or it
could make you eat a tire or have a lot of fun but
unfortunately it is not for everybody. If it was, we
would feel a whole lot better, just like the Greeks
and the Romans. I hope it wasn't crushed with
                    stinky
                    feet
                    good
                    if you
                    are 21.
                    Well
                    it also
                    could
                    be if
                    you
                    are not.
Wine is the food or drink of the gods.
And many other people throughout the
world. Wine is the key to all the parties!
            Or not

Robert E. Haney
River Trail Middle School
Mount Prospect
Grade 7

The Life of Little Leon

When Leon was a little boy,
he was only given one small toy.
He played with his toy for days on end,
with no one to talk to, not one friend.

When Leon started school,
everyone thought he was a bit odd, not cool.
Because of his height, he was called Little Leon.
Little Leon was made fun of because he wore neon.

Little Leon sat by himself at lunch,
and at recess and didn't hang out with the cool bunch.
Leon's nose was too big for his face,
he was clumsy and he had no grace.

But one day Little Leon grew,
and he was no longer three foot two.
Little Leon's nose now fit his face,
and he was no longer a disgrace.

Little Leon is no longer taunted and teased,
He has good self esteem and is very pleased.

Erin Delaney
Queen of Martyrs School
Chicago
Grade 8

Winter

I love the winter
Even the fierce wind that's bitter.
It whips at your face
At what seems like haste
To give the Earth its blanket
That dazzles and sparkles like trinkets.
The trees are beautiful, outlined in white.
My, they're a pretty sight!
You can smell a crisp freshness in the air.
The snow has washed it, like you wash your hair.
All in all, winter's fun
Because it's the season, that's number one.

Stephanie Brooke
Harrison Elementary School
Wonder Lake
Grade 7

Grandmother

I love my grandmother; she's the best.
She's very different from all the rest.

She doesn't act like my grandma, but like a friend.
She's always there to give me a hand.

I love my grandmother; I love her very much.
Nothing and nobody can part us.

She's the only one, and there's no other
Who can take the place of
        My
            Grandmother.

Latariah Little
Thomas J Kellar Middle School
Robbins
Grade 7

Confused

Every time I look into my dad's eye
I see many bad memories
Then I start to think about them
Sometimes I get sad
So I turn around and look at him
He turns around and looks at me back with a smile
I look into his eyes once more
That is when I start to see many good memories
I start to think again
I begin to feel happy and smile back
This is what causes my confusion
But he always tells me he loves me
So that changes everything.

Christian Chazaro
Children of Peace-St Callistus School
Chicago
Grade 7

Antz

They don't even give you a chance.
They just run straight up your pants!
Then you do the funniest dance!

Ryan Taylor
St John The Baptist School
West Frankfort
Grade 7

Peace/War

Peace
Nonviolent, neighborly
Admiring, accommodating, calming
Harmony among the people
Troubling, disturbing, attacking
Hostile, angry
War

Jenny Schwartz
Holy Angels School
Aurora
Grade 7

I Hope I'll Never Say Good-bye

As we graduate,
Our great 8 years come to an end.
We say good-bye to many people,
but you my friend,
I hope I'll never say good-bye to.
You have been there for me,
and I have been there for you,
through thick and thin,
we stuck together like glue.
Although in high school we may part,
you my friend will stay in my heart.
As we grow older,
our friendship may grow colder,
but to even think of losing you,
I don't know what I'd ever do.
I want you to know,
I'm just a phone call away,
so don't hesitate to dial my number,
or even come my way.

Julie Crinion
St George School
Tinley Park
Grade 8

The Airplane

Up and down the airplane goes.
Twisting and turning as it flows.
Flying and flying,
Look at it go.
With power and speed the airplane goes.

Frances Ward
St Michael School
Orland Park
Grade 7

Rain

I love the way rain cries;
When rain falls, I feel like it is reaching down to kiss me;
When I look out my window, I will see the rain dancing in puddles;
When I walk down the sidewalk, I feel like the rain is chasing me.

Brittany Weiser
Holy Cross Lutheran School
Collinsville
Grade 7

Day

The grass so green, the sky so blue
The sparkling sun, the cold wet dew

The outdoor smell, the sight of clouds
The feel of rain, the thunder so loud

The splish splash of puddles, the water jumping so high
The amazing place of nature, then you think and sigh

The world is so wonderful, everywhere you go
The world is so beautiful, everyone should know

The sparkle in your eyes, when you smell a rose
The shimmer of your smile, the feel of grass on your toes

The way the colors are so bright, the way you love this wonderful place
The way the world's full of light, the feeling you'll admit face to face

The grass so green...
The sky so blue...

Annie Rohrhoff
Clifford Crone Middle School
Naperville
Grade 7

Feelings

I know that feeling, that happy feeling of being way up high.
I know that feeling, that joyous feeling of flying in the sky.
I know that feeling, that longing feeling of wanting to be free.
I know that feeling, that hopeful feeling of getting to be me.
I know that feeling, that confused feeling not knowing what's happening.
I know that feeling, that lonely feeling of having no friends at all.
I know that feeling, that dreamy feeling of singing lullabies.
I know that feeling, that wondrous feeling of being on the top.
I know that feeling, that doldrum feeling of being really bored.
I know that feeling, that frightened feeling of staying awake at night.
I know that feeling, that emotional feeling of mourning someone's death.
I know that feeling, that guilty feeling of knowing I did wrong.
I know that feeling, that innocent feeling of knowing what I did not do.
I know that feeling, that anxious feeling of where I get to go.
I have feelings!!

Brittanie Wilczak
Hamlin Upper Grade Center
Alsip
Grade 7

A True Friend

A true friend is someone kind
Someone with a great mind
A true friend will always care
Someone who will always share
A true friend won't betray
Someone who will be there every day
A true friend won't talk bad
Someone who will be there when you're mad
A true friend will always know
Someone who won't keep you low
A true friend is someone true
Someone just like you!

Laura Aguilera
St Mary of Czestochowa School
Cicero
Grade 8

My Little Man

Little boy with eyes of blue,
how come I love you like I do?
I love to watch your little eyes close,
and marvel at your tiny nose.
The things you say and the things you do,
remind me that you're not brand new.

Now you're a bigger boy,
the source of all my pride and joy.
Someday, oh yes, you'll be a man,
and I will be your biggest fan.
But, for now I'll hold you close to me,
and treasure every memory.

And when you're old and I am too,
you'll know how much that I love you.

Bridget Blake
Nathan Hale Middle School
Crestwood
Grade 7

Springtime

Springtime is a time
When dragonflies and butterflies
Come out to fly so very high.
Kids come out to play
When their parents say
If they could play outside on any given day.
On the ground all around you hear
The sound of the birds getting rowdy
And seeing the clouds getting cloudy.
At this point, springtime has come to shine.

Benny Garcia
St Mary of Czestochowa School
Cicero
Grade 8

Summer Paradise

As the sun comes up one morning
Its booming rays spread across the land
Enticing the world with a feeling of hope
Which is difficult to understand

The gentle waves of the ocean
Flow steadily onto the beach
Like a child leaning over the edge of his crib
For a toy he cannot reach

The ocean seems to stretch forever
For a man can see no trace
Of what may lie beyond our sight
Is a distant and mystical place

Lying down on a velvet towel
The light softly hits the sea
While listening to the seagulls sing
And the ocean play its symphony

As the summer day comes to an end
The sun comes melting down
And forms a breathtaking canvas of colors
From the heavens to the distant ground

Ryan Bittle
Jonesboro Elementary School
Jonesboro
Grade 8

The Sky Is an Amazing Thing

The sky is an amazing thing you know
Sometimes it rains sometimes it snows
Sometimes it's dark sometimes it's light
Sometimes it can give you such a fright
With lightning that crackles and thunder that roars

The sky is an amazing thing you know
The sun and rain helps make things grow
When it snows that's okay too
It lets me get an extra day off at school

The sky is an amazing thing you know
Sometimes after it rains and the sun shines down
A colorful rainbow comes out of the sky
And ends on the ground at night

After the sun goes down
Beautiful stars are all around
You never know what the sky is going to bring
That's why I think the sky is such an amazing thing

Jonathon Klostermann
Beckemeyer Elementary School
Beckemeyer
Grade 7

I Made a Wish

Last night I made a wish
upon my lucky star
I wished I could find you
or at least know where you are

We all have a special someone
at least that's what they say
In the sea of our being
we must find our own way

How do you want me
patient eyes or dark
Must I be really nice
or have a hardcore heart

You said to turn out another
then there must be love
Was there hatred between us
did push come to shove

The fear of feeling things
that may not be true
Feeling infinite affections
does that make you blue

How do you want me

Billie Meyer
Tri-City Jr-Sr High School
Buffalo
Grade 7

Like a Dream

Life is like a dream
Or so this it might seem

When you are born you sleep
And you die, only to awake

You live your dream to the fullest
Every moment in time
Is a moment cherished forever

Until you lie in your death bed
Not knowing whether you want to
Die or live

Do you realize what you live,
Is only a dream?
Because your body has died
But yet your soul is still alive

Taylor N. Richmond
Holy Angels School
Aurora
Grade 7

Listen, Look, and Feel...

Listen...
Can you hear the wind?
Whistling and screaming in the night...

Look and listen...
Can you hear the dogs?
Running and barking in the night...

Feel...
Can you feel the breeze?
Gently brushing against your face...

Just listen, look and feel...
And you shall feel the way
... I feel

Rhoda Faye Tomines
Trumbull Elementary School
Chicago
Grade 8

Shine

Light is a good thing
Beavers like it a whole lot
It is all around

Eric Wiberg
Holy Angels School
Aurora
Grade 7

Flower

Flower why do you
hide from the world?
Why don't you open
up and show your
majestic beauty to the world?
Tell your story to me and everyone
in the world?
Don't hide your secret forever!

Diane Montez
St Barbara School
Chicago
Grade 7

If I Were a Bird

If I were a bird
Soaring through the air
With the wind beneath my wings
Staring down at the treetops
I would drop down for a bite to eat
And rest for another flight

Griffin Gher
Parkview Jr High School
Lawrenceville
Grade 7

Flowers

Flowers are natural beauties
From their petals down to their toes
They hardly need any makeup
Just pollen to powder their nose

They nod as though to say hello
Whenever we pass them by
They charm us and disarm us
Just ask a passing butterfly

Silently in their loveliness
They have messages to impart
In the area of romance
Affairs of the heart

Even the tiniest daisy
Can often reveal a lot
If a certain someone loves you
Or if that someone loves you not

Most flowers greet the morning
By opening up to the light
Then at days end close their petals
Drawing their curtains for the night

Andrea Mlot
St Philip The Apostle School
Addison
Grade 8

For All Eternity

Love...
Is a book read.

Love...
Is a song heard.

Love...
Is a story told.

Love...
Is an emotion expressed.

Love...
Is a flame burning.

For all eternity,
Love has been,
And will,
Take on many aliases
That will shadow its true meaning.

Bridget Madden
Queen of Martyrs School
Chicago
Grade 8

The Moon

A pale white orb in the darkness hangs there.
I wish to meet that god of the cold night.
But he, a harsh god, rises and unfair.
To all who try to touch him, he does smite.
And ev'ry night on his high throne he schemes.
The silent, sleeping world at his command;
He mocks the mortals down below who dream.
Yet, lonely he sits, eyeing all the land.
His starry troops ascend his palace dark.
He leads his Legion on with expert skill.
And always victor'ous though is stark;
Nothing to fear but the morning lark's trill;
But his immortal enemy awakes,
This god takes command and a new day breaks.

Ruthanne Swanson
Washington Jr High School
Naperville
Grade 8

My Bed Is the Center of the Night Landscape

My bed is the center of the night landscape.
It is endless and dark as the possibilities of the shadows
and ancient indigo mysteries of the sleeping house.
Together the pillowed walkway that sleeps with the dark park
under the plumes and blankets of the stars
stand as guidance for night riders.
In the center is my bed
which has grown from the dark of the good night room
where only the soft lines of many blues becomes
that sea of tender sleep.
And there is nothing I want less
than that piercing yellow light.

Russell Perkins
Nichols Middle School
Evanston
Grade 8

Seasons

Fall, winter, summer, spring
These are the seasons that bring good things.
My favorite season of all
I would definitely have to say is fall.
Because my birthday is in November,
I hope you will always remember.
Summer is fun,
I get a lot done.
Winter is cool,
So bundle up, don't be a fool!
finally spring is here,
So stand up and cheer.

Dalina Adorno
St Gerald School
Oak Lawn
Grade 8

My Friend

My friend is different don't you see
she has a secret no one knows, no one except me
her skin it glows
at night when no one sees
she pretends to be a human
but it's a disguise
looking into her glowing eyes
she pretends to be like you and me,
but really, my friend's an alien you see!

Christina Moran
Pleasant Hill Elementary School
Peoria
Grade 8

Sister Forever

Out of everyone in the whole wide world
my sister, Shelly, is my best girl.
She's a very special person to me.
I'll tell you about her and then you'll see.
She's the sweetest and nicest person I know,
she never tries to steel the show.
Ever since she was 19 years old,
she's been independent and on her own.
To me she makes the most sense of all,
whenever I need her I only have to call.
She listens carefully to what I have to say.
Then she shows me the right way.
I've always cared and looked up to her.
As if I was told to know for sure,
that she is my sister here to stay.
We'll be together forever, she won't go away.

Kelli Newman
Smithton Elementary School
Smithton
Grade 8

Camp Wonderland

Such a great place, such a wonderful place
to camp out and to have fun! You meet new people
and swim in the lake while watching the fish go by.
There are many cabins, and great food to eat,
and beautiful flowers to smell.

When it's hot you jump in the pool to cool off
and to splash around. You have fun playing
basketball and volleyball and sailing in the boats.

When the day is over you sleep in the warm
and cozy beds, in your cabin and dream of what
you had fun doing that day.

Jennifer Makol
Mayer Elementary School
Chicago
Grade 7

I Like That Stuff

Souls are soothed by it
Hearts are smoothed by it
Music
I like that stuff

Kids gaze at it
Our ancestors are amazed at it
Television
I like that stuff

Stomachs are filled by it
Hoboes are thrilled by it
Food
I like that stuff

Many would die for it
Hopefuls try for it
Baseball
I like that stuff

Rachel Gurley
Jonesboro Elementary School
Jonesboro
Grade 8

Flowers

Flowers are pretty
Don't you think?
They're purple, red, yellow
Green and a pretty pink.

There are lilies, and tulips
Roses and more!
There are so many flowers
Flowers galore!

They're in my yard, your yard
And his yard too
But if you're allergic to pollen,
Watchout!! A-CHOO!!!

Loren Laslie
Parkview Jr High School
Lawrenceville
Grade 7

A Mid-Summer Evening

The moon shines brightly.
The tiny stars twinkle dazzlingly.
The pleasant warm air,
And a gentle breeze.
The fireflies lighting up the night sky,
And the cicadas buzzing noisily.
All this on a mid-summer evening.

Harry Thompson
St Matthew School
Champaign
Grade 7

What Does He Need?

He is very lonesome. He has a nice job.
He is very smart and makes good choices.
He is only missing one thing.
He needs a wife to make his life perfect.
He tried to meet women different ways to meet the right one.
He just couldn't find the woman he was looking for.
He didn't give up trying to find the woman he was looking for.
Finally after waiting so long he found her.
He knew to keep trying because sometimes it is the only way to succeed.

Tyler Emlund
Finley Jr High School
Chicago Ridge
Grade 8

The Change

Our break-up was very dramatic;
It was torture having to live without you.
I thought it would be impossible;
You knew my dreams;
My dreams were your dreams.
You coped with my pain.
Your suffering was my misery.
Words were said, and tears were shed.
Friends you say!
I can't see you with another.
Nor can I stand here talking to you;
Knowing just a week ago we spoke the language of love.
When we were together I shared my most precious possessions with you.
Never did I think we would be no more.
I was your Baby;
You were my Boo.
Few people had that.
You say maybe in the future.
For me that's too much torture.
So let me save the agony.
I'll miss you.

Shauntia Evans
Hillcrest High School
Country Club Hills
Grade 9

I Look Outside

I look outside and all I see is hurt, pain, fighting, and killing.
For all these stupid reasons.
A man once said he had a dream.
A dream that one day people would be judged
not by the color of their skin but by the content of their character.
I also have that dream.
I dream that one day there will be no more racism or hate or killing,
but I look outside and I see that my dream,
our dream, is far from becoming reality.

Stephanie Ortiz
St Nicholas of Tolentine School
Chicago
Grade 7

Grandma

G reatest alive
R eliable
A lways right
N ever wrong
D ependable
M om's mom
A lways around

Danielle King
Beckemeyer Elementary School
Beckemeyer
Grade 7

Mark McGwire

Let me tell you about Mark McGwire.
When he hits the ball his eyes blaze like fire.
He is also known as Big Mac.
When the pitch comes in he gives the ball a big smack.
Mark McGwire is my hero.
In '98 he hit home run number 70.
He has more power than anyone can recall
by the distance that he slams the baseball.
He is sure to go into the Hall of Fame
for playing so well in many a game.

Jonathan Mueth
Smithton Elementary School
Smithton
Grade 8

Questions

I do not know why
Apples are green.
If they were peach,
Would they be as sweet?
I do not know why
Clouds are shaped the way they are
Like grizzly bears and dinosaurs.
I do not know why
The earth is round? If it were square,
Would it still spin round and round?
I do not know why
The sky is blue. If it were a different color
I would probably wonder about that too.
I do not know why
I wonder about so many things.
If I didn't wonder, life would be a mystery.
When I lay down on my pillow
Half asleep, I sit and think,
Does everyone wonder about the same things?
Or are they not like me
Living their life a mystery.

Chelsea Magnusen
Blessed Sacrament School
Belleville
Grade 7

Stars

I dream, I wish, I look, then wonder.
Who wished upon you and what they wished for?
Storing dreams, wishes, wants, and worries.

I dream, I wish, I look, then wonder.
You are like fireflies that won't stop glowing,
or like water that has never been touched.
Swoosh, swoop,
until something hits and the water sparkles.

I dream, I wish, I look, then wonder.
You are like a blanket filled with bright lights.
The brighter, the more I hope my dreams come true.
Dreams and wants everyone has.
They just hope or wish someone or something will listen.

I dream, I wish, I look, then wonder.
Will my dreams come true?
I'll wonder and sit still waiting, like I already do.

Lauren Fournie
Blessed Sacrament School
Belleville
Grade 8

An Unforgettable Journey*

The bus has stopped
Our trip is through
We say our farewells,
And go our separate ways.
Together we have been through it all,
The bumpy roads and the stormy days,
Not only the bad times but the good times too.

The journey has been difficult and full of challenges,
But together we have been through it all.
Together we laugh,
And together we cry.
Through this journey, we have been together,
Side by side,
Hand in hand.

Now the bus has stopped,
And we must go our separate ways.
Savor the memories,
And keep the good times close to you.

The bus has stopped; our trip is through.
I'll never forget you guys;
I'll remember you each and every one.

Valerie Haeger
St Colette School
Rolling Meadows
Grade 8
*To my eighth grade class.

Page 189

Outside My Window

When I look out my window,
I see a variety of things.
Children playing in the park,
Swinging on the swings.

People walking their dogs,
Or just passing through.
People running for their lives,
But running from who?

I see this place that should have peace,
But all I see is crime and fear.
I want this to change as soon as it can,
Today, tomorrow, but hopefully this year.

Please help me out,
This is not what I wish to see.
Take a stand against violence,
If not for you, do it for me.

Emily Grady
St Matthew School
Champaign
Grade 8

Final Seconds

The clock is ticking down from ten.
It's tied at fifty each.
The other team now has the ball.
Far from my team's reach

10....9....8....

We go into our defensive stance,
There isn't any time to wait.
Our team now has stolen the ball.
This could take us to state.

7....6....5....4....

We have scored with four seconds to go.
The other team just need two more.
They bring it down. We have to press!
Just don't let them score!

3....2....1....0....

In desperation they throw up a 3.
Right as the buzzer sounds.
The whole room freezes and stares at the ball.
It's off! Our victory resounds!

Bethany Sullivan
St Matthew School
Champaign
Grade 7

My Room

In my room I can be whatever I wish,
superman, an airplane, or even a fish.

I can imagine that I can jump over a sea,
and maybe, be as quick as a bee.

I could pretend I am floating in space,
and during this time, see an alien in a race.

But I know, for in my room I can be,
a kid playing happily.

Michael Minor
St Irene School
Warrenville
Grade 7

My Crazy Friend

My best friend is like a firecracker about to pop.
He loves to jump around and have a good time,
but also knows when to stop.
Our friendship will always last like the great redwood trees,
there's no limit to its massive height.
Conflicts come and go like the running water of the stream,
through the palisades of pine trees.
We stick together like glue; once we're together it's like
a massive fireworks display, very loud and crazy and fun.
Whenever I'm feeling low he'll comfort me like the comforting
sound of the wind through the trees.

David Baczewski
St George School
Tinley Park
Grade 7

Confusion

Where do you turn when there's nowhere to go?
Or what do you say when you are asked why?
Why is our world filled with such a hatred
When all everyone wants is to be loved?
Why are simple questions asked constantly
When nobody knows the correct answer?
Why do people always judge each other
When equality is a common goal?

These questions don't have a set of answers,
But if you look deep inside, you may find
A special little feeling, or answer.
Sometimes we try to run from our feelings,
To banish those emotions from our mind,
But banishing isn't worth the struggle.

Kristina Hartmann
Fenwick High School
Oak Park
Grade 9

I Will Remember

I will remember my 22 rifle
Because my grandpa gave it to me
I will remember my knife with my nature scene
Because my grandpa gave it to me
I will remember my knife with my fish scene
Because my mom gave it to me
I will remember my cane
Because my grandpa gave it to me before he died

Tom McBride
White Oak Academy
East St Louis
Grade 8

My Very Favorite Sports

Basketball, baseball, and football,
these are all sports that I think are fun.
I think basketball is my favorite of all,
especially a game called one on one.

Baseball is the next in line,
hitting and bunting and throwing.
It consists of a team of nine,
this is a sport that I think is growing.

Football, touch or tackle, two types of this game,
object of this sport is to punt, pass, and score.
Rules are different but the outcome is the same,
this game is the most physical, after you may really be sore.

These are all games that I enjoy to play,
to be the better team you have to win by one.
I could play these games day after day,
now I can rest, because our team has won.

Jeffrey C. Webster
Scales Mound Jr High School
Scales Mound
Grade 8

A Sonnet of Springtime

Spring has come upon us again this year.
We know it's here when the snow melts away.
From the south birds fly back and bring good cheer.
In the morning, sun brings light to the day.
Then with its vibrant rays, sun warms the earth.
But sometimes in the spring rain wets the ground.
And birds get slimy worms for their new birth.
From the sun, all trees and flowers awake.
Then the flowers bloom and start to smell sweet.
Some flowers look so real they seem so fake.
When trees wake up in the spring it's so neat.
You can see the little leaves start to grow.
And when spring comes you're glad there's no more snow.

Catrina Kopel
Sullivan High School
Sullivan
Grade 9

The Hall of Fame Pup

There once was a baseball playing pup
Who loved to play this game,
He was really good at it, too
And got into the Hall of Fame!

Some of his best friends were mad
And others started to cry,
When he got into his limousine
Stuck his head out and waved "Good-bye!"

His baseball playing career went great at first
Until he started to plot,
He was getting sick of this game
So he became the team mascot!

"Oh my!" he finally realized
After many mascot working years,
When he left home to go play ball
He caused his friends many, many tears.

He then flew a long way back home
On his first class private jet,
When he saw all of his friends again he said...
"Being a friend is the best job yet!"

Kelli Kroeplin
Holy Family Catholic School
Rockford
Grade 7

Daddy Could You See?

When I got A's instead of B's
Daddy were you proud
When I disobeyed you and did things that were bad
Daddy would you forgive
When I didn't win first prize
Daddy were you ashamed
When I was hurt and would start to cry
Daddy were you sad
When I wandered off out of your sight
Daddy were you scared
When you left me that afternoon
Daddy, I was sad that day.
Daddy, I'm still sad today.
When you were here I learned from you
To be the best I can be.
I'm sorry if I ever hurt you
I never meant any such thing.
Because I always tried to make you proud
Daddy could you see?

Virginia Lisa Torres
Thompson Jr High School
Oswego
Grade 8

Rockies

O Rocky Mountains hard to see at first
I must climb you if I can
Through the valley fields
Up the mountain slopes
Destiny awaits me...
The cool air in my face
The rocky slopes
The howling wind
At last I've reached the top
"YEAH!"
I am victorious
In my very own way
I'm on top of the world
The river is magnificent
As anyone can tell
Now there's just one problem
How do I get down?

Steven Creasey
Tri-City Jr-Sr High School
Buffalo
Grade 8

The Sea

Take a look at the sea
What do you see?
I see waves and
mysterious caves.
Do you see sand,
on a faraway land?
As dolphins leap high into the air
You'll see them everywhere.

Edwin Afante
Armstrong Elementary School
Chicago
Grade 7

Best Friend

B eing there for me all the time
E xcellent friendship
S pecial person
T rustworthy

F air all the time
R eally good relationship
I ncredible times together
E ntertaining each other all the time
N ever ignoring one another
D oes what is right for everyone

My best friend

Kenia Chavez
John F Eberhart Elementary School
Chicago
Grade 7

Spring

Spring is so pleasant
In the day all the birds chirp
At night it is calm.

Nichole Saxour
Holden Elementary School
Chicago
Grade 8

Daddy's Little Girl*

I did what he said,
I ate what he ate,
I followed his rules,
I tried to make him proud.

I got passing grades,
I stayed away from harm,
I stayed home,
I always obeyed.

I grew up to be wonderful,
I will go further,
I will achieve,
I will conquer.

I will not do wrong,
I will not do the opposites,
I will not disobey...But,
I am intelligent.

I am capable,
I am free,
I am not uncontrolled,
I am Daddy's Little Girl...
I am now and always will be.

Jennifer Torres
St Ferdinand School
Chicago
Grade 8
*Dedicated to Dad

Friends Forever

Friends are the best.
They are better than all the rest.
They'll help you through the worst.
They'll be with you through the best.
And still friends are the best.
They'll be with you forever
In good and bad times.
Friends are forever.
And will never leave your side.

Nicole Duran
St George School
Tinley Park
Grade 8

The Sky

The sun and the moon
They glow very brightly
In the morning and at nighttime
Bright stars

Rebecca K. Sedano
River Trails Middle School
Mount Prospect
Grade 7

My Cousin

Why?
It happened so suddenly ...
Then a boom!
He went down in an instant –
Why?
Just an innocent teenager,
Never hurt anyone ...
Why?
That Friday –
After the game ...
Why?
For attention,
Or for fun ...
Why?
My cousin!

Jeff Itbal
Nathan Hale Middle School
Crestwood
Grade 7

Conscience Is a Light

My conscience is a lighthouse
Guiding me through the darkness
Of my decision makings;
No matter what I will do,
It always keeps coming back.
Reminding me, telling me;
Sometimes it leaves me alone
Yet, I would be lost without,
It will warn me of danger
Not letting me go too far.
It is stable on a rock
Within my treacherous brain;
Shining its light over all.
I must see what will happen,
For it will never be wrong.
It lights at a certain time
When it is shady and dark;
Continues 'til safety arrives.
Then it waits, and starts again.

Clare Kennedy
Fenwick High School
Oak Park
Grade 9

Emotions

I quarreled with my grandmother;
Now she is filled with pain.
My anger won't let me apologize;
Now I feel left in the rain.
The grief is eating me up inside;
No one loves my grandmother like I do.

I feel like such a bad guy;
My sky is dusty blue.
I love my grandmother with all my heart;
So I'm going to do the right thing.

I apologized; you should have known I would.
She did the same;
Still I felt a lot of pain.
In the end we started talking again.

Whitney T. Brown
Cairo Jr High School
Cairo
Grade 8

Friends

Friends are always there for you.
They know how to help you
during all the hard times.
Friends cheer you up
when you are down,
and you can tell them anything.
Friends know how you are feeling
even when you don't tell them.
They always tell the right jokes,
and they always tell them at the right times.
Friends watch out for you.
Friends always know what you are thinking.
Friends are special.

Meghan Gallagher
Queen of Martyrs School
Chicago
Grade 8

Purple Rain*

Purple rain is still the same
Purple rain will never change.
But up above in the sky
It won't change you and I
Throughout my life I've looked near and far
But now I don't know where you are.
And now I've felt purple
And I know it will never change
And I know it is still the same.

Daniel Whitehead
Children of Peace-St Callistus School
Chicago
Grade 7
*Love that you just can't find.

The Place I Can!

The place I can relax my mind
The place I can lay back and rewind
This place I may call home
This place I may speak my feelings and not get made fun of
Just because they deal with family and love
It's time we grow up and be mature
And not make others feel the pain you endure
Take them to the place you can
Show how to be a real man
Now this may sound hard
But it isn't that malodorous
Don't make them feel like it's no holds barred
That'll make them so frenzied
Take it easy, once at a time
And just remember the rhyme
The place I can relax my mind
The place I can lay back and rewind
This place I may call home
This place I may speak my feelings and not get made fun of
Just because they deal with family and love

Dave Dorman
Francis Granger Middle School
Aurora
Grade 7

The Wall

Here, in memory of
Heroes who died–
Heroes who loved
No longer at our sides.
Those who gave their all
Immortalized on this dark wall.
So here we stand
On this sacred land,
To remember them.

We have forgotten
Most of their names–
But we try to remember
So is it the same?
These men were not loved for their bravery.
We did not like their "battles won,"
We thought each a tyrant with a gun.

We come here today in hopes
That someday we won't have to.
That all this war,
Fighting, and anger
Can be stopped by you.

Mason Donahue
Grayslake Middle School
Grayslake
Grade 8

The Power of Love

We fell into the sweet romance so quickly
Everything fit, we seemed to match perfectly.
Until I found the one flaw — the division
That broke the connection between us —
And everything we had worked so hard to accomplish was lost.
We were so alike and knew what we had between us was special, and yet
So much was breaking us apart, and nothing seemed to work between us anymore
The loneliness began to set in once again
I felt unworthy of the love that I had once known.
I had abused the power of one's heart,
Given to me under deepest authority and respect
But, in the midst of the worst,
A fallen angel swooped down, and rescued all that was lost between us
And we learned to move past our differences
With the thought of how much we meant to each other
And everything in the world was righted once again.

Rachael Hoffman
Fenwick High School
Oak Park
Grade 9

March Clouds

Still clouds on a peaceful March day
Only appear still.
Amorphous shapes, continuously ephemeral.
In reality, they glide swiftly across a rainbow crowned sky.
Perfect spring weather preserved by massive marshmallows.
Ever changing bodies held in place, though moving, by pastels of pollution streaking the horizon as
Afternoon fades into dusk.
The neophyte sunset merely blends colors, sinking lower upon Earth synchronizing with the sun.
An atmosphere teeming with clouds.
Blue shades of sky, concealed by curtains of clouds, peek out like little ballet dancers
    waiting in the wings, anxious, yet overcome with butterflies of stage fright.
The sky patiently waits to perform as the clouds exit the stage.
Street lights flicker on automatically, reminding those of us with heads buried in clouds
    that life on Earth is changing – unpredictably and rapidly as clouds.
Afternoon diminishes into evening, evening dissolves into night.
Twilight dawns different cloud creations as a new day is born,
    carried high on a golden stair of clouds.
Soon mystical March clouds become ethereal April clouds, ever changing.

Kimberly Reishus
Madison Jr High School
Naperville
Grade 8

Tribute to the Moon

Sometimes late at night I wish to stay awake and stare at you.
Your silvery glow against the ebony backdrop puts me in awe.
Awe struck, with how simple, yet beautiful you are all together.
You're just a simple light in the night that God thought about to put out with the stars.
Such a simple thought with such a powerful meaning.
A meaning that there's always light in the dark and that God has thought of everything.
That's why I like to stare at you, deep into the night, your glowing beauty shining upon me.

Megan Hutchison
Pekin High School East
Pekin
Grade 9

The Gypsies of Seville

Swirl, Taratatata, swirl, CLAP!
Seville's gypsies dance around with a snap.
Tambourines jingling,
Excitement tingling,
Bright cloth flowing,
Bugles blowing,
Taratatatata.
Cymbals clanging,
Big drums banging,
Nights on the desert full of light—
Illuminating a gypsy's feet in flight.
Quick little tapping,
Big sharp rapping,
Tralalalala, Seville's gypsies chant.
Boom, they're gone,
In a cloud of mist.
Where did they go?
We shall never know,
Until we see the dancing lights of the gypsies of Seville.

Marcy Capron
North Park Elementary School
Chicago
Grade 7

Fear? Where?

I see the stars, big and small,
But that's not what I think at all.
I only notice the bright and dim,
And so I step out of my body, to look at him.

He talks in his mind
  Because he can't be left behind,
    And he continues to walk through
      Only because he has to,
        It's a thing of survival,
          Defeat all rivals

Fear? What fear? A bear? That's mere!
He won't even shed a tear,
  But he's afraid to tell,
    That eternity in Hell,
      Bothers him a bit
        But until he loses his will, he won't quit.
          Accepting these things are, almost a fear
            But until then,

He strives on,
Longing to hear cheers,
At the end of his road.

Peter Lewis
St Cyprian School
River Grove
Grade 8

Alex

Alex is my best friend in the whole world,
she is so pretty with her hair nicely curled.
She is always there,
she will always care.
She is very trusting,
even if our friendship is breaking and busting.
But it will never come to that,
because when we have problems we will sit and chat.
We will always have fun times together,
even if we cannot depend on the weather.
So in the end what I am trying to say,
is that Alex is my friend that *no one* can take away!

Katie Peterson
St Irene School
Warrenville
Grade 7

Where Were You?

Where were you when kids made fun of me,
when I fell on my face and scraped up my knees?

Where were you when I went on a hike
and the first time that I rode a bike?

Where were you when I first learned to skate,
or the first time I went on a date?

Where were you when I turned 16
and filled up my own car with gasoline?

Where were you when high school came to an end?
You were with me because you're my friend.

Richard Larson
St George School
Tinley Park
Grade 8

Lament for a Young Warrior

You look at his things,
his socks, his boots,
his uniform, his gun.
Yes, his gun.
You see a life you'll never have,
flashing right before your eyes.
You'll never see him again because of war.
War is evil, war is death, war is fighting.
Alas, I have to face my day,
so young warrior rest in peace.
You, I'll never forget.

Francesca Schleiss
Kennedy Elementary School
Spring Valley
Grade 7

Words

Words can make or break a person's day
Words can be laughter
Words can be sadness
Words are the best gift of all
If said with thought and kindness
Megan Hutson
St Matthew School
Champaign
Grade 7

Winter

Winter is coming
You can smell it in the air
Snow is falling down
Jessica Fisher
River Trails Middle School
Mount Prospect
Grade 7

Confirmation

Religious moment
Holy Spirit fills us all
Time to celebrate
Heather Nowak
St Michael School
Orland Park
Grade 8

Football Practice

They said, "We have practice."
I went to practice.

They said, "Run."
I ran.

They said, "Do leg-lifts."
I did leg-lifts.

They said, "Do push-ups."
I did push-ups.

They said, "Do jumping jacks."
I did jumping jacks.

They said, "Go get water."
I got water.

They said, "Run again."
I ran again.

They said, "Sit on the bench."
I *QUIT*
Mike Murphy
Queen of Martyrs School
Chicago
Grade 7

Best Friends

As I walked through the doors on the first day of school,
I saw this girl standing all alone.

She came up to me, with these big blue eyes.
And filling up with joy, she asked if I would be her new friend.
I smiled a big smile and said "Yes," and together we played.

Over the years, we told each other secrets and together we walked,
Down one long road called "life."

When we were twelve, we made a playhouse,
For just the two of us, the way it should be.
Then we became fourteen, and didn't leave each other's sides.
We went to homecoming together, all dressed up without our dolls.

We got the news that she would be moving soon.
The days were coming fast while the memories were running through my head.
Us as little girls, playing with our dolls, and telling secrets.
It seemed like we had eternity together to play with our dolls in our playhouse.

As I saw her leaving that day, I was flashing back.
When her big blue eyes asked me that question that changed my life.

All I want to say is thank you for all your advice.
Thank you for always being there for me, and for being my best friend.
Without her I wouldn't be who I am today.
After all, that's what best friends are all about!

Jamie Hagerman
Hoffman Technical Center
Machesney Park
Grade 9

My Best Friend Forever

I haven't had my best friend for a long time,
But no matter how short we've known each other we still are best friends.
My best friend is there when I need her,
to change all those bad things into good.
She cares about me and loves me like a sister.
When I'm with her I feel like I'm in heaven,
But, I guess....
it's because she's there to take me through the good and bad times.
I hope I will have my best friend forever,
because when I see her,
all the dark gray things turn
into bright and wonderful things.
I hope I will have her for the longest time,
she's all I have in the dark gray times.
She's like a friend for life to me!

My best friend.

Andrea Kruszka
Clifford Crone Middle School
Naperville
Grade 7

My Paradise

Florida is the perfect place,
Where they launch shuttles into space.
Swimming up and down the beach,
Jellyfish just out of your reach.
Let's take a walk along the sand,
Doesn't it just make you feel grand?
The air whistles by without a care,
This peacefulness is just so rare.
Now it is time to part ways,
I must return home for the rest of my days.
But do not fear,
For there is always next year.

A.J. Tomich
L J Stevens Middle School
Wilmington
Grade 7

Wanted

I am wanted for...
Not cleaning my room
Not eating all my food
Not doing my chores
And also,
For skipping school.

But other than that,
I am not wanted at all.
Alejandra Carrizalez and Vanessa Gutierrez
Logandale Middle School
Chicago
Grade 7

I Have a Dream

I have a dream, that one day
Everyone will be happy, and everyone could say
That they are happy:
With what they have, not what they want,
With who they are, not who they want to be,
With what they wish, not what everyone else wishes,
Will be concerned more about how they act, not how they look,
And everyone would care not for themselves
But more for each others,
When that day comes and if I live to see it
My dream then will come true, and I'll be very happy
And happiness is something that we need to live our lives,
And not to waste them, our life is something precious,
Something that's priceless and given only once.
Live it, so you won't regret what you have done
Or maybe haven't done.
Live your own life how you want
Not how someone else has once lived theirs.
It's your life.

Anna Hommadova
Bartlett High School
Bartlett
Grade 9

The Dance

Music, dancing, twirling about
You wonder is the music going to stop
Then a thought runs through your head
Then you think, why would you want the music to stop.
For the night has just begun.
One song after another you dance,
And the music just goes on.
Then you realize that this is where you want to be,
At the dance.....

...Where you can meet someone,
Someone who will keep you company,
Someone who understands you,
Someone who will lift your spirits when they're down,
Someone who cares for you as much as you care for them.

But, then the music stops,
And it is time for you to go home.
Then you leave the fantasy that has finally come true.
Then you realize that you had the time of your life.
This is the time that you'll never forget
You'll never forget
The Dance

Lauren Fox
L J Stevens Middle School
Wilmington
Grade 7

All at That Moment

All at that moment,
a small piece of time,
I heard the waves crashing,
I felt the warm sunshine.

As I stood in the water
knee deep,
I could feel the sand below
at my feet.

All at that moment,
I knew nothing could go wrong.
For the wind blew softly
and the birds sang
their peaceful songs.

I took all my feelings
and let them go free.
Now they're exactly where they should be.
At the bottom of the sea.

Katherine Howard
Norman Bridge School
Chicago
Grade 8

Apples

A ppetizing
P ie filling
P eels easily
L ots of people like them
E xceptionally good
S old almost everywhere

Brent Schlarmann
Beckemeyer Elementary School
Beckemeyer
Grade 7

Black and Blue

I like the color blue
Because the days are blue
And the sea is blue.

I don't like the color black
Because my sister died on a black day
And I didn't see a blue sea that day.

She was one year old.

Edgar Guallpa
Logandale Middle School
Chicago
Grade 7

Break a Leg

My mom drops me off
"Break a leg"
We practice
Jump ball
Up by twelve
Crack
Ouch!
I broke my leg

Brenna Kelly
Sacred Heart School
Lombard
Grade 7

Balloon

Balloon, Balloon
In the air.
Watching, waiting,
For you to appear.

Balloon, Balloon
In the air.
Where are you?
Are you there?

Ashley Mangum
Parkview Jr High School
Lawrenceville
Grade 7

Road Kill

R ancid and
O ld
A lso
D ead

K illed
I nnocently by the
L eft tire of the
L amborgini

Ryan Peacock
Fremont Elementary School
Mundelein
Grade 7

Dear Storm

Dear storm,
You can be a tornado
Or a hurricane
You can cause floods
You do cause pain
You can be like a thief in the night
And leave right away
Or stay a very long time
For days and days
You make lots of noise
You light up the sky
With a flash of lightning
You kill
You steal
You make children cry
BOOM! BANG! BAM!
There you go again
You kept Noah afloat
For days on end!

Morgan Prestridge
Francis Granger Middle School
Aurora
Grade 7

Friends

Friends are people to count on.
They're someone to hang out with.
They're someone to talk to.
They're someone to look up to.
Someone to be there for you.
They're someone really cool.
They're there when you're feeling down.
They're always there for you.
They're there for you in difficult times.
That's what friends are for.

Chris Hollock
Queen of Martyrs School
Chicago
Grade 8

The Snow

It's the snow
Look! Look!
Do you see
something white
something that goes
swish
slish
slosh
shwee
shwof
shee
sha
do you see?
Falling down from the sky
really, really high
the snow very white!
And then I heard a SWISHHHHH!
It's the
SNOW

Angelica Morales
River Trails Middle School
Mount Prospect
Grade 7

Snow

Upon the mountains
Twinkling in the cold air
Flakes of white lie down
Comfort for many children
Clouds broken into pieces

Ashley Damato
Holy Angels School
Aurora
Grade 7

Bowling

As the ball twisting and turning
makes its way toward the pins,
you can never be sure where it will go.
Will it go right,
will it go left.

As the ball's going down
greasy lane number nineteen,
you start to notice that it is
turning toward the head pin.
You get a strike, but it is then
you realize bowling is like life.
If you hit the head pin,
the rest will fall.

Jim Hillman
Owen Scholastic Academy
Chicago
Grade 7

Love

Love is like an eagle,
It flies so briskly and so free,
Over the mountain peaks
And through the weightless floating clouds,
Above the canyons of unending depth,
Over the river, over the sea, and into the heavens.
The love that is shown will never die.

Caitlin Ludden
Queen of Martyrs School
Chicago
Grade 8

Make A Difference*

Teachers and students, lost in the tears;
As the world can't help but express it's fears.
"Which school is next?" and "Where will it be?"
Yesterday Denver, maybe tomorrow you and me.
The answer here, is not violence.
Where there once was laughter, now is silence;
All because of useless killing —
We all should help — are you willing?
Be a friend, understand, give a hug, hold a hand.
Life is too short, too sweet, too great;
Don't throw it away, overcome the hate!
Wash the sadness off someone's face,
And put a smile in its place.
Make a difference – because you can.
This is the way towards a better land.

Stephanie Drone
Murphysboro High School
Murphysboro
Grade 9
April 22, 1999 — The day after the Columbine Shootings

Graduation

It's a time to say good-bye
But also a time to say hello to new places

You might cry
But you will be happy for your accomplishments

It's a time to remember all the memories
Good or bad

It's a time to be with friends
Some of them for the last time

Graduation will be an exciting time
But I will miss all the fun times I had at my school

Neal Stephenson
St Matthew School
Champaign
Grade 8

My Mommy

Her final days
Slowly drifting past.
Full of pain
And discomfort.

I always thought she'd be with me...forever,
I am not whole without her.
But I know now
She'll be with me only in my heart.

The cancer has spread.
A forest fire,
Destroying her body.
Taking away her life.
Taking her away from me.

Who's to blame,
For taking her away?
Who's in charge of,
Leaving people lonely?
Who takes pride in ruining people's lives?
Who can I scold for stealing my mommy?

Don't worry mommy,
Don't be scared.
I will be with you one day soon.

Joseph Adamji
Nichols Middle School
Evanston
Grade 8

Pain

As I'm sitting here, writing this sonnet
I'm thinking of all the pain you caused
You shattered my heart, caused me to fret
In thinking of you makes my life paused

You were so special, you were all I had
Since you have left me, I felt tons of pain
You have made my life miserable and sad
Leaving me alone with nothing to gain

And time will take its course to relieve me
Your face will be no longer in my mind
You will control me no more, I am free
I will leave my sad memories behind

Today is a new beginning for me,
My options are open like the ocean sea.

Darek Bialon
St Ferdinand School
Chicago
Grade 8

a new spring
red
eyes open
a red tulip blossoms

breath leaves its lips
softly as a mountain scent
enters its nostrils

fingers move as the grass sways
trees sway in the breeze
never before has life been so beautiful
so simple

the beginning of new life
a blossom in the road to come

Daniel Dresner
New Trier Township High School
Winnetka
Grade 9

Determination
I keep my eye on the prize,
But today I must realize,
That we must retreat,
And ponder our defeat.
It was not our day to win,
It almost feels like a sin.
I must not get too downhearted,
The season has just started,
We will get them some other day,
The victory will be ours, I pray.
We will prove to everyone,
That justice will be done,
After years of try and fail,
We will finally prevail!

Ashley Lievers
Hardin County Jr High School
Elizabethtown
Grade 8

Got
Got
Milk
White
Snow
Cold
Frozen
Yogurt
Healthy
Choice
Mind
Own

Amanda C. Bosley
River Trails Middle School
Mount Prospect
Grade 7

Youth
When I was young I used to do whatever, now it's all work.
When I was young it was a great time to do fun things.
Now it's do this and do that.
When I was young I used to sleep and sleep now it's up at dawn and bed at midnight.
Playing in the garden to tending the garden.
From eating anything to watching my diet.
From doing this and that to just do this and nothing more.
The days just being spent lying around to nothing but work.
Ah youth is a beautiful thing.

John Page
Scales Mound Jr High School
Scales Mound
Grade 8

Valentine
V is for a very important day
A is for an arrow from Cupid
L is for love, which is the mood people have today
E is for everything, which is what makes them happy
N is for nobody else like him
T is for today, which is Valentine's Day
I is part of those three words your boyfriend would like to hear you say to him
N is for nothing else would make him happier than being with you and
E is for the last letter in Valentine

Brenda Salazar
John F Eberhart Elementary School
Chicago
Grade 7

Welcome to Horse Country
As you enter this new country,
the scene begins to change.
Tall buildings and paved roads,
now reveal open lands.

The dark clouds clear,
and the puddles dry.
Dead grass and trash
melt away with tall grass now in its place.

As the sweet aroma of the fresh spring flowers fill your nose,
you can hear the soft buzzing of the many busy bees filling your ears.
And off in the distance you can see,
a group of magnificent animals running wild and free, racing with the wind.

Then you can feel your hair growing,
as it grows it moves to just one single strip,
running down your neck and back.
You now know that you will never want to leave,
the peaceful and free *horse country.*

Matt Gette
Thompson Jr High School
Oswego
Grade 8

Winter

The sun is pale,
Like the flowers in midsummer.
The snow is so soft
Like the bushy tail of a rabbit.
The wind carries all joyful and sad memories.

Liliana Salgado
St Mary of Czestochowa School
Cicero
Grade 7

I Am

I am a God-fearing girl.
I wonder what the perspective is from heaven,
I hear all the marvelous things of God,
I see all the miraculous miracles,
I want to know Him a lot better,
I am a God-fearing girl.
I pretend I am always happy,
I feel love from my family,
I touch the bible everyday,
I worry about those gone on without me,
I cry at the thought of losing a love,
I am a God-fearing girl.
I understand with death they go away,
I say I'm OK, I don't feel that way,
I dream of time when heaven will come,
I try my very best to go on with life,
I hope I will one day see that perspective,
I am a God-fearing girl.

Kimberly Carter
Marya Yates Elementary School
Matteson
Grade 8

Sweet Love

I shall miss you until your return
My longing for you cannot be mistaken
I see your eyes still with a passionate burn
I yearn for my heart to be once again taken
Once this great trek is over please come home
I will do my best to stay pure for you
I remember your love, sweet as honeycomb
And to me your love was always true
No matter what anybody may say
I will wait for you till the day I die
I will watch for you each and every day
No one still believes there's still hope but I
Our story is a sad one for me to hear
But my heart will ache until you are near

Cara L. Morgan
Hinsdale Middle School
Hinsdale
Grade 8

I'm Sorry

I'm sorry for falling in love with you
for believing the things you said were true.
I'm sorry we couldn't work things out
maybe we had too much doubt.

I'm sorry for the bad times we had
for all the times I made you mad.
I'm sorry for the things I did wrong
for never singing that special song.

I'm sorry for not believing
for always grieving.
I'm sorry we moved too fast
for making that kiss our last.

I'm sorry for never taking the time to listen
for never watching the way your eyes glisten.
I'm sorry for being apart.
for not having a big enough heart.

I'm sorry it didn't last forever
and for us not staying together.
I'm sorry my friend
for letting our poem end.

Jill Smith
Laraway Elementary School
Joliet
Grade 8

You Stick Out Like a Sore Thumb

In a small town,
In the 19th century,
Lived a little girl.

They were celebrating the start of a new town,
In a barn.
She wore a bright orange dress.

That was when the first idiom was spoken...

"You stick out like a sore thumb!"
Her thumb started to grow,
And grow some more.

"It was the idiom that made her thumb grow!"
It turned purple and black,
And nobody ever said an idiom again,

EVER!

Maggie Novotny
Sacred Heart School
Lombard
Grade 7

Spring

Spring is the most beautiful season of all
Most times prettier then the fall.
With gray and white clouds passing by
It's fun to watch the birds fly sky high.

The sun brings out it's new light
As little kids fly their new kites.
The days become long
And so does the bird's new song.

In April and May there are lots of rain showers
Those showers will bring those beautiful flowers.
The tulips and roses start to bud
And don't worry there will be mud!

New signs of new life living
That our mother nature is giving!
Happy Spring.

Erin Fisher
St Irene School
Warrenville
Grade 7

Candle

Sometimes when you read a poem
you can smell a sweet, wonderful aroma
like a candle that has been lighted
for the first time.
As you read the poem the candle melts fast
and the poem fades away
and the sweet aroma fades as well.
As the sweet smell leaves,
you will recall the aroma forever.

Monica Vera
River Trails Middle School
Mount Prospect
Grade 7

As I Strolled Down the Street

As I strolled down the street,
The sidewalk curved anxiously.
Each crack with dirt and rocks
each chip off
showing the pain
Through the times it's been stepped on.
The dirty road,
with rocks all over.
The sound of cars,
rolling by busily.
I stand there,
searching above.
Wondering what the streets in heaven look like.

Sparkle Jackson
Francis Granger Middle School
Aurora
Grade 7

Soldier

He stands alone all by himself
On a battlefield of life and death.
His men fight to win a war.
He stands strong in the vicious core.
Far in the distance he sees the flag.
The one so many had often bragged.
Planted was that flag in the ground.
For all to see far around.
Suddenly he is hit, by an enemy's fierce bullet.
Pierced savagely through the heart,
As if by a speeding dart.
Knowing that it was his end,
His soul had a single tear to send.
In his mind all he sees,
Is all the precious memories,
Of his wife and child as they waited,
For the hero in their mind they created.
As he dies all alone,
No one to touch, no one to hold, he would go strong and bold.
"...I give them love, I give them peace,
As I lay down for this eternal sleep."

Angela Malzow
Lundahl Middle School
Crystal Lake
Grade 8

The Perfect Girl

The perfect girl would be so fine
and would take me out to dine.
The perfect girl would have long hair
that would go with her dark green eyes.
The perfect girl would be so smart.
She would be brave and bold.
The perfect girl would share my love for animals,
especially for the rattlesnake.
The perfect girl would be sweeter than a lamb,
but fiercer than a lion.
The perfect girl would be the one
that is always on time.
She doesn't care how she looks,
but when she thinks she looks her worst,
she really looks her best.
The perfect girl would like to exercise,
but only at home.
She would like to ride her bike,
and take lots of healthy hikes,
and that would be perfect,
and just for ME!!!

Roy Leinweber
Harrison Elementary School
Wonder Lake
Grade 8

The Loss of My Friend

It seems like yesterday when my dad died.
I wasn't with him on this day,
But I was still sad.

When I went to the funeral,
I felt as if my heart
Broke in half.

When he was buried,
I felt as if
I lost my only friend.

John Belsky
Logandale Middle School
Chicago
Grade 7

Danny

I remember the day I saw you.
At that moment I knew I liked you.
I wanted to be with you,
But I knew you didn't feel the same way.
You and I have not really been close,
But I hope that could happen one day.
Right now the pain is so great.
I realize you would never think of me as more than a friend.
The pain will be gone over the days, weeks, and months.
I hope I can face you and say that I'm all right,
But today I need the pain to go away.

Jenny Yun
River Trails Middle School
Mount Prospect
Grade 7

Out of Love

When I think of how I used to be,
  I was always apart.
Then you came along
  leaving footprints in my heart,
Standing up when you knew it was right,
  comforting me through the night.
Being there
  is the best thing you've given me.

You were my guiding light,
  made everything right.
I've been blessed
  with an angel from above, and
Everything you've given me was out of love.

Cherisse Guinid
St Jude The Apostle School
South Holland
Grade 7

Snow

Snow is endless bliss.
It is like an empty void.
It doesn't have a care in the world.

Snow is silent
But at the same time, loud and noisy.
It follows no rules
And waits for nobody.

Snow shows no mercy,
Many people can get lost in its blizzards.
Snow can be peaceful and caring.
It likes when children build snowmen from it.

Snow is an unpredictable force,
And what it does next is never for certain.

Martin Kouba
Queen of Martyrs School
Chicago
Grade 8

Just a Game?

There were few seconds remaining,
The score was tied.
Our opponent drove down the lane,
In the ball went and we all about died.

With tears in our eyes,
We walked off the court.
The doors closed behind us,
And our season was cut short.

The loss is close at heart,
And the memories remain,
Of the basketball season we'd played as a team.
They all said not to worry, it was just a game.

A few lessons were learned that game,
We got discouraged and our game faces fell;
We made mistakes, not normally made;
We couldn't come together, we just didn't gel.

We all learned that game,
Trust in each other and play as a team.
We can work together,
And fulfill our team's dream.

So now you tell me, was it more than just a game?

Katie Holcomb
St Matthew School
Champaign
Grade 7

The Sun

The sun moves around
while plants grow all the day long
and rain starts to fall.

Crystal Garcia
Trumbull Elementary School
Chicago
Grade 7

One Day

One day
I hope to be pretty
One day
I hope to be skinny
One day
I might actually be loved
One day
People may care for me
One day
Is all I wait for
One day
I will be like you
One day
Is all I have these days
One day...

Kristina Losh
Elmwood Jr High School
Elmwood
Grade 9

Neglecting the Unfavorable

Everyone is always there,
Where the glorious sun glows,
The ground is bare,
Where no one knows,
Everyone runs to the happy places,
To get rid of all their fears,
To see all the happy faces,
And worry only about their cares.

Kyle Schultz
Stratford Jr High School
Bloomingdale
Grade 8

Summer

In summer you can go on vacation
In winter you are in school
In summer you can sleep all day
In winter you go to school
In summer you can play all day
In winter you go to school
That is why summer
Is a lot better than winter!

Michael Cooney
Pope John XXIII School
Evanston
Grade 8

One

I am one. You are one. Everyone is one.
I have two ears, two eyes, two arms, two legs, but I am still one.
I am smart, I am cute, I am and always will be me.
I am nice, responsible, helpful, and fun, but still I equal only one.
Everyone is someone and they are special too,
Everyone knows something no one ever knew.
There are secrets inside of me and inside of you,
There are regrets and mistakes but I learn from them too.
Sometimes I forget how cute I look or how smart I am,
But then I realize how wrong I am.
So dear God, if you are listening let everybody know to appreciate
Themselves for who they are and how they look, and never to put themselves low.
Because everyone is someone, no matter their color, religion, shape, or size.
Because everyone and everything is equal in God's eyes.

Amanda Danielle Gabel
Shiloh Village School
Shiloh
Grade 7

Raiders

In the beginning we all goofed around,
But that only led to more running, we soon found.

Basketball has made us all better athletes.
Almost every team we played, we beat.

It was best when we won,
Because that meant we could celebrate and have fun.

Losing was still okay,
Because we could learn from our mistakes when we play.

We did a whole lot of running and worked on our shot.
As we got better, we learned this helped a lot.

We soon won regionals playing this wonderful sport, basketball.
Everyone tried and gave their all.

Then came sectionals and we played Fisher, a team we twice beat,
But they got better and learned to move their feet.

It was Fisher's ball, 0.9 seconds on the clock. The game was on the line.
I thought to myself, "It's okay, we'll win it in overtime."

They got the ball in the hoop when they threw it in the air.
All we could do was look on with disbelief and a blank stare.

Some of us showed our emotion with tears,
Because this one loss meant our season was over, we fear.
Please don't worry, my friends, there will always be next year.

Erin Mears
St Matthew School
Champaign
Grade 7

The Gift

Learning is a constant cycle of life that shouldn't be broken.
Treat it as you would a gift,
Hold it, never let it go.
Because once it's gone there is no second chance.

Ted Dimiropoulos
River Trails Middle School
Mount Prospect
Grade 7

Fall

It would be a cool night,
But it was bright.
The stars would twinkle,
And look like sprinkles.

The wind blew lightly,
But still, you would have little goose bumps.

The night was silent.
All you could hear were crickets,
And they would be singing together, side by side.

Your mother just made lemonade.
You would drink it all,
And all you would hear would be gulp, gulp, gulp.

At the end of the night you would fall asleep,
And your father would carry you to your room.
The dog would jump on your bed,
And snuggle by your feet.

The next day when you awake,
You think it was a dream.
Until your pup bites your toes,
Thinking they're toys.

All this would happen in fall.

Lizzie Sendejas
Blessed Sacrament School
Belleville
Grade 8

It Doesn't Matter

My name, it doesn't matter.
Even though I don't see eye to eye with my parents.
I always love them.
Even though I lie, talk back, or swear, they will always love me.
At the beginning to end.
We all love each other,
no matter what happens.
So no matter what the conditions are in your relationships,
everyone love themselves and their parents.

Santos Cabrera
Taylor Elementary School
Chicago
Grade 8

Changes

When I was younger I was a bad little girl.
I was always in trouble and always got punished.
My mother never let me do anything
Because I was the youngest.
I used to curse at my brothers
Because they got on my nerves.
Back then, I never understood them.

Things change.
Now I am crazy about my mom.
I treat her with respect
And understand what she went through
Raising my two brothers and me by herself.
I don't curse at my brothers anymore
Because I love them.

I've changed.
I guess it's because I've seen a lot
In my short life.
I want to be better
Than the people I know
Who have let their lives slip away.

Yesenia Vargas
Logandale Middle School
Chicago
Grade 7

Great Grandpa

Lying in bed, silent as night,
Waiting for that special light.
As I lay so silent, so dead,
So calm and quiet.
I wish I could be alive again,
Play again, feel free.
But I think I'm trapped for eternity.
Still waiting for a loved one to kiss me goodnight.
Then I might be able to be in flight.
Then in my dreams I wish for that special light,
But I should finally say good-bye once and for all.
I'm going away slowly.
My eyes getting watery.
My body getting still.
Now I say good-bye as I close my eyes.
Lying in bed, silent as night.
He comes for me and I finally feel free.
Now I lie safe in his arms, far away from harm.
No more silences, no more suffering.
Now keep me close in your heart and we'll never part.

Sarah Marshall
Grant Community High School
Fox Lake
Grade 9

Kids

The way they kick the ball,
The way they run in the hall,
Kids
I really like them all.

Luis Gonzalez
Jonesboro Elementary School
Jonesboro
Grade 8

Here With Me

Words can mean enough
Whether it is in the right or wrong.
You were always there for me
Loving me and holding me
Now and forevermore.
You'll be in my heart
No matter where you are,
We'll be together
From now until forever
We'll have each other
In the right or wrong.
I'll protect you from all around you
I will be there always.
Flying in your arms, so close together
How I'm loving you so much,
You'll always be right here with me.

Diana Camacho
John F Eberhart Elementary School
Chicago
Grade 7

I Think of You

The sun is slowly rising,
The oceans are serene,
The earth is silent,
All is peaceful but my heart,
Beating incessantly,
I think of you,
I envision your face,
You walking,
Such a vivid, lucent view,
Then. . .
It all vanishes,
You are no where in sight,
You are gone,
At that sudden, painful moment,
I realized that you. . .
You were only an illusion,
A figment. . .
Of my imagination.

Vy Nguyen
Trumbull Elementary School
Chicago
Grade 8

Winter

Reds, greens, and silver,
Winter is already here.
Christmas is coming,
Snow is falling,
Laughter fills the air.
Children are playing,
Carolers are singing.
We say good-bye to '99,
And hello to the new year.

Melissa A. Mulrooney
St Joseph Elementary School
St Joseph
Grade 7

Fast Food

I always wanted a little dog
like the one from "Taco Bell."
Wouldn't that be so swell?

When I go to "McDonalds"
I order a fish fillet
then I like to play;
in the balls, slides, and tubes.

If I go to "Burger King"
I'm afraid that I might meet a bum
who would break my thumb,
just for my Whopper.

When I get a craving for pizza, I race
my brother to "Roseangelos" Pizza Place.

Nick Pentek
Owen Scholastic Academy
Chicago
Grade 7

Birds

Birds are the animals of the sky,
Where they fly very high.
How high can they go,
Is a mystery that we don't know.
Birds have many feathers.
That keep them warm in cold weather.
Some are big and tall,
While others are short and small.
There are blue and red birds,
There are also brown and black birds.
Birds are beautiful features.
So many pretty designs,
That change over time.

Shannon Pugh
Harrison Elementary School
Wonder Lake
Grade 7

Grandmas

Grandmas are sweet and cuddly.
They are like teddy bears
Grandmas spoil us rotten;
They smell as sweet as honey!
Grandmas love to plant gardens;
Grandmas tell neat stories.
They love to bake
They also love to take care of you
When you're sick.
Grandmas like to play games.
Grandmas are special
That's why we love them so.

Bonnie Wittrock
Harrison Elementary School
Wonder Lake
Grade 7

God's Grace

Words cannot describe the call of the sea
or the effect that it has on me.
For I must have a ship to sail in
and I must have a wind in my sail
I have to have a place to roam in
where the lonesome cannot fail.
Oh, to feel the thrill of a summer's gale
and to soak in the frightening storm.
All I need is some wood and a sail,
I don't want to be safe and warm.
I want to feel the salt spray in my face
and let the wind carry me
where I'll see everyday God's grace
for all eternity.

Dusti Rose Hendricks
Schuyler Middle School
Rushville
Grade 7

Myself

I love myself as you can see.
I'm always happy as can be.
I love myself as you should know.
I always have to let it show.

I love myself and that is true.
Like the sky when it's bright and blue.

I love myself in every way.
Constantly and every day.
I love myself as you can see.
I'm always happy as can be.

Tamika Houston
Cairo Jr High School
Cairo
Grade 8

I Am

I am a girl who adores and treasures life.
I wonder what life is about.
I hear the world speak.
I see me as a grown-up and being fortunate.
I want to explore the world.
I am a girl who adores and treasures life.

I pretend to be in charge.
I feel an urge to love and be loved.
I reach out with open arms.
I worry about all people in the world.
I cry when violence strikes.
I am a girl who adores and treasures life.

I understand that the world will not be sleek.
I say, "Try your hardest, it's the best you can do."
I dream about high hoped places.
I try to help others.
I hope to be the best person I can be.
I am a girl who adores and treasures life.

Brittney Rautio
Francis Granger Middle School
Aurora
Grade 7

King of the Ice*

he walks in
the self proclaimed King of the Ice
he can glare through the boards
share the ice with a mighty beast
 (also known as a zamboni!)

lacing up skates he does with ease
on the ice–those first few strides
then a fury of cutting blades
this kingdom is in his blood
 (how could he ever leave it?)

almost an hour of bliss
his kingdom being reclaimed every minute
heart pounding he instructs the little soldiers
who must one day carry on his legacy
 (like anyone else could hold the position!)

he exits the ice
 (when will he return...?)

Stephanie Kaplan
Highland Park High School
Highland Park
Grade 9
*Dedicated to Marco Santi for helping me to learn to play
hockey and for adding wood to the fire that is my passion.

Tears of a Child

When you aren't near
It's hard to see clear
But in a way even I can't say "hurray"
You see you've hurt me bad
And now I feel so sad
Because you've let my image go...
Now you can't see me play or grow
You've gambled on taking on some other kids
I guess I was lost amongst all the bids
You've made me angry and now I fight
You've left me hanging here with no father in sight
You've hurt my feelings, with tears they do flow
This pain you've left is something you'll never know
Acknowledge me and turn around
Do you think I'm buried in the ground?
As the open space in my heart hangs with air
A dying love of a father... A father who doesn't care...

Alyssa Dickerson
Parkview Jr High School
Lawrenceville
Grade 7

Friends

No matter what happens, no matter what goes wrong,
a friend will always be here standing by your side.

If anything should happen, or not go your way,
a friend will do all they can
to make things the best they can be.

If you're ever down or feeling sad,
even just talking on the phone
will make you feel better.
A friend to laugh with, a shoulder to cry on,
and with you every step of the way.

Lauren McGuire
Queen of Martyrs School
Chicago
Grade 8

Under Moonlight

As I walk, on this night,
Down along an empty beach,
As I walk, under moonlight,
I feel a cool ocean wind.
As I walk, silver moonbeams shine from above.
And under moonlight,
I fall asleep and dream...

Tara Edwards
Forest Trail Jr High School
Park Forest
Grade 8

The Colors of the Rainbow
RED is the color of your heart,
ORANGE is the color of your sweet tart,
YELLOW is the color of your brightness,
GREEN is the color of your niceness,
BLUE is the color of your pretty eyes,
INDIGO is the color of no lies,
VIOLET is the color of your sweet smell,
This rainbow fits you well!
Katie Savage
St Irene School
Warrenville
Grade 7

Tornado
In the empty sky
I see a tornado
Wild like a Tasmanian
Devil
Swirling vanilla sundae
Cone with a
Blueberry
Touch
Brenda Tovar
Hubbard High School
Chicago
Grade 9

River
The river roars around the bend,
The river murmurs around the rocks,
The river splashes on the rocks,
The river gurgles on the sand,
The river hisses by the land.
Elizabeth Greenland
Shirland C C Elementary School
Shirland
Grade 7

You
Of all the people in the world
people care, people share
I respect you as the flowers, or as the sun
giving great gifts as you go
When the wind is fast, and the sky is blue
I sit on this step, on my porch waiting
watching for you to come my way
I know that day may never come,
where that special you passes by
So I wait just for you
on this step
on my porch
just for you
Dustin McNichols
Thompson Jr High School
Oswego
Grade 8

True Friends
A friendship is a wonderful thing,
Through thick and thin,
Your true friends will always be there.
When you're feeling sad and low,
And you feel there is nowhere to go,
Remember you can always come to me.
I am there for you no matter what time of day,
I'll listen to whatever you have to say,
Even if it is something dumb like who you're dancing with in gym
Even when we get into a fight,
We could care less who was wrong or right,
We'll be friends till the very end.
When that one special boy breaks your heart,
I'll be there for you.
I have you,
And you have me
That is all two real best friends need.
Each other
Amanda Frederick
Stratford Jr High School
Bloomingdale
Grade 8

Death
I wonder of the cloud of death that puts a blanket on people every day
And the coldness it brings to your breath.

It grabs me to think of the effect my
Death will give to my friends and relatives.
Will my children be able to understand?

I search for the answer to this question.

I think death's vision would be a bright light
Descending like an afternoon bird in the quiet blue sky.
And though the light seems so bright
Death closes the windows of happiness.

The dark cloud of death darkens day by day
Like a just-received bruise to the arm
For as we live, we also die.

Death is a scary event, and is hard to comprehend
But there are some who do not need to worry.
People who know there's another path around the bend.
I am one of them.

Do not gasp and lose your breath at the sound of death
For I tell you
There is a ray of sunshine after the storm.
Paul Fischer
St John's Lutheran School
Buckley
Grade 8

Snow

Snow is so fluffy and white,
I love having a snowball fight,
It only comes once a year,
Or until spring is near,
But sometimes snow can be a pain,
Like when there's a freezing rain,
With snow there's so many things you can make,
You can even make a snow cake,
But since it's spring, all I have to say,
Is I can't wait till the next snow day.

Jessica McAlpin
Grant Park Middle School
Grant Park
Grade 7

America

Home of the brave, land of the free
Or so we say
I walk home from school and see a man with no money
I ride my board and see a kid get beaten up
though the gangbangers find it funny
But maybe there is good in all that is bad,
not all make others sad
and no matter how bad the world may seem
God will keep us strong and keen

Christopher Zaccaro
St Ferdinand School
Chicago
Grade 8

Today!

The world to me is just a blur,
It's filled with anger and hidden hate,
The world is built up of tragedies,
That no one wants to face,
I see children's minds grow,
And show love and respect towards each other,
Based on their achievements and not their color,
I see that the force of a bullet can kill,
And that the ability of fire can burn,
I see that the energy of water can drown
And that the power of a smile can heal a lonely heart,
I see people who are giving up hoping,
And people who dream with their eyes open,
I see a young child dying,
Because of the violence in the streets,
Throughout all the days I have lived on this earth,
I've seen a change from day to day,
A chance to succeed and build a new,
You just have to believe in rising above and succeeding,
The most important thing that I see makes the world up,
Is God's creations.......US!!!

Annette Brzozowski
St Ferdinand School
Chicago
Grade 8

A Picture's Beauty

The artist quietly sits in the corner.
He thinks and thinks and thinks;
Not sure what his next painting will be,
Uncertain what the world wants.

Wait! An idea erupts in his brain.
He is certain that it is a brilliant idea.
He knows that the painting will be magnificent
And that people will cherish it forever.

He decides on the picture's medium,
The painting will be oil;
And then he gets to work,
Working for a year on this single, splendid showcase.

Then the artist's work is unveiled,
But as he views his work on the canvas,
He does not see the beauty in the entirety that he imagined.
The picture is not complete; it is not a gleaming masterpiece.

After careful consideration, he makes a hard decision.
The painting is not a masterpiece; it will be destroyed.
He destroys it, and afterwards he thinks how it is
Funny that the mind can depict a picture that truly is not real.

Brian Bauer
Fenwick High School
Oak Park
Grade 9

My Heart Still Smiles

I sit beside your grave,
Crying and reminiscing over times we've shared.
All those times you've shown you loved me, and cared.
My mind ponders for an answer,
I ask why did you have to go, why were you put at rest?
I guess it's because God wished to have the very best.
We grew so close and developed a great bond,
I told you all my secrets and we advised each other,
You always were the best loving godmother ever.
I feel so lost and lonely inside,
My mind is always full of thoughts of you,
Some happy and some blue.
I am full of grief and mournful sorrow,
My tears express melancholy and sadness,
Because all our times together, I strongly miss.
However, throughout all my pain and sorrow,
My heart still smiles all the time in every way
Because in my heart, I keep you with me night and day.

Krissy Abene
Garvy Elementary School
Chicago
Grade 8

Summer's Here

Wisps of cool night air are fading,
Dark green grass is getting lighter,
Showers that replenish everything,
Shade is worth the price of gold,
Sun is closer by the day,
Days are winning,
Nights retreating,
School's leaving, so is spring,
Summer's here,
What will it bring?

Matt Picchietti
St Matthew School
Champaign
Grade 7

Rainbow

Red is ruby, it's the color of a rose,
Blue is my favorite, it sometimes even glows.

Yellow is bright, it wakes up the night,
Orange is kind of dull,
It's darker than it's bright.

Green is rather different,
It's the color of a tree,
Purple is pretty, it's never boring to see.

Red, blue, yellow, orange, purple, and green,
Look up at a rainbow and that's where they'll be seen!

Danielle Bert
Chester Community Elementary School
Chester
Grade 7

Hip, Cool Clothes

Hip, cool clothes,
You want them more and more,
When you go to your favorite stores.
You walk around and spot,
The hottest jeans in stock.
Your outrageous mind is telling you to give them a try.

Hip, cool clothes and accessories,
Your eye spots a tie-dye shirt,
It's gold and orange.
And then you know once again,
To put that eye back to work.
It spots out a backpack with a peace sign,
A silver smiley face necklace, a bucket hat, and —
Some silver platform shoes.
And you're saying to yourself, "What do I have to lose?
I'll give them a try."

Melanie Lucas
Owen Scholastic Academy
Chicago
Grade 7

I'm Sorry

This world is full of mortal things,
Of sin, and wrath, and hate.
With people outside in the streets
Up early, noon, and late.

Where guns ring clearly everyday
And fights are lost and won.
Some people say, "I had no motive."
Some say, "It was for fun."

To take another person's life,
And have no better excuse
Than, "It was just a game for fun,"
Is something I'd never do.

How can it be that everyday
These horrible things go on?
While here, in my own little world,
I see happiness, laughter, and fun.

I'm sorry you've gone through this
I'm sorry I wasn't there.
For you to cry on my shoulder.
Please know I'll always care,
Because I'll always care.

Lizzy Ozee
Hardin County Jr High School
Elizabethtown
Grade 8

I Am Not Yet Ready

I am not yet ready to be out on my own,
To spread my wings and fly
I am not yet ready to have my own place with bills to pay
I am not yet ready to walk down the aisle,
With my one true love in sight
I am not ready to give life to something so tiny and weak
I am not yet ready to provide for a family
I am not yet ready to grow old and have wrinkles and spots
I am not yet ready to lose the ones I love,
Or to leave the world myself

I may never be ready to let go of the hands
I am still holding on to so tightly right now
I may never fall deeply in love,
Or to marry a man I may in the future love
I may never be ready to give life to a fragile little person
I may never be able to provide for a family of my own
I may never be willing to let myself grow old
I may never be ready to let go of my loved ones
I may never be ready to die

Whether or not I am ready, my life will go on
I am just not ready yet to realize this

Rachel Anderson
Libertyville Community High School
Libertyville
Grade 9

The True Story of Love

Love is a wing of an angel that only comes once,
But lust is the flame from a demon's fist.
Love can never be broken by a demon,
Only an angel's arrow can pierce a loved one's heart
Love, it only comes once and never again or does it...

Shaun Moats
Southeast High School
Springfield
Grade 9

Stop and Listen

Stop and listen,
Listen to your friends,
Listen to their hopes, dreams, and even their problems.
You will probably be surprised by what you hear.

Stop and listen,
Listen to your teachers,
Listen to their lessons,
Not just on classwork but on life itself.
They have a lot more than one would think to say.

Stop and listen,
Listen to yourself,
Listen to what you say,
Listen to the world,
Listen to others.
Don't interrupt or talk,
Just listen.
Their words might be subtle but powerful,
So just listen,
And let the message sink in.

Sandi Roznovsky
Thayer Jay Hill Middle School
Naperville
Grade 8

Grandma's House

It's very exciting at grandma's house,
I get so happy I squeal like a mouse.
I have so much fun when I visit her,
We laugh when she says, "Life is like a ball of fur."

Grandma has two big cats,
They play all day and sleep on mats.
They get into a lot of things,
But love it when my grandma sings.

Now it's time to say good bye,
But she insists we make a pie.
Then we exchange kisses-n-hugs,
Then grandma has to vacuum the rugs.

Karleen Kingman
Immaculate Conception School
Morris
Grade 7

Untitled

You are much more beautiful than a rose,
Yet roses in the winter do not bloom.
But my admiration for you still grows,
In the sun, the snow, or in days of gloom.

Still, you are much more than a pretty face,
Although a pretty face you do possess.
For a thousand birds couldn't match your grace,
And to hear your voice, indeed, I am blessed.

Even if you leave, I will not forget,
For my memories, rarely do they die.
And even if my destiny is set,
To come back to you I will always try.

So to you, amazing in every way,
I really hope I, will meet you someday.

Matt Kasperowicz
St Ferdinand School
Chicago
Grade 8

There Once Was a Friendship

There once was s friendship long ago,
but time had to pass and we to grow.

I guess you could say it was love at first sight,
we never would bicker, or quarrel, or fight.

But now as the years go by,
there's not much time to laugh, but more time to cry

It seems as if with each new day,
the past mem'ries seem to fade and slip away

We "talk" and say it's growing,
but I think all just going

Going away that is,
the life long friendship of hers or his

I know this is may be hard to admit
but I think our friendship finally is down to the pit.

It's done,
it's through,
I don't know about you,
but I'm leaving now, for in my heart I know it's true.

Tee Reynolds
Holy Angels School
Aurora
Grade 7

A Wish!

A penny in a wishing well,
a wish on a shooting star,
blowing out the birthday
candles hasn't worked so far.

Wishing that you come to me
I feel won't ever come true.
I finally gave up, on having you.

These feelings of emptiness
without you by my side,
My heart is filled with
sadness and feelings
I just can't hide.

Chimere Lauren Scott
Armstrong Elementary School
Chicago
Grade 7

A Brother

A brother is the best friend
anyone could have.

He helps with everything
such as math.

He plays with you all of the time
even when he's not feeling well.

A brother will be true to you
he will always be there.

A brother is everything
a kid could ever want.

A brother is a special person
so keep him in thought.

Ronald King
Laraway Elementary School
Joliet
Grade 7

Loneliness Is...

A boy all alone in a classroom corner,
Waiting for someone to approach,
But no one comes.

A kitten being sold
Shortly after meeting its mom.

A homeless man searching for friendship,
Yet finding nothing.

Eminia Negroni
Logandale Middle School
Chicago
Grade 7

My Dog

My dog is named Abby.
When we leave home she is so crabby.
She can perform just like a clown.
Because she jumps up, down, and twirls all around.

When we come home we let her outside.
When she goes outside she hurries to come back and meet us.
She runs really fast like a wild cheetah coming to catch us.
But once we turn that corner she flies right past us.
My dog is named Abby.

When she runs right past you, you can see all her colors.
Black, brown, and bright, white that just seem to be so pretty.
But when you try to catch her, she has been known to say, "You can't catch me!"
When she sees food on the table just sitting all by itself she thinks it's butter.
My dog is named Abby.

Her tail is so long and slender.
When she eats food she likes it nice and tender.
Her eyes are so pretty brown and in the shadow, green.
When she gets out of the bathtub she smells fresh and clean.
My dog is named Abby.

Nick Murray
Blessed Sacrament School
Belleville
Grade 7

I Am an Unstoppable Athlete

I am an unstoppable athlete
I wonder if I'll make it pro
Playing softball in the stinging summer sun or maybe skiing in the icy winter snow
I hear the crowd roar, "Let's go Lowenstein!"
I see the grand prize as I zoom across the finish line
I want to keep going, though I'm sure we'll be beat
I am an unstoppable athlete.

I pretend to smile, when I really want to frown
But I don't let my teammates down; they look towards me to be their clown
I reach out like a starving animal for that ball
I worry I won't be able to play because of a bad fall
I cry when I lose either a game or a meet
I am an unstoppable athlete.

I understand that I can't always win
I say to myself, "If at first you don't succeed; try, try again."
I dream of winning the gold medal in the Olympics or a winter Xgame
I try to be energetic and strong, and fight my way to fame
I hope I can compete all of my life, and be that star,
That girl the competition can Never Defeat!
I am an unstoppable athlete!

Sarah Lowenstein
Francis Granger Middle School
Aurora
Grade 7

Being Young

I watched him play.
He looked as though he didn't have a care in the world.
The rain danced on his petite head,
As the mud climbed up his tiny boots.
How great it must have been
To go about what you like to do
With no one criticizing you.
I stood there with jealousy.

Brittany Mondane
Garvy Elementary School
Chicago
Grade 8

Springtime

Springtime is a joyous time,
A happy girl and boy time,
We will laugh and sing all spring,
In the morning sunshine.
Springtime is a joyous time,
A happy you and me time,
We will dance and play,
All the day long,
Singing a you and me song.
Springtime is a joyous time,
A happy family time,
We will laugh and sing and dance and play,
All the live long day.
Springtime

Annamarie Ciardullo
Owen Scholastic Academy
Chicago
Grade 7

A Midnight Prayer

Many nights I pray
God give me strength
I'm a sinful man by mind
But deep down in my heart
You're my Lord, my Savior, and forgiver
Many gifts you give me
And yet I use your name in vain
I get angry and do things not of your will
The somehow you look over my sins
If I ask for your forgiveness

Please help me to conquer the temptations of sin
Make me able to stand for you
Even on the darkest hours
Help me to learn with a desire
Help me with my temper and anger
Especially when I don't understand
Amen.

Heather Ewell
Hardin County Jr High School
Elizabethtown
Grade 7

Doc, the Short Little Basset

Doc is a short little Basset
He is fat and real funny
He has short legs and GIANT paws.
With his tail in the air,
He is off to find his tennis ball
He hands the slobber-coated ball to you,
He runs half way down the hall
Bounce, bounce, bounce, bounce, SMACK
Is the sound of the tennis ball hitting the hall door
And he is off after the ball
Wow! He is surfing on the hall rug
SMACK! He slammed his head into the hall door
Click, click, click, click, click, click ...
And he is on his way back
THUD!!!
His head butts the couch
Well, you tug and tug for the ball and ...
POP!
You got the ball
It has even more slobber dripping from the ball
Well, here we go again

Brandon Hunter
Jonesboro Elementary School
Jonesboro
Grade 8

I'll Never Know

I'll never know what could've been
If you and dad were still together
You got divorced when I was only two
I never knew what happened
I know now that I'm older
If you had stayed together, it would not have been pleasant
But it's hard for me you know
I remember when I was little
I would always miss my daddy
But when I got to dad's
I would always cry for mommy
Parts of life have been hard for me
Having to live in two separate worlds
Never really having the best of both parents at the same time
But I've gotten used to it
Getting dependent on either parent for different things
Yet there have been times
Where I wanted both or the other
And my wish was not granted
I'll never know what could've been
And I'm sure I never will

Emily Cotterman
Jean Baptiste Elementary School
Chicago
Grade 8

Dipping in Ice Cream

It was a very special dream,
I went swimming, in a pool of ice cream.
Strawberry was not the only kind,
There were so many, it blew my mind.

I had a hard time maneuvering though,
Through the cherries and cookie dough.
Eating different kinds here and there,
Soon I had toppings in my hair.

Every stroke was another flavor,
These memories, I would, forever savor.
Swimming in ice cream was lots of fun,
Now I have a tummy ache, and should be done.

Ken Hudziak
St John the Evangelist School
Streamwood
Grade 8

Unseen

I beg one day, oh one day alone,
to put together what I have not yet shown.
To be the one seen through everyone's eyes,
and for them to treat me as a beautiful surprise.
But no, I am shoved in a closet and locked behind the door.
Then I am noticed no more.
I obviously don't appear to be attractive to many,
or else I would be seen as much as any.
I would love one day to be seen by all,
and instead not behind but in front of the wall.

Erin Steinwart
Holy Angels School
Aurora
Grade 7

In Peace You Lay*

Waiting, waiting, waiting
for my dad to pick me up
to see you one last time

Then I got the shocking call
all of a sudden I started crying
I just couldn't believe it

Then came the funeral
it was too emotional
couldn't look at you just lying there

My favorite grandpa, acting like a dad
and you are dead
I just can't believe it

Karissa Fourman
St Joseph Jr High School
St Joseph
Grade 8
*Dedicated to my grandpa who will always be in my heart

The Endless Tunnels

The endless tunnels are like life
You can't go wherever you want, or go back
There are good times and also strife
There may be hatred there may be lack.
When you suffer over pain
Be sure to keep your head up high
Because in life, there is love to gain
Only if you look up towards the sky.
Your tunnel doesn't stop, it has no end
But in heaven as a wanderer in the sky
You will have many messages to send.
In this part of the tunnel all you see is light
Nothing to fear, for God's love is there to seal
Have nothing to be ashamed or have no fright
For God is there to heal.
The life you go through is not only on land
But the Kingdom of Heaven is a life of joy
For everyone has a tunnel in God's hand
Even for little girls and boys.

Rachel Pavel
St Irene School
Warrenville
Grade 7

On a Wednesday Night

My savior is Jesus. My savior I love.
He listens when I pray. He watches me everyday.
He saved me on a Wednesday night,
When I prayed one little prayer.
I was saved when I said,
"In Jesus' name, Amen."

When people ask him into their heart
They will be saved.
Their sins will be forgotten,
And they will be forgiven.
When He calls I will come.
When He says it's time to go.
When I die I know where I will go.
He will let me go to Heaven,
Because I was saved one Wednesday night.

My savior is Jesus. My savior I love.
He listens when I pray. He watches me everyday.
He saved me on a Wednesday night,
When I prayed one little prayer.
I was saved when I said,
"In Jesus'" name, Amen."

Leroy Epperson
Harrison Elementary School
Wonder Lake
Grade 8

Hockey

Hockey is the best sport in the world
when we play, we beat the other team

When we are celebrating
we see the other team so sad because they lost

We go over to them and say
"Good game."

Joey Guthrie
Beckemeyer Elementary School
Beckemeyer
Grade 8

A Poem About Soccer

You can play this sport in all types of weather
Because it stands above the rest.
This sport is so exhilarating,
Especially if you are the best.
This sport is very fun to play,
It's cool to play it at night,
However, even better if played in the day.
If this sport was non-existing,
I am sure my life would be a bore.
Thanks to whomever invented it,
I now play it more and more.
You play this sport with a special ball,
In fact, I keep one in my locker.
I am sure you know what sport this is,
Of course, it is soccer.

Concepcion Rodelo
Stratford Jr High School
Bloomingdale
Grade 8

The Girl I See

When you look in the mirror, what do you see?
A face, your face, but I see different.
You say you're ugly, but looks don't phase me.
What I see, a kind face, is permanent.

You may think you are unimportant.
You may think negative, I think you're wrong.
I think you're wanted, become confident.
Don't be afraid, go out and sing your song.

I don't understand why you have this thought.
Who cares what they may say, follow your heart.
Believe in what you do, teach what you've sought.
Have trust in yourself, God will never part.

Don't give in, you will forever succeed.
Trust in yourself always, let your heart lead.

Dane Hansen
St Ferdinand School
Chicago
Grade 8

Friends

When your friends turn away
You don't know what to do
It leaves you sad, confused, and lonely
In these times
People change so quick
And they're not the ones you knew
Nobody here is like me
Now I'm the odd one out
And it seems so wrong
That all of them
Should get to have another
If you're not in, you're always out
That's so much harder than you think
Long, dark hallways inspire fear
Of all the kinds there are
When on one's there to catch you
You must be careful not to fall
You can't look back upon the past
And ever really know
If you could have changed with your friends
Or if you were destined to walk the path now that you must go.

Bethany Willeford
Tri-City Jr-Sr High School
Buffalo
Grade 8

My Good Friend

You're a good friend
You always will be
You helped me out in my bad times
When I needed you
You never really knew
That you were helping me
Till this letter that came
You never knew me

You're a good friend
You always will be
You stood up for me
When you never had to
You make me laugh
And brighten my day
You sent me signs that you cared that day

You're a good friend
You always will be
You won't know me now
Till the clouds roll away.

Sarah C. Goad
Pennoyer Elementary School
Norridge
Grade 8

High School

The school year is coming to an end
It's time to say goodbye to my friends
High school is just around the bend.

High school can be a scary place
Sometimes you will see a new face
Maybe one of another race.

So now that I am in High School
You still have to follow the rules
But I think High School is really cool.

Brian Lanter
Beckemeyer Elementary School
Beckemeyer
Grade 8

Raindrops

cold drops falling down
blue drops splashing on the flood
dripping from the trees
"drip" on the green grass and streets
to the soil and up again

Daisy T. Reyna
Holy Angels School
Aurora
Grade 7

The Spell

I think I saw the devil,
He came riding in so fast,
And suddenly he vanished,
He lingers in the past.

He put a plague upon us,
He cast a sinister spell,
Then he went on his evil way,
To the sweltering pits of Hell.

The spell he cast on us was harsh,
A spell of greed and hate,
What would the world be like today
If he came a century too late?

He gave kids visions of violence,
He told them that fighting was right,
He taught them to flirt with all that's bad
And filled their dreams with fright.

He suggested they should play with guns,
He assured it would be okay,
He raped them of their innocence,
And stole their souls away.

Emily Homa
Stratford Jr High School
Bloomingdale
Grade 8

Follow Your Heart

Life's path can sometimes be difficult.
Like the waters of a flowing river, it is ever-changing.
It is hard to know which choices to make or which turns to take,
for there is so much in life to behold.
But if you listen closely to the sound of your own dreams,
to the voice of the wind, and the wisdom of the trees,
you will soon discover a strength inside you,
and you will understand.
The answers you seek are already within you,
just waiting for your grasp.
So look with more than your eyes,
and never ever be afraid to follow your heart.

Eboney Grant
Quincy Jr High School
Quincy
Grade 8

Try

Don't always wait for helping hands
to lead you through the mist.
Maybe you should try yourself and go on without assist.
And now you know that you can fulfill the dreams you've always had,
protect those dreams with all your heart or ill forces may turn them bad.
Just believe in yourself and you will succeed in
whatever you want to do,
just follow your dreams and mind the light,
that will always bring you through.
For it will guide your soul through light and dark,
and sleet and rain and snow.
This light is your conscience,
and don't ever let it go.

Stephanie Zare
Highland Middle School
Libertyville
Grade 7

Dancing for Myself

My heart pumps faster to fit the oncoming rush of excitement
And yet my face tries to stay calm as it flashes a strong smile.
I hear the applause as the curtain slowly rises and the music begins.
"One, two, three. One, two, three," it says as if talking to me,
Waiting for my first movement so that the melody can join in.
My arms begin to stir, carefully at first and then easily.
Quickly I add my feet hoping they won't mess me up.
Suddenly I look out into the audience it becomes one dark blur
And I begin to think I'm the only one there, dancing for myself,
As if I were a little kid dancing in the living room.
As my dance slowly ends I am transported back to life
For the applause has awakened me. Quickly I bow, and run off stage.

Emily Fields
Nichols Middle School
Evanston
Grade 7

Mexico, My Soul

Black and blue.
A feeling that won't go away
when I remember,
when I wish to turn back time
and not receive the harm that others have done.
Moving away
from my homeland and heart,
the only place that described me
deep inside my soul.

Alma Martinez
Logandale Middle School
Chicago
Grade 7

India's Children

The shortage of food makes them fight one another.
They cry for food, shelter, and most of all for a mother.

Few are there to dry their eyes.
No one sings them lullabies.
Throughout the hardships of the years,
They have shared the same types of fears.

Their stories are sad, but very true,
They need help from people like you.
Your support might be the best of all,
So be the one to hear their call.

Please take a few minutes of your time,
To spare as little as a dime.
Your contribution will make a difference,
To these poor children of India.

Liz Paunicka
St Matthew School
Champaign
Grade 8

Tears of War

The wind is blowing with the gunshots in the air,
Happiness is lost because pain we can not bear,
So many are lost,
So many are gone,
Never before something like this,
I've looked upon,
When will all this suffering end,
When will this broken heart mend,
Holding back the tears,
Who's to blame,
Because of all the lives we've lost,
So many we can't name,
One day this country will be free,
But the pain still will be.

Benazir Chhotani
River Trails Middle School
Mount Prospect
Grade 7

Basketball

Basketball is my favorite sport
Watch me as I run the court
Forward, guard, or center position
Making shots in fast repetition
I steal the ball
But while I'm driving I get the call
I missed the first
And I think I'm cursed
Offense, defense, it's nearly the same
We play this sport for the love of the game
If my ball sails and whooshes the net
Everyone in the crowd would cheer I bet
Indoors, outdoors, day or night
It's fun anytime there's a hoop in sight
Winter, spring, summer, and fall
All the seasons are great for basketball!

Brian Paplaski
Highland Middle School
Libertyville
Grade 7

Sister

Being best friends with you
Is what I love to do

We are together every day
Telling secrets without delay

We have fun when we laugh and play jokes
Even when we talk to our old folks

Every once in a while, we are not that sweet
But without each other we'd never be complete

Most of the time we get along
Through there are times when things go wrong

When I have bad days where I'm sad
You come along and make me glad

We have our fights over the littlest things
But once they are over, oh, the joy it brings

Many times we wish the other was dead
But those are only harsh words in our head

We will always be sisters to the end
But you are considered as my best friend

Rachel Minard
Beckemeyer Elementary School
Beckemeyer
Grade 8

Searching

I'm searching for the day
When I may find a way
To get it through to you
Until then what do I do?

I'm searching for a guy
Who will keep my eyes dry
Who will always keep me smiling
And never get me crying.

I'm searching to find and see
More to the life God has given to me
To find my happiness
And to see everyone's kindness.

Jaclene Bellinder
Harrison Elementary School
Wonder Lake
Grade 8

Kindness

Kindness is. . .
Willing to share
Showing respect
Showing you care
Not being mean
Not judging people
Giving people chances
Being nice to others

Maggie Cruz
Mayer Elementary School
Chicago
Grade 7

What Is Life?

Life.
Is there a meaning?
Or do we create our own?
Is life a riddle to be understood
Or a lesson to be learned?
Have we learned it at death
Or forgotten it at birth?
What is life?

Our meaning is our own.
We choose our own meaning and dreams
For ourselves to work toward.
Life is both a riddle and lesson.
The riddle, which is given at birth,
And the lesson is learned at death.
Life is a way to experience and learn.

Skylar Patridge
V I T Jr High School
Table Grove
Grade 7

The Young Mallard Drake

There was a young mallard drake,
Who loved to swim in the wake.
A hunter came by
And said "You must die!
For supper the drake I will make!"

Joshua Ashmore
St John The Baptist School
West Frankfort
Grade 8

lantern

sun
shining
glowing bright
leaving tonight
gone

Josh Wilson
Pleasant Hill Elementary School
Peoria
Grade 7

Morning

The destructor of night
winds through the hall
bouncing through doorways
reflecting off the wall
stripping dark corners
of their murky light
shooting in every
direction taking flight
throughout the room
the shadows scatter
perilous dreams
die thereafter

Rachel Van Ryn
Albright Middle School
Villa Park
Grade 8

Young Poets
Grades 4-5-6

Spirits

My spirit is my soul,
My spirit is free.
My spirit is my life,
My life within me.

When I think of my spirit, I think of myself,
Without my spirit I would have nothing left.
I wouldn't know right, I wouldn't know wrong,
Without my spirit all hope is gone.

My spirit is like a treasure, a treasure to behold,
My spirit is precious, as precious as gold.
My spirit is inside me, my heart keeps it whole,
A spirit is priceless, it costs nothing to own.
Everyone has one, one of their own.

So take care of your spirit,
And guard it close.
Because your spirit is the one thing,
You need the most.

Roddrick Bowers
Meridian Elementary School
Mounds
Grade 6

Top Poems Grades 4-5-6

The Loon

Sitting on the dock in a cedar chair
I gaze at the still mirror spreading across the lake.
A ripple comes to me.
Looking for its source I hear a faint tremello.
A loon.
A graceful bird dives into the mirror that stays ever still.
Getting off the chair, I sit at the edge of the dock and kick my feet back and forth.
I see in the distance a black and white blur.
I stop kicking as the blur takes form.
As still as a statue I wait. . .wait. . .
The bird appears, sailing to me
In the golden beam of sunset, shining on that mirror.
It swims up to my feet and releases its sorrowful wail,
Turns around and swims into the distance.
The sun is gone. The lake is still.
I get up and walk into the cabin, my feet dripping on the soft carpet.
I sit on my bed, lay down and close my eyes.
On the edge of sleep, I hear a tremello.
A soft, warm-hearted tremello.
The loon. . .the loon. . .the loon.

Pier T.C. Debes
West Middle School
Rockford
Grade 6

The Bard

As the sun sets in the horizon
"Listen!" says the Bard.
All who sit around his fire
Are silenced by his charm.
He spins a yarn
And weaves a tapestry
Of tales from ages past;
Of warriors in battle—
Their valor is renowned;
Of mystic animals in faraway lands
And plants with healing powers;
Of lords and ladies, princes and princesses—
Their noble deeds are told.
As the first star is sighted
In the evening calm and still,
The dying fire is smoldered
And the Bard says, "Farewell!"
As mothers carry their sleepy ones
And ponder o'er his words—
Though the Bard may be forgotten,
His words will live on still.

Joyce Fan
Highland Middle School
Libertyville
Grade 6

Top Poems Grades 4-5-6

The Lion

The lion slowly walks about
In his lion way.
Soft and quiet as he creeps,
Searching for his prey.

The lion yawns and down he lay
His furry lion head.
He then closes his big eyes,
And sleeps in his lion bed.

The lion soon then awakens,
And lets out his lion roar.
He then begins his brand new day,
As he has done before.

Kaitlin Fink
Iroquois West Upper Elementary School
Thawville
Grade 5

Music to My Ears

Music is a useful tool. It can achieve many things.
It has a special meaning to anyone who sings.
Everyone plays music by just walking down the street.
As our shoes hit the ground, you hear the rhythm in our feet.

Music is a language that we all can comprehend.
We only have to choose what kind of message we will send.
More music evolves every day. That we know is true.
We can even take old songs, mix them up, and make them new.

The graceful music of ballet is played beautifully in tune.
There is music of the outdoors, wolves howling at the moon.
Rigid, hard, rap beats, words spoken fast.
The upbeat songs of pop groups, who some say will never last.
Rock 'n Roll is very loud, but that's okay with me,
Because you can tell they play their music very honestly.

You may think that music is a single commodity,
But music can be many things, which you soon will see.
Music has a different meaning to anyone that will hear.
It's for the people who love to dance with those that they hold dear.

So sing your song and beat your drum; it won't take long to start.
You will make great music, as long as it comes from your heart.

Melissa Janes
Blessed Sacrament School
Belleville
Grade 6

Dusk

Natures red sandstone sculptures dominate the land.
They wait eagerly for sunset, because they know
that the suns last fleeting rays
add greatly to their beauty.
But while they wait
the violet clouds amass to form
a different kind of mountain.
Then even the vain sandstone must admit
that its beauty has been equaled
by its brothers in the sky.

Jacqueline Jankowski
Quest Academy
Palatine
Grade 6

A Lab in a Basket

In my Easter basket
I thought I would find eggs
Instead I opened it
To a set of four hairy legs

At first I thought I was going crazy
But I looked again and found
That what I saw was really true
Mom said she got him from the pound

We named him after the New Year
Millennium became his name
He is as naughty as my brother
Soon we hope they will both be tame

No matter what the bunny brings to me
In the coming years
Nothing will make me as happy
As the memories we share

Brittany Nichting
Kellar Central School
Peoria
Grade 4

Color Doesn't Matter

She took my hand. It wasn't her color.
She eats. It's not what I eat.
But when she laughs, it's how I laugh.
And when she cries, it's how I cry.
And color doesn't matter.

Bruce Scott
St Anthony's School
Streator
Grade 5

Storm

When rain is pounding on the roof,
And lightning fills the sky,
I'm suddenly lost and scared and cold.
But I sit and wonder why.

What's so scary about water?
And sound and flashing light?
What's so scary about storms,
That shake up the whole night?

Maybe it's the darkness,
Or the way that I'm not warm.
Maybe it's just mental.
I'll never like a storm.

Amanda Walsh
Kennedy Jr High School
Lisle
Grade 6

Top Poems Grades 4-5-6

Angels

Sweet angels watching over me
Making sure I'll be the best I can be
Always on duty, reassuring to all
A protective net, in case I should fall

Loving and caring through my pain and sorrow
Confirming my safety, will be here tomorrow
With an innocent smile, blessing an adult or a child
Letting my expression of my heart flow wild

God is so blessed to have such great creatures
With an innocent quality and blossoming features
Always at my side, I am forever glad
My angel, I know him; he is my dad

Alison Yuhas
Northlawn Middle School
Streator
Grade 6

Can You Imagine

Cars without tires, kids that are not liars.
Houses without roofs, no cowboy boots.
Windows in a house, a 3,000 pound mouse.
Fridges not cold, letters not bold.
Trucks with no wheels, geese with no corn fields.

Michael Sadler
Jonesboro Elementary School
Jonesboro
Grade 6

Friendship

Friendship is like the sky

It never ends.
The universe is smaller than true friendship,

If you think about it.
In case of a fight a wise friend forgets his or her anger,
Before she goes down to bed.
Nothing can keep two friends away from one another,

Not candy,
Not money,

NOTHING!

Kelsy Rezansoff
Bolin Elementary School
East Peoria
Grade 5

What Is Yellow?

Yellow is a sunflower,
a banana,
a color in your box of crayons.
Yellow is a bird,
a color in the rainbow shining its way.
Yellow is a moon,
a bright golden sun,
a twinkling star in the blue sky.
Yellow is a gum-ball,
a bird flying by a school bus full of kids.
Yellow is a color a light bulb gives off,
a diamond,
a streetlight that tells you to slow down.
Yellow is a pencil,
a stripe on a flag,
a buzzing bumblebee.
Yellow is a lemon,
a fish,
a strand of blond hair.
Yellow is my favorite color because it's loud, mellow
and screams hello...

Kathy Laba
St. Richard School
Chicago
Grade 5

Revolutionary War

F or freedom they fought
R iding on horses they came
E veryone was sad by the dying of people
E vents happened as the war went on
D eath was everywhere north, south, east, & west
O verall Washington led them to victory
M any people died grandpas, dads, & children

Allie Rush
Booth Central Elementary School
Wilmington
Grade 4

Madiline

One day Madiline walked the beach,
Along the sizzling sand.
Her feet got so hot,
Continuing she could not,
So she sat down and played in the sand.
And while she played,
Her mind drifted away,
And a brilliant idea she got.
She ran home and got,
Some glue and paper,
And back to the beach she did trot.
To the sand she did add the glue and the paper,
A new form of scraper she sought.
She called and she called,
For people to buy,
Newly made sandpaper.
But she is still mine,
My dear old Madiline.

Brennan Tracy
New Hebron Christian School
Robinson
Grade 4

Grandma,
My Guardian Angel

God sent you from heaven a gift for me.
To put in my pocket or watch over me.
Made with love, care, and hope.
Do you think I'd ever lose her...nope!
She sits in the clouds and watches me play.
I hear her singing while I lay.
She talks to me and tells me secrets.
She whispers in my ear, "you don't have to fear."
I talk to her in my dreams, we visit France, Florida, and the seas!
We play games and laugh a lot.
She tickles my head while I lay in bed.
"Close your eyes," that's what she said.
Then she gave me a kiss and flew away.
I hope I'll see her again someday!

Tiffany Hall
Geraldine Kerkstra Middle School
Oak Forest
Grade 6

The Backpack

I am the backpack that gobbles the stack
Of books and papers you carry on your back.
Books and papers I like best
But let me tell you about the rest.
There are colored pencils of different flavors
If you give me some you'll do me a favor.
I like lunches in bags or boxes
Just don't give me any sockses!
Notebook covers I like to munch
Sometimes they're better than your lunch.
Test results I like to taste
So please don't throw them in the waste.
Crayons and markers I love to bite
So try to keep them out of site.
So when you put something in your pack
Keep in mind that it's my snack!

Tara Cesario
Anderson Elementary School
St Charles
Grade 5

A New Day

A new day begins,
From the long night of drizzles,
To a new beautiful day.
The water flowing
As the sun rises.
The wind is blowing,
But in a way, nothing is going to go wrong.
The birds are chirping,
I yawn to see myself awake,
Awake from the terrifying nightmares.
As I go downstairs to see my family,
I know nothing can go wrong today.

Nadia Zoubareva
Meridian Middle School
Buffalo Grove
Grade 5

The Dream

I had a dream at night,
While I was in bed.
It was scary...
There was a monster under my bed—
And this is what the monster said:
"Little boy I want to be your friend,
So open up your heart and let me come in."
I hid under my blanket
Then I slowly came out.
I heard a loud voice as it started to shout.
"Little boy don't be scared of me!"
It was just my brother playing a trick on me.

Zaheen Rupani
Solomon Elementary School
Chicago
Grade 4

My Goal

My goal is like your goal; something I want in life,
and is something that will never cost a price.
It seems like how hard we worm and squirm,
it always gets harder to reach it.
You may only be inches away,
but it will seem like eternity.
So you may reach it or you may not,
so go and never stop!

Emily McClain
Manteno Middle School
Manteno
Grade 6

Gone

The whirling winds surrounded my cold and empty heart.
The waters crashed around the open sea,
Dampening my flamed feelings.
Love and life were no longer important,
As I felt hurt and betrayed.
Sand was being thrashed at my tear struck face,
Sticking to me like a rough outer core.
The journey home would be a long winding trail,
Of sadness, anger, and loneliness.
He was gone.

Melissa Shamberg
Meridian Middle School
Buffalo Grove
Grade 6

I Wish I Had a Little Sister

I wish I had a little sister as small as me.
I wish I had a little sister that's not afraid of a bumble bee.
My mom and her would be as happy as can be.
Oh? Now I wish I do not have a little sister.
Because my mom might forget about me!!!

Courtney Underwood
Diekman Elementary School
Dolton
Grade 5

Balloon

Slipped from the boys' hands.
Getting
higher,
higher,
higher,
so high it went out of sight,
floating over a football field
almost popped by a bird's beak
flew into a house
went up to the ceiling
finally it comes down back into the boys' hands.

Tyler Hunsinger
Grand Prairie Elementary School
Joliet
Grade 4

The Dream

I'm plunging into this well of soullessness – Falling toward the golden
    coins of those who did not wish for this.
I see the blank, cold faces around me, searching sleeplessly to find
    what was once themselves, but was replaced by material things.
They checked each golden coin for dreams they might have had in their innocence.
For shimmering memories they could steal as a last attempt at saving
    what was left of their meaningless existence.
As my hands move in a liquid motion, I see a blanket of snowy white
    cover them and I feel the faith leave me.
Panic takes over. My head turns wildly, seeking that which gave me
    life, memories, and feeling.
These were all kept in a glistening gold sphere – which, as I looked closely at,
    held living pictures of colorful seasons, sunlight, and intervals of laughter and sobs.
As I gazed at this precious globe, I felt the color come back to my body and a rush come under me.
I was put back into my pearl of existence.
I stood at that well and saw no more than the shimmering coins –
    Left by those who did not wish for this.
I tossed in my own glistening brass wish – That turned into gold as it struck the bottom.

Celena Rhoads
Century Oaks Elementary School
Elgin
Grade 6

Your Mind is the Most Powerful

Your mind can take you anywhere. It's only up to your imagination.
You can land in the world of princesses and unicorns, space, or under the sea.
Your mind has the power to make your own private wonderful world with your imagination.
It makes no difference how old you are, everybody has an imagination and should use it.
Not only does your mind hold inside of it your imagination;
There is also an amazing power that is almost like super powers.
Whenever you do something and tell yourself whether or not you can do it,
That super power inside of you goes along with what you have told it.
If you have confidence in yourself; and if you want to do well on something
Use your imagination and show your magic powers what you want to happen.
Show yourself how good life is going to be.
To be successful you need confidence in yourself, practice, and positive thought.
But until you do know how to use your mind to be positive
Use your mind to be a princess down under the sea.

Angela McBride
Still Middle School
Aurora
Grade 6

My Grandma's Eyes

When I look in my Grandma's eyes I never know what I'll find.
Sometimes I'll glance over and see her smiling at one of us and all I can see is kindness and joy's reflection.
Or in church I'll turn to see her eyes closed showing nothing but respect and admiration of God.
When we watch the news together and crime scenes come on I'll look over and see her shake her head.
Then there is anger and disappointment in her eyes.
Or when someone mentions a family member who is no longer with us I'll see sadness in her warm, soft eyes.
But no matter when I look over I know there is one thing that never changes in her bright blue eyes
and that is a background of love.

Mandy Lewis
St Mary School
Alton
Grade 6

Hershey's Kisses

Kisses, kisses, kisses are so tempting. Ahh!
Kisses, kisses, kisses, looks like a chocolate mountain.
Oh kisses, kisses, kisses, stop luring me with your smell.
Mmm! Mmm! That was delicious!

Tammy Wruck
Hiawatha Elementary School
Kirkland
Grade 5

What You See at the Zoo

The gorilla is jumping up and down
wondering when it can touch the ground.

Then you see the monkey swinging on the trees
wondering when he can sneeze.

There's the zebra moping around
thinking of when he can leave this town.

There's the wolf looking upside down
looking at his playground.

Then there's the lion roaring loud
surrounded by a big crowd.

Everyone is yelling loud
in this very big crowd.

I'm sorry but it's time to go
grab a balloon and let's go.

Christina Fanucchi
Barbara B. Rose Elementary School
South Barrington
Grade 5

On the Farm

Every morning on the farm,
I wake up to be not alarmed.
To me it felt just like the zoo,
The birds were chirping, the cows said moo.
The roosters crowed to attract the hens.
The pigs were oinking in their pens.
I knew my job, to milk the cows,
Collect the eggs, then in the house.
Crack some eggs to make a meal,
With Dad I made a morning deal,
To do all this and don't break glass,
Then grab my backpack and off to class.
And don't forget, remember this,
I'm not a Mrs., I am a Ms.
Remember I live on a farm,
To the animals I mean no harm.

Anne Turner
Washington Jr High School
Naperville
Grade 6

What God Is

God is good.
God is powerful.
God answers our prayers.
God doesn't always answer
How we want Him to.

Almighty God You are great.
You rule the world,
Forgiving sins,
Welcoming more people.
You sent Your Son to save us.
For we were born under Your power and might.

Jimmy Mulcahy
St John Of The Cross School
Western Springs
Grade 5

Running

I really like to run a lot, run, run, run, along.
I run then stop and visit people or run and sing a song.
I like to run to places where I cannot ride or drive.
But if I don't run anywhere, then I stay at home and jive.

Mike Randall
Iroquois West Upper Elementary School
Thawville
Grade 5

My Life Is Like a Present

Life is like a present
Waiting to be opened,
Just like me waiting to be born,
With all my family members waiting, too

Life is like a present because
You don't know, what, why and when
They got you this present.

Life is like a present because
Once it is unwrapped,
You can't wrap it up again.

Life is like a present because
It is a surprise when you unwrap it,
Since you don't know what's going to be in that present....
Just like you never know
What's going to happen tomorrow.

Life is like a present because
When you open it up you might not like it,
Just like in life
Where there might be some things that
You like and dislike a lot.

Natalia Ruiz
Barbara B. Rose Elementary School
South Barrington
Grade 5

Animals

Animals,
Animals in the park,
Animals,
Animals in the zoo,
Animals
Animals in the city,
Animals in the country,
Animals,
Animals in the sky,
Animals,
Animals in the ground,
Animals.

Loralea Bean
Ina Comm Consolidated School
Ina
Grade 5

Spring Weather

Spring is a wonderful time,
Filled with Maples, Oaks and Pine;
I love to climb so high in trees,
Flowing with the air and leaves;
I love to go to school each week,
I like it when the teacher teaches;
This is why I love spring,
It is such a wonderful thing

Andrea Coulter
Ontarioville Elementary School
Hanover Park
Grade 5

Star

O star
O star
So far and bright
O star
O star
Who shines in the night
I see your glow
Your slow and gentle flow
Your touch, your feel
O it seems so real
O star
O star
So mighty and gold
O star
O star
So warm, but cold
I wish you may
I wish you might
Give me a ride
Into the deep, blue sky!

Katie Fehrenbacher
East Richland Elementary School
Olney
Grade 5

I Lost a Friend

I know you're not going to listen to me talking.
Or pay attention when you see me walking.
Even though we've known each other for so long.
I'm beginning to think your thinking is wrong.
I may have been your best friend by my friendship for you will never end.
Yes, of course, you may be mad,
But there is a part in my heart where I am sad,
Because of the way you said goodbye.
The opposite around is I want to begin to say, "hi."
I've said all I have to say,
And will pay for what I have said to make you feel wrong,
Just as long as it isn't strong.
I hope we can meet again someday.
But just as long as it doesn't rain.

Vanessa Corral
St Procopius School
Chicago
Grade 4

Myself

Dishwater blonde hair, brownish greenish eyes,
and light skin I am a sister of Derek, Kyle and Brandon.
Who loves family, friends, and my cats.
Who feels good about others.
Who needs love, compassion, and parents
to help me behave and make decisions.
Who shares my friendship, my joy, and my feelings.
Who fears life forever, not going to Heaven, losing my only friends:
Rosie, Jessica, and Lindsay.
Who would like to see Ireland, even though there is always wars going on.
Who dreams of more nice people in this world.
A student of Mrs. Ross, Mrs. Sefton, and Mrs. Millar.

Mandi Dorworth
Wells Elementary School
Grayville
Grade 5

Spring

The silence of winter is fading away,
And the soft, sweet sounds of the birds can be heard.
The whiteness on the ground melts away,
And bright green grass grows in its place.
Green leaves and colorful flowers
Take the place of the raw branches on trees and bushes.
The dark, gray clouds in the sky vanish,
As the radiant, yellow sun peeks out.
The cold, violent winds slowly disappear,
And a light breeze can now be felt.
The small, frisky animals that were hibernating for the long winter
Are now peeking out of their hiding places.
A light rain falls and everybody is happy,
For spring is now here.

Perri Kofkin
Meridian Middle School
Buffalo Grove
Grade 6

Caterpillar

I am the caterpillar, they are the weeds
Laughing, joking over me with
Their yellow faces turned towards the sun.
Waiting to be cut by the lawn mower
Just to grow again and spread
The cruelness towards me, the caterpillar.
While they die, I live and
Become a butterfly,
Beautiful
Just flying along the breeze.
The weeds are the popular,
The caterpillar, the unpopular.

Rachel Daum
Nelson Ridge School
New Lenox
Grade 6

Thoughts

Thoughts are a part of life.
There are good thoughts and bad thoughts.
And there are also thoughts that are wrong and right.

But the thoughts I have are special.
The kind of thoughts that brighten up your day.
The thoughts that make me want to say.
If I could have these kind of thoughts all the time,
It would certainly make my day.

My thoughts aren't only special,
They're soft and sweet,
But at times they can get weak.

Destiny Autman
Laraway Elementary School
Joliet
Grade 6

Smile

You should smile every once in awhile.
Even when you're sad, you should smile.
You should smile if you get something
you have always wanted.
You should smile when there are jokes that are funny.
You should smile if you like roast beef.
Even if you don't like peas, you should still smile.
When you smile then you make someone else smile.
And someone else and someone else and
Someone else and someone else and
Someone else and someone else and
Someone else and someone else and
Someone else and someone else and
Someone else and someone else and
So forth.

Christena Zeanah
Manteno Middle School
Manteno
Grade 6

The Night

The sky darkens
And the gentle breeze is brushing past your face
Then a sudden stillness
Everything is quiet
Except for the crickets
The temperature drops
And luminous lamps
Are placed outside
The moon comes out
Quiet and shy, it lights up the sky
The stars come out from hiding
One by one clouds are moving in
They cover the moon and stars
Silent screams, wind storms in
And then FLASH!
Lightning comes down, angry and bold
CRACK!
Thunder is heard across the land
It starts raining
The clouds and mad storm move away
As peace resumes

Caitlin Cronin
Frances Xavier Warde School
Chicago
Grade 5

Dreams

I'm dreaming though I cannot feel my skin.
The softness of my sheets brings my spirit from within.
My spirit roams the world in search of something more.
My spirit wants adventure so it goes into the core.
The core inside myself lets my spirit through the door.
My spirit is back within me though it is worn out.
It has had a busy night roaming about.
In my dream about my spirit, I've had a lot of fun.
Until my mom comes in my room and says get up
Sleepy one.

Stephanie Pieczynski
Channahon Middle School
Channahon
Grade 6

Spring

I think spring is when...

The sun is out to brighten up our day.
The beautiful flowers start to bloom.
The birds are flying through the air.
The trees and grass are turning green.
The beautiful butterflies come out to fly around.
You are able to ride your bike and play with your friends.
This is what I think spring is.

Amanda McGinnis
St John Fisher School
Chicago
Grade 4

Cat

Cat
Fat, smart
Running, walking, standing
Purr's around my feet
Feline

Evelyn Solano
St Procopius School
Chicago
Grade 4

Basketball

B alls bouncing around
A ir ball
S coring 3 points
K ids having fun
E nthusiasm
T raveling
B oxing out to get a rebound
A thletic
L eagues after school
L eaping for the ball

Tyler Baldwin
Manteno Middle School
Manteno
Grade 6

Christmas

Christmas is a very cool day,
It's awesome in every way.
I hop out of my bed,
And I run to the tree,
And right there,
Was a present twice the size of me!
I ripped it up.
Look what I see.
Right in front of me,
Was a big screen T.V.!
But what matters,
Is not the presents and the tree.
What really matters,
Is being with my family.

Joe Renardo
Geraldine Kerkstra Middle School
Oak Forest
Grade 6

Sports

Sports are fun
Like football and soccer.
But volleyball is not fun
Baseball and swimming are fun
But softball is not fun.

David Otto
St John Fisher School
Chicago
Grade 4

The Day the Sea Dried Up

The day the sea dried up,
All the fish cried.
The day the sea dried up,
Most of the fish died.
Cod moaned,
Salmon groaned.
Clown fish wept,
The crabs just slept.
Then, the rains came,
To crabs this was a shame.
Their wish came true,
This tale I tell you.

Virginia Sutfin
New Hebron Christian School
Robinson
Grade 4

Dogs

All dogs give me joy.
Dogs come in many colors.
They can run and play.

Tiffany Tutor
Booth Central Elementary School
Wilmington
Grade 4

Ballerinas

Ballerinas on their toes,
walk across the stage.
Their hair tied up in little bows.
They come in every age.

Their mothers sit and smile with glee
as their child spins and twirls.
They squint their eyes so they can see,
all the precious little girls.

Tondu, posé, plié
go the dancers on their feet.
The mothers like to watch the ballet,
and listen to the dancing beat.

Ashley Ubik
St Irene School
Warrenville
Grade 6

Wild

Wild
Big killer
Attacking, destroying, eating
Creature in the forest
Grizzly

Michael Holcomb
St Anthony's School
Streator
Grade 5

God

Come and watch over us
guide us in all we do
you know we love you
God creator of all
you are my savior
you are my God
love for the world
was made for you and me.

Jessie Yocum
St Frances Cabrini School
Springfield
Grade 4

Winter Fun

Last winter,
In the white fluffy snow,
I went sledding and skiing,
I flew down the biggest hill and slope,
It was fun!

Samantha Werner
St Mary School
Mundelein
Grade 6

A Glacier

A glacier is able
It is very willing
To be very killing
A glacier is unstoppable.

Craig Dailey
Tri-County Christian School
Freeport
Grade 4

Leah

pretty, funny
she is very special
I love Leah with all my heart
sister

Jerica Lynn Harweger
St John's Lutheran School
Buckley
Grade 5

Kitty Cats

The new kitten
is very playful
he runs and attacks little balls.

The older cat
just moped around
he was very unplayful.

Whitney Kincheloe
Central Elementary School
Lincoln
Grade 6

Spring

Thank You for every tree and flower
Thank You for every sky of blue
Thank You
We should spend every hour truly thanking You

Greg Daniels
Virginia Elementary School
Virginia
Grade 6

My Wish

I wish I had a million dollars.
I guess because I would buy everything for myself.
Wait . . . that doesn't feel good.
I wish I had no school,
I would play and play
But no, that doesn't feel right.
I wish I had a pony
I would ride it everyday.
Wait . . . that doesn't feel good either.
I wish I owned every store in the whole world.
Wait . . . that doesn't feel right either.
I wish I had a perfect life.
Yes, that feels just right.

Christine Ozarowski
Our Lady of Mt Carmel School
Melrose Park
Grade 5

Spring

In the spring before the flowers bloom
there is rainfall and thunder goes boom.
Deep in the ground the seeds start to grow
with sunny days they will start to show.
All the colors so bright
they glow in the sunlight.

Devan Spears
St Mary's of Kickapoo School
Edwards
Grade 5

Fishing Headquarters

Fishing all over the store.
I am not selling hunting any more.

I like sharp fishhooks.
I love Bass Pro Shop books.

I get a hundred visitors a day.
Shoplifters I shoo them away.

I love the visitors I get.
They are better than any old baseball mitt.

Dustin Eilers
Beckemeyer Elementary School
Beckemeyer
Grade 4

Friends

Friends will be here to the very end,
A sign of care they always will send.
Friendship is something that will always be there,
To find these type of friends is not so rare.

They come in every shape and size,
With green, brown and big, blue eyes.
Their appearance will never matter to you,
It's their friendship that counts, sincere and true.

Some friends may come and go,
The parting tears will quickly flow.
In your heart they will always stay,
Every minute of every day.

True friends will listen; true friends will hear,
True friends will walk you through your darkest fear.
But in times of trouble and in times of need,
Just remember, a friend is a friend, who's a friend indeed!

Carli Siebert
Northlawn Middle School
Streator
Grade 6

A Walk Through the Field

Through the field nothing on my feet;
I smell the flowers fresh and sweet.
I pick a tulip and a daisy.
They just sit still in my hand so lazy.
I throw them in the air so high.
They twirl and spin up in the sky.
With the wind blowing through my hair.
I walk a little farther with nothing to bear.
As the ants glitter past my toes.
Going somewhere no one knows.
The butterflies dance and fly past me.
They flutter and flip so everyone can see.
The wind blows and the dirt flies up.
I hold out my hands and catch it like a cup.
Then I see the flowers fall to the ground.
And I know by another girl they will be found.

Amber Johnson
Iroquois West Upper Elementary School
Thawville
Grade 5

A Man from Sand

There was an old man from sand
Who liked to walk the land
He walked for three days
No money did he raise
But the people in the town gave him a hand

John Hochstetter
Kennedy Jr High School
Lisle
Grade 6

Butterflies

Butterflies floating
Throughout the sky, quickly,
Then stops on a flower.

Pamela Spyrka
St Mary of Czestochowa School
Cicero
Grade 6

Summertime

Summertime is a time for fun
When kids and children play and run

A time to relax, a time to be glad
A time to be happy and not to be sad

A time for smiles and happy faces
A time for swimming and many races

A time to be good, a time to sleep in
A time for loving and a time to win

Bridget Kelly
Most Holy Redeemer School
Chicago
Grade 5

Recipe

Soft nose and long neck
Big body, lots of hair
Head so big
Looking so fair
Nuzzling and kissing
Hooves so coarse
Beautiful, beautiful
This makes a horse!

Brita E. Morland
North Park Elementary School
Chicago
Grade 4

My Fears

I know a girl, who is afraid of snakes.
She fears them even more,
Than drowning in a lake.
If she ever met a bear,
All she'd do, is sit there and stare.

She's afraid of the dark,
Likewise, a shark.
She's afraid as you can see,
Of a big, fat, scary bee.
But most importantly,
That girl is me.

Alyssa R. Bauer
St Mary-Dixon School
Dixon
Grade 6

The Millennium is Coming

The millennium is coming
It will soon be here.
Lots of people are coming.
To my house this year.
We will have yummy treats.
Let's just hope my room stays neat!

Kristen Wilke
Riverwood Elementary School
McHenry
Grade 5

Wind

Cold or warm
Fierce and strong
So loud in the trees
make the bells go ding dong
Blowing pushing
you can't get it pinned
Hear it at the door but it can't get in
this makes wind.

Casey Strickler
North Park Elementary School
Chicago
Grade 4

Rain

It drips and it drops
And chills my housetop.

It drips and it drops
When it hits the ground.

It showers the flowers
And makes them lively.

It showers the streets and roads
And out come the toads.

It washes the streets
And it smells sweet.

It floods the field
And makes a muddy shield.

It makes us cold
And it chills our toes.

It wets our town
As it falls around.

It comes in spring
For all these things.

Erika Pimentel
Nixon Elementary School
Chicago
Grade 5

What Is Red?

Red is a color of a rose,
a cherry,
a cranberry,
and Rudolph's shiny nose.
Red is lipstick
that you can pick.
Red is a crayon,
a marker,
a colored pencil,
and some dark red tinsel.
When I think of red,
I think of apples,
tomatoes, red berries,
bows, hearts,
and strawberries.

Michelle Magat
St. Richard School
Chicago
Grade 5

The Ghost

I thought I saw a ghost
A walking midnight ghost
As pale as the moon itself
Every night I could hear it scream
It screams help... help... help...
On Friday the 13th

Nicole Nugent
Booth Central Elementary School
Wilmington
Grade 4

Nascar

The cars flew by at record speed,
The race had already started.
Tires squealed and gears ground,
The car fumes filled the air.

Ten more miles of deafening noise,
The roar of the engine blared.
Speeds so great the colors blurred,
The need for speed was definitely there.

Tim Ludwigson
Schiesher Elementary School
Lisle
Grade 5

Lolly As a Flower

Sunshine yellow,
Spring prettiness,
Singing about things of spring
On the green grass.

Claire Mullen
St John Of The Cross School
Western Springs
Grade 5

The Day

The sun is shining nice and bright
The birds are singing with delight.
All the May flowers are blooming just right.

The grass is green the sky is blue
This is the best day to read it to you.

Mike Doolan
Channahon Middle School
Channahon
Grade 6

Peace, Love and Kindness

Where there is peace
There is love

Where there is love
There is kindness

Where there is kindness
There is God

Where there is God
There is no killing, dying, fighting or suffering.

Lindsey Williams
Evangelical Christian School
Chicago
Grade 4

A Sailor Past His Prime

A sailor once lived in a tree,
Completely unhappy was he!
In his earlier days,
He'd ridden the waves,
On a ship in the rollicking sea.

So one day this man said to me,
"I'm through with life up in this tree.
I plan to go home,
To a sea white with foam,
And contented is what I shall be!"

Then he set off for wide and deep ocean,
Without contemplating his notion;
When he got to the sea,
He sadly did see,
At sixty he couldn't stand motion!

So he realized it wasn't so bad,
That he couldn't remain a Sinbad,
It was not a disgrace,
Staying in his old place,
In the tree which had once made him sad!

Alexander English
Kennedy Jr High School
Lisle
Grade 6

Kenny and Jenny

There once was an old man named Kenny.
He really like a girl named Jenny.
So they got married,
the ring she still carries,
and Kenny found a best friend in Jenny.

Carrie Meyer
Beckemeyer Elementary School
Beckemeyer
Grade 5

All About Me

My name is Andrew,
I live in Breese.
I love to ride my bike,
and rollerskate at D's.
I am ten years old,
and go to school.
Sometimes it is hard,
and I feel like a fool.
I've got a pet dog named Yo-Yo,
and a deer named Daisy.
I would ride my deer,
but she is lazy.
I've got a sister named Amy, who just got a car,
so stay off the sidewalks, because she is bizarre.
I play with my dog, but sometimes she bites,
she even bit her own tail when we were in a fight.
I do flips on my trampoline and swim in my pool,
but when friends come and play with me, it is so cool.
Now you know about me, so I am through,
I've got to go now, and find something to do.

Andrew Gildehaus
Beckemeyer Elementary School
Beckemeyer
Grade 5

My Family's Sadness

Once my cousin had a dad
He was the best friend you could have ever had.

He did not have much to say.
That's what I wondered day after day.

If I were him the jobs would have drove me crazy.
But I could see why he could handle it day after day,
Because he was not lazy.

When he died we cried and cried
As he watched in Heaven every tear that fell from our eye.

He was my friend but now he's dead,
But if only I had the chance to see him again.

Christopher Matthews
Evangelical Christian School
Chicago
Grade 4

My Dog Molly

My dog is Molly
She is jolly

We have fun
Playing in the sun

She's not small
She's not tall

She barks at the mail
Wagging her tail

Running after her ball
She doesn't always come when we call

We love to run
Having fun in the sun

Kevin Zwickl
St John Fisher School
Chicago
Grade 4

Sports

hockey is awesome,
baseball is cool,
volleyball is boring, basketball is too,
soccer is snoring,
tennis is too,
snow boarding rules,
and skiing drools,
football is hitting,
that's all the sports there are.

Billy Keiss
St John Fisher School
Chicago
Grade 4

Soccer

Here they come
Dribbling the ball.
I hope none
Of our players fall.
The closer they are,
The more nervous I get.
Pretty soon they'll give it
A great big kick.
I am hoping it won't go in,
So we can be ahead in the end.
Here they are, they kick the ball.
But to my surprise,
I am the one to fall,
But I get up and save the ball.

Drew Westendorf
St Anthony of Padua Grade School
Effingham
Grade 5

In Dreams

In dreams you can fly like a bird in the sky,
Or go back to the beginning of time.
You can talk with the animals,
And swim in the deep seas.
You'll never have to worry about losing your keys.
In dreams the world could be a wonderful place,
Or you could ride on a ship to outer space.
You could run through a cold desert in Africa,
Or live in Antarctica where it never snows,
And battle the deadliest of foes.
In dreams nothing could ever go wrong,
And something short could be long.
In dreams there would be nothing to worry about until you awake...

John Metz
St Mary School
Alton
Grade 6

A Basketball Game

Dashing down the court as I move my feet
I feel like I am running down a long, long street.
I can hear the crowd yelling as I try to get the ball.
I push and pull until I have that round, rough ball.
I shoot and score, hurrah, I hear!
As I run back down that long, long street, I push to get the rebound.
I jump to get the ball, and foul. I can hear the referee
Saying foul, number forty three!
The other player gets two shots. I rest on number one.
I have to get the rebound; the score is very close.
She misses number one and scores on number two.
I look up at the scoreboard. The score is all tied up, 20-20.
I hear the buzzer buzz as loud as a siren on a police car.
We have one last time out.
I go to get a drink, the freezing water down my throat refreshes as it flows.
I can feel the sweat dripping down my face.
I run back on the long, long court. We have to get the ball and shoot.
We have only seconds left. We cannot lose this game today.
I can feel the pressure building up as we try to break the press.
I get the ball and shoot and score. That means WE WON!

Anne Orlet
Blessed Sacrament School
Belleville
Grade 6

I Love Them but They Don't Love Me

I love my brother but he doesn't love me.
I love my sister but she doesn't love me.
I love my cousin but she doesn't love me.
I love my niece but she doesn't love me.
I love my dad, he loves me; and I love my mom, and she really loves me.
That's my family and it doesn't matter that all of them might not love me,
What matters most is I LOVE THEM.

Jamie Caesar
Morton Career Academy
Chicago
Grade 4

Food

I like food.
My favorite food is pizza, but I still like
Candy, chocolate, chips, gum, doughnuts, and ice cream.
I steal a lot of food.
My hobbies are eating, drinking, and running.
Sometimes I watch TV and eat.

Mike Ryan
St John Fisher School
Chicago
Grade 4

If Only

If only we were all the same color
If only everyone was rich
If only no one got judged
If only everyone lived in Florida
If only boys would admit that girls were always right
If only singers lived next door to us
If only I could stop saying "If only".

Bianca Sanchez
Emerson Elementary School
Berwyn
Grade 6

Riding a Horse

By riding a horse through the woods,
Or through the mountains,
Or on an open plain,
You feel the joy to do it again and again.
And my horse can tell when it is time to go home,
And turning around he knows the way to go too.
So I doze off and when we get home,
He gives a little lurch,
To wake me up.
And I hop off,
And walk him to the stable.
And the horse is so calm,
And so smart,
He can do almost anything.

Levi Brush
New Hebron Christian School
Robinson
Grade 4

Snow

Snow, snow, why won't you go?
You're blocking our roads, you're mean when you blow,
You're closing our schools and freezing our pools,
You're making us mad the visibility's bad,
All the dogs are barkin', all the cars are honkin',
The snow's so deep, I can't see my feet,
Snow, snow why won't you go?

Jason Piper
Grant Park Middle School
Grant Park
Grade 6

Spring

Spring! Spring! What a fantastic thing!
Picking flowers for hours and hours.
Going hiking and biking down
A long winding path.
Going to the park, or having a snack.
You can go to the mall,
You'll have quite a ball!
You have no time to waste, not at all!
So when spring comes be aware,
You have all these fun things to do and share!

Liz Brandt
St John Fisher School
Chicago
Grade 4

The Seasons

In the fall the leaves on the trees fall.
In the summer you can see me at the beach.
In the spring the flowers grow.
In the winter the roads are blocked and we can't go to school.
This is my favorite season because there's no school!

Stanley Pheteau
Forest View Elementary School
Mount Prospect
Grade 4

Dreams

I am famous.
I can swim like a fish,
I can fly like a bird.
I can skate across the ice and win the gold.

I can live underwater,
I can sleep in the sea.
I am an artist, I am a singer.

I am an actress,
I am a queen.
I own a palace,
In England and Paris.

I have seen the world.
I have seen all the sights.
I live in all the countries,
I am there all at once.

I am a doctor,
I am a lawyer.
I am a comedian.
I am an engineer.

And all I have to do is fall asleep.

Danielle Marshall
St Irene School
Warrenville
Grade 6

Bubble Wrap

Clear as a drop of water.
Bubbly as a bubble.
Crackles like popcorn in the microwave.
Slick as a newborn chick.
Makes music when you step on it.

Lisa Devereux
St John Of The Cross School
Western Springs
Grade 5

My Mother

My mother is so sweet,
She always helps me.

When she goes to the store,
I am always bored.

When she takes me to school,
She never forgets a hug.

When I get home,
She helps me with my homework.

When I brush my teeth,
She loves me.

When I go to bed,
She never forgets a hug.

I have always loved my mom,
And she has always loved me.

Kyle Eggleston
Evangelical Christian School
Chicago
Grade 4

Spring

Colorful flowers
Butterflies flying around
The wonderful spring

Diana Zenteno
St Mary of Czestochowa School
Cicero
Grade 6

War

Charging and racing of men
Women crying and singing sad sorrow
Piles of death and piles of blood
What has this become?
Just madness
That is war

Anaese Duran
Alexander G Bell Elementary School
Chicago
Grade 6

Where Is Poetry?

Where is poetry?
In a dog's legs when it runs
In a cat's purr,
In a frog's legs when it jumps,
In an apple you eat,
In your voice when you talk,

I know, here it is—
In the poetry book
That the teacher read to us.

Antoine Bouzi
Walker Elementary School
Evanston
Grade 5

Friends

Friends stick together
Kind of
Like, well, Elmer's Glue
They can't break away
Because it is dry
So you'll always be with them
From start to end

Abby Schwarting
Deer Creek-Mackinaw Middle School
Deer Creek
Grade 5

Look at Who You Are

Look down deep inside you,
Find out who you are,
Express your feelings,
Do what you want,
Because you are who you are.

Look from the inside,
Not the out,
Remember that,
You are who you are.

Remember that you make a difference,
No matter how small or large
The deed is
Say you did it,
And you'll like yourself,
Because then you'll remember,
You are who you are

No matter what anyone says,
You shall always know,
That I am who I am,
And you are who you are!

Abigail Livingston
Beverly Manor School
Washington
Grade 6

Glasses

My glasses are quite delicate.
They mean so much to me.

So whenever they fall,
I feel like I could scream.

You see without my glasses,
I might think that you're a tree.

So I guess my glasses,
Are a-ok with me.

Joseph Peckenpaugh
St Joseph Catholic School
Harvard
Grade 5

Nikki

Nikki is very energetic
She runs around the house
like she is in a panic
Whenever we leave
she puts on that puppy face
and acts so tragic.
She eats everything from A to Z
including things for people's needs.
By late at night she finally gets tired
so she sits on the couch
and acts all snuggly.

Marilyn Jacques
Indian Knoll Elementary School
West Chicago
Grade 6

Falcon

falcon in the air
painting the landscape above
spreading its wonder

Aditya Salunkhe
Stone Creek Elementary School
Roscoe
Grade 4

Dinosaurs

Dinosaurs, dinosaurs long ago
I believe in dinosaurs,
How about you?
I believe in all kinds of dinosaurs,
How about you?
I hope you do, too!
So come on,
Let's rock with dinosaurs,
How about you?

Aaron McCann
Hickory Bend Elementary School
Glenwood
Grade 4

My Friend

I have a friend, just like me,
We play all day, with such glee,
Though he's not very smart,
He's a great friend at heart.

I teach him every day just because, you see,
He wants so very much to learn,
I'll teach him how to do two times two
Every day the more he yearns,
To be as smart as I.

Steve Wakeman
Northlawn Middle School
Streator
Grade 6

Books

I like to read books all day
I buy them even though I have to pay.
Everyday I go to the library and read
If my parents won't let me I always start to plead.
I like books that are interesting
Mysteries are very convincing.
So books are like a friend
Without an end.

Yamilett Villegas
Our Lady of Mt Carmel School
Melrose Park
Grade 4

I Am

I am silly
I am free
I wonder how planes are built
I hear the ocean from a far away land
I see people shaking hands
I want people to do to others as they want to be treated
I am silly
I am free

I pretend to soar above the Earth
I feel as if I am very brave
I touch the sky above
I worry about bad weather
I cry when friends leave me
I am silly
I am free

I understand reading
I say it is wrong to lie
I dream our world would be a better place
I am silly
I am free

Arthur Lee
Kellar Central School
Peoria
Grade 4

To Asthma

Asthma, I hate you so much,
I just wish that someone could scare you away,
And I know it is not that easy,
But I still wish it could be that way.

You stay in my lungs like a spider on a web,
You make me cough and wheeze,
You scare me,
Sometimes I just sit and think, oh geez!

You make me take too much medicine,
You always annoy me,
You keep me from doing things that I love,
Why can't you just let me be?

Jessica Reed
Argenta-Oreana Elementary School
Oreana
Grade 6

Friends

Friends are people who take your side.
When it rains a friend gives you a ride.
Friends give each other joys.
They don't come over just to play with your toys.
Friends give each other high fives.
Friends don't give each other the hives.
Friends walk with you on the shore.
I couldn't ask for anything more.

Michael Watson
Iroquois West Upper Elementary School
Thawville
Grade 5

Basketball

A ball, a hoop, and you need a gym
Dribble it, pass it, we want a basket.
3 pointer! Slam dunk!
Don't get any fouls and of course no technicals!

Maura Harrington
St John Fisher School
Chicago
Grade 4

Friends Forever, I Hope

Friends can be helpful but, sometimes annoying
They can make you laugh or cry
Either way you still may love them
And you know they always care
Even though you may be mad
They love you just as much
So because of that I have to say
That's what my friends are for.

Nicole Pelton
Laraway Elementary School
Joliet
Grade 6

Snow

I like the way that God made snow
This is something you'll never know
God made snow all shiny and white
It can reflect the light so bright.

Aaron Johnson
Tri-County Christian School
Freeport
Grade 4

Can You Imagine ...

Beds without springs,
weddings without rings.

Kids without toys,
the world without boys.

Me without drumming,
Kids without humming.

Summer without pools,
Earth without schools.

The world without pens,
an eye without a lens.

C.J. Fricks
Jonesboro Elementary School
Jonesboro
Grade 6

Birds

Birds are very small
Birds are not big or strong
And birds have to build nests.

Jacqueline Hernandez
St Mary of Czestochowa School
Cicero
Grade 6

Green

Green is dark,
Green is light,
Green is always in my sight,
I see green in my chair,
I see green everywhere.
When I see green,
It makes me happy,
I love green very much,
I love green to the touch.
Green is clothes,
Green that flows,
I see green in the air
I see green everywhere.

Shaun Whitaker
Summit Elementary School
Collinsville
Grade 4

Girls

Long hair, pretty dresses
Buddies and friends
Wearing nice earrings
Not people to offend
Loving and caring
Wearing diamonds and pearls
Really smart, really nice
This makes girls

Alex Zorn
North Park Elementary School
Chicago
Grade 4

Frog

Ribbit, ribbit,
hippity, hop.
a frog.
All day,
non stop.
Lily pad to lily pad,
it goes, going,
going,
until the day it snows.
Ribbit, ribbit,
hippity, hop.
That frog.
Will it ever stop?

Samantha Hickey
St John Of The Cross School
Western Springs
Grade 5

Lost

I am lost.
I am standing here, lost.
I am waiting for you.
I am asking myself,
Where have you gone?
Where....am I?
I am frozen....in time,
Waiting for you....
I cannot find you.
I am lost.
Where are you?
The world is still changing,
But I am NOT moving on without you.
My world seems to have stopped turning,
Because you are not here.
You have hidden yourself,
And I cannot find you.
Where are you?
Come back.

Caitlin Keturi
Bolin Elementary School
East Peoria
Grade 5

Friends

A friend is someone you talk to
someone to go shopping with.
A friend is someone that comes over
someone to play sports with
and someone to go ice skate with.
A friend is someone who cares.

Jacqueline Keane
St John Fisher School
Chicago
Grade 4

Sara

S he wants to have fun
A person that likes art
R eally good at recess
A n animal lover

Sara Brall
Grand Prairie Elementary School
Joliet
Grade 4

Knights

Strong, brave
Training, riding, fighting
In tournaments and wars
Warriors on horseback

Andrew Olshefski
Manteno Middle School
Manteno
Grade 6

Rainbow Color

Rainbow
Colorful, bright
Arching, bending, flexing
Huge, sections of colors
Colorful

Emily Mullen
North Elementary School
Marshall
Grade 6

The Letter

This is my letter,
Which I send to you with care,
To soar above the highest clouds,
Through the brisk morning air.

I send to you my letter,
With friendship and with love,
As it soars above the highest clouds,
Like a patient, flying dove.

Tim Bauer
Nelson Ridge School
New Lenox
Grade 6

My Friend

I had a friend who was dear to me.
She would invite me to go to her house.
She might buy some candy bars—1, 2 or even 3.
Her cat would sniff my hand, then chase a mouse.

We would sit in her house and talk for awhile.
On her kind, gentle face there would always be a smile.
Her cat would jump up and sit in her lap.
Her dear husband was, and still is, a jolly old chap.

Recently, I found out about certain things,
That I really didn't want to know.
Those certain diseases that life can bring,
Linda had one of those, though it never showed.

I miss her now 'cause she is not here,
But still, I feel that Linda's soul is near.
I feel that her spirit is with me now.
I don't see her, but I feel her presence some way, somehow.

Caitlin Henson
Northlawn Middle School
Streator
Grade 6

My Guardian Angel

Watching over me day and night,
making sure I don't get into a fight.
Although invisible to my sight,
I know I am right,
for if I only had the right light,
I would see the graceful white wings,
and the bright golden halo.
For if I only had the right light,
my guardian angel is what would be in sight.

Jessica Norman
Butterfield Elementary School
Libertyville
Grade 5

Spring

Spring is a time
    for nature to bloom.
Spring is a time
    to bring the little kids out to play.
Spring is a time
    to plant your flowers, vegetables, and your fruit.
Spring is a time
    to go on trips and not think about snowstorms.
Spring is a time
    to put joy back in your lives.
Spring is a time
    for animals to give birth to their babies.

Brittney M. Haynes
Diekman Elementary School
Dolton
Grade 5

My Life

I love to fish,
and eat them on a dish.
I have one wish,
that is for more wishes,
and to not have to do the dishes.

I have one dog,
that eats like a hog.
In the summer my brother looks under logs,
hoping to find a few frogs.
Our neighbor has four dogs that chase our cats,
and those same cats like to chase the rats.

I love to play football and baseball,
but boy is it hard to hit that ball to the wall.
I've got to go,
My mom says I'm doing my homework too slow.

Danny Kampwerth
Beckemeyer Elementary School
Beckemeyer
Grade 5

Tiger

Tiger
Lazy, scary
Running, jumping, hunting
Jump up, jump down, jump up, jump down
Eating, chasing, sneaking
Mean, mad
Cat

Roy Moya
St Procopius School
Chicago
Grade 4

Golf

Golf is the game you just have to love.
Compared to baseball, it's a cut above.
Football and hockey cannot compare
To the powerful feeling when your drive's in the air.
A day on the course. Some time on the links.
It's fun just to practice, and it helps you to think.
A nine-iron approach shot that's right at the pin
Might make your palms sweaty, it might make you grin.
When you step on the carpet to line up your putt,
Your hands sometimes tremble, there's a knot in your gut.
But when you set up and spike a ball true,
The ball starts to travel, and all you can do...
Is wait for your Top Flight to fall into the cup.
And just when it does, your foursome gives up.
Because when you drain that 30-foot putt,
The other three players know it's time to pay up.

Stephanie Signore
Geraldine Kerkstra Middle School
Oak Forest
Grade 6

The Storm

Thunder and lightning
Raining and hailing all night
It's dark and gloomy

Jamie Weber
St John's Lutheran School
Buckley
Grade 5

I Am

I am Travis who loves sports.
I wonder if I'll be a star someday.
I hear the cheers of the crowds.
I see players trying hard.
I want to be like them.
I am Travis who loves sports.

I pretend I play like them.
I feel the pressure and excitement.
I touch my heart for good luck.
I worry about losing.
I cry seldom over sports.
I am Travis who loves sports.

I understand it takes a lot of practice.
I say I'll do my best.
I dream of being a superstar!
I try my hardest.
I hope my dream comes true!
I am Travis who loves sports.

Travis Kalmer
Damiansville Elementary School
Damiansville
Grade 6

Teddy

My name is Casey.
I have a new puppy.
I named him Teddy.
My mom bought him in Selmaville,
From some lady named Mrs. Benedoli.

I can't wait 'til after school,
Just so we can go out and play.
We go for walks to the park.
It's best when it's a warm sunny day.

Neither one of us like bedtime,
Teddy gets put in his carrier.
I go upstairs to my room,
While he whines from behind his barrier.
I whisper to him to be quiet,
Which always creates quite a riot!

Casey Thoele
Beckemeyer Elementary School
Beckemeyer
Grade 5

Dr. Seuss

D r. Seuss was born in 1904. He made
R hyming books.

S euss made many books.
E ditor of the school paper in college. Seuss at one time
U sed the name Theo Lesieg, which is his name spelled backwards. By
S ix he spent more time in the library than at home.
S euss died in 1991.

Brad Vander Zanden
Manteno Middle School
Manteno
Grade 6

Fairy Ponds

One day it was raining, it was such a gloomy day.
Janie sat inside moping, she wanted to go out and play.
Once it had stopped raining, Janie ran outside.
It was very wet and slippery, she could easily slip and slide.
Janie looked down at the sidewalk, and there was a tiny puddle.
She saw something that surprised her, she thought she was seeing double.
She saw a pair of wings, and a body to go with it, too.
The thing was about twenty times smaller than even me or you.
Her mother came outside and said, "Oh a fairy pond!
And look at all those fairies, of whom I'm very fond!"
Fairy ponds appear in spring, when winter is all gone.
They are very beautiful things, but they don't last for long.

Emily Cashman
Butterfield Elementary School
Libertyville
Grade 5

The Ram's Miraculous Season

To many Ram's fans it may seem
That this past season was a dream

They started out as the very worst
But soon after, they skyrocketed to first

With each touchdown, they performed the bob and weave
The success of this team, no one could believe

Victory after victory, win after win,
The Rams would never be made fun of again

As the season progressed, they pictured a goal,
They wanted to play in the Super Bowl!

This team's wish soon came true
Not only did they make it there, but they won the Super Bowl too!

When the Rams returned, the crowd let out a cheer:
"We want to see it happen again next year!"

Jennifer Riebold
McCray-Dewey School
Troy
Grade 5

Kobe

Kobe Bryant young and strong,
He practices basketball all day long,
He is a Laker from LA,
He hopes to play with MJ someday.

Another teammate's name is Shaq,
When they get together they go on attack,
Could Jackson let Rodman reunite,
And he could help the team fight.

Kobe Bryant is my hero,
He doesn't ever score zero,
I hope to grow up to be like him,
Play basketball and hang on the rim.

Greg Hoerr
Kellar Central School
Peoria
Grade 4

Weather

Weather, weather, it's always changing,
Somehow it seems to be rearranging.
Rain, sleet, snow, hail, all of it comes,
It sounds sometimes, like it hums.
When it thunders, I get scared,
Will it make me hearing-impaired?
When it snows, I like to play,
When my mom calls, I wish I could stay.
When it hails, I run for cover,
Above my head, it seems to hover.
When there is wind, I get scooted around,
If I get blown off the road, I might not be found.
When it floods, things get swept away,
Hiding in a tree, I begin to sway.
When it's foggy, I cannot see,
Hope I don't run into the trunk of a tree.
All these things have to do with weather,
I hope it doesn't affect my friend, Heather.

Caitlin Harrington
Channahon Middle School
Channahon
Grade 6

Sunny Day

It was a sunny day.
No one could come out to play.
I looked here, there, and everywhere.
At 3:00 I went to get my friends.
No one could come out to play.
So at 3:30 I went out again.
Everyone had homework so I'll try later.
Finally they come out before the day ends.

Jovon Fears
Diekman Elementary School
Dolton
Grade 5

Spring Storm

Spring Storm
I like a spring storm.
It makes flowers bloom in spring.
It makes life bloom with a new beginning.
Spring Storm

Rebecca Lessenberry
Hyde Park Elementary School
Waukegan
Grade 4

Merry Christmas Birds

I wonder if the squirrels and birds
Can understand any of the words
We hear at Christmas time.

I wonder if they dream
About gifts they give and get.
I wonder if their little ones are told
How to keep warm in the cold.

I wish they never had to go to bed hungry!

Merry Christmas
To the birds,
And all other creatures without words

Kristin Taylor
Hickory Bend Elementary School
Glenwood
Grade 4

My Music

The music flows out of me.
I open my mouth wide and raise my voice in song.
I put my whole being into the music and
My heart leaps with the excitement
Of knowing I provide
Enjoyment of some sort for
Someone, somewhere.

I feel.
I concentrate.
I think hard on
Rhythm, words, fingerings.
But soon the music lifts me away
And I wrap myself
In my sounds and the sounds of others.
I am transformed by the music.
I am lifted up until
It feels I am flying away,
Floating on the intertwining melody and harmonies.
Until I sink back, remembering myself,
And smile in the memory.

Eleanor Good
Kennedy Jr High School
Lisle
Grade 6

Beautiful Nature

Beautiful nature
Animals, flowers, and fresh air
Ideal for camping
Animal tracks everywhere
It's being destroyed by us

Erin Mahan
McCray-Dewey School
Troy
Grade 5

My Hope

Life gives us all hope,
That God loves us all so much.
In return, make peace.

Katie Roberts
Prince of Peace School
Lake Villa
Grade 5

What Lies Out There

What lies out there,
Beyond the front and back door,
If only I could have a little freedom,
To go out and explore a little more.

I wonder what lies out there,
Beyond the old maple tree,
So many cool things to do out there,
So many cool things to see.

Oh, I can't take it anymore,
I've got to have a look,
And as I left my back lawn,
My entire body shook.

Two words describe my sight,
All was magical and supreme,
But I think it would've been better,
If it hadn't been a dream.

Julia Spiotta
St Irene School
Warrenville
Grade 6

Sunset

Sunset
Over the ocean,
Color flooding the sky
Alike my soul with emotion.
Sadness or happiness
I will never know,
For he has gone.

Stephanie Nudelman
Meridian Middle School
Buffalo Grove
Grade 5

Spring Rains

Springs rains have come,
But haven't gone,
The rain will last twice as long,
Don't matter what you say or do,
The rain will last as long as you.

Amy Wells
New Hebron Christian School
Robinson
Grade 4

Time

Time is a constant thing
It wakes you with a morning ring
It tells you the time you go to bed
That time I do dread

With all of the seconds,
The minutes, and hours,
The days, the months, the years
Time will go on forever and ever
With a little tick-tick-tick
To hear by all the ears

Eric Lechner
Northlawn Middle School
Streator
Grade 6

Treasures of Life

Up the anchor goes
And then the wind begins to blow.
For the ocean's like a desert of blue ink
Slipping around staining the ground.
But at the end of the can
What have we found
But the treasure of life.
Sea horses, dolphins, whales,
And sharks with teeth like knives.
These are the treasures of life
But all I am is a sailor and a sailor I be
And all I seek are the treasures of the sea.

Emily Gumm
Kellar Central School
Peoria
Grade 4

Basketball

I like to play basketball,
Hopefully I do not fall.
It is very hot in the sun
It is also very fun.
It's good to be on the winning team,
It could be somebody's dream.

Ryan Dart
New Hebron Christian School
Robinson
Grade 4

Sports

Basketball, soccer, softball, too.
These are the sports I like to do.
Softball in the summer,
Soccer in the spring and fall,
Basketball in the winter,
I like to do them all.
I would like to do them every single day.
But I might get kind of tired,
Wouldn't you say!

Casey Larkin
St John Of The Cross School
Western Springs
Grade 5

War

Their blood is everywhere.
People screaming for help.
Men riding on horses or in chariots.
People shouting in the air like an echo
That will never end.
And finally the war is over.
And the whole town is destroyed.

Cristina Robledo
Alexander G Bell Elementary School
Chicago
Grade 6

My Sister

My sister is a fashion goddess
at least that's what she says,
and when I try to prove her wrong
she always has her ways.

She says that for eternity
her perfume will always smell,
and over Lent when she ate chocolate
I always tried to tell.

When she wears her diamond earrings
it always makes me smile,
she says she'll save them for her kids
but that's a long, long while.

It makes me very happy
when she dreams of love and life,
and then I know in my heart
she'll be a lovely wife.

Yes, I am going to miss her
Oh, with all my heart
but then I know, way deep down
we're never going to part!

Bianca Goutos
Oak Ridge Elementary School
Palos Hills
Grade 5

Man Will Destroy

The forest is asleep and quiet
The animals do not know of the impending danger
Then, morning rises
The river is peacefully babbling
The animals are just waking
A little fawn is walking when
Lo! A tower of smoke rises above the foliage!
The animal called man hacks at the trees
Not caring for the residents
The sky blackens with exhaust
And the animals flee for their lives
Night comes and the loggers are gone
So are the forest and its life
Then, a sapling rises out of the ashes
From death, life is created
All is calm and peaceful
Life goes on for eternity
But man will destroy forever.

Paul Axel
Meridian Middle School
Buffalo Grove
Grade 6

Friends

A friend is someone who will stand by your side
A good friend will never make you cry
Through thick and thin they will be there
When you're sad they're always here
A friend who talks about you bad isn't something,
Maybe nothing
A friend is always there to care for you
To all of my friends I want to say, "I love you!"

Sunni Krengel
Parker Jr High School
Flossmoor
Grade 6

The Hard Planet

Jupiter has a big red spot,
Venus I could cook soup with a pot because it's so hot.

Pluto is the farthest from the Sun;
As Mercury is the coolest one.

Uranus spins on its side;
As Saturn's rings hide in the dark sky.

On Mars I'd go bizarre;
On Earth I'd collect jars.

Neptune is blue;
As water is too.

Jonathon Strawn
Beckemeyer Elementary School
Beckemeyer
Grade 4

My Grandma

My grandma lives in a nursing home
She stays in her bed all day.

She is very sick
And she doesn't move around.

She doesn't even know who I am.

I don't get to see her very often
But I love her and she is my grandma.

But deep down inside I know she loves me
And that's all that matters.

Tricia A. Sloan
St Mary School
Alton
Grade 6

Family and Friends

My name is Grace,
and I love to race.
I have a brother named Ben,
that I sure would like to put in a pen.
My parents won't let me,
but you just wait and see.
By the way, I love school,
I think it is so cool,
I have four good friends,
and when we are together, the fun never ends.
Shasta is one of my friends' names,
we like to play lots of different games.
Now my poem is through,
and I have to find something else to do.

Grace Herbst
Beckemeyer Elementary School
Beckemeyer
Grade 5

The Grinning Moon

The candle flares all night long,
Lighting up the house.
The wind, strong and rumbly,
It whistles all night long.
On the clearest nights the stars are bright,
Lighting up the sky,
The moon seems to have a face,
A smiley little grin.
That lights the earth with joy.
You never have seen a moon wink?
But it does it very suddenly.
To your surprise it does catch your eye.
In the sweetest little way.

Lauren Chapman
New Hebron Christian School
Robinson
Grade 4

America

America
Beautiful, united
Free, love, mellow
America the free world
U.S.A.

Nicole Schuett
St. Mary School
Mundelein
Grade 6

Bowling

Heard yelling and screaming.
Got to a table.
Put on my shoes.
Got my ball.
Put my ball by the lanes.
Put my hand by the air blower.
Got my ball in my hand.
Walked up.
Let the ball go.
Got a strike.
Then I screamed.
Everyone was happy.

Miranda Bourland
Grand Prairie Elementary School
Joliet
Grade 4

The Wind...

Oh how it blows...
It gives me chills
All the way down to my toes
As I watch the fields sway
Just like small ocean waves

Oh how it blows...
For those cold winter nights
It makes all have a nasty winter cold
Leaving frostbite
To see such a sight

Oh how it blows...
Taking all kites
Into its dark hole
With its great strength and grace
Which makes all go around in haste

Oh how it blows...
It does not scare me
So I can put it on hold
Just as I please
With my protection, the trees

Danielle Auth
Channahon Middle School
Channahon
Grade 6

Falling

Falling up falling down
I hope I don't hit the ground.
There goes a tree past me.
I hope I don't get too close
f
a
l
l
i
n
g
!

SPLAT! ....Ouch.

Nate Cooling
St James School
Rockford
Grade 5

Questions

Why did the wind bring tears to my eyes?
Why did it leave me in its shadow?
Why did I cry when the wind left me?
In my darkness and endless peril?
Why didn't walls bring peace to my head?
Why did the wind howl outside my door?
Why did my thoughts whirl in pain?
Why didn't I cry when the pain began?
Why did my heart race with love?
Why did it beat at the pain?
Why did it sleep, cold in silence?
And then begin again?
Why did I trust you through my hurt?
When it was only you who caused it
Why did trust deceive me and maim
My heart just once again?

Alice Baumgartner
Chicago City Day School
Chicago
Grade 6

Life

How do *you* look at life?
A story without an end
A flower waiting to bloom
A feeling of waiting to be let out
A secret edging to be told
A bird trying to fly away
A poem waiting to be read
A child screaming for a way out
A beginning of greater things yet to come
A feeling without a purpose
What does it mean to *you*?

Samantha M. Edidin
Meridian Middle School
Buffalo Grove
Grade 6

Stars in the Night

Stars are big,
Stars are bright,
Deep in the Solar System,
Burning in the night.

Andy Jones
Brick Elementary School
Beardstown
Grade 4

Stars

Stars
Bright, light
Blinking, winking, twinkling
Little balls of light
Stars

Kimi Olson
St Mary School
Mundelein
Grade 6

Basketball

It's just a sport,
But a fun one,
It's competitive,
Active, and hard.

David Lindholm
Laraway Elementary School
Joliet
Grade 6

Semi Trucks

I like semi trucks that are big,
they are also called big rigs.
Some are red and some are white,
they can be 8 feet in height.
They all have transmissions,
some have big missions.
You can shift gears,
some have big mirrors.
Some carry gas to race car tracks,
some had sleepers in the back.
Some are in the shape of a box,
others carry rocks.
Some deliver ice cream,
others deliver whipped cream.
They all have heat,
some carry meat.
They have codes,
some had side loads.
Some drivers have maps,
other drivers take naps.
I think it would be neat to own a Pete.

Joel Goldenstein
St John's Lutheran School
Buckley
Grade 5

Basketball

Basketball is one of my favorite sports.
You have to run up and down the court.
My favorite position is the guard,
even though it can be hard.
I play guard most of the game,
and if we lose, I share the blame.
Forward is a spot, I can't play.
"That kid's too short," the people say.
Center is not the spot for me.
I'd get slam dunked, I'm 4 foot 3.
Maybe someday, I'll be in the NBA.
Then you'll say, "That boy can really play!"

Andrew Weidner
St Joseph Catholic School
Harvard
Grade 6

Too Much Homework

Today I had too much homework.
I mean I have every subject.
Science, Social Studies, Reading too.
But that is only the beginning.
English, Spelling, Band, and even Music.
But the worst of them all 152 math problems.
Oh cruel teacher...why, why, why,
Do you give me too much homework

Jared Smith
Deer Creek-Mackinaw Middle School
Deer Creek
Grade 5

Dream Sky

Go on, ride the wind, soar the skies, fly free.
Open your eyes to a new galaxy.
Follow the path through the rising mist,
For this is the place of legends' tryst.
A world that glints on the edge of dreams,
Floating in shimmers of a rainbow's beam.
Stars' majesty fuels the blaze.
An aurora's veil casts its rays.
Feel the heartbeat of clouds' glowing sea,
Pulsing like the echo of a memory.
Watch the horizon for a sphere of light.
Catch it before it slips out of sight.
A pounding heart, a curious eye,
A brilliant flash across the sky.
Keep on searching, keep on trying,
Keep your dreams, keep them from dying.
Find your wind, your guiding light.
Follow your dreams and rise into flight.
Then maybe, someday, you'll be allowed,
To glimpse the wonders of the dreamer's cloud.

Esther Shyu
Kennedy Jr High School
Lisle
Grade 6

The Blizzard

The weatherman said snow was on its way,
But only one or two inches by the end of the day.
At two o'clock the snow started to fall,
By midnight the snowdrifts were four feet tall.
The weatherman was very wrong. . .
He didn't think it would come down that strong!
The next day we got off from school
All the kids thought that was very cool!

Angela Schwarz
Wayne Elementary School
Wayne
Grade 5

Friendship

I never want my friendship with my best friend to end!
What would life be without friends?
I can't even imagine it.
She helps me.
She cares for me.
She never tells a lie.
She tells me her ideas and I tell her mine.
We share so much in common,
Likes and dislikes.
But in the same way we are also different
With our own special things that we do!
Friendship, now that's a powerful word!!!

Lauren Hetrick
Indian Knoll Elementary School
West Chicago
Grade 6

A Rose

The sweet scent of a rose.
Beautiful, yet harmful.
Its thorns sharp, a needle.
Petals as soft as a delicate lace.
It suffers and dies in the harsh weather.
but when the bees come back, so does the rose.

April Baity
Nelson Ridge School
New Lenox
Grade 6

The Girl I Like

I used to go out with a girl
Her name was Kayce,
Everyone would make fun of her
And of me also,
I would defend her from a kid named Mike K,
Even though we broke up
I defend her to this day,
I even think about her all day.

James Parypinski
Emerson Elementary School
Berwyn
Grade 6

Riding a Palomino Horse

Riding a Palomino horse,
Is the most fun you can have of course.
Flying through the ocean waves,
By the power of his legs.
Kicking up the sand and surf.
His long legs pounding on the turf.
By the sun setting my horse knows,
It is time to now start home.

Chrissy Gilbert
New Hebron Christian School
Robinson
Grade 4

School

School is a fun place,
A palace, a cabin or even like a cottage
It can be small or big.
Teachers make you think real hard,
So heads are full of brain wattage.

Evan Schrock
Tri-County Christian School
Freeport
Grade 4

Books, Books, Books

There's a book about books,
Whatever they are.

There's a book about hooks,
That is lined up in bars.

There's a book about cooks,
That is very neat.

There's a book about millions
And millions of feet.

Natalie Faculak
St John Fisher School
Chicago
Grade 4

Spring

The sky is blue.
The grass is green.
The wind smells like spring is here.
The sun is bright yellow.
The clouds are white like snowflakes.
The flowers are blooming.
The trees are tall and green.
Spring is finally here.
It is warm.
Spring is finally here.

Jessica Wingren
Iroquois West Upper Elementary School
Thawville
Grade 5

Angels

They play with us, they look after us.
They hear us, touch us, comfort us
With invisible warm hands.
And always they try to give us what we want.
Angels look down upon us
So that we can look up to heaven
For guidance, peace, and protection.
An angel of compassion is like a bowl of chicken soup made by mom.
It makes you feel all warm inside.
It makes you feel loved,
Every time you meet a stranger,
Is also a chance to make a friend,
And perhaps be touched by an angel.
The angel on your shoulder whispers in your ear,
"You are loved, so love others, you are my friend, so be a friend."
Angels help us believe in those things we can't see and understand.
Angels give us the gift of faith to know things are possible.

Alejandra Yniguez
McCormick Elementary School
Chicago
Grade 5

Angel

Fiery flames engulf all happiness,
And sorrow shadows the land.
Demons with devilish eyes and wicked souls loom about.
There is no happiness, only gloom
Suddenly, a bright light penetrates the evil and fills one's soul with hope.
It diminishes the suffering
And lets God's voice of joy cry out and fill one's heart with faith.
There is no more pain, no more anguish.
An angel, sent to cleanse the corruptness
And let happiness sweep over the demonic place
That one has been confined to.
She cleanses the soul, cleanses the mind, cleanses the spirit.
There will be no more sadness, and no more despair.
Peace reigns over the land.
There is no more misery,
In a place that we call heaven.

Vivienne Zhao
Meridian Middle School
Buffalo Grove
Grade 6

Summer

Summer is the time of year where it is always happy.
There are pools, sports, games and no school.
There are happy kids all over playing with friends, doing what they like best.
Getting to stay out late and playing all day.
... One of the happiest times of the year for all kids.
Hot weather all day and it never gets cold.
... My favorite time of year.

Steve McGowan
Most Holy Redeemer School
Chicago
Grade 5

Frogs

Frogs jump, hop, and pop out of the water,
And splash around just like a little kid.
A frog falls asleep like a president.
A frog sits on a leaf like a madame.

Patricia Peralta
Hyde Park Elementary School
Waukegan
Grade 4

My Alien Visitor

It's 5:54
There's a knock at the door

"Hello," they said
"Want to buy a bed?"

"Need a good night's sleep?"
"I'll install it—don't make a peep."

In a few minutes he was back
And he stuffed me in a sack.

He talked with such persuasion
I didn't know it was an invasion.

He said all of Earth had been taken
At this news I was badly shaken.

But all this I earned
The lesson I learned...

...was, "Don't open the door to a stranger."

John Kenealy
St Irene School
Warrenville
Grade 6

When I Grow Up

When I grow up I can scale the seven seas, or,
I can save people from fires and be a hero.
I can swim and win the Gold or,
I could skate, run, ski, or fly.

I could become another Bill Gates
Or I could be a carpenter and make gates.
I can be whatever I want to be.
I could be an astronaut and fly through space.

I could be a writer, or
I could be a comedian and make people laugh.
I could even be a teacher if I want to.
But until I'm old enough I think I'll finish school.

Kathryn E. Folz
St Irene School
Warrenville
Grade 6

Friends

Appreciate your friends,
Without them life would have no meaning.
Life without friends is a forest without trees.
Be good to your friends.
Without them life is a book without pages.

Paul Kato
Pilgrim Lutheran School
Chicago
Grade 4

Mom

laughing
talking
shopping
driving
playing

at the end of the day she's too tired to even think.

Greg Berns
Walker Elementary School
Evanston
Grade 5

Eternity

Our lives have no true end you see,
We live and roam the world.
After death we become spirits.
Some might guard their most loved ones,
While others want revenge.
No matter what the purpose is,
No matter where they go,
Our spirits roam the great big world for eternity.

Kristeen Fogarty
Northlawn Middle School
Streator
Grade 6

I Live in a Van Down by the River

I live in a van down by the river.
For dinner, I eat onions smothering liver.

For breakfast I eat roadkill, mostly raccoon.
I dropped out of school way too soon.

I ain't the smartest or the wealthiest.
Let me tell you, I ain't the healthiest.

I have no money in my wallet.
But I do have a dog, name of Paulette.

Now I live in a van down by the river.
And for dinner, I always eat onions with liver.

Scott Nemecek
St John Of The Cross School
Western Springs
Grade 5

Birds

Birds sing lovely songs
Flying around in the blue sky
Making sweet music.

Tom Conlan
Solomon Elementary School
Chicago
Grade 4

Nature

Nature
Sunny flowers
Growing, blooming, sprouting
See beautiful Mother Nature
Nature.

Cian Martin
Solomon Elementary School
Chicago
Grade 4

The Truth

What is the truth?
Could it be a small child,
Tiny fingers, toes, and eyes.
A delicate, soft flower,
With a silky, sane petal?
What is the truth?
The pure smile of an old woman,
Sitting quietly in the park.
Crystal clear waterfalls,
Falling down toward faithfulness.
What is the truth?
A tall, old tree,
Wise, yet, certain for sure.
A floating, fine feather,
Sailing swiftly through the air.
What is the truth?
So many things,
Yet, still underneath,
Will we ever uncover,
The real story beneath?
What is the truth?

Danielle Grunloh
St Anthony of Padua Grade School
Effingham
Grade 6

Wind

Wind
Gentle
Dangerous
It's cold and hot
Air

Mike Jenkins
McCray-Dewey School
Troy
Grade 5

Champions

The crowd roars
As he soars
In the air
As he squares
The shot goes up
Then you hear umph!
He falls down
To the ground
Free throws in
They win

Marcus Myer
Virginia Elementary School
Virginia
Grade 6

Bed Bugs

The bed bugs that bite
Are out tonight!
You better watch out
Those things are stout.
They will get in your clothes
And crawl up your nose,
Climb on your pens
And get in your den.
And worst of all
You just can't catch them!

SO DON'T LET THE BED BUGS BITE!

Kate White
St James School
Rockford
Grade 5

Love

Some say love is forever
Kids think it is gross
I think love is a beautiful thing

Everyone can feel it,
Every living thing

Some say love means caring,
And showing and understanding

Others say love means being there
When people need you

You can love anything
Animals, like your stuffed animal.

I think love can be
Anything you want it to be.

Aubree Jerome
McCray-Dewey School
Troy
Grade 5

Clouds

Wispy shadows
High in the sky
Like rolling meadows
Soft to the eye

Color so bright
Like the sparkling sea
They shine in the light
Just like me!

Fluffy and white,
Or sulky and dull
Oh what a delight
To have a sky so full!

Blinding white
Or gray and cold
But oh what a sight
One can behold!

Rachel Knisley
Nauvoo Elementary School
Nauvoo
Grade 6

Frogs

Frogs are little.
Frogs are sweet.
Frogs have such little feet.

Frogs can hop.
Frogs can leap.
Frogs can zoom by in such a heap.

Frogs are neat
Frogs are unique.
Frogs can crawl right under my feet.

I love frogs.
And there is nothing wrong...
With loving frogs.

Jessica Leal
Leland Elementary School
Leland
Grade 6

Mom

Mom, you mean so much to me,
You held me in your arms,
You gave me life, you're the best,
I don't care about the rest.
I have a few things to say to you,
It's three words—here goes—I Love You!

Danielle Keltner
Parker Jr High School
Flossmoor
Grade 6

Space Exploration

High in the sky
Past the sun
Lay all nine planets
Waiting to be explored

High in the sky
Quickly goes a spaceship
Manned with five astronauts
Excited to search and discover

High in the sky
The astronauts examine
Make new discoveries
To share with the world

Down to earth
All five astronauts come
Bringing new knowledge and understanding

Megan Smith
Channahon Middle School
Channahon
Grade 6

Grandma

Wrinkled hands, face, arms and legs.
Pretty, short brown hair.
Ten grand kids but still no sign of gray.
Smells like fish that's cooking in the kitchen.

She lays down in bed
I lay down too.
I talk to her
She talks to me
And all that comes out
Are three little words.
I LOVE YOU!

Michelle Thomas
Walker Elementary School
Evanston
Grade 5

Goodbye 20th Century

As the 20th century drew to a close,
The Y2K bug gave us many woes.
We had a big celebration bash,
And Bill Gates came in with a lot of cash.
Before there was St. Patrick's Day clover,
The calendar year had to roll over.
We thought the computers were going to crash,
When we had our big celebration bash.
Then we found out Y2K was a fib,
As babies lay fast asleep in their cribs.

Matt Sampson
Schiesher Elementary School
Lisle
Grade 5

Yellow

Yellow is the color of lemon trees,
of dandelions and honey bees.

Yellow is a slow down light,
a sunny crayon and a star so bright.

Yellow is a pot of gold,
a jellybean and lemonade that's oh so cold.

Yellow is the sun and the moon.
They are always so bright in June.

Yellow is cats' eyes in a pair.
Yellow is everywhere!

Annie Kellogg
Most Holy Redeemer School
Evergreen Park
Grade 5

There's a Dragon Under My Bed

There's a dragon under my bed,
His claws are ruby red.
His scales are green,
His teeth are bright white,
He goes to bed but doesn't sleep at night.

He gets up at about 12:00 A.M.,
Gets a snack,
Goes back to bed,
But then sings a short lullaby hymn.

Of course in the daytime he sleeps,
But never gets up for playtime.
This dragon of mine
Is a pretty good friend most of the time.

In the morning I say, "How do you do?"
But then he just says, "Boo-hoo-hoo!"
What a weird dragon of mine.
Well, that's the dragon under my bed.

Cassie Holt
St Joseph Catholic School
Harvard
Grade 5

The Wrestling Tournament

in the wrestling ring
with your coach cheering you on
you get him in a pin
the crowd is roaring
you are feeling good when the ref slaps the mat
he says pin

Jimmy Rusenovich
Grand Prairie Elementary School
Joliet
Grade 4

Lost Forever

All I can feel
Are the waves beneath me

The sky gray
My mood depressed

Friends being washed away
Gone into the sea's gentle wind

Lost forever

Until I find myself
In that same wind

Britta Monson
Meridian Middle School
Buffalo Grove
Grade 6

My Sister

My baby sister loves her bottle,
she looks adorable and little.
She smiles so big,
she needs a wig,
I still think she will be a model.

Jacob Johnson
Beckemeyer Elementary School
Beckemeyer
Grade 5

Dakota

My dog Dakota is dying,
And all the while I'm crying.
He's really loving, caring, and sweet,
And sometimes I give him a treat.
Dakota is the best dog you can get,
He's the sweetest dog you've ever met.
I'll give him hugs,
And lots of love.

Allison Henry
Wells Elementary School
Grayville
Grade 5

Friends

Friends are nice;
Friends are cool.
Friends are always
Company for you.
Friends always care;
Friends always share.
Friends are always
There for you.

Priscilla Lopez
Nixon Elementary School
Chicago
Grade 5

Wrestling

Spike, cradle, pin, mat
You will see all that
When you wrestle on the mat
You do not want to wrestle someone fat.

Sean Whalen
Grand Prairie Elementary School
Joliet
Grade 4

A Rainy Day

The rain outside makes me want to hide.
I wish it would go away
so I could go out to play.

It makes the day gloomy and dark,
sort of like Noah's Ark.

Rain, oh rain, go away;
Come back some other day.

Laura Brady
St James School
Rockford
Grade 5

Castle

C an have people in it,
A nd a king and queen.
S ometimes standing
T all on a mountain.
L arge and tall.
E veryone was protected.

Jesus Calderone
Manteno Middle School
Manteno
Grade 6

My Unlucky Day

I was walking by the park,
When a dog started to bark.
Before I knew what hit me,
That dog turned around and bit me!
All my blood was gushing out.
That dog was mean, without a doubt.
It kept biting and nipping,
Chewing and ripping.
I called for help.
No one heard my yelp!
Finally that dog let go
But I was missing my big toe!
I realized as I limped away,
That was just the beginning
Of my unlucky day.

Samantha Powers
St John Of The Cross School
Western Springs
Grade 5

My God

You are the one God
To me you are my only God
You're my Holy Ghost.

Stephen Lemons
Ina Community Consolidated School
Ina
Grade 5

My Forever Star

I have a special star,
I can see it from afar,
Wherever I go
It follows me,
It is not a he,
It is not a she,
It's just my star.
My star is a special star,
It's like no other
I can even see it from the car.
My star is blue and white,
My star is very bright,
It always shimmers on my birthday,
When it shines in my window,
It always makes me feel happy,
It's *bigger* than any other.
That's MY FOREVER STAR!

Danielle Meischner
Bolin Elementary School
East Peoria
Grade 5

Flowers Are All Different

Violets and roses and daisies too
Tulips in yellow, orange and blue.
They are all so pretty and smell so good
I'd fill my house with them if I could.
They almost smell as pretty as me.
I think I'll plant them under a tree.

Natalie Jansky
St John Fisher School
Chicago
Grade 4

Clouds

When I look up at the clouds,
I see cats and trees.

When I look up at the clouds,
I think, that's where I'd like to be.

For one day I will be in a cloud,
Where it's always silent and never loud.

Annie Littrell
Manteno Middle School
Manteno
Grade 6

Tobacco

Every day 4 million kids light up a smoke,
The tobacco companies think it's a great joke!

They push their ads at kids through magazines,
And get 3,000 new smokers, daily, in their teens!

Every year kids smoke almost one billion cigarette packs,
It's hard to believe that so many people ignore health facts!

Over 400,00 Americans every year, from smoking, die,
From advertisements, kids and teens seem to buy!

With tobacco companies losing customers by the day,
I see why they advertise in many a way!

The tobacco industry spends $5 billion a year on advertising,
To keep people puffing away with the death toll rising!

Kara Salin
Grant Park Middle School
Grant Park
Grade 6

Icicles

Icicles are like shiny diamonds twinkling in the wind.
Water is like a blue cloud in a bright sky.
Snow is like a white polar bear in Alaska.

Daniella Cahue
St. Richard School
Chicago
Grade 5

Life

People expect so much from life
but you really have to go through some strife.
In life it's hard and you must be smart.
You can't just expect sudden success.
And another thing is the way you dress
you can't go around having baggy pants
because you must be a smart man.

Erik Tunstall
Evangelical Christian School
Chicago
Grade 4

Untitled

Summer is when flowers grow tall.
Summer is when you go swimming in a pool.
People love summer because you are out of school.
I like to stay out late
And play games play ball and skate.
Play games all night.
Summer might be the best season of all.

Victor Q. Beard Jr.
Diekman Elementary School
Dolton
Grade 5

My Friend Sue

I have a dear friend whose name is Sue.
She picks me up when I'm feeling blue.
Sue loves her music and she can dance.
When I get nervous she says, "Take a chance!"
With Sue I'm brave, I'm never shy.
I hope we're friends until we die.

Cynthia Vargas
Plainfield Elementary School
Des Plaines
Grade 5

Frogs

Frogs are tiny and green
but they only come out in the middle of spring.
Every time they come out from the mud,
they hop up on a flower bud.

Sam Flowers
Brick Elementary School
Beardstown
Grade 4

Sleepiness

My sleepiness is a silent tree
That whispers a soft sound in the black of night.
It beckons, "Come to a peaceful sleep."

William Howard Ross
Pilgrim Lutheran School
Chicago
Grade 4

When I Cut My Knee

It was so bad when I cut my knee,
because that ball got a piece of me,
that I got stitches
but I screamed to the whole hospital that I hate stitches!

It didn't hurt when it came out
when they came about
but it hurt when I got them in
because they used a pin.

Sometimes it doesn't hurt
if you touch me there
but other times it does
because it is just like my cuz'
(It goes away, but it always comes back).

I don't care
if anyone stares
because it is almost gone.
I almost went to the great beyond
(Trying to get it off).

Randy Gilpin
Nauvoo Elementary School
Nauvoo
Grade 6

Dog-Gon-It

When I got my dog, all he did was snore.
He kinda was a bore.
My dog is very lazy.
He drives my family crazy.
He always howls.
I should have got an owl.
My dog is a pest.
He always makes a mess.
He has to be in charge.
My dog is very large.
Even though my dog's a pain.
We all love him the same.

Kelsey Pliner
Riverwood Elementary School
McHenry
Grade 5

Alone

As I sit here alone
In the darkened night
I think of you
And picture you in my sight

I want to run
Away from here
To find you
And never shed another tear

But as I try
I wonder and worry
If maybe all this pain
Is caused by fury

But I figured it out
So it's time to say goodbye
Well it's just the beginning
So I guess I'll say Hi!

Sarah O'Keefe
Manteno Middle School
Manteno
Grade 6

What Is Green?

Green is like a frog on a lily pad
that sits there all day.

Green is like the cool crayon
in the box that you color with.

Green is like a green car on a road
with a motor that doesn't
stop running.

Ricardo A. Tijerina
St. Richard School
Chicago
Grade 5

Spring

S pring is the one time of the year when the flowers have time to grow.
P eople fall in love.
R ooting for your favorite baseball team.
I ce cream for the first time.
N ight walks.
G etting good grades.

Jennifer Leon
St John Fisher School
Chicago
Grade 4

Junk Drawer

Things   scattered
                    all
                                                around
Garbage
that
                                    was
                                            not
        thrown   away
                    Small   trinkets
                            have
                            no
                            home
        A
                                                Junk
            Drawer
                                                            that
                                        is
                        BIG!

John Waterman
Nelson Ridge School
New Lenox
Grade 6

Outdoors

Flowers are as sweet as honey that bears like to climb and eat.
A butterfly is as pretty as a horse running free in the midnight air.
A tree is as big as a whale swimming in the big blue ocean.
A rose is like a ripe strawberry getting ready to be picked.

Heather Reed
St. Richard School
Chicago
Grade 5

Sisters

They comfort me when I'm down, just maybe when I have a frown.
Whenever I want to laugh and play, just ask and they will almost every day.
Sometimes they're mean and they'll hit, but they never mean it not one bit.
Helpful, partner in life, loving, friendly, and generous.
These are my sisters!

Emily Redd
St Mary School
Alton
Grade 6

Red

Red is the sun beating down
Red is the nose of a funny clown
Red can be happy
Red can be sad
It can be the devil, who is always mad
Red is the finish line of a race
Red is the lipstick on a girl's face
Red can be the best
Red can be the worst
Red can be a time bomb ready to burst
Red can be a candle flickering its light
Red can be blood after a fight
Red is a cardinal ready for flight
Red is a firework that's a wonderful sight
Red is the color of a beautiful rose
Red is the color of a runny nose
Red can be the best friend of yellow
Red can be rowdy or it can be mellow
Red can be your feet if you walk on hot sand
Red can be your body when you get a tan

Gregory Gotsis
Kennedy Jr High School
Lisle
Grade 6

The Eclipse of the Moon

It was a dark, and startling night,
But the moon was gleaming bright.
I could hear the excitement of my family,
As I looked up through the spy glass.

I looked up to see the bright, starry night.
Then I said to myself, what a wonderful night,
All I heard was absolute silence. Everything was quiet.

Then I looked up, and what did I see?
But the big, black moon was staring at me.
It was just sitting there all alone.
It looked like it was on a quilt ready to be sewn.

Then I asked my mom for the spy glass.
I looked up through it, and what did I see?
But the man on the moon wasn't smiling,
But the man on the moon was frightfully crying.

It usually looks happy like a ball of fire,
But now it has lost its desire, to become big, and strong
Like its brother, the big bright sun

But now, oh look, it looks like a rebirth.
Oh, it's not, it's the moon coming back
To its old bright self, like the coming of a star.

Eddie Szewczyk
Blessed Sacrament School
Belleville
Grade 6

The Man Who Had a Plan

There was a man who had a plan that was dumb for some.
The man was smart, but didn't start the plan.
He started when the technology came.
He did the plan and made millions and trillions.
The man with the plan was forced into early retirement.

Pat Miller
Most Holy Redeemer School
Chicago
Grade 5

My Vacation in San Francisco

The people all rushed around,
Like toys that had just been wound.

The cars honked as they flew by.
The birds chirped as they flew in the sky.

With all the people and stores around,
A lost child could not have been found.

The buildings around me were very tall.
So tall, they seemed that they should fall.

The weather was very cold,
And, many businesses were being sold.

We got in line for the cable car.
When we got on, we didn't get very far.

The next day the people came into the city.
The sky looked pink and blue and very pretty.

We got on an airplane and flew away,
The cars were ants running out to play.

The trees looked like broccoli stalks.
You couldn't see people on their walks.

Then we got into a car and drove away.
But, I still remember clearly today.

Melanie Mueller
Blessed Sacrament School
Belleville
Grade 6

A Spider

A spider went in a mouth
Teeth came down and spit him out
A foot came to him and squashed him flat
Squashed him right on the mat
There was a tragedy today
And that is all I have to say

Dave Lauer
Sycamore Trails Elementary School
Bartlett
Grade 5

I Wish Upon a Star

I wish upon a star
That I would go so far
Up in the sky
Like a butterfly
I would see so many things
So then I would start to sing
Just like a feather
In the bright sunny weather
But I know I cannot fly
In the sky so high
And I know I cannot go so far
But I can always wish upon a star

Tiffany Jones
Chaney-Monge Elementary School
Crest Hill
Grade 6

Santana

Carlos Santana,
He wears a bandana!
He sings very bad,
Just like his dad!

Carl Frantz
Grand Prairie Elementary School
Joliet
Grade 4

Snow

When snow comes, winter is here,
The most wonderful time of the year!
When you go outside to play,
You can have fun in many ways.
But after a while,
When the snow is all in a big pile.
I wish summer was here,
The next best time of the year!

Brittany Bird
Grant Park Middle School
Grant Park
Grade 6

My Best

Basketball is my game,
Emily is my name.
I dream of going far.
Maybe even becoming an all-star.
But if I don't, that's okay,
I'll just try again another day.
I will practice hard and try my best,
To put the others to the test.
It will not be easy, I won't get much rest,
But I can always say I did my best.

Emily Kuhl
Beckemeyer Elementary School
Beckemeyer
Grade 5

My Team

I was on a team that won
Boy did we have fun

We practiced day and night
Until we were ready to fight

We beat the Yankees.
They needed hankies
Because they cried all night

Chris Mack
Parker Jr High School
Flossmoor
Grade 6

My Dog Blue

I once had a dog named Blue,
Who never missed his cue.
I'd jump up and down,
He'd dance all around.
And I'd say, "I'm proud of you!"

Zachary Wagner
Garvy Elementary School
Chicago
Grade 6

A Friend

Nice and fun
Running and playing happily
Jacob

Matthew Doty
McCray-Dewey School
Troy
Grade 5

Little Mouse

Little mouse,
in a house,
trying to get some cheese.
He ran and ran,
into a pan,
and began to sneeze.
Oh no!
It's...cheese!
Round and round
he went back down,
to eat some barley.
His friend named Charlie,
came over with some cheese,
and offered him a piece.
Yes please!
So, the little mouse and Charlie,
ate barley and cheese in peace.

Maryann Manatt
Parker Jr High School
Flossmoor
Grade 6

Ready to Explore the World

I feel ready to explore the world.
To Africa or to find some gold.
To explore undiscovered islands,
With monsters never seen before.
I will travel from sea to sea,
It is an awesome experience I do believe.
I can explore everything through books.
I have never left my bedroom
But, I know I have explored the world.

Hannah Benson
New Hebron Christian School
Robinson
Grade 4

Soccer

Soccer is fun
You will always get to run
The goals weigh a ton
Kick it off your foot like a gun
And remember to have fun

D.C. Cusanelli
McCray-Dewey School
Troy
Grade 5

Hard Day

He's coming from work
a hard day he had
looks, sees dishes in the sink
I know that he is mad

A cold beer is waiting
gets it and sits down
it is 11:15 pm it is late
No one is around

Not yet asleep I come out
I want some water I said
I notice he is angry
so I go back to bed.

Katarina Miletic
Emerson Elementary School
Berwyn
Grade 6

The At-At

An At-At looks like a rock
It sounds like a vacuum
It also has fumes as bad as a car
It has a lot of armor
It also is like a bomber
It is big and grey like an elephant

Ryan Werntz
Tri-County Christian School
Freeport
Grade 4

Ode to *NSync

I love *NSync oh so much!
Justin, Joey, J.C., Lance, and Chris can sing!
Justin is so cute with that curly hair,
He makes you want to walk on air!
All day long I think of you,
I just hope you could say that too!
Chris is so crazy,
To see him dance makes me dizzy!
J.C. has eyes that make me weak,
So I just can't speak!
Lance *loves* horses oh so much.
Joey's hair is so bright,
It makes boys turn and run in fright.
Their hair could be white, red, purple, or blue
(as long as they sing too.)
It makes no difference to me,
I will always love *NSync

Meghan Kuchta
Parker Jr High School
Flossmoor
Grade 6

A Friend

A friend is someone
　　On whom you can depend,
Someone who will care,
　　Love, promise and defend.

A friend will keep a secret,
　　When everyone is against you,
You can trust that they will be there for you,
　　Even when you're down and blue.

No one can break a friendship,
　　Of its very solemn vows.
For truth a friendship brings,
　　Even when one person bows.

You can trust a friend with all your life,
　　A broken heart they can mend,
Through the good times and the bad times,
　　One will be there 'til the very bitter end.

Meghan Mitchell
St Irene School
Warrenville
Grade 6

Fall

Fall is the time when leaves start falling.
Fall is the time that animals start leaving.
Fall is the time that flowers stop blooming.
Fall is the time that wind starts blowing.

Cicero Porter Jr.
Diekman Elementary School
Dolton
Grade 5

Tears

A tear is magic
That comes from your eye

It comes unexpectedly
When you're mad, sad, or just plain glad

They sparkle in the light
As warm as the sun down you're lowly little face

You may cry when you're hurt
Or when somebody dies

You might even cry
'Cause someone does something nice

You might even cry
When you say something you shouldn't

A tear is magic
That flows from your eye

Amber L. Vann
Our Savior Lutheran School
Chicago
Grade 6

Big Thoughts

Giants! Giants! They're after me!
Monsters! Monsters! Under the sea!
Kings! Kings! With all you desire!
Dragons! Dragons! They breathe fire!
Lions! Tigers! I have no fear!
Aliens! Aliens! They've landed here!
Ghosts! Goblins! I hear their screams!
Soldiers! Soldiers! Shooting laser beams!
Knights! Knights! Of the table round!
A dinosaur! A dinosaur! It's bones I found!
Rockets! Spaceships! Zoom! Zoom! Zoom!
And it's all happening right here in my room!

Erik Jensen
Butterfield Elementary School
Libertyville
Grade 4

Summer

Summer is my favorite time of year because it's hot.
My friends and I go outside a lot.
We ride bikes,
We rollerblade,
Sometimes we go to the arcade.
When summer is over, I'm not mad.
I'm kind of low.
But at least fun fall winds will blow!

Meghan Jarema
Most Holy Redeemer School
Chicago
Grade 5

Hershey's Kiss

As I touch my Hershey's Kiss,
I feel the gooey sensation of it all.
It trickles down my throat,
And tickles my tongue.
The wrapper crumbles in my hand.
It crackles near my ear.
It smells delicious,
And tastes even better.
It looks like the Statue of Liberty's flame.
Suddenly it is gone.

Kristen Mattison
Hiawatha Elementary School
Kirkland
Grade 5

Big Question

Every day I ask myself why is life unfair?
Why is earth solid and air clear?
Then I answered my question.
Life is just one big question.

Today I asked why are people mean,
And why do people die?
Then I answered my question.
Life is just one big question.

Sinclaire Joyce
Gavin Central Primary School
Ingleside
Grade 5

I Love the Way

I love the way she creeps into my room,
the way she sneaks
and carefully lies beside me.
She whispers jokes into my ear
the way she tickles
tickles
tickles
and finally I awake.
I love the way she wears her hair
and asks me how it looks;
the way she wants my opinion
for lots of stuff.
I love the way she lets me cook
and I get to crack the ooey gooey
slimy
squirmy eggs.
I love the way she loves me.
I have no way
to get along without her.
And yet I say
this is only the beginning.

Mandy Hileman
Jonesboro Elementary School
Jonesboro
Grade 6

Freedom

F ighting for our freedom
R ights
E qual men
E ar splitting noises
D istant gun shots
O pen wounds
M oney spent on weapons

Annalise Randall
Manteno Middle School
Manteno
Grade 6

Brothers

They're in the way
Lazy as can be
When they do their work
You want to spree

I love him
Even though a nuisance
He can be a bother
Or a prince.

My heart would feel empty
If he was not here
Through messes and noises
Through having a career

All the while I know
Somehow, some way
He will always be close by
Even if far away

Lydia Parker
Manteno Middle School
Manteno
Grade 6

Summer Vacation!

I love summer the best,
when I can rest.
I love to swim,
especially with Kim.

I can ride my bike,
or even hike.
I love to be out in the sun,
where I always have fun.

Summers go,
but I always know,
they always come back
next year.

Cindy Pratscher
St Irene School
Warrenville
Grade 6

Water

W aves
A qua
T ide
E rosion
R eflection

Kiley Kruger
St Anthony's School
Streator
Grade 5

Basketball

Gather some friends,
Toss me a ball.
Then come watch,
The one and all.
See me shoot,
Watch me score.
See me drive,
Down the floor.
Bounce! Bounce! Bounce!
Swish! Roar!
Listen to the ball soar.
Bounce! Bounce! Bounce!
Buzz!
Let's go team,
We have just won.

Barbara Payonk
St George School
Tinley Park
Grade 6

Stars

Stars
Bright, beautiful
Shooting, sparkling, dazzling,
Shooting across the sky,
Light

Stephanie Serna
St Mary School
Mundelein
Grade 6

War

What is this?
Blood is here.
Blood is there.
What has happened?
My family is not here.
It must have been a war.
But now I am alone!
What shall I do?
And there isn't anymore.

Mackenzie Krey
Alexander G Bell Elementary School
Chicago
Grade 6

Busch Stadium Strikes Again!

Everyone is at the game.
It's just like the hall of fame.

The umpire makes the calls.
Balls bounce off my walls.

Every seat is nailed to my floor.
I get headaches from people slamming on my door.

Who needs football?
When you have fastball?

It was built many years ago.
There's never an empty seat in any row.

Cody Prince
Beckemeyer Elementary School
Beckemeyer
Grade 4

Spring

Winter, spring, summer, and fall.
Winter is no fun at all.

I prefer summer better
But spring is my kind of weather.

Winter is cold and dead
As for summer, hot and dread.

Spring is warm, fresh, and new.
It has beautiful flowers, daisies, roses, and sunflowers too.

It's exciting and has so many reasons
That's why I think it beats all three seasons.

Angelica Josephina Rosario
Nixon Elementary School
Chicago
Grade 5

Summer

Summer is a time to hang out with your friends.
Summer is when school is out.
Summer is made up of mostly sunshine and fun.
Summer is time to go to the beach.
It is also time for picnics at parks.
Summer is a time to smell the flowers around you.
Summer is a time to eat watermelons.
Summer is full of bright colors.
Summer is a season full of warm, hot weather.
As you can see summer is full of FUN!!

Colisha Poston
Diekman Elementary School
Dolton
Grade 5

A Friend

A friend is like a special toy,
it doesn't have to be a boy.
Whenever you feel lonely or down,
your friend will always be around.
You never want to let them go,
it's hard to move away, I know!
But you will always remember them.
They won't leave you and go for him.
Sometimes times can get too tough,
and make you think you've had enough.
But when those times come around
you can escape to a place where a friend can be found.
So when you need someone to talk to
or help your heart mend
you can always talk to the one you call a friend.

Jessica McDonald
East Richland Elementary School
Olney
Grade 5

Door County

It's 10 to 2 what should we do
We will go to the pool
That's what we will do
It's wet and fun
You could soak up sun
Play in the sand
Put your hair back in a white head band
Smell the chlorine
See the diving board shake with a bang and a boom
Feel the sand munch and crunch under your feet
Getting ice cream—mmmmmmm what a tasty treat!
Walking on the path leading to the pond
Look at that green frog!
Go home to the trailer to have some lunch
Play a game or two
That's what we will do!

Lindsay Berghuis
Grand Prairie Elementary School
Joliet
Grade 4

Raindrops

Blue, wet, big, small
Raindrops in every direction
Let them all. Let them fall.
I'm sitting inside on a rainy day,
Look at the sky, and what do I say,
"Raindrops are falling so quick and so fast,
Makes me think they're always gonna last."
But when the rain is over
The sun comes out to say,
"Come on, the rain is over,
So come on out and play."

Stephanie Stefanik
St John Of The Cross School
Western Springs
Grade 5

Fire

Burning logs turn hot
Make animals run away
Snowflakes fall and die

Alex Faulkner
Kellar Central School
Peoria
Grade 4

Recipe

Concord and juicy,
spherical and good.
It is small, it is tasty
and really good food.
Hanging and picking,
it fell in a lake.
It's scrumptious! It's delicious!
This makes a grape.

Wade Julstrom-Agoyo
North Park Elementary School
Chicago
Grade 4

My Family

My name is Kayla,
and I live at home
with my mom, dad, sister,
and a dog of my own.

My sister has fish,
She thinks they're nifty.
I have a guinea pig,
Whos' name is fifty.

My aunt and uncle
live on the East coast,
with my two cute little cousins,
don't mind if I boast.

One set of grandparents
live twenty minutes away,
we go to the park in the summer
to picnic and play

My other grandparents
also live near,
in a house in the woods,
you can even see deer.

I come from a family
that is nice and small,
but that's quite all right,
because I love them all!

Kayla Carnahan
Beckemeyer Elementary School
Beckemeyer
Grade 5

Friendship

She rides with me, she cares for me,
She brings out my laugh, always concerned on my behalf
Will she dump me in the cold, does she think me strong and bold
Does she laugh at me or with me?
Should she tackle or control me or just give me advice
Is she my friend?

Should he hold me close or give me room
Should he leave me be when I'm angry
Does he care like he says he does
Does he snicker behind my back, does he think I am weak

How do I know what he/she is thinking?
I don't and that's just it.
We need to trust and hold and care
Let each other know we're there.
We need to feel a friendship that's real.
We need to laugh and cross paths.
And be fair and just
But most of all we need to trust.

Kimberly Wehr
Indian Knoll Elementary School
West Chicago
Grade 6

Anne Frank

Anne frank was a marvelous child.
She had to stay in hiding and could never go wild.
She was never able to love and grow old.
When Anne was caught, she died of hunger and cold.
Anne had a diary whom she called Kitty.
And people who cared for Jews, thought the whole thing was a pity.
Anne wanted to publish her diary after the war.
Wanting to know when the war was to be over, her curiosity grew more and more.
Anne's last pages of her diary are as white as snow.
What Anne was to fill them up with, the world will never know.
Anne is what she wanted to be.
And will never be forgotten in my memory.

Sarah Teuber
Riverwood Elementary School
McHenry
Grade 5

Best Friends

Anne you are my greatest friend and that I won't deny,
Sure we get in fights a lot and sometimes even cry,
But even though we do those things and maybe even more,
If you weren't my best, best friend from my eyes tears would pour,
Sure you can have other friends like Mallory or Lana,
Just don't have them be your only buds and treat me like a banana,
That is all I have to say so I guess this is the end,
Just remember that you're great and always my best friend!

Claire Barnhart
Circle Center Intermediate School
Yorkville
Grade 5

The Storm

The loud roars of thunder shook the house.
The wind howled like a freight train.
Shutters banging against the bricks.
Panic set in with beads of sweat rolling down my cheeks.
Lightning lit up the gray sky.
Hail crashed on the roof with the sound of breaking glass
    with the mixture of rain splatting against the window.
Thump, thump, thump...We ran down the stairs.
Under the playpen as we crept like scared puppies.
But soon the thunder fell hushed in the background.
The wind became calm, the shutters fell silent.
My state of panic soon became composed.
The lightening soon became very distant.
Soon the hail and rain became a light shower
    and that is when I knew the storm was over.

Bridget Buckley
St Mary School
Alton
Grade 6

Future

Over the moon and around the sun
lets take a look at the future and have some fun.
You never know what the future will bring,
maybe exploding food – boom! pop! zing!
Maybe good times or bad, happiness or sad
    even a bizarre new teenage fad.
Stores may carry long range indiglo glasses
    or VW space passes.
And jet powered shoes
    guaranteed not to lose.
But what ever this bizarre new age brings,
    I hope it's good things.

Joseph Haine
St Mary School
Alton
Grade 6

Schoolwork

Spelling comes first,
Saying all the letters gives me a thirst.
Next comes math,
That's leading on a job path.
Then there's science,
That gives you science learning appliance.
Language teaches you writing skills,
That gives me lots of thrills.
Social Studies is fun,
But I usually get homework by the ton.
Last is reading,
We read a story about two friends meeting.
That's schoolwork.

Trae Mottet
Virginia Elementary School
Virginia
Grade 4

The Castle

Hidden doors and hallways,
Who knows what lies ahead?
A ghostly painting with knowing eyes
That fills your heart with dread?
A cheery, sunny window
With a view of birds in trees?
A chilling, empty bedroom
That sends shivers to your knees?
A corridor leading to a dungeon deep?
A door behind which the princess sleeps?
A prince on a stallion
Carved onto a wall
Saving the lady
From the witch who will fall
Down! To the dungeon
Down! To the deep
Down! To the place where the skeleton sleeps.
Hidden doors and hallways,
Mystery lies ahead.

Julia Spangler
North Elementary School
Marshall
Grade 6

I love cats and dogs

I love cats, they are so cute and playful
I hate bats, they are so mean and painful.
If cats are here stay and have fun,
If bats are here you'd better run.
I LOVE CATS!

I love dogs, they are so fun
And sometimes they are whiny when they are sad.
I hate frogs, they are so slimy and jumpy and bad.
If dogs are here stay and recline.
There will be action in no time.
If frogs are here you'd better watch out
You just might be wearing slime.
I LOVE DOGS!

Shauna Walat
Riverwood Elementary School
McHenry
Grade 5

Birds in the Sky

When I look in the sky and watch the birds flying,
it makes me wonder if I can get in the sky and fly too.
When I see the birds eating bread around the tree,
I start to see them grow day by day.
And when I hear them singing musical songs in the sky
it brings music to my heart and then I say,
"Can I be a bird one day too?"

Kendall Rapheal Sullivan
Evangelical Christian School
Chicago
Grade 4

I Do Not Understand

I do not understand why people hit each other.
I do not understand why people talk about each other.
I do not understand why people disrespect each other.
But most of all, I do not understand why moms and dads have to work all the time.
I do understand that people need each other.

JuTaun Wright
Barbour Elementary School
Rockford
Grade 4

At the Beach

Waves approaching the sand
Then getting scared and backing away
The soft sand at your feet
Full with shells and other things
The fish swimming gracefully in the water slowly and then with your approach disappearing again
Sitting beneath the sun sipping lemonade
Carefully making a sand castle sifting the sand though your fingers
What a fun day at the beach

Christiana Hinders
St Matthew School
Champaign
Grade 4

Thinking

As a boy sits on a boat, he thinks about his life and what he's been through.
He thinks back to the time he first tottered and the happiness of his parents.
He remembers when he first walked into school and what was going through his head.
He puts to mind the first time he learned how to read, write, solve math problems and how proud he had felt.
He recalls the first time he broke his arm and the pain he felt.
He treasures the first time he went to an amusement park and how much fun it had been.
He looks back to the time when he first learned how to play basketball and how good he became at it.
He goes back to the times when he got in trouble and how horrified he'd been.
And now as he rides down the river on the boat he wonders why he ever decided to leave his home
And start a new life in a whole new world.

Jason Jiang
Meridian Middle School
Buffalo Grove
Grade 6

A True Friend

A true friend is somebody you can count on when no one is around.
A true friend is someone you can lean on instead of falling to the ground.
A true friend will stay by you, when you are against the wall.
They'll pick you up each time you fall.
There are some people who will say that you're a friend to them.
But when times get tough and the going gets rough all you have to do is grin and bear it,
because there is nothing you can do.
When they are mean to you, they don't care how you feel.
This person you call your friend, has now turned into someone you wish that they would die.
So when you find someone who is a true friend to you,
who would rather give than receive something, then you'll know that this is the friend for you.

Gretchen Buhrke
Our Lady of Mt Carmel School
Melrose Park
Grade 5

Happy

Happy is pink like bubble-gum ice cream.
Happy slides slowly through my mind like a slippery banana.
It makes me want to jump!

Rebecca Brown
Pilgrim Lutheran School
Chicago
Grade 5

Volleyball

Volleyball, volleyball
Doesn't matter if you're short or tall.

The game's real fast when you play indoors.
You can move very quickly on the hardwood floors.

Playing on the beach is the most fun.
You're enjoying the sand, the water and the sun.

Volleyball, volleyball ...
Volleyball is very fun for all.

Erin Casey
Most Holy Redeemer School
Evergreen Park
Grade 5

Spring

The season of spring is filled with great things.
Many flowers are blooming, while the birds loudly sing.
The wonderful aroma of roses is here.
The air is mild and the sky, crystal clear.

Softball is coming and I cannot wait.
A bat in my hands again will feel quite great.
When the ball hits the bat and makes a loud ring,
To the bases my feet surely cling.

Children are outside having fun.
It's getting warmer, due to the sun.
Spring is ending, what a bummer.
Now it is time for a fun-filled summer.

Lyndi Araujo
Northlawn Middle School
Streator
Grade 6

Soccer

soccer is an awesome sport
offense is the position I play
center is a good position
coaches have to yell a lot
energy is wasted all the time in soccer
right midfield is one of my favorite positions

Matt Quiter
St John Fisher School
Chicago
Grade 4

New Lenox

New Lenox, a small town?
Not so small, people all around.
Cars screeching.
Trucks rumbling.
Dogs barking.
Birds squawking.

Winter snow falling, snowballs flying.
Kids zooming in sleds down hills.
Snowplows knocking down mail boxes.
Neighbors shoveling snow from their drive ways.
Someone doing donuts in a snow covered parking lot.

Town's getting larger everyday.
Cornfields shrinking.
Houses being built by the hundreds.
People moving here from everywhere.
Cars screeching.
Trucks rumbling.
Dogs barking.
Birds squawking.
New Lenox, my hometown.

Justin Fleck
Nelson Ridge School
New Lenox
Grade 6

There's a Mouse in Our House!

There's a mouse in our house
and he won't get out!
We don't know where to find him.
We looked under all of the beds
and I even looked on my sister's head.

There's a mouse in our house
and he won't get out.
One day I heard him say,
"I've found a pretty good house for myself;
I think I will stay!"
My grandma tried to kill it with a frying pan
and missed by a mile.
My sister just stood there with a great big smile.

My mom tried to hit it with a broom
and missed by an inch and said, "Oh, shucks."
She hit a glass pitcher that cost fifty bucks.
Finally we set the traps easily with cheese
then we tried peanut butter.
By this time I just gave up and said, "Oh, geez!"

There's a mouse in our house and he won't get out
and we probably never will find him!

Emily Cartmill
East Richland Elementary School
Olney
Grade 5

Lolly

Lolly is a nice spring day
Lolly is water flowing gently in a pond
Lolly is a soft pink color
Everyone would like to hug her.

Alyssa Schmiege
St John Of The Cross School
Western Springs
Grade 5

Life Is Like a Game

Life is like a game,
The starting of the game
Is like the starting of our lives...

Life is like a game,
In the middle it is really hard
Just like in the middle of life
It is hard to keep up —

Life is like a game,
Skipping levels is like
Moving up a grade each year.

Life is like a game,
Finally when you
Think you are going to beat the game
You get the game over.
Like you could be having
A good time and die!!

Brett Anderson
Barbara B. Rose Elementary School
South Barrington
Grade 5

How a Duck Feels About It

I'm brown and
yellow
in the sparkling
water.

This warm water
feels
good on my bottom.

I see a small
fish
I dive down to
get it.

I see the grass
move
I fly away.

Kin Barnard
St Boniface School
Quincy
Grade 6

Fat Cat

I have a fat cat that likes to nap.
She loves to sit on everyone's lap.
My cat is like me,
It fills me with glee,
Because she loves to nap on my lap.

Katelyn Garrett
Beckemeyer Elementary School
Beckemeyer
Grade 5

Home

H eart of family
O utrageous place for fun
M y place to be me
E veryone needs one.

Sarah Berry
St Anthony's School
Streator
Grade 5

Reading

Reading! Reading!
I love reading!
Reading makes me feel
Sad
Happy!
Glad!
I love reading!
Yes I do,
I love reading
More than candy!
Some books are happy!
Some are sad,
Some are boring!
But when I read books,
I love them all!
Reading is a good hobby,
If you are interested.
Reading! Reading!
I love reading,
More than candy!

Nichole Harris
Bolin Elementary School
East Peoria
Grade 5

Horse/Donkey

Horse
Strong, powerful
Running, galloping, fast,
In the grassy meadow flowers.
Donkey

Nicole Michelle Ballou
Hiawatha Elementary School
Kirkland
Grade 5

Spring

The grass is green
The trees have leaves;
It's nice and warm all around;
It is time to grow your plants
    around your home.
It's time to play!
Other reasons why spring is nice,
Several sports have started:
McGwire,
Sosa,
Professional baseball players.
This is why I like spring.

Nathan Springmeyer
Cisne Middle School
Cisne
Grade 6

Anger

Anger,
It's bottled
up inside
me way down
deep inside,
It doesn't want
to show it self,
it just wants to
hide, If someone
gets me really mad
I think I just might
pop, because of all
the anger inside me
that stays there
bottled up.

Matthew Morales
Emerson Elementary School
Berwyn
Grade 6

One Night

One night
I had a big fright.
I got out of bed
to see who was there.
I walked out of my room
and I heard a big boom.
I jumped back into bed
and I saw something near my head.
I screamed really loud
and I fell out of bed.
I lifted my head
and I said
Oh, it was just my shadow.

Marcus Bradshaw
Parker Jr High School
Flossmoor
Grade 6

I Am

I am a person who loves basketball
I wonder if I can play for the rest of my life
I hear that I can play for the Bulls
I see basketball games
I want to be in one
I am a person who loves basketball.

I pretend I don't play
I feel happy when I play
I touch the ball
I worry about getting hurt
I cry about nothing
I am a person who loves basketball.

I understand that I can play
I say I don't play
I dream I play for the Bulls
I try my hardest
I hope I play for the Bulls someday
I am a person who loves basketball.

Brad Wegmann
Damiansville Elementary School
Damiansville
Grade 6

God

God is here
God is there
God is everywhere

God sees this
God sees that
God sees everything that he chooses

God sees the sun
God sees the moon
God sees the stars at night

God is here
God is there
He's everywhere
He was even there when His dear child was born

Nikki Rhodes
Jefferson Elementary School
Springfield
Grade 6

Baseball

Baseball you try and catch the ball.
Sometimes you fall when you go for the ball.
Some kids are tall, some are small.
It's better to be tall so you will catch a fly ball.

John Fenton
St John Fisher School
Chicago
Grade 4

Jack, My Science Lab Partner

Jack is my science lab partner,
His whole name is Jack Hartner.
That's all I can say about him that's nice.
Yesterday, he mixed something and said it was lice.

He likes to mix things all together
Then try to pour it on my best friend, Heather.
Jack always slacks off on reports,
I hope he mixes up some warts!!!

We better switch science partners soon.
If we do, I hope I get June.
"Jack is a bad kid," says my mother.
The scary thing is, he's my brother!!!!!

Ashley Yates
St Mary School
New Berlin
Grade 6

School

Fun, lasting
Brains blasting!

Kindergarten, first grade, second grade more
My brains can possibly get sore.

Class is over as the lunch bell rings.
Let's go see what the lunch lady brings.

One thing is groovy
Like watching a movie.

Science is fun — guts and glory
Mopping the floor — a janitor's worry.

And even doing math
Worse than a bath!

Phillip Winkeler
Okawville Grade School
Okawville
Grade 5

The Squirm Worm

The squirm worm cannot stand still
He never has and never will.
He's always jumping up and down.
And when he's not turning around.
Or somewhere on his head.
Sometimes he runs up the stairs,
Then he stops and runs back down again.
The squirm worm is always turning around.
Watching him will make you dizzy.

Elizabeth Echeverria
Our Lady of Mt Carmel School
Melrose Park
Grade 5

Jack's Money

When Jack gets his money
he's running down the halls.
When Jack gets his money
he's jumping on the walls.
When Jack gets his money
he's as crazy as can be.
When Jack gets his money
he stings like a bee.
When Jack gets his money
he's gone to the store.
When Jack gets his money
it's spent and there's no more.

Christa Anders
St Mary School
New Berlin
Grade 6

When I Think of Blue

When I think of blue,
I think of the sky
I think of the water
I think of my eyes.
When I think of blue,
I think about you
I think about love
I think of my gym shoe.
When I think of blue,
I think of my school
I think of my cat
on the blue and black mat.
I love blue, do you?

Julie Grismanauskas
St. Richard School
Chicago
Grade 5

Earth Day

Earth Day,
is a beautiful day,
when every one,
does their share!

Recycle,
clean,
we can do the job,
for the wonderful Earth Day!

Earth Day,
should be a,
wonderful day,
for every living thing,
to enjoy!

Ashley Mathew
Garvy Elementary School
Chicago
Grade 6

When Friends Leave

As you go on through your life,
You will have many friends.
Some are friends of the road people say,
Others are friends for life,
So you stay,
Friends forever and much longer than that.
But sometimes something happens to a friendship so strong,
One of the friends moves away for so very long,
They leave you with memories that you hold so tight,
That you think of when you are laying in bed in the night.
But every now and then you find a special friend,
that you know will keep in touch no matter how far away they go.
When you find that friend,
Make sure that you tell them how much you cherish them so,
Or else they will leave you and you will never know,
if they were a friend for life,
Or just a friend of the road.

Caitlin Anne Tucker
Meridian Middle School
Buffalo Grove
Grade 6

Ode to Abraham

Abraham Lincoln was an honest man.
He earned his living by the sweat of his brow and the work of his hand.
His family was very poor you see,
So he worked in a store, to make money for his family.
A lady once forgot her change,
So he walked five miles across the open range
To give that lady back her change.
He married a woman named Mary,
And happily they lived, VERY!
This great man became president,
In writing a speech, he was not hesitant,
How I wish that great man was still president,
May this great man rest in peace in the presence of God.

Molly Fisher
North Elementary School
Marshall
Grade 6

Most Dreams

Most dreams have perfect people
Most dreams in my life are enjoying
Most dreams have first loves
Most dreams don't have to do with boxing gloves
Most dreams you can find your true love
Most dreams have to do with the future
Most dreams you can do as you please
Most dreams occur during daylight
Most dreams will be about good things as well as the bad
Most dreams end up with happy endings.

Candice Sanchez
Emerson Elementary School
Berwyn
Grade 6

I Am...

I am a student,
Going to Solomon School,
Who loves to read (especially mystery books)
Any will do for me—
Scary or fiction it can be.

I am also a brother—
To a little sister
I am in a family of five.

I have a big sister,
And a little sister—
Which makes me the middle child.

I also like sports
My favorite is football,
Where the ball is thrown
And the ball is caught.
It is a lot of fun—
To watch and play.

So, that is me—
Who I am happy to be.

Kevin Dam
Solomon Elementary School
Chicago
Grade 4

Red

Red is a beautiful color,
It reminds me of many things,
Roses, and berries, and sugar plum fairies,
Red is the fireworks on the 4th of July,
And a heart that beats fast when a baby cries,
It makes me picture flames in an old fireplace,
Where you cuddle up with a smile on your face.

Brittany Mackowiak
St. Richard School
Chicago
Grade 5

My Dog Bub

He was on his own until he was found,
we got our dog Bub at the pound.
My dog Bub is brown, black, and white,
and he gets on the couch late at night.
Bub's fat and lazy and he doesn't play
he sleeps on his bed for most of the day.
Bub's supposed to be a hunting dog,
but my mom says he looks more like a hog.
Bub is fat and he's lazy and he doesn't play,
but I love my dog Bub anyway.

Becky Westerdale
Kellar Central School
Peoria
Grade 4

Nascar

Nascar races
Excited faces

Nascar fans all come to see;
Nascar fans like you and me.

Flipping, spinning, and crashing all around the track
When it comes to racing, there's no slack.

Drivers drive and drive.
All racing fans thrive.

It's fun to watch all day.
We'll watch it instead of play.

Drivers love it, too.
It's challenging to do.

Matthew Elliott
Okawville Grade School
Okawville
Grade 5

Varnack

Varnack is as sharp as freezing snowflakes in winter.
As cold and lonely as Pluto.
Its action is crunching and chewing.
Its favorite food is irksome little sisters.

Andy Muscarello
St John Of The Cross School
Western Springs
Grade 5

Flying

Flying, flying, up in the sky,
Soaring with bluebirds, way, way up high.
You can see rainbows, as you pass by,
Looking at trees, bowing good-bye.

Sailing, sailing, sailing the seven seas,
Being the captain, steering as you please.
Using a compass, you guide the ship safely,
You collect tickets, as passengers pay fees.

Racing, racing, racing without fear,
As you accelerate, you switch the gear.
As you race, laps zoom by,
Your engine is so loud that you cannot hear.

Running, running, running really fast,
The speed of your running, of course, will not last.
You dash down to the finish line,
The speaker's announcement makes a loud blast.

Frank Yan
Butterfield Elementary School
Libertyville
Grade 4

Poison Plants

Rhododendron is a plant
It can poison even an ant,
So is a wild mushroom too
It is smaller than a kangaroo.

Jesse Castle
Tri-County Christian School
Freeport
Grade 4

Butterfly Fly

Butterfly fly
all through the sky
so very high
My oh my
you've flown so high
up to the sky
oh little butterfly
you're so very high
in the sky
come down my butterfly.

Mallory Halvorsen
Ontarioville Elementary School
Hanover Park
Grade 5

The Cocker Spaniel

So kind and shy always
Looking for a friend.
So calm and friendly
The cocker spaniel.

Kelly Lancaste
Richmond Elementary School
St Charles
Grade 5

Anything Is Possible

Anything is possible,
like riding a rocket to outer space.
Anything is possible,
like tying your own shoelace.

Anything is possible,
like reading a book.
Anything is possible,
like crossing the brook.

Anything is possible,
like riding a bike.
Anything is possible,
like having friends you like.

ANYTHING IS POSSIBLE!

Alyssa Catlett
Lewis & Clark Elementary School
Wood River
Grade 4

Scary Ghosts

Ghosts are clear
Ghosts are white
They can scare you in the night
Please don't yell
Please don't scream
They won't be too awful mean.

Megan Force
Brick Elementary School
Beardstown
Grade 4

Paintball

Laying low, among the trees,
I'm in my crouch, upon my knees,
I can scan the field far and wide,
from my opponent I shall hide.
I scan to the left, and I scan to the right,
I put my target on my sight,
raise my marker, aim it high,
I pull the trigger and the ball will fly,
it takes its flight straight and true,
at that moment my opponent knew,
the game was over and he was through!

Thomas Feicco
Spring Brook Elementary School
Naperville
Grade 5

The Birds

Birds fly high in the sky
When they come down they fool around
Chirping in the trees
Making nests with grass and greens.

Aubree J. Rhoades
Brick Elementary School
Beardstown
Grade 4

Boys

Some are nasty,
Some are cute,
Some I wish I could just mute.
Some are fun,
Some are boring,
When I'm around some
I feel like mourning.
Some are rude,
Some are cruel,
Some of them even drool!
And some of them wink,
But all boys, I'm sure,
Forget to think.

Missi Davis
St John Of The Cross School
Western Springs
Grade 5

Birds

The birds are chirping
The birds are flying back north
They are wonderful

Christine Pedroza
St Mary of Czestochowa School
Cicero
Grade 6

Freedom

F light of the missiles
R emembrance of those who died
E motion of the determined heart
E nding of the battle
D efending what you believe in
O n going love of those who fought
M aking America a better place

Brandon Provost
Manteno Middle School
Manteno
Grade 6

I Hear Music

I hear music in the air,
I hear music everywhere!
I hear things my mind says,
I mostly hear things my heart says.
That's what I hear.
I hear music!

Katrina Jefferson
Diekman Elementary School
Dolton
Grade 5

Poor Puppy

I had a puppy dog.
The poor puppy dog.
My father was painting my room.
The paint spilled and my puppy is now
blue!

Molly Condon
St John Fisher School
Chicago
Grade 4

Imagination

An unrealistic journey has begun,
There, all meaningless words are spoken,
This place is the world of imagination,
Mystical angels stand by my side,
Looking at me with only happiness,
I fly in this world with gorgeous wings,
While brightness fills the air.

Kara Werner
Meridian Middle School
Buffalo Grove
Grade 5

My Loony Granny

I'm going to tell you a story,
About when my granny came to town,
But may I warn you, about my granny,
Who can be somewhat of a clown.

Let's start with her clothes,
They are absolutely funny,
She wears cowboy boots,
And the ears of the Easter Bunny.

She wears polka-dotted socks,
With huge earring that don't match,
She wears a dress full of fur,
And a belt with a silver patch.

Once I was eating dinner,
And suddenly granny screamed,
"Come on folks! Let's go dance!
Then let's eat some whip cream!"

When we were in the snow,
In five degree weather,
And she came out in a bathing suit,
And said, "Surfs up, Heather."

So, yes, she's weird, but she's my special friend.

Bridget Flores
St John Of The Cross School
Western Springs
Grade 5

Heaven's Light

It's a shimmer that glitters in your soul,
A glow that burns in your heart,
Whispers filter through it,
And it dances.
It shows a freedom like sunlight on the earth,
Proves that a golden heart is a stairway,
And it speaks.
Like a beacon in the night,
It is your candle.
It is what uncovers the mountain peaks in morn,
What graces the grass with dew,
And it spreads.
The clouds that roll silently across the sky,
The silhouettes that dance in the night,
It is the path to an endless road,
And it leads.
The mountain may bow to the wind,
Or the soft colors that paint the sky at dawn,
Whether we wake to death or life,
It is heaven's light.

Shaila Naughton
Elizabeth Ann Seton Catholic School
Fairview Heights
Grade 5

My Father

Have you seen my father, who gives his love to me,
who tells me funny stories while I'm sitting on his knee.
Who gives his emotions to show that he does care,
to everybody's crystal eyes we make the perfect pair.
I write this poem thanking him for all the things he's done,
he's smart, funny, loving, and caring. But most of all he's fun.

Erica Curry
Parker Jr High School
Flossmoor
Grade 6

Lanky Lenny

Lanky Lenny is a basketball star.
He earns so much, he drives the finest car.
And you bet,
He'll hit the net,
When shooting hoops on the dark tar.

Aaron Minard
Beckemeyer Elementary School
Beckemeyer
Grade 5

About The Immigrants

Left their country
and they wanted to have freedom.
Some of the immigrants had to go back because of a disease
others didn't.

Ryan Snow
Central Elementary School
Pontiac
Grade 4

God

God is the one who created you
So be grateful for what He gave you.

He sent His only begotten son to save you
So go to heaven with Him too

Our God is an awesome God

He raised from heaven above
With wisdom, power and love

Our God is
An awesome God!

The Devil tries to capture us
But He can save us

To get to heaven Jesus Christ is the way
So get saved today!

Kiani Love
Evangelical Christian School
Chicago
Grade 4

Water/Rocks
Water
Wet, cold
Swimming, drinking, diving
Liquid, drink, gravel, boulder
Throwing, breaking, cracking
Hard, rough
Rocks

Miguel Huerta
St Procopius School
Chicago
Grade 4

Spring
Spring is here
Spring is here
Spring is here again

During the winter
All flowers are dead
But during the spring
Flowers come alive

Daffodils, tulips
Daisies, and roses
The pretty colors
Bring the smell of spring

Spring is here
Spring is here
Too bad spring can't stay

Rebecca Lee
Forest View Elementary School
Mount Prospect
Grade 4

A Flower Named Gale
There once was a flower named Gale
She hated the sleet, snow and hail
It started to rain
And she was in pain
But nobody could hear her wail.

Alexander Blank
North Park Elementary School
Chicago
Grade 4

Summer
Summer is my favorite season,
to fish, swim and ride bikes is the reason.
Enjoy these in the sun,
you are bound to have fun.
So don't stress out and enjoy the season.

Michael Arnold
Beckemeyer Elementary School
Beckemeyer
Grade 5

20th Century
In 1908 the cathode ray tube
Marked the beginning of T.V.,
For kids everywhere the greatest
Invention of the twentieth century.

Nick Marchese
Schiesher Elementary School
Lisle
Grade 5

Rainbow
Sparkling is the sun
Sparkling wonderfully
Beautiful rainbow

Michael Holmes
North Elementary School
Marshall
Grade 6

Lolly
Lolly is the season of summer
Lolly is a happy place
Lolly is smiling happily
Lolly is the color pink

Deirdre Burke
St John Of The Cross School
Western Springs
Grade 5

All Alone
Standing here, all alone,
wondering where I am,
in a land of strangers.
Wishing, Hoping,
that someone I know,
will walk by,
and give me directions,
so I can get home.
Safely.

Vanessa Ruesch
Emerson Elementary School
Berwyn
Grade 6

Football
It is fast, exciting, and complicated.
It takes a lot of guts, and hard work.
On offense it is end zone to end zone.
On defense it's hard to the bone.
You don't play on a court.
It is not for the gentle sort.
It is played in fall.
It is *football*

Rory Keigher
Iroquois West Upper Elementary School
Thawville
Grade 5

What Your Senses Can Do
Oh, what your nose can do,
Like sniff a flower or an old shoe,
Oh, what your nose can do.

Oh, what your eyes can see,
Like clouds on a rainy day or a lit Christmas tree.
Oh, what your eyes can see.

Oh, what your mouth can taste,
A sour lemon or peppermint toothpaste.
Oh, what your mouth can taste.

Oh, what your hands can feel,
Like a soft pillow or the skin on your heel,
Oh, what your hands can feel.

Oh, what your ears can hear,
Like a buzzer or a resounding cheer,
Oh, what your ears can hear.

Oh, what your senses can do,
Your senses can do everything for you,
Oh, what your senses can do.

Erin Kasson
All Saints Academy School
Breese
Grade 4

Duke

I always wanted a dog;
It was a need that surrounded me like fog.
But mom said, "No,
I like my house clean."
Dad said, "Whoa,
We don't need one more thing!"

A new century dawned;
And my 12th birthday was here.
After a basketball game in New Harmony;
We had an errand to run quite near.
I fell asleep on the far ride;
My parents said, "Open your eyes!"
Through a basement door they disappeared;
I followed to find a big surprise.

Suddenly a furry ball was placed in my arms;
It was a beagle pup full of charm.
Duke's quite a hound;
With a sensitive nose.
Soon he'll be hunting rabbits;
In those old fence rows.

Patrick Dee
St Mary School
Mount Carmel
Grade 6

The Vine

My hyperactivity is a vine
That spurts and flourishes wildly in the warm day.
It tells everyone, "Guess what I found out?!"

Nicolas Nootens
Pilgrim Lutheran School
Chicago
Grade 4

Who Do You Think I Am

Who do you think I am,
Who do you think I am,
I am a sparrow from an egg.
Who do you think he is,
Who do you think he is,
He is the bluest blue jay I have ever seen.
Who do you think she is,
Who do you think she is,
Well, if I am a sparrow,
And he is a blue jay,
Then she must be a robin but,
Not an ordinary robin, a bright robin.
Who do you think you are,
Who do you think you are,
You are the nicest person in the whole wide world.

Crystal Moody
Morton Career Academy
Chicago
Grade 4

Hamburger

I walk through the door after a long day at school.
I hear the sizzling of the pan and my mother's singing voice.
I'm starving.
I see a plate on the table,
Buns, pickles, lettuce, burgers
I feel the bun in my hand and the burger in my mouth
Smells like juicy lettuce, meat
My hamburger.

Leah Peinovich
Grand Prairie Elementary School
Joliet
Grade 4

My Brother Pete

My brother Pete, nice and kind
But he can never make up his mind
He is skinny and kind of funny
He never likes to spend his money
My brother Pete is very smart
Except for when it comes to music and art
He likes soccer and basketball
But he doesn't like going to the mall
My brother Pete likes to play
But only in the light of day
He never likes to stay up late
Unless it is a sleepover with his friend, Nate
My brother Pete is very fast
Even if he was wearing a cast
He is silly and sweet
That's why I want to be like my big brother Pete

Matt Chambers
Kellar Central School
Peoria
Grade 4

I Want To Go Home

I wish I would have been there more,
I always seemed to be walking out the door,
Our family is never together,
It's been like that mostly forever.
She kept the family closer,
And we'd really hate to lose her.
Then my mom came to me to say,
That my grandma passed away today.
But how could she tell, like it really truly is,
In a melancholy moment just like this.
It doesn't feel like she's really gone,
Even though her life was so happy and long.
She knew she was ready to go,
She'll be my angel, whatever I do she'll know.
I don't want her to be sad or alone,
My grandma's last words were, "I want to go home".

Sheila Boyer
Dakota District 201
Dakota
Grade 6

Friends

Friends are kind,
with heartful minds.
They care for you,
and hope you will, too.
You are always together,
from the beginning through forever.
They stick up for you,
just like you would do.
There is one gift they give to thee.
Something that is very free.
The gift is them,
FRIENDS.

Kris Roberts
St Matthew School
Champaign
Grade 4

My Secret Crush

I feel like telling you how I feel
but when I see you I can't reveal
my feelings for you are really deep
and when I think of them I want to weep
I feel alone, I feel left out
I wonder if you like me
but there's still a doubt
my feelings for you will never go away
but I have to deal with them day to day

Alyssa Hernandez
Nixon Elementary School
Chicago
Grade 5

Happiness!

Happiness is a joyful thing!
It makes you happy.
It makes you sing, clap, and dance.
It brings great pleasure.
Happiness is a joyful thing!

Shannon Carter
Diekman Elementary School
Dolton
Grade 4

Little Masked Bandit

Rings all around these little guys,
Big, beady, shiny, saucer eyes.
Think you're the masked bandit master?
This guy will steal it much faster.
Sneaky, sneaky yes he is,
Shiny things will soon be his.
His eyes are as shiny as the moon.
Yes, he is the impressive raccoon!

Christine Holm
Anderson Elementary School
St Charles
Grade 5

Dreams

Dreams, dreams, what a sight!
  Sometimes they wake you in the middle of the night.
Dreams, dreams, who knows what will happen.
  Like the dream I had in my grandfather's wagon.
Dreams, dreams, sometimes they're weird
  Like the one last night when my aunt had a beard.
Dreams, dreams, sometimes they're funny
  Like the one where my uncle was telling jokes with his monkey.
But most of all, dreams are great.
  And I'm sure all of you can relate.

Holly Thomann
Pilgrim Lutheran School
Chicago
Grade 4

The Beauty of Spring

Spring is coming.
The evening night is becoming bright again.
A new life is coming into everything.
The restless flower petals are swaying in the night sky.
The dew is beginning to shine.
The mist is starting to fall among the beautiful sprouting green grass.
The air smells fresh as fresh as rain.
The flowers are as bright as the glimmering sun.
The beauty of spring is here, again!

Samantha Liametz
Forest View Elementary School
Mount Prospect
Grade 4

No More Sorrow

As a girl walked to the sea,
She wondered about her family.
They long long passed so long ago,
She could not express her sorrow
She wondered if she could hear or see,
But all she saw was a tree,
She saw lots farther on,
As the wind blew her down.
Then it struck her, like a burst of light,
They were with her all along, since the day they passed so long ago.
Her mother was the sun,
Shining so bright in the summer days.
Her father was the moon,
Glowing in the dark, starry night.
The winds were her brothers and sisters,
Playing so strong in the day.
Her grandma and grandpa were the clouds,
Different shades of goldish browns and bluish skies.
Aunts and uncles were the waters, rivers, lakes, and oceans too,
Now she knew that she was not alone,
Together in happiness and forever in love!

Natalia Burzynska
Channahon Middle School
Channahon
Grade 6

The Pillow

White as a puffy cloud.
Smooth like a piece of thread.
Reminds me of angels wishing me a happy dream.
Take a nap on it.

Madison Tolomeo
St John Of The Cross School
Western Springs
Grade 5

Upside-Down Day

One day I got out of my bed,
and something fell upon my head.
I looked to the ceiling, only to see,
the floor that was supposed to be beneath me.

A toy had fallen on my head,
just above my little bed.
I went downstairs, just to see,
if things were happening to them, like me!

Sure enough, things were wrong,
our cow started to sing a song.
Our bird was mooing, oh what a sight,
I went to the parlor to turn on a light.

I went outside to get some fresh air,
and then I turned away in despair.
I screamed, I yelled, I ran to my room,
and then something just went kaboom!

I checked my closet and then I saw,
the old pictures I used to draw.
I forgot about the kaboom,
and went into another room.

Then I woke up.

Katie West
Riverwood Elementary School
McHenry
Grade 5

Rumors

Secrets passed through the quiet halls.
They don't care if it's TRUE or FALSE
only your true friends stand by you.
Sometimes it's forgotten sometimes it's not.
But you feel the pain it hurts a lot.

Nobody cares if it's RIGHT or WRONG.
But you must stand tall and must be strong.
For people will spread them. FALSE or TRUE
they can be about anyone even you.

Anca Covaliu
Emerson Elementary School
Berwyn
Grade 6

My Dad

Oh, Daddy-O, how I love you so,
I never want to let you go,
I love you down to your big hairy toe.
It's funny to watch your stomach grow.
Your hair is almost as white as snow.
So I'm writing this note to let you know,
I love you and admire you more than you'll ever know,
Because I think you're the best Daddy-O
That I'll ever know!

DeAngela Futch
St Paul Lutheran School
Rockford
Grade 4

Flowers

Flowers are in every place and spot.
You normally find them in temperatures that are hot.
Beautiful lilacs, lilies, petunias, and roses,
Are all flowers that tickle our noses.
Flowers can come in bunches or just one.
No matter where they are, always in the bright, shiny sun.
Flowers are beautiful in the morning dew and spring.
A smile to your face they will always bring.
Flowers can be big or little and smell good too.
No matter what, they bring happiness to you.

Kelsey Dubree
Iroquois West Upper Elementary School
Thawville
Grade 5

Changes

Changes always happen whether you want them to or not.
You may have a death in the family or turn 12
either way there's a change in your life.
It may be good or bad no one knows.
Changes are good sometimes and awful others.
I hope the next is good 'cause I can't bear another bad.
I wish upon a star there was never another bad change,
but I know in my sad heart that's how life works.
Changes are what you want them to be.
Please help me through these changes I'm going through.
I know you can only do so much
But do your best to help me through these times.
You have the power to heal my broken heart so please do.
I'm sure glad you brought me here.
I know you can only try to heal me so I am asking you to.
To try and help my wound by the changes I go through.
Some changes are good some are bad,
no matter what they happen to all of us
and I wish I could say I will never have another bad change
but that would be a lie.
The last will be when I die and go to Heaven.

Danielle Hughes
Indian Knoll Elementary School
West Chicago
Grade 6

Space

Space is wide and open,
Like the prairie sky so blue.
The stars are diamonds in the sky,
Glittering down on you.

Space is black as ink,
Blotted on a page.
Space is old,
And it doesn't age.

Space is different,
Than any place that I'll ever see.
It will not perish nor disappear,
It will be there to the end.

Meagan Anderson
Iroquois West Upper Elementary School
Thawville
Grade 5

Springtime

S wimming in the spring
P eople meet
R eading a good book
I s when you visit someone
N o one fighting
G etting good grades
T oys to play with
I s when you play with your friends
M y mom
E verything that you have

Patrick Clancy
St John Fisher School
Chicago
Grade 4

Sun

Sun is to sun
smart and bright all day,
Shining its face,
always to us and never away.

Carissa Wozny
St Mary School
Mundelein
Grade 6

Heather

Heather
She is a doll!
She is like a chatterbox.
She talks, runs, and laughs.
She is my sister.
Heather

Brittany Lucas
North Elementary School
Marshall
Grade 6

Singing

Up in the clouds,
where the angels sing alto,
Down in the ground,
where the devil sings bass,
It doesn't matter what you sing,
it's how you sing it.

Steph Snethen
Manteno Middle School
Manteno
Grade 6

Life Is Like a Room Full of Boxes

Life is like a room of boxes,
Open one at a time—
Do not rush or go too slow...

You don't always know what you will
Come up with,
But have to do it anyway.

If you can't get the box open
Don't give up,
Just do your best all the time.

Once it is open into your mind,
Always use it
Never forget anything about it

Life is like a room of boxes;
Sometimes it's easy,
Sometimes it can be very hard.

Kevin Deacon
Barbara B. Rose Elementary School
South Barrington
Grade 5

An Angel

Down the hill yonder,
'Twas light brought to God.
To see forth baby Jesus,
Through rain, soot and sod.
'Twas an angel as bright as can be
Who crossed everything just to see
A newborn baby laid in a manger.
She came to see Jesus,
And spoke only this,
"Forth lay this baby,
Mary gave God.
This baby as powerful as I,
Jesus will not die.
He cannot die.
He will live in our hearts forever!"

Nikki Warner
North Elementary School
Marshall
Grade 6

To Trees

Ever growing, always calming,
White oak, birch, and evergreen,
Housing squirrels and singing birds
Darkened branches of foliage green.

Willow, apple, beech, and maple,
Holding memories and forgotten things
Nesting ancient and tweeting birds,
It softly, quietly, sweetly sings.

Cloaked in time-hardened bark,
Putting forth cones and flowers
Where tired birds wing home,
Soothing with its unseen powers.

Daniel Scott
Argenta-Oreana Elementary School
Oreana
Grade 6

Spring

Robins in the air
Light blue eggs in their small nests
I hear a chirping

Jaclyn Taylor
Stone Creek Elementary School
Roscoe
Grade 4

Dreams

Soft,
cloudy things,
that come from somewhere.
Where?
No one knows.

People can track them,
remember them,
and study them.
But no one
knows them.

Shrouded in mystery.
If you try you will
get nowhere.
A dead end,
starting over again.

Soft,
cloudy things,
that come from somewhere.
Shrouded in mystery.
Sleep.

Kyle McKay
Nelson Ridge School
New Lenox
Grade 6

Our Faces Looked Funny

Bars rising up and down
Sitting next to people screaming everywhere
Black, red, yellow and white
You try to put your hands up
Dropping them back down
Hold on tight
Here we go
Going down the unseen hill
Your stomach dropping down
When going down a curve, picture taken
I try to smile, but I can't
When we looked at our pictures
Our faces looked very funny

Andrea Mackley
Grand Prairie Elementary School
Joliet
Grade 4

Slave

Running through my master's field,
which consists of corn, soybeans, and cotton.

Hiding in my family's
small, cold, and old shack.
Eating anything that is given to me,
which is often nothing.

Playing with my old, tattered corncob doll.
Thinking about my home in Africa,
so far, far away.

Watching out for my master:
his whip, his fists.
Dreaming about freedom,
escaping—at least away from this place.

Toni Frederick
Wells Elementary School
Grayville
Grade 5

Immigrants

Some immigrants looked really nice
but some looked like dried rice.

On the ship some of the rats
were bigger than the cats.

Some immigrant ships got lost at sea
and those immigrants never saw land that was free.

Some immigrants caught some sharks
and they were pulled in water that was dark.

Jose Guerrero
Central Elementary School
Pontiac
Grade 4

Friends

When you have a friend your friendship will never end.
You will spend many times with each other.
It will be like having a sister or brother.
You will stick together like a bird and a feather.
Depending on the wind and depending on the weather.
No matter what, you will always have a friend.
And when you do it will never end.

Brittany Majka
St John Fisher School
Chicago
Grade 4

One Person

One person can make a difference,
One person can love, hug, kiss, and cuddle,
One person is unique,
Not one exact copy of them
In any way, shape, or form.
One person has power like Napoleon,
Queen Elizabeth or Charlemagne,
They can rule over a country or household,
They still have power,
One person has feeling,
Feeling that could change the rest of your life
Or the rest of your day.
One person's feeling that could make the happy,
Sad, joyful and sorrow,
One person has their say, black,
White, yellow, red, or even purple,
They have their say, whether wrong or right;
A lie or the truth,
One person can do anything.

Simone Hall
Parker Jr High School
Flossmoor
Grade 6

Good-Bye

Good-bye old friend.
I knew this time would have to end.
The times were fun.
I still remember when you got stuck in gum.
He was my best friend and our times will never end.
Your final day is here.
Good-bye, friend.
You're always in my heart.
Our last day was the best
and now you're put to rest.
All of your pain is gone.
Don't worry, friend.
I'll be there.
It won't be long.

Andrew Jacklin
Emerson Elementary School
Berwyn
Grade 6

Night

The middle of the night is the scariest time,
when the light goes dark and the big chime chimes.
The wind blows fierce, the big dogs bark,
I can even hear the echoes from the park.
The song of the ghosts, the mumbling of the mummies,
and the rum tum tum going on inside my tummy.
I try to hide, but where is there to go?
If you ever hear of such a place, please let me know!

Jami Normann
McHenry Jr High School
McHenry
Grade 6

Snow

The snow falls through the night
leaving the ground a blanket of white
I wake up in delight
for I will have a snowball fight!

I go to my friend's door
but all I hear is a snore
Then behind me, I hear a roar
that I wish I could ignore

Suddenly, I get hit on my back with a splat!
there is my friend with his orange hat
He is not really my friend— he is kind of a brat!
his face is scrunched up like a fat rat

So we fought all day
under the sky, which was all gray
So we played by the bay
as the day drew to an end, I went my separate way

To my house I walked in the snow
the moon made the snow glisten and glow
When I woke up, I wondered *Where did it go?*
and there went the snow, with one single blow!

Elyse Pieper
St Irene School
Warrenville
Grade 6

Bricks

Bricks are big,
Bricks are red,
One just hit me on the head,
Now I'm dead,
They made my grave,
Out of hardened clay,
There then my body lay on that dreadful day,
Too bad it happened in beautiful May.

Peter Hackley
St Matthew School
Champaign
Grade 4

Quiet Snow

I listen to snow,
music, snuffle-luffing,
and friends and my family.
I was mystified by the snuffle-
luffing, people sleeping, relaxing,
perfect, resting alone in the sweet
music of the snow. It excited me. I was
mystified by the sweet pond exploring the
white,
soft, snow. I was alone practicing, relaxing,
sleeping and resting. Relax, sit back,
and enjoy. Then settle in, start
snuffle-luffing, listen, sleep,
and imagine. Then fall
asleep, alone. In
the snow . . .

Marylyn Presutti
Nelson Ridge School
New Lenox
Grade 6

Fuzzy Wuzzy Creepy Crawly

Fuzzy, wuzzy, creepy, crawly caterpillar funny.
You will be a butterfly when the days are sunny.
Winging, flinging, dancing, springing butterfly so yellow.
You were once a caterpillar wiggly, wiggly fellow.

Yessenia Gutierrez
Ontarioville Elementary School
Hanover Park
Grade 4

The Sword Fight

I slashed out my sword ready to fight,
When I first started I bowed right.
Then I bowed up and to my left,
I won't let my victory be from theft.
Then I blocked one going down,
I didn't even show a frown.
I jumped back high into the air,
I was ready and I had no fear.
I turned and swiped my sword around,
Then there was a clanging sound.
I climbed up a pole to get away,
My dueler followed me up at midday.
I thought fast but there was no time to think,
A thought came in an eyeblink.
I grabbed onto a flag and spun around,
Suddenly I slipped and fell on the ground.
My dueler's face I could clearly see,
I feared the winner would not be me.
But I swung my sword and it was done,
I had become number one.

Shimon Castle
Yeshiva Tiferes Tzvi
Chicago
Grade 6

20th Century

20th century you were so grand
How powerful you stand
The color barrier broke
Martin Luther King stepped out and spoke
We had so many wars
Technology began to soar
Cars suddenly drove by
Next airplanes started to fly
As we say to the 20th century bye-bye
We await the next millennium
With excitement sky-high

Cory Zomick
Schiesber Elementary School
Lisle
Grade 5

The Working of Life

Start of a new universe,
Beginning of a new world.
One hundred miles of forests and fields.
Magical
First opening of eyes,
Delicate and fragile motion,
Relaxation.
Surprise battle,
Incredibly horrifying attack,
Start of World War III,
Terrifying, devastating and overpowering war,
Over ruling one hundred survivors.
World vanishing in the dusk.
Death and mourning.
Wind blowing away the sorrow,
Waves washing away the sadness.
HEAVEN!!
Dreamy and imaginary land.
That is the way life works,
So use your life wisely!

Steven Klein
Meridian Middle School
Buffalo Grove
Grade 5

The Way I Feel

The way I feel is special,
so special it's hard to describe...
When I look at you I melt.
Hoping someday I'll be in your arms
holding you and never wanting to let go.
When I tell you how I feel, there's a gut feeling,
hoping you feel the same.
So keep it in mind that that's the way I feel
and it'll NEVER CHANGE!

Nicole Valle
Logandale Middle School
Chicago
Grade 6

Me

My shoe is like mud
My teeth are like yellow
My glasses are like dirty
My heart holds secrets
That are blue as a cloud
I live in a cardboard box
And eat fried chicken and tacos and drink alien goo

Matt Steele
Matherville Elementary School
Matherville
Grade 5

Feelings

They hurt my feelings when they call me names
little do they know I'm going to be the fame.

People get their feeling hurt when people call people names,
I really think that mean, all we have to do is be a great team.

People say they're sorry but do they really mean it?
If they put their hearts and minds into it maybe they will feel it.

Eboni Brown
Sunnydale Elementary School
Streamwood
Grade 5

Snow

The snow comes, the snow goes
The snow comes, knocking on my door.
It is so beautiful covering the ground.
For kids to play in all for the day,
But when the sun goes down
The snow sparkles and gleams
For everyone to enjoy!

Jessica Lowe
North Elementary School
Marshall
Grade 6

Summer

Summer is a wonderful season,
for many, many, many reasons.
In summer you don't have to go to school,
instead you can go to the swimming pool.
You can stay up late and sleep all day,
and when you get up – go ahead and play!
You can go places with your friends,
it just seems like the day never ends!
And of course you can go on vacations to places to see,
that's one of the best parts for me!
Summer is my favorite season,
for all of these reasons!

Heather Schaefer
Garvy Elementary School
Chicago
Grade 6

Spring

The birds are flying,
The sky is brightly shining,
The sky is pretty.

Alysia De Leon
St Mary of Czestochowa School
Cicero
Grade 6

What's a Hero

A hero might be someone small
Or they could be someone tall.
For a hero doesn't have to fly
Or have the power to never die.

A hero could be as a helpless flower.
Does a hero have to have power?
The power to run, the power to sing.
What, really, do these things bring?

The power for right, to do your best
You never know what will happen next.
A hero might be someone small
Or the hero could be inside us all.

Kara Puccinelli
St John Of The Cross School
Western Springs
Grade 5

Brother

B old
R ambunctious
O dd
T reacherous
H ugger
E ager
R eally short

Sean Hallin
Emerson Elementary School
Berwyn
Grade 6

Spring

Spring is when bells ring,
  children sing
And flowers bring a scent that
  fills the air.
The crazy daisies blow in the wind,
  with all the other flowers blooming.
The children are swinging
  with their friends.
That's what brings the joy
  of spring to everyone in the world.

Meghan Williamson
Most Holy Redeemer School
Chicago
Grade 5

Dandelion

There was this lion,
whose name was *dandelion*.
They called her names,
and never let her play games.
One day she walked along in the woods, to see what she would find.
She did not find anything but she left something behind.
While she was walking,
she saw a friend and to her she started talking.
Dandelion told her that she lost something in the woods.
They went and searched.
What they found was a beautiful *dandelion* that was like the lion
whose name was *dandelion*

Carmen Grace Puentes
Our Lady of Mt Carmel School
Melrose Park
Grade 4

I Am

I am a caring girl who loves rabbits.
I wonder about them all the time.
I hear them running around in their cages.
I see them every day.
I wish they would never die.
I am a caring girl who loves rabbits.

I pretend they are always with me.
I feel them when I go out to feed them.
I touch their ears.
I worry that they could die when they get old.
I cry when my mom says she will let them go if I do not feed them.
I am a caring girl who loves rabbits.

I understand them.
I say they will always be in my heart.
I dream happy and sad dreams about them.
I try to remember to feed them in the morning.
I hope they will always love me.
I am a caring girl who loves rabbits.

Ashley Hitch
Damiansville Elementary School
Albers
Grade 6

A Little Bit of Heaven

As I sit on this hill looking over the lake,
I think this is what heaven must be like.
I think of all the things God's done,
Like making the moon, stars, and sun.
I see birds soar through the clouds,
That look like cotton balls thrown up into the sky on a summer day.
There may be some reason I think of heaven in this spot today.
It's because it is perfect in its own little way.

Elly Newell
Most Holy Redeemer School
Chicago
Grade 5

Best Friends

Best friends are the ones that you can trust.
You could never let them down.
Best friends are like your brothers and sisters.
Best friends are always there for you when you need them!
They never stop being your best friend.

Kelly Tresslar
St Matthew School
Champaign
Grade 4

Gaylen's Car

Gaylen bought a muscle car
He had to haul it very far.
Hugger orange is the color
A perfect car for my brother.
A built 350 lies under the hood
Boy that orange and black really looks good!

Jenna Wurmnest
Deer Creek-Mackinaw Middle School
Deer Creek
Grade 5

Rainy Day

Stuck inside, no fun at all.
I'm losing my mind, I hate the fall.

Thunder booms, lightning strikes.
Trapped in my room, this really bites.

Look out the window, the storm roars.
I think I will die if I don't go outdoors.

Picked up a book, it was really bad.
A little girl dies, it was really sad.

The lights went out, the candles are lit.
I search the basement for the storm-warning kit.

Funnel clouds pass, I hope they don't drop down.
There's too much excitement, and I feel a frown.

I begin to cry, a perfect day wasted.
The sirens sound, and I run for the basement.

I pray that I'm safe hiding down here.
I'm being taken over, I'm filled with fear.

Hours have passed, the sirens have silenced.
The damage is done, and the storm has triumphed.

I feel a smile start to emerge.
I feel so brave, that took so much courage.

Laura A. Blaskey
Channahon Middle School
Channahon
Grade 6

Revenge of Dirt E. Mirror

It was just him and me, me and him.
"There's no room in the bathroom for the two of us and...
the dirt you've got there." I said in my most westernly voice.
He answered back in a snotty voice—
I knew this wouldn't be pretty.
I stepped closer—
He seemed to look away.
I quickly sprayed him with soap
and then...
I wiped him with my rag.
I did it—
Again and again
UNTIL
He was all clean—
AHHHHHHHHHHH!!!!!
I quickly turned away and—
Dirt E. Mirror
was no more!!!

Katy Dunlap
Longwood Elementary School
Glenwood
Grade 4

May

The flowers are blooming, the trees are curled,
the forest is alive, it's a rainbow world.
The trees are growing and church bells are ringing,
frogs are croaking; every creature is singing.
Every color you can think of; in the forest you'll see,
every bee has its own flower, every bird its own tree.
It seems that the sound will never die,
the smell of barbecue embraces the sky!
Not a flower or insect in the forest can hide,
what is it about May that brings people outside?
There is everything outside; I see an egg a robin has laid,
in May everything is alive; all that God has made!!

Trevor Sutton
St Mary School
Alton
Grade 6

War

War, what a disaster!
People running shooting guns and some screaming.
Women are praying,
Children left alone.
When finally the war is over
Blood and people just lying there.
Children looking for their parents
Trying to find them until they
Find them lying on the
Ground surrounded by blood.

Virginia Reyes
Alexander G Bell Elementary School
Chicago
Grade 6

Bright
Sun is bright.
The moon has light.
How many stars are in the night.
When it's night I wish I had some light.
And when the sun comes out it is bright.

Jonath Lasenby
Diekman Elementary School
Dolton
Grade 5

Chocolate Frosting and Sprinkles
Chocolate is as dark as the sky
when it is a gloomy, dark, stormy night.

Sprinkles are as colorful as a rainbow
and as tasty as candy.

Frosting is as smooth as silk
and as gooey as gum.

Eden Munoz
St. Richard School
Chicago
Grade 5

Spring
Spring is sprung.
Life has just begun.
Spring is a time to have fun.
Spring is a time to go outside and run!

Lawrence Parks
Diekman Elementary School
Dolton
Grade 5

A Far Off Land
A far off land
with unicorns grazing,
swans swimming on crystal waters,
and stags galloping across the land.

A far off land,
with a castle sitting proudly,
gardens bright with dew,
and a beautiful princess too.

A far off land,
with rolling hills,
valleys deep and mountains high.

A far off land,
oh what your imagination can see.

Margaret E. Molitor
Butterfield Elementary School
Libertyville
Grade 5

Ocean
Feel the wind and sun
Hear and see the ocean waves
A nice green and blue

Marissa Rae Saint Germain
North Park Elementary School
Chicago
Grade 4

Snow
Snow
White, soft
Falling, melting, settling
It's beautiful when it sparkles
Winter

Michael Rocha
Barbour Elementary School
Rockford
Grade 4

Baseball
Baseball is fun
Baseball is easy
Baseball is the best
Baseball is something to play with friends
Baseball is fun to watch
Baseball is for anyone

David Fried
Parker Jr High School
Flossmoor
Grade 6

R.I.P.
Things die. Some are small
and some are tall.
They can be bad
but I know they are sad.

I get sad when things die
and when it happens I say why.
When they do I get mad
because it almost happened to my dad.

If that happened it would be sad
and that would be bad
because it was my dad
and I would get mad.

That's why dying is sad
and it makes you mad
and it would be very, very bad
if it was your dad.

Jamie Leonard
Nauvoo Elementary School
Nauvoo
Grade 6

The Ocean
The lovely, smooth ripples
All just gently flowing,
A cool breeze blowing,
The sun beating down,
You can hardly hear a sound.
Way down deep
The fish hardly make a peep,
Sand clings to my toes,
The dolphins put on shows.
The oh so pretty shells.
And when the day is done
An explosion of warmth fills the sky.

Kelsey Puttrich
Meridian Middle School
Buffalo Grove
Grade 5

Art
Art
is fine
projects too
painting papers
Blue

Rajda Samsuri
Westmore Elementary School
Lombard
Grade 4

Nature
The trees in the forest,
The leaves on the ground
The fish in the streams
It all seems like a dream
The doe and the fawn
The trout on the spawn
The bird singing
The frogs croaking
It's like a song to me
The gentle wind in my face
It's all the beauty of nature's grace.

Amos Elam
Moweaqua Elementary School
Moweaqua
Grade 5

Varnack
A cold, hard,
December snowstorm.
A dark blue,
Storm rumbling
Terribly loud.

Todd Salerno
St John Of The Cross School
Western Springs
Grade 5

God's Creations

God's creations are beautiful things
You see them everyday
Like beautiful nature and animals
And even the sun's bright ray
When you go outside and smell a flower
Thank God because he made it with his power
God made the beautiful stars at night
So to thank God do something nice
Don't get in a fight
But the most beautiful thing God made
Is every single human being
Some people already realize
How grateful they should be
But some people are just now seeing.

Shannon Murphy
Most Holy Redeemer School
Evergreen Park
Grade 5

My Backyard

The yard is full with lots of trees.
The air is full of bumble bees.
They pollinate the plants.
The ground is full of ants.
They move the dirt from here to there.
They can move it anywhere.
The bushes give a home to birds.
When the bushes bloom they are too beautiful for words!
The rabbits hop with lots of ease.
The mice scurry for some cheese.
The squirrel sat on the fence post.
The butterfly flew on our bright red roast!
That's what happened that day.
It was a beautiful sight, that's what I have to say.

Allie Liss
Ontarioville Elementary School
Hanover Park
Grade 4

Saying Good-Bye

Saying good-bye is very hard to do
especially when it's your best friend leaving you
I tried to say please stay
but she just had to move away.
The fun we had
was hardly ever bad.
We used to always walk.
But now we hardly talk.
We used to always come over
but now it's all over.
We used to have so much fun
but now it's all done.

Danielle Willette
Nauvoo Elementary School
Nauvoo
Grade 6

Love Heals

It is said that the human being, be it man, woman, black or
white, has equal rights.
Rights to prosperity and well being, and the right to have and to
hold, until death do you part.
But still so many victims of grief wander the streets of life alone,
and cry, not because of poverty or hunger, but lack of love
and welfare.
And we ask, when will mankind be generous and kind to the
earth's victims of sadness, and when will it end?
For we are put on this world by God Almighty only once, and
why not make a difference?
We know our rights, but what about those of other people?
What will happen to those people who cry silent tears in the
castaway places of mankind?
For no one person, be it man, woman, white or black, deserves
to have tears fall from their eyes.
And all people of this earth should be free, and the rights equal.
Love heals.

Eric Lander
Durand Elementary School
Durand
Grade 6

Cameron

Cameron is a handsome little boy,
he sometimes could be very coy.
He likes to eat anything,
he really, really likes to sing.

My daddy is a big, big man,
I have to admit I'm his biggest fan.
I love it when he gives me lots of kisses,
especially when he wants me to do the dishes.

My mommy's the best in the world,
she shines like a big fat pearl.
She helps me with my homework every day,
I wish I could be that way.

Fransisca Elizondo
St. Richard School
Chicago
Grade 5

Castles

Castles were big structures made out of stones,
Inside them sat kings high on their thrones.

The queens wore dresses that touched the floor;
The knights did battle with shields and swords.

Castles had moats and heavy gates to guard their door,
So that they could live on forever more.

Kristina Kubal
Manteno Middle School
Manteno
Grade 6

Tall Trees

Trees are very tall
The big ones are the best ones
I like the tall ones
Liberdy Daniell
Booth Central Elementary School
Wilmington
Grade 4

The Lake

When you want to take a walk,
Or go swimming in the sun,
Go to the dock,
And have some fun!
While you're there,
Make sure you are wet,
Or sun block you will need to get!
Erica Stanley
New Hebron Christian School
Robinson
Grade 4

Christopher Had a Hamster

Christopher had a little hamster
little hamster, little hamster
Christopher had a little hamster
his fur was brown as bark

He followed him down the stairs one day
stairs one day, stairs one day,
he followed him down the stairs one day
and bounced into the dryer
Christopher Pierce
Phillip May Elementary School
Rochelle
Grade 4

Baby Poem

Crying
   Crying
   Crying
All day long   Night and day

Eating,
Spitting,
Rolling,
Screaming,   Boasting,
                     Banging,
on
  people.

Babies cry all day long.
Yolanda Mercado
St Procopius School
Chicago
Grade 4

Friends

Friends are **F** un,
Friends are **R** espectful,
Friends are **I** ntelligent,
Friends are **E** njoyable,
Friends are **N** ice,
Friends are **D** elightful,
Friends are **S** miley.
Friends are all of those things and more,
They do everything to make you happy.
Jacquie Hoeflich
Prince of Peace School
Lake Villa
Grade 6

Kitten

The little kitten,
Sitting in a barn,
Plays with a ball of yarn.
Thinking of the world,
And it's creations,
With her wondrous,
Imagination.
Now the kitten,
Thinks of things,
While playing with,
A ball of string.
Kaci Weirich
St Mary School
Mount Carmel
Grade 6

Immigrants

Immigrants
sailing on a ship
hoping that the people can be free
wishing to meet the new land
come to the free land
Immigrants
Liam Champlain
Central Elementary School
Pontiac
Grade 4

Seasons

winter
cold, frost
snow, snowflakes, snowmen
grey clouds, ice, pools, sand
vacations, flowers, sun
hot, beach
summer
Erik Esquivel
Emerson Elementary School
Berwyn
Grade 6

My Family

My family is very nice
They help me every day
I love my family very much
And I hope they love me

My family is very big
I have one mother and father
I only have two sisters
And I don't know how many cousins

My family likes to work
My mom is an assistant dean
My dad is a medicine provider
My family has a lot of jobs

My family likes vacations
Even though we like to work
Everyone needs a vacation
And so do we
Charia McKee
Evangelical Christian School
Chicago
Grade 4

Skating

Skating
hard, challenging
wheels are rolling
souls are grinding away
fun
Justin Schott
Jonesboro Elementary School
Jonesboro
Grade 6

The Mountain

I am the mountain.
I stand high and
proud against the
howling breeze.
I am as still as
a rock but yet I
have feelings.
I can feel the
ocean beating
at my feet yet
I do not hide
from the children
playing on me.
I laugh silently
yet I am the mountain.
Andrea Moreno
St Matthew School
Champaign
Grade 4

Silkworm

Listen to the conversation of the silkworm
As she munches on the dark mulberry leaves,
What a sweet, cold breakfast from nature's icebox
In patches of drifted snow in the great trees.

Listen to the conversation of the silkworm
As she wriggles under a barb-wire fence to the graveyard.
There she burrows in a rotten plum in the Wisconsin forest.

Listen to the conversation of the silkworm
As she dreams of a gray-haired magician
Who has a rabbit and an overactive imagination.
His face has perfect wrinkles like Grandpa's.

Listen to the conversation of the silkworm
As she dreams of exploring caves.
Her imagination takes her off to paradise . . .
Sweet plums, mulberry leaves, and great trees.

Katie Corradetti
Nelson Ridge School
New Lenox
Grade 6

Fear

My heart is pounding in my chest, trying to escape.
Thump, thump, thump.

Sweat pouring down my face, blinding my eyes.
Drip, drip, drip.

My legs aching with pain of running so long.
Running from fear.

Tripping over rocks and stumps.
Falling into the wet mud.

Scrambling to get back up.
Up from facing my fear.

Running for miles until I fall.
Struggling to get up.

Using my last ounce of energy.
Pulling with all my might.

Only to fall back down, unable to move.
My body sinking into the wet mud.

My body unable to move.
My fear has finally pulled me under.

The fear of dying.

Jocelyn Mellen
St Mary-Dixon School
Dixon
Grade 6

Memories

You were here,
but now you're gone.
All I have left are memories.
I remember when you rocked me to sleep,
and the way you were always there for me.
When I had a nightmare,
you were beside my bed telling me
everything would be alright.
But then the fire came
and destroyed my life.
The lifeless bodies of you and dad
destroyed my heart.
You were here,
but now you're gone,
and all I have left are memories.

Katelyn Green
Channahon Middle School
Channahon
Grade 6

Snow

I love how the snow looks on the trees,
The way the snow blows in the breeze.
I love the way the snow falls,
The way the snow sticks on walls.
I love the way the snow tastes in your mouth,
I love the way that birds migrate south.
I love the way the snow nips at your nose,
I love the way Jack Frost nips at your toes.

Brad Dulin
Grant Park Middle School
Grant Park
Grade 6

Goodbye

Oh me, oh my,
Has the century flown by.

The Wright brothers flew the first plane,
Ford's car roared down Cherry Lane.

Hippies thought that war was wrong,
Beetles sang a very good song.

Ann M. Martin can write a good book,
The atom bomb made the world look.

So I'll say goodbye to the old,
And welcome in the new.

21st century, lets give it a cheer,
Celebrate the new and have a happy New Year.

Ruth Kakumanu
Schiesher Elementary School
Lisle
Grade 5

Summer

I like lemonade
In the summer with cookies.
My friends come over.

Jenna Bennison
Varna Grade School
Varna
Grade 5

6th Grade

Our survival skills paid off
We're out of here in June
Farewell to classmates
Graduation came too soon
Our classroom was the coolest
We really are unique
We wear all the latest fashions
Our hair changes by the week
We dream of being sport stars
Basketball or football
Defense, offense, full-back
We can play them all
Recess is my favorite
Wrestle, topple, and "The Wall"
The Lunch Moms are impatient
When we play suicide ball
Just like a birthday candle
This year went by so fast
Sixth grade was the bomb
I really had a blast

Pedro Vasquez
Emerson Elementary School
Berwyn
Grade 6

Spring

Spring is a time
of happiness.
Spring is a time of joy.
Spring is a time
when you see birds flying,
Crows crowing,
and children playing.
Spring is a time
you can go to the park
and play with sticks
and make art.
Spring is a time
when you can play
with your friends
and have a good time.
And that's what
spring means to me.

Charcie Little
Hyde Park Elementary School
Waukegan
Grade 4

The Blooming of Spring

The icy, frosty snow is melting away.
Winter is almost through.
The sparkling, freezing snowmen melt dry; the snowball fights cease.
Ice fishing is over; fishing begins.
Green grass grows as flowers bloom.
Winter is through, and *spring* is here.

Danny Rockoff
Meridian Middle School
Buffalo Grove
Grade 6

I Am

I am a goofy guy who likes basketball.
I always wonder if the shot I take is going to make it.
I hear the dribbling of the ball, the sound of the swish,
   and the crowd go wild, the buzzer go off, and the winning congratulations.
I see the ball go high in the wondering sky.
I want to be in a game of a lifetime that never ends.
I am a goofy guy who likes basketball.

I pretend that I'm the greatest basketball player in the world.
I feel the excitement in the other players.
I touch the rim's smooth, shiny, bright metal.
I worry about the points at halftime.
I cry when a game is lost, but there's always tomorrow.
I am a goofy guy who likes basketball.

I understand the frustration of missing a shot, thinking you let the team down.
I say that anything is possible.
I dream of doing the impossible, stretching to the limits, going all the way.
I try to keep the team together.
I hope to go to the NBA.
I am a goofy guy who likes basketball.

Roger Nuxoll
St Anthony of Padua Grade School
Effingham
Grade 5

Great Grandmother

There once was a little girl,
That had hair full of curls.
One year her great grandmother died.
And at the funeral, the little girl cried.
She couldn't believe it,
And didn't want to receive it.
Then, about a week later,
The little girl realized that she really missed her great grandmother.
She remembered the good times they had together.
And then she remembered that her great grandmother wouldn't live
Forever,
But as she moved on with her life,
She still remembered her great grandmother.

Abby Williams
North Elementary School
Marshall
Grade 6

Social Studies Is History!

Social studies is history!
It's all just a big mystery!
Social studies isn't for me!
Can't you see?

Pyramids in Egypt!
What a reject!
MESOPOTAMIA!
Too much for your crania!

Here's where we all moan!
BONES AND STONES!
Cro-Magnon, Homosapiens Sapiens, which was first
Oh! Social Studies, what a CURSE!!!

Emily Reid
St Mary School
New Berlin
Grade 6

Space

Russia started the great space race.
USA won the great space race.
USA won when we landed on the moon.
We built 4 space ships.
Apollo got us to the moon.
That ends my story about the great space race.

Brendan Carey
St John Fisher School
Chicago
Grade 4

I Am

I am a boy who loves cars.
I wonder what the new styles are going to be.
I hear the roaring of the engines.
I see the beautiful exterior.
I want a good looking car
I am a boy who loves cars.

I pretend to drive one.
I feel the hard metal shells.
I worry if they'll stop making them.
I cry when they crash.
I am a boy who loves cars.

I understand all the car terms.
I say that they all look cool.
I dream that I'll own a Corvette.
I try to get one for my mom and dad.
I hope I'll own one when I get older.
I am a boy who loves cars.

Eddie Brickeen
Damiansville Elementary School
Albers
Grade 6

Life Is a Maze...

Life is a maze because
sometimes you take the right paths and sometimes
the wrong ones.
Sometimes it has obstacles
that get in your way and are difficult to overcome;
but don't give up, go on.
Sometimes it has rules,
Sometimes it has too many frustrating walls but eventually
it will end and you will be wild and free again.
It's long and hard, sometimes even boring
but a maze is a maze mystifying your mind, telling you to stop,
but go on.
I think life is a maze,
but that's my opinion,
What's yours?

Anuraag Tripathi
Barbara B. Rose Elementary School
South Barrington
Grade 5

Snorkeling

Right beneath the sea
Is a life that's just for me.
With my snorkel and mask I am one with the sea
Swimming with the fish is the life for me.
They come in all colors, orange, yellow, and blue,
Looking more closely you can see a starfish too.
Gliding alone I come upon the colorful coral reef,
It's 100 years old, that's the natives' belief.
You can see a giant sea urchin and great black rays,
And maybe a shark that hasn't eaten for days!
Coming closer to shore there are shells in the sand,
I gather them up holding all that I can.
Swimming along feeling free as can be,
And that is why the sea is the life for me!

Chris Duff
Butterfield Elementary School
Libertyville
Grade 5

Life

My name is Josh.
I hate to do the wash.
I have three brothers, they are a pain,
all they like to do is watch the choo-choo train.
I have a dog named Daisy,
but she is not lazy.
My parents are very nice,
They always remind me not to play with knives.
My favorite sport is baseball,
but I do hate to chase that ball.

Josh Pitt
Beckemeyer Elementary School
Beckemeyer
Grade 5

Butterfly

Butterfly butterfly, fly in the air.
Butterfly fly over there.

Butterfly butterfly you are so pretty.
Butterfly butterfly why are you steady?
Butterfly make us ready.

Butterfly butterfly, what am I seeing?
Butterfly butterfly, I feel like squealing.

Butterfly you look like a moon.
Butterfly butterfly, is that your cocoon?

Justine Nuguid
Costa Catholic School
Galesburg
Grade 4

Angel

Angel sitting on a cloud
Soft like a cotton blanket,
Sweet like a vanilla cherry cake,
Pretty like a white butterfly
Lighting on a flower
Playing with her friends.

Maryann Gewarges
Pilgrim Lutheran School
Chicago
Grade 4

Suddenly You Turn Around and See:

Suddenly you turn around and see a...
sleek face,
poker ace,
jolly, holly,
gardens great,
master trait,
bubble blowing,
good at throwing,
rocks, socks,
bad at mowing,
likes sewing,
computer freak,
likes meat,
baseball playing,
dancing, swaying,
singing, swinging,
beautiful,
suitable,
lovable,
huggable,
Mom!

Danielle Gibbins
Sandburg Middle School
Elmburst
Grade 6

Peace

Peace blows
like the wind.
Peace could be everywhere;
on the moon,
on Jupiter,
on Earth,
or right in your hand.
When you are in fear, just think
of your inner deep feelings,
and from inside
you will get
Peace.

Zohaib Ali
East Prairie Elementary School
Skokie
Grade 6

Oh Egypt

Land of shrouded mystery,
And the cobalt blue Nile,
Wavy green palm trees,
And the sand that goes for miles.

Egypt, you keep a secret,
Of the mummies in their tombs,
Hieroglyphics in your pyramids,
And the smell of incense fumes.

Ever since I've been there,
I never will forget,
The people, food and culture,
For this I have no regret.

Andrew Naber
Argenta-Oreana Elementary School
Oreana
Grade 6

Trust

Take my hand.
Follow me.
Close your eyes,
For you are not to see.
Can you trust me?
Take my heart.
Believe in me.
Don't think just act.
Can you trust me?
Here we are
You are now free
See see,
You can always trust me.

Julie Alexander
Geraldine Kerkstra Middle School
Oak Forest
Grade 6

Family

Uncle Henrik
Helpful, brave
Helping, caring, fishing
Harbor, boat, kitchen, house
Cooking, cleaning, hurting
Caring, gentle
Mama

Andrew Frame
Manteno Middle School
Manteno
Grade 6

Football

Football is fun
the tackling has begun
right guard is fun
my team has always won

Travis Tissiere
Central Elementary School
Pontiac
Grade 4

Who Is She?

Who is she?
The one that gave me a life.

Who is she?
The one that gave me a name.

Who is she?
The person I can talk to.

Well, I know, she's my mom
From her head to her toes.

Arianna Gaytan
Nixon Elementary School
Chicago
Grade 5

Black Lab

A big black lab.
It can run fast.
But after a while
It becomes hungry
So I must tell it not to eat
Anything except for what ever
Is in her bowl.
But it won't help.
She is not obedient.
So I sent her to school
And she never came back.

Matt Nowaczewski
Indian Knoll Elementary School
West Chicago
Grade 6

How I Feel About People Drinking and Driving

here I am so cold
in the dark
shivers run down my back
I feel scared
seeing flashes of these
red and blue
I feel a fear
of death
seeing no longer
why do people drink and drive

Natalie Szulyk
Forest View Elementary School
Mount Prospect
Grade 5

The Smell of Roses

One day I went outside to play,
I saw something that had caught my eye.
It was a beautiful spring day in May,
I looked right at it and then I sighed.

It was so beautiful, so little, and so bright,
The colors were streaming through the air.
You could see it if it were night,
It was much prettier than blond, shiny hair.

The thing I just told you about,
It is called a rose.
They come in so many colors I have to shout,
When I smell them they itch my nose.

All the roses come in pink, yellow, and red,
The significant rose is everywhere.
They make a magnificent flower bed,
One can smell the roses in the air.

Shannon Lynn Whitley
Northlawn Middle School
Streator
Grade 6

Spring

Spring makes you feel so clean,
Makes you want to go sing
And say "Blink, blink!"
Flowers blooming, grass is green,
Rainy weather is spring, spring, spring!
Spring is when it's not too hot nor too cold.
Spring and me are like two things
That never go green.
That's what I like about spring
Blink, blink!

Charlene Key
Washington Irving Elementary School
Chicago
Grade 5

Astronaut

Astronaut astronaut fly in the sky.
Oh how long have you been in that sky
You see the stars above you
The Earth below you
Is it boring being in that sky?
If it is why don't you try to get back to Earth?

Bryan Lowery
St John Fisher School
Chicago
Grade 4

Playing

Soccer, soccer, seasons blue.
Running, kicking, scoring too.

Legos, Legos, so fun to build.
Boy you give me such a thrill!

Blue, blue, blue, if I only knew.
I would take you home and color with you.

Blading, blading, what a thrill.
Doesn't it give you a chill?

So if you need to find me soon,
I will be playing in my room.

David Mauhar
Central Elementary School
Lincoln
Grade 6

Baseball

Baseball is a wonderful sport,
You don't play it on a rink or a court,
On a diamond is where it is played,
All the players get heavily paid.

If I played pro baseball, I would play for free,
Even if I would have made a very high fee,
Baseball is such a beautiful game,
It can make you disliked or bring you fame.

All the players are diving for balls,
The outfielders taking very hard falls,
All the backhands by the shortstop,
Then turning and throwing, while on the hop.

Basketball and football just won't do,
There are many others, not just those two,
Hitting a homer is the best of all,
That is why I love baseball.

Brandon VanDuzer
Northlawn Middle School
Streator
Grade 6

Friend

Friend
Cool, helpful
Caring, forgiving, sharing
Sticks up for you
Lasting, never-ending, loving
Nice, fun
Buddy

Kris Norman
Chaney-Monge Elementary School
Crest Hill
Grade 6

Fall

Fall leaves fall to the ground
As the cold weather blows
them down
As the leaves say good-bye
my friends.
As the trees' leaves are off
the branches.
As the winter
comes.

Kimberly Marzullo
Leland Elementary School
Leland
Grade 6

The World

I look at the world twirl
like a giant pearl
I see the glimmering lights
shining through the night.
The world is so big from the inside
But from the outside it looks like
a little ball guiding me around the sun.
The world is beautiful
and it is wonderful.

Brandon Zhang
Forest View Elementary School
Mount Prospect
Grade 4

Red

Red is the color of my shirt,
Red is the color of my skirt,
Red is the color of a box,
Red is the color of a fox,
Red is the color of chicken pox,
Red is the color of some clocks.
Red is not the color of air.
Red is everywhere.

Karabeth Moses
Summit Elementary School
Collinsville
Grade 4

Mice

We once had a house full of mice.
Oh, but they were so nice!
Yes, they ate all our cheese.
But they remembered to say please.
Oh, they feared our cat!
But we took care of that!
Now he lives upstairs,
With old clothes and underwears!

Lindsey Tuntland
Ontarioville Elementary School
Hanover Park
Grade 5

Snow

Snow falls down
Without a peep.
Lighter than air,
Fluffier than sheep.

Whiter than White,
Colder than cold,
I'll want to see snow
When I get old.

Snow makes me feel
All warm and happy.
I ask to play,
And my sister gets snappy.

So remember
That when it snows,
Get bundled up
In your winter clothes!

James Foster
Nelson Ridge School
New Lenox
Grade 6

Fall

I see a raven brilliantly flying
The once beautiful flowers are now dying
For my birthday, it's presents galore
For Thanksgiving, I get some more
The leaves are rusty
The wind is gusty
Animals play
People are at home, always happy to stay
Acorns silently fall to your head
Cold days make me thankful for my bed
Fall, fall, fall
Oh, how I love fall

Mike Martin
Porta Central School
Petersburg
Grade 5

My Dad

I had a dad,
Who died too young
He had a heart attack
He died April 17, 1998
I was the saddest of all,
Except my mom of course.
The night when my mom found out,
She sent me to a friend's house.
The next morning she told me
I cried for hours on end
April 22, 1998 was his funeral
I cried longer than life has been
We went in a limousine to my church
We got gift's that were great
I thought my dad was too young to die
He was only 38
My friend Catrina
Told me he wouldn't forget me
That's my tragic tale about my dad.

Emily Pearson
Deer Creek-Mackinaw Middle School
Deer Creek
Grade 5

Sounds at Dawn

Beginning of a celebration
Sounds bouncing off each other
Bells listening to one another
Harp sounds floating in the air
Flute notes dancing across the sky
Sound has started its day.

Karen Gluskin
Meridian Middle School
Buffalo Grove
Grade 5

Flame Dancers

The dancers are twirling and twisting
With a bright orange steady glow
As agile as a ballerina
As quick as a fox
I close my eyes starting to see
The hearth turn to a marble dance floor
The flames turn to graceful dancers
Their dancing a waltz, the minuet in G
I open my eyes, what I see
Is only one flare and a couple of embers
Soon they go out
But tomorrow I'll be glad
To see their lair glaring
Tomorrow at 7:30 p.m.

Rob Binder
Westmore Elementary School
Lombard
Grade 4

The Game

Wristshots flying through the air
Slapshots going everywhere
Goals are scored left and right
Overtime is a fright
First one to score wins the game
Oh yeah, we won, the crowds going insane!

Nicholas Brown
McHenry Jr High School
McHenry
Grade 6

Jumble

My mind is in a jumble
and it's the test day!
Oh Golly! Gee! All I can do is grumble!
Can I stop this madness? Is there any way?
My mind is in a jumble!
Oh, golly, what a day!

Sean Brennan
St John Fisher School
Chicago
Grade 4

Music

When I play in band I see,
How much music means to me,
My flute I play,
Most everyday,
The music can be soft or loud,
Our concerts always draw a crowd,
I love the music that I make,
And every opportunity to play I always take.

Katy Ortigara
St George School
Tinley Park
Grade 6

It's Spring

The birds sing,
the flowers bloom
but not in the month of June
the trees and bushes are filled with buds
not suds
so this means...
if the birds sing,
and the flowers bloom
and this is not the month of June
and the trees and bushes are filled with buds
not suds
this must mean...
it's SPRING!

Callie Zindel
Moweaqua Elementary School
Moweaqua
Grade 5

Out in Space

Flying through the air,
Wind blowing in my hair,
I see a shooting star.
My problems seem so far.
The sun is blazing on my face,
While the moon is somewhere out in space.
I see the planets come and go.
I feel so happy,
Do you know?
Flying through the air,
Wind blowing in my hair,
I see a shooting star.

My problems seem so far.

Samantha Toeller
Meridian Middle School
Buffalo Grove
Grade 5

Where Does Poetry Hide?

Where does poetry hide?
Does it hide above the steeps of the Rocky Mountains,
Does it hide through the thick morning grass in the prairie,
Or does it hide underneath my pen cap as I write this poem?

Poetry is everywhere
When you step your foot on the dew grass
Or clap your hands to applaud
Or smell the scent of a rose
Or taste food like green tortillas

We shall never know
Where poetry will take you
If
You
Just imagine
It's there!

Michelle Redmond
Walker Elementary School
Evanston
Grade 5

Who Am I

Who am I?
I am someone.
I am a person who believes,
I am a person who believes that I can achieve.
I believe that I can achieve my goals,
I'm succeeding.
Who am I?
I am someone!

Jillian Henry
Diekman Elementary School
Dolton
Grade 5

Summer/Winter

Summer
hot, warm
swimming, playing, partying,
joyous, sandals, fun, icy,
snowing, freezing, piercing
foggy, sick
Winter

Lauren Kelly
Diekman Elementary School
Dolton
Grade 5

Friends Forever

We have been friends
for what seems like forever,
but now our friendship fades,
the promise that was spoken
now lies broken
forgotten in some way
every day I sit and think,
whatever happened to the friendship
we said would never sink?

Amber Bergmann
Indian Knoll Elementary School
West Chicago
Grade 6

Team

MY class is a team,
not just any team.
A class team
a chain that will lead me
to my dream.
If we work together
we all are in a dream
a thing to capture in a journal
and keep in a safe
to look at each day.

Boye Adefeso
Walker Elementary School
Evanston
Grade 5

Rainbow

One day in early April
I saw a pretty thing in the sky.
It had red, orange, yellow,
Green, blue and purple.
It was a rainbow.
On that day it was raining.
"Oh how I wish it would rain again
To see the rainbow in the sky."

Liliana Torres
Nixon Elementary School
Chicago
Grade 5

Life

Life is a journey of happy times and sad,
Times when you're angry, all uptight, and mad.

Although there are times when things will go wrong,
Just fight all your fears and try to stay strong.

People will live, people will die, but their souls are never gone,
Just know they're in a better place and memories will still hold on.

Enjoy life, like every day just might be your last,
Because someday you'll grow old and you'll look back at your past.

Try not to judge people by their looks or popularity,
But what's inside is what really counts, both kindness and personality.

Sometimes you'll be scared and afraid and things might be somewhat strife,
Just try to overcome these hard times and make the best out of life.

Mark Simek
Riverwood Elementary School
McHenry
Grade 5

A Day With Sunshine

There was a young butterfly whose name was Sunshine.
She shed her cocoon in a day's ago time.

Sunshine was very tired of being cooped up for awhile
She was so happy to be free that she started to smile.

"I can feel it," Sunshine said, "The world for me is an adventure,"
So she decided to fly around, and from her cocoon she did venture.

First she flew to a meadow and there she let loose.
She wanted to taste a flower; "Oh me, oh my, which one should I choose?"

She decided to taste the yummiest-looking flower, which was a tulip,
She uncurled her long tongue and took a sip.

"This is delicious! I'm going to try some more!"
And then she tasted flowers for many an hour.

After tasting flowers Sunshine found a friend—Pixie was her name,
They played together the whole day through, playing a fun butterfly game.

In just that one day they became the best of buds,
But it was soon bedtime, and they parted, giving each other butterfly kisses and hugs.

She yawned a big yawn as she flew back to her bed,
Thinking all the while, "What an exciting day I had!"

She curled up in her bed of moss and drifted off after awhile.
Her last thoughts were of all the fun she would have tomorrow.

Jacqueline Brosius
Kennedy Jr High School
Lisle
Grade 6

My Sister Mandy

This is my sister Mandy.
She is rather dandy.
Although she thought it was funny.
When I sat on my chocolate bunny.
It was really mean.
When she ate my lucky jelly bean.
She drives a lot.
When it is hot.
But she doesn't turn on the air.
Because she'll mess up her hair.
She plays volleyball like a pro.
But she doesn't like to wear ruffles or a bow.
She likes cats.
But doesn't like to wear hats.
Because she'll mess up her hair.
Well, we've already been there.
Sometimes she is nice.
She is afraid of mice.
She would like to have a dove.
This is the poem about the sister whom I love.

Kaila Kuester
St John's Lutheran School
Buckley
Grade 5

Hockey

H ockey is a physical sport.
O ffense's job is to score goals.
C hecking is against the rules.
K ey to winning is to skate hard.
E veryone goes crazy when the home team scores.
Y ou have to watch the game carefully.

Dave Brankin
St John Fisher School
Chicago
Grade 4

Shel Silverstein*

Shel Silverstein could make anybody laugh
even if his story was about
a tree,
a sister,
or a clumsy calf.
He's been writing since 1964, straight
and since then his books have been great!
Kids didn't care if his poems were short in length.
It doesn't matter to us either if we're in Kindergarten or in 8th.
Everybody thought you were a pretty cool dude.
You were so keen no one will ever forget you
Shel Silverstein!

Taylor Stinson
John F Kennedy Elementary School
Schiller Park
Grade 5
*In memory of Shel Silverstein, a great poet!

Palm Trees

Palm trees, palm trees, palm trees
And more palm trees.
Palm trees in the morning.
Palm trees in the evening.
Palm trees in my breakfast.
Palm trees in my lunch.
You know, it's not a very good brunch.
People laugh and scream at you.
It's not too bad when you get used to it.
Actually, the coconuts aren't too bad, either.

Erin Walsh
St John Fisher School
Chicago
Grade 4

What Matters to Me

The world has rainforests, oceans, and trees,
Pollution and people are ruining these.
Trees in the rainforest disappear,
While water in the ocean is no longer clear.
The thought of the air, in the wind, in the breeze,
Polluted with smoke, dust, and debris.
When I think of these things, and I know you'll agree,
We need to help our surroundings for you and me.

Ashley Marks
East Richland Elementary School
Olney
Grade 5

My Mom

Caring,
Loving,
Hard worker.

Wishes to do her best.
Dreams to be a perfect person.
Who wonders what is beyond Earth.
Who fears snakes.
Who is afraid of droughts.
Who likes people, short and tall.
Who believes in herself.

Who loves me and her husband.
Who loves to play outside.
Who loves her job.
Who loves all kinds of foods.
Who plans to be a good person all her life.
Who plans to love her parents forever.
Who plans to live a good life.

Whose final destination is home.

Brook Wibben
Central Elementary School
Lincoln
Grade 6

Katie

Katie
Katie is a chatterbox.
Katie is like an alien from Mars.
She talks, laughs and yells.
She is my sister.
Katie

Jenny Beard
North Elementary School
Marshall
Grade 6

My Cat Ying

I have a cat
that's named Ying
He hisses and groans
and looks mean.

He can be scared
just like me
That's what I know
and what I've seen.

He's black and white
and scared at night
He's a cute cat
that you can pet.

That's all right now
but I'll be back
To tell you more
about my cat.

Bridgette Smith
Nixon Elementary School
Chicago
Grade 6

Flowers

Flowers are yellow, red,
pink and green

They open their leaves
and have funny cheeks

When the morning comes
they come out to see
the yellow sun with you and me

When the sun goes down
some of the flowers
turn their cheeks upside down
and turn all around.

Mayra Maldonado
Nixon Elementary School
Chicago
Grade 5

Can You Imagine

Dogs without tails
Sand without pails

A board without chalk
Feet that don't walk

Birds that don't sing
A diamond without a ring

Clouds without rain
Fields without grain

Hearts that aren't red
Kids without beds

Mary Toler
Jonesboro Elementary School
Jonesboro
Grade 6

My Best Friend

Friends are nice,
And friends are kind,
But my friend:

B est ever
R espectful
O ut of this world!
O utstanding
K ind
E nergetic

P olite
O utgoing
T errific
E xcellent
N eat
D epend on
Y aps on the phone
K eeps our friendship

Is different

Melissa Gamber
Bolin Elementary School
East Peoria
Grade 5

Rain

Rain, rain, everywhere,
Rain, rain, in the air,
Falling like a giant's tear.
Now it's falling everywhere.

Maggie Musso
Summit Elementary School
Collinsville
Grade 4

Flowers

The clouds pass by the sky.
Knowing that every season
They will be there,
Watching the seasons go by,
And hoping to see the flowers
Blooming in the spring.
Staying flowers through out
The summer, quenching the
Rain that falls from those
Clouds, wilting in the fall
Waiting for their blanket.
The snow, when the snow comes
After all the seasons,
The flowers know it's time for
A good nights sleep.

Nicole Palmer
Sunnydale Elementary School
Streamwood
Grade 5

The Hot Days

I love summer sun,
I love swimming, splashing,
Flowers blooming,
Showers bursting.
Splashing in puddles,
Causes rainbows to muddle.
In the summer I have so much fun,
Fun in the sun.

Krystina Guess
New Hebron Christian School
Robinson
Grade 4

The Heart of the Girl He Loved

On a cool autumn day
A faint breeze blows
And takes me away
To a summer of sand covered toes

And the way that he laughed
On the beach where we sat
Could take any girls heart away
But he could not stay
He had to go away

How I would miss my dear friend
For I was in love
Packed away with his clothes is the
Heart that he stole
The heart of the girl he loved

Samantha McKeever
St Mary School
Alton
Grade 6

Friendship

Friendship shouldn't be based on the clothes you wear,
or your hair.

It should be based on the fun things you do together,
the fun times you share

When friends are friends you never try to break them up
'cause it hurts them so much.

You always want to tell the truth to your friend
'cause if you don't, your friendship might end

To me, best friends are people who share one soul
until they grow old.

Enjoy your friends and be nice,
and you and your friend will be friends for life.

Stephanie Crosier
Parker Jr High School
Flossmoor
Grade 6

Friends

I've had lots of fond experiences with friends
I'll tell you a story from beginning to end.
One summer Mandie and I
Went camping at the Green River
And my, did that time fly!

We played and we swam
We even found river clams!

We went fishing and inner tubing
Wow! Mandie's a good fisher!
And my, how time flew
That summer at the Green River!

Jaime Magnafici
St Mary-Dixon School
Dixon
Grade 6

My Father

My father means so much to me.
If he was not there I don't know where I would be.
He is a great father.
He listens to what I have to say.
He knows what is wrong or right with me.
When I am sick he takes care of me
And when I am crying he makes me happy.
I love my father so very much.
I remind him every day.

Rosa Camacho
Nixon Elementary School
Chicago
Grade 5

The Color Of

Blue is the color of the sky in the light.
Black is the color at night when it is not bright.
White is the color of my shoes that come in pairs of two's.
Green is the color of the grass this spring—
We will have a blast.
Brown is the color of my hair—the same as a bear.
Red is the color of my coat and the color of a boat.
We look at color every day.

Deonté Sabbs
Diekman Elementary School
Dolton
Grade 5

A Tree, a Father

A
Tree stands,
A father of the Earth,
As you are a father to me.
He guards and protects the Earth,
Just as you guard and protect me.
When the tree drops its colorful leaves,
It whispers a soft, sweet lullaby; it sings,
"Baby go to sleep. Go to sleep, slumber, my love."
The tree, the old maple tree has watched me grow up,
Just as you have watched and cared.
A tree remembers all, years, seasons, times.
The way you have remembered me as a small baby.
I remember, too. I remember the chilly autumns
When you would take me bundled outside
In front of that old maple tree, red-orange, brown.
It is like me,
Waiting to reach
The shining moon,
But still having
A long way to go.

Brittany Wanner
Wauconda Elementary School
Wauconda
Grade 5

Jingles

I own a lot of pygmy goats,
But one stands out the very most.
His name is Jingles, and you should see
What he likes to do when I go to feed.
In a feeder, I put the hay,
The next thing you know, he's up and away!
He won't come down, he'll stay there all day.
He'll eat the hay and he'll eat the hay.
There's not much else that I can say,
He's one of a kind and he's all mine!

Carissa Clawson
North Elementary School
Marshall
Grade 6

Pollution Poem

I went to the ocean
And what did I see
A lot of fish
And trash for me

I dug down deep
And found a dish
And a very old jeep
And some smelly old fish

I saw some more trash
And a dirty old can
And a lot of cash
In a very old pan

I saw a meanie
That was really mean
We need a genie
To clean up this scene

Adam Curran
Stone Creek Elementary School
Roscoe
Grade 4

School Year

School
children, kids
prepared, homework, papers
exciting, difficult, winter, spring
fun, dry, windy
tired, lazy
summer

Mike Toledo
Emerson Elementary School
Berwyn
Grade 6

The Time I Was in the Super Bowl

Time was running down
And I had to kick
For a field goal.
I kicked it,
And the defense
Knocked me down.
All I heard was
The crowd roar with joy,
And when I saw we won,
I woke up.
And that is when I was in
The Super Bowl.
It was only a dream.

Mike Dow
St Anthony of Padua Grade School
Effingham
Grade 5

Ocean and Land

Ocean
blue, sparkly
bubbling, splashing, salted
water, liquid, solid, ground
boring, rolling, hard
dirty, rough
Land

Connor Haxel
St Boniface School
Quincy
Grade 6

One in a Million

One falls,
a million follow,
no one dares to show,
happiness or sorrow.

No emotion is dared sought,
walk in a line,
is what all thought.

But I stood out,
and walked my own road,
and now emotion,
my own I could show.

Soon little by little,
and one by one,
few joined me for their life run.

And soon a hundred,
or maybe more,
were standing beside me,
hidden no more.

All it takes is one to follow a dream,
and forever onward,
people's lives will be seen.

Innessa Kipnis
Meridian Middle School
Buffalo Grove
Grade 6

Changes

Changes, changes, my what changes
Changes can be good
Changes can be bad
Changes can make you devastated
Changes can make you happy
Changes can be sad

Kevin Smith
Indian Knoll Elementary School
West Chicago
Grade 6

Snakes

I fear snakes
Their teeth are just
As sharp as rakes.
Their prey slides
As it winds inside
The snakes body.
So if you see a snake
Just run away
And start to pray.
That will keep
The snakes away.

Matt Kipping
St Mary-Dixon School
Dixon
Grade 6

Fleeting Moments

These days of ours
are fleeting fast.
These moments we take for granted
leave us so quickly.
It's in these times
we have to
help each other,
choose our actions wisely,
and above all
live in the moment.

Ben Gielow
East Prairie Elementary School
Skokie
Grade 6

Look at Me

Look at me.
What do you see?
Do you see me,
Or someone else?
Listen to me.
Do you hear me,
Or bells?
Do you know who I am?
I am not them,
But me, Alice.
I am my own person,
I am unique.
I have my own mind.
So when you look at me,
Don't be blind.
See what I see.
See me.
Look at me.

Alicia Feliciano
McCormick Elementary School
Chicago
Grade 5

Library

I go to the library
I check out lots of books
There are no sounds
Because if you talk you will hear shhh!
The colors of red, green, blue, yellow
The colors of imagination
I read books like Harry Potter and Judy Blume
I have a great time
Lost in the places of the books I read

Zack Bakewell
Grand Prairie Elementary School
Joliet
Grade 4

The Princess With the Broken Heart

Born into this world with the wail of a train
And the cry of a bird, and the gently tapping rain
The princess was destined for a life of ease
She could get all she wanted without a whine or tease
But the princess was not happy; no, she shook her curly head
And she sighed a gusty sigh and she frowned and sadly said
"Listen, the train is coming. Even it has places to be
Just like everyone else in the whole wide world
Except poor, little, sad, lonely me.
Listen, hear the bird calling? It's calling 'I am free!'
Just like everyone else in this whole wide world
Except poor, little, sad, lonely me.
Listen, hear the rain tapping? It's as happy as can be
Just like everyone else in this whole wide world
Except poor, little, sad, lonely me."
Don't wish to be a princess; it's not an easy part.
If you do you'll be just like the princess
With the broken heart.

Martha Schmid
Cissna Park Jr High School
Cissna Park
Grade 6

When Spring Comes

When spring appears,
I am always near.
When flowers start growing,
my eyes start glowing.
It's finally warm enough to swim in the pool.
The season spring is really cool.
The grass is green, the trees are tall,
and the leaves from autumn aren't brown at all.
Other seasons are okay,
but the first day of spring really makes my day.
I love to feel the warm breeze,
blowing on my bare knees.

Alicia Aronson
Parker Jr High School
Flossmoor
Grade 6

20 Word Poem

As I blow out the candle I quickly fall asleep.
I begin to dream something very unique.
I am alone in the classroom everyone went home.
The hair on my arm sticks straight up, I try to scream.
The windows and doors are locked, I cannot get out.
It becomes a matter of survival.
As I look out the window, I see a classmate.
He waves farewell and I run to the door.
I pull back on the knob and I topple over and wake up.

Mike Koehler
Emerson Elementary School
Berwyn
Grade 6

What Is Blue?

Blue is the sky I look up and see.
It is the world big and round.
It could be an ocean, lake, or sea.
It could be your jeans.
Your twist-tie in your hair.
Blue could be a book cover.
It could be a chair.
Blue could be a pen, an eraser
Blue could be a window.
Blue can be anything in the whole wide world.
Well that's all I have to say to you about blue.

Crystal Wojciak
St. Richard School
Chicago
Grade 5

What Is Red?

Red is a ladybug,
A wire,
A candle on fire,
The hot air,
The best color of the year.
When I think of red,
I think of Christmas and Valentine's Day.
Red is a lollipop, red is a heart
It's one of the streetlights and a color in art.
Red is a planet, red is a vein
The stripes on a candy-cane.
Red is a watermelon, also a cherry
Red is a fruit like the strawberry.
Red is the color of a fire truck,
If you wear red you'll have good luck.
And in the garden
The butterflies are flying
On top of the roses
Which the people are buying...

Angelika Piwowarczyk
St. Richard School
Chicago
Grade 5

A Fond Memory

A fond memory for me is
Making forts out of pillows and blankets
For all of my friends to see.

Chris Kreger
St Mary-Dixon School
Dixon
Grade 6

Shairice

You are the sunshine
That helped me grow.
From scared and insecure,
Confidence rose.

You saw in me
Courage and pride,
More that I knew
That I had inside.

A new star in heaven,
My guiding light,
You have touched so many
With your special, loving care.
Your impact is endless
With all it will stay.

You'll always be missed.
But never forgotten

Ashley Kunke
Chaney-Monge Elementary School
Crest Hill
Grade 6

The Day I Lost My Tooth

Today was the bestest day!
My tooth fell out!
I got to feel it and touch it
It was sooooo cool!
I felt so proud
To lose that big tooth!
But the best thing is the penny
That the tooth fairy gave to me.

My mommy said
That I could spend it on a piece of candy
So I did.
You'll never guess what happened.
I lost another tooth
And another
Until I had none.
Now I can barely speak
And that is a really bad thing.

Kathleen Brosnan
St John Of The Cross School
Western Springs
Grade 5

My Waterfall

The foamy bottom feels so fresh.
Moss grows all around it like a fuzzy green blanket.
It sounds so refreshing—like a new day ahead.
The rocks are mossy, damp things that sunk a long time ago.
The waterfall is so huge, it can reach the sky.
It rushes down the steep mountain like the water was flowing and gliding.
It changes its way.
It's calm to furious—nothing to.....something!
It's my

w
  a
    t
      e
        r
          f
            a
              l
              l

Jenna Brandon
Forest View Elementary School
Mount Prospect
Grade 4

Basketball

We're on the grassy battlefield. The blare of the trumpet has begun.
Playing this game grants me so much fun.

The first battle, we blow their gangly troops out.
We get praise from the crowds, the fair weather friends,
Who love us now, now that we've won,
But after we lose, we'll be off and gone.

The second battle is brutal, the troops are catching up.
You try to keep your plays in disguise, and take the advice,
"Keep your head up and your eyes on the prize."

The second battle is over, and we still are ahead,
But that was truly a horrible battle,
And on top of that, there was much bloodshed.

The third battle has begun, between my troops and theirs
You can hear the clashing of swords and the blasts of guns.

This battle we have lost, but luckily not many were hurt,
And still the very horrifying smell of a brutal bloodshed lingers in the dirt.

All of the sudden, in a split second, I hear a victorious blast from a trumpet.
"VICTORY! VICTORY!" I cry and shout.
I dance and sing and wail all about.
I do not know what to say,
Except, no man could have a happier day!

Theresa Lisch
Blessed Sacrament School
Belleville
Grade 6

Fly Swatter

Fly Swatter
killer, airborne
hitting, swinging, killing
comedy, assassinator, exterminator, splat!
exciting, fighting, flying through the air
· full of holes, plastic
Fly Swatter

J. Taylor Hudkins
Wells Elementary School
Grayville
Grade 5

Beauty of Springtime

I sit in the grass;
I feel the cool breeze;
I'm concerned of it's source;
But I still feel at ease.

The flowers are blooming;
How beautiful their shades;
Lilacs, and roses, and lilies;
It's so sad it all fades.

But still the beauty surrounds me;
I have not a bit of fear;
A tear then dripped down my face;
As I shudder at the thought of cold throughout the year.

For now I shall not worry;
I must enjoy it while it's here;
For when winter shows its fury;
I'll remember this moment, year after year.

But now the sun has laid its head;
I know, shall too I;
But in this moment of springtime;
My dreams can freely fly.

Brianna Pursell
Channahon Middle School
Channahon
Grade 6

Courtney's Faith

C ourage and strength, that's what I have.
O ver my shoulder lies a guardian angel.
U nder my feet is the ground God created.
R ound and round and round the world goes.
T op to bottom everyone knows
N o matter if you look or feel different,
E ven if you're not smart or pretty,
Y ou still are loved by God!

Courtney White
St John Of The Cross School
Western Springs
Grade 5

Shadow

Your shadow is black.
Your shadow is your reflection,
Your shadow reflects whatever you do.
It is a copy cat.
It copy cats everything you do.
Your shadow is your shadow,
Your shadow copies the way you move.
It's mysterious though, when you move your mouth,
You cannot see your mouth move.

Jonathon Neal
Hickory Bend Elementary School
Glenwood
Grade 4

Animals

Dogs, cats
And bats

Long haired, pointer, short haired, setters
Some can be real go-getters.

Siamese, Persian, calico, fat, skinny, slow, fast, lazy
Some get to lie in the soft daisies.

Black, white, brown, gray
Some sleep all day!

Weasels, ferrets, fish, hamsters, birds, mice,
For pets, these would be nice.

A four-legged friend
Until the very end.

Erika Hankins
Okawville Grade School
Okawville
Grade 5

I'm Thinking of You

When I see a bright red rose,
I'm thinking of you.
When I look up at the pretty blue sky
and see the bright yellow sun,
I'm thinking of you.
When I see a kind gentle person with a warm heart,
I'm thinking of you.
When I feel safe and sound and nothing else bad
is going to happen like the way I feel when I am
with my best friends,
I want you to know that deep down inside of me,
I truly am
Thinking of you!

Crystal Cast
Manteno Middle School
Manteno
Grade 6

The Shadow

A shadow.
Just a phantom.
Or maybe nothing at all.
Lost in its world of imagination and darkness.
Lost without a soul.
In a temple of traps and hallucinations.
A temple full of hate, lies and hurt.
A temple of death and ill.
Nobody there; just the shadow.
By itself, trying to find its way out of this temple full of mazes.
It is trapped.
It can't get out.
No matter how hard it tries.
It dwells in there for eternity, finally knowing and understanding it.
It joins the darkness, knowing its way around, joining it, but still lost within it.
It scares the shadow, but it doesn't care.
This is where it belongs, no matter what.

Walter Beversdorf
Meridian Middle School
Buffalo Grove
Grade 5

Snow

Snow.
Gentle, bright, cold, and quiet.
Snow flakes drifting in the brisk night air.
Waking in the early morn to see fresh animal tracks in the backyards' snow.
Snow day from school and other activities.
And there are so many things to do in the snow.
Building snowmen, making snow angels, and sledding down the biggest hills.
Helping Dad shovel the endless driveway and trying not to get frostbite on my nose.
Snowball fights with the neighbors, using our own snow fort for protection.
Now I start to feel a touch of the cold.
Snow pants are soaked right through my clothes.
Time to warm up with a cup of hot cocoa.
Bundled up in a blanket close to the warm fire.
Resting up for the next winter's play.

Jinger Walrath
Channahon Middle School
Channahon
Grade 6

Why?

Why is everyone so happy today, I'm not. What about me, don't I count any more?
Why does everyone have on the new Jordans' I don't. What about me. Don't I count anymore?
Why does everyone have a bike, I don't. What about me, don't I count anymore?
Why does everyone have their own room, I don't. What about me, don't I count anymore?
Why does Mom come and I forget everything. What about me, don't I count?
WHY WHY WHY TELL ME...why isn't everything about me?
BECAUSE I am not the only person on earth!

Stephanie Stone
Posen School
Posen
Grade 4

Stars

Stars are out all day and night,
Making the sky very bright.
Never can see them in the day
But they are there when the sun clears the way.
They are stars, and they make the day.

There are little stars and big stars.
Stars that explode and fall from the sky.
Stars that disappear and we do not know why.

There are stars that shine better, on any kind of day.
Stars can comfort you every night
For the stars are bright lights.
Stars live forever and ever
Never leaving the dark sky for they are stars,
They are the children of the sky.

Jacquetta Redd
Barbour School
Rockford
Grade 6

Homework

I think homework is sometimes hard and sometimes easy
Sometimes I wonder why was it invented?
I think Albert Einstein invented it
Or maybe Thomas Jefferson invented it.
Homework—it wonders me.
WHY?
Did cavemen have homework?
I am very curious on homework.
Homework is always on my mind even in spelling.
Nothing else bothers me except HOMEWORK.

Megan Sanchez
St John Fisher School
Chicago
Grade 4

Mountains

There's pretty mountains everywhere around
There's steam coming up from the rocky ground
The sky looks gray like it's going to storm
It looks like the Grand Canyon
It is so beautiful like the summer breeze
I wish I could be there so badly
Mountains mountains beautiful mountains
They're prettier than the light in my bright green eyes
I love those mountains
They're the most beautiful thing I have ever seen
Mountains mountains bright shiny mountains
Mountains mountains look at the world around you
Mountains mountains such a beautiful sight.

Jessica Sagle
Tri-City Jr-Sr High School
Buffalo
Grade 6

Math

In math there are many different strategies;
We add, subtract, multiply, and divide.

In math we figure out different numbers;
Greater, less, and equal to compare numbers.

In math we can use fractions to divide things up.

We can use shapes — to build buildings.

In math we find area to find
How much carpeting we will need.

We can draw pictures,
To figure out word problems.

We can figure out word problems
To figure out how many apples...
To give each person.

Jessica Vargo
Barbara B. Rose Elementary School
South Barrington
Grade 5

Long Lost Brother

I went to my house there was a kid there
I didn't know him I was not aware
We had the same hair we had the same eyes
He looked just like me I could not despise
I was so curious I started to stare
Where did he come from where oh where?
I didn't know so I ran up the stairs
He didn't know where I was going and he didn't care
Then I went and asked my mother
"What's that you say, he's my long lost brother?"

Kevin McNerney
Emerson Elementary School
Berwyn
Grade 6

All Alone

When I am home alone
And everything is still,
I turn on the TV set
And with sound the house is filled.

Or sometimes when the house is full
And my brother is bugging me,
I go to my room to be alone
And I make sure to lock my door because...
He doesn't have a key.

Jason Blumstein
Solomon Elementary School
Chicago
Grade 4

Corvette/Chevy

Corvette
Beware, road king
Cruising, winning, spinning
Keep off the road here's a hot rod.
Chevy

Tim Loomis
Hiawatha Elementary School
Kirkland
Grade 5

Life

What is life?
I don't think anybody knows.
Is life an obstacle to slow you down?
Maybe it's here just because.

Why are we here?
There has to be a reason.
I guess we'll all find out, someday.
But for now, we'll all just
have to wonder...what is life?

Doug Phelps
Varna Grade School
Varna
Grade 5

Relaxation

My name is Lucas,
I live in Breese.
I'm a ten year old boy,
and I rarely sneeze.

I go to Outback Video
to rent a game,
they're always fun,
and never the same.

Late in the night
when it is dark,
I go play soccer
at Southside Park.

On Tuesday nights,
I am a Scout.
In the summer
we camp out.

Like I said,
I am a boy who is ten
and I live in a house,
not in a pen.

Lucas Richter
Beckemeyer Elementary School
Beckemeyer
Grade 5

Friendship

F ighting over a silly thing
R emembering old memories
I n and out of conversations
E ternal
N ever fighting again
D epending on them to be there
S pecial bond between each other
H elping one another
I gnoring bad choices
P romises that never end!

Maria Cuevas
Indian Knoll Elementary School
West Chicago
Grade 6

Dare Rap

When you smoke
It's no joke

Smoking turns lungs
Black and it makes you hack

If you go ahead and smoke
You are going to croak

If you smoke pot
Your brain is going to rot

When you drink beer
You're not thinking clear

Luigy Lima
Emerson Elementary School
Berwyn
Grade 6

The Celebration

Last night I went to celebrate
The celebration ended late
When I got there I had to wait
But I don't care because it was great

Andy Barlow
Edison Middle School
Champaign
Grade 6

Cats

Cats are very, very tall,
Cats always have paws,
Cats may claw only if you bother them,
Cats are very small
Cats can be small or tall.

David Lee
Summit Elementary School
Collinsville
Grade 4

Leaves

Winter, spring, summer, fall,
Leaves are the best of all!
Green, yellow, orange, red.
They make a nice cushioned bed.

Lauren Martens
Grant Park Middle School
Grant Park
Grade 6

Gym

Gym is fun.
Gym is excellence.
Gym is fitness.
Gym is healthy.
Gym is great.
Gym is fantastic.

Kenan Kinney
Laraway Elementary School
Joliet
Grade 6

Popcorn

popcorn
butter, salt
pops, explodes
I feel excitement at the smell
good food

Chad Pacey
St John's Lutheran School
Buckley
Grade 5

If I Were in Charge of the World

If I were in charge of the world,
I'd cancel chores,
I'd cancel eating veggies, and
I'd also cancel school.

If I were in charge of the world,
There would be no violence,
There would be no drugs, and
There would be no littering.

If I were in charge of the world,
You wouldn't have a bedtime,
You wouldn't have a curfew, and
You wouldn't have to clean.

If I were in charge of the world,
All scary movies would be rated G, and
All videos and games would be free.

Jessica Lynch
Emerson Elementary School
Berwyn
Grade 6

In My Dreams

In my dreams I am a princess loved by one and all.
The center of attention at a royal ball.

In my dreams I am a pirate fighting for the gold.
X marks the spot, or so I'm told.

In my dreams I'm a mermaid, gliding through the sea.
A creature full of magic, questions, mystery.

I'm also a butterfly fluttering with the birds.
How beautiful am I! You cannot describe with only words.

In my dreams I can be whatever I want to be.
I simply let imagination take hold and let me free.

I can be all these things. It's more than it seems.
But not in real life, only in my dreams.

Brittany Leigh McDermott
Jefferson Elementary School
Springfield
Grade 6

The Last Game

I was on the court giving it my all
When someone passed me the basketball.
I wanted to shoot and be very cool
Because if I missed, I'd feel like a fool.
My family yelled "Go Spens, go!"
I nearly fell and broke my toe!
Some guys on the other team treated me very mean.
They hit me high, they hit me low
They nearly broke my other toe.
If you don't play the game right
You won't look like a fighting knight.
My team passed me the ball
And I took a shot for victory.
The game was tied and I took the shot.
Everyone cried that I wouldn't make it.
The ball made it in and we won the game.

Spenser Svehla
St Joseph Catholic School
Harvard
Grade 5

Flowers

Flowers, flowers how pretty you are.
Flowers, flowers you are so many different colors
pink, blue, yellow and purple too.
Flowers, flowers so many different kinds,
roses, carnations and tulips too.
Flowers you brighten the world.

Carly Condon
St John Fisher School
Chicago
Grade 4

School's Out

When school is out
Kids are happy that's no doubt
Kids are running to and fro.
It's so hot they melt like snow.
Down to the lake is where we go
We all want a chance to row the boat
The boat is so heavy is won't float
Two days later we're at summer camp
And mail letters home with a postage stamp
In those letters we say hello and good-bye
Camp is soon over and we just want to cry
Now we are home and summer is near its end
And we see school coming just around the bend.

Carrie Schmitt
St Mary's of Kickapoo School
Edwards
Grade 5

Thank You Family

Thank you family for always being there
Thank you family for letting me know you care
Thank you family for saying you love me
Thank you family for showing you're proud of me
Thank you family, I LOVE YOU!!

Kelly Ayers
Emerson Elementary School
Berwyn
Grade 6

The Paradise

A new paradise opened
All spirits are welcome
As if a long journey is over
And their destination is inviting them
With a delicate and fragile
But wondrous call
Water flowing softly
Bells chiming
As the sun rises slowly over the horizon
Glistening ever so brightly
Streams of sadness being lightly washed away
By the river of wonder
Sickness being curved
Dead seas awakening
The celebration of life
Happy to have family, talent and knowledge
Happy to be who you are,
To have feelings,
To be different,
Time to reflect on the lives we've lived
Long live peace in this joyous magical paradise.

Taylor Blevons
Meridian Middle School
Buffalo Grove
Grade 5

School Days

Teacher
Smart, fun
Interesting, teaching, enjoying
Telling, loving, smiling, learning
Laughing, reading, achieving
Educated, small
Student

Jeni Wright
Varna Grade School
Varna
Grade 5

At the Plate in the World Series

Bottom
Nine, two outs,
I'm at the plate.
Missing the ball
Could be my fate. I'm
Very nervous, yet happy.
The World Series comes down
To me. I can feel the triumph,
Yet taste defeat. I'm cherry red,
From head to feet. The pitcher stands
Looking at me, hoping to get almighty
Strike three. Sixteen seasons I have
Played. People ponder if I will fade.
I wish to show them right now. Hit the
Ball; make it go KOPOW! He starts his
Windup, throws with might. I hit the
Ball; it has much height. There it goes
Some five hundred feet. I have felt
The triumph, and killed defeat.

Stephen Azar
Blessed Sacrament School
Belleville
Grade 6

Cool Facts About the Nine Planets

Mars is made of rust;
And Venus is made of dust.

Mercury is the closest to the Sun;
As Pluto is the smallest one.

Neptune is blue;
And the Earth is too.

Jupiter has gas;
And has the most mass.

Uranus is blue;
As Neptune is too.

Emily Prince
Beckemeyer Elementary School
Beckemeyer
Grade 4

Sister Jean

Sister Jean is our principal; she keeps the school running.
She gets all of her work done and she plans field trips for our school.
All of the trips are fun.
Sister Jean is a cool principal and when kids get hurt,
Sister Jean puts a band aid on their cuts.

Caitlin Clancy
St John Fisher School
Chicago
Grade 4

Grandparents

What are grandparents? To me grandparents are like a
second life just bursting when you go to their house,
or even when I think about them. Listen to the word
grandparents. It has two words, grand and parents.
For I know why it has the two words grand and parents.
Grand goes with what you are, because you are indeed grand.
And so the word parents means that if my parents were to pass on,
I would go to you. To go to you would be like having a whole new life.
A life that would be full of mystery and fun. I cannot tell you enough
how grateful I am to have you as such wonderful grandparents!
I can tell you how much I love you though. I love you as much as
the wolf cries to the new fallen moon or as an eagle feeds its babies
to keep them alive. You are that wolf and the eagle. I could not
live happily if it were not for you. You have cared for and loved me.
My parents could mostly fill the gap, but you would finish it.
I love you and always will, for even if we get in fights, I will
always forgive you.

Heather Brown
Channahon Middle School
Channahon
Grade 6

Dreams

A dream is like a secret place.
It is created at your own pace.
A vision in your head, mostly when you go to bed.

A dream might be during the day.
Sometimes it's when you break from play.
It might be of a memory in your past, or of what is to come at last.

A dream brings a happy feeling.
Maybe it's even when you are staring at the ceiling.

Sometimes it feels as if you are being hugged.
Then it is impossible to be bugged.

A calmness is there.
To leave it, I would not dare.
A dream how I wish I was there.

Nicole Fortuna
Geraldine Kerkstra Middle School
Oak Forest
Grade 6

My Grandmother

My grandmother was a sweet grandmother.
I loved her dearly.
She loved me dearly too.
I'm happy she's in Heaven.
She is not with us, but she's still in our hearts.

Brandi Elaine Bonner
St Paul Academy
Rockford
Grade 4

Life Is Like a Baseball

Life is like a baseball,
You get knocked around...
Never knowing where you're going to end up.
Only living for a period of time
Not always feeling fine
It always has to come to an end.
It could be soon,
If you get hit up to the moon
Or it could happen later.
If you're in a swamp and get eaten by a gator.
Not knowing until it happens.
The baseball having feelings...
As it gets hit around,
Getting hurt.
Then people get scrapes or cuts.
Not enjoying their short period of time living
Giving itself to someone else
Then it's over.

Brady Booth
Barbara B. Rose Elementary School
South Barrington
Grade 5

Life

Life doesn't frighten me at all
that is what I say, to conquer my fear
I am scared of life
because one day if I think something negative
and I still think about it
you never know if it will come true
I am scared of walking at night alone
creepy noises, loose wild animals
people fighting by me
snakes or reptiles or even creepy girls
life doesn't frighten me at all
that is what I say to conquer my fear
I am going to conquer my fear
by standing up for myself
and being strong and proud
that life doesn't frighten me at all

Giana Hutton
Parker Jr High School
Flossmoor
Grade 6

Nature

Being in nature gives one a great feeling,
Away from the city's shoplifting and stealing.
You may absorb all the sights, and relax in the peace,
And also hear the sounds of bullfrogs, chipmunks, and geese.

Chickadees and cardinals all sing in their choirs,
While all of the crickets loudly chirp from the briars.
They will all chirp and sing for a time that is long,
Until the other animals join in their song.

You can feel the soft, spongy grass prickle your toes,
As the pollen from flowers tickles your nose.
Nature is God's garden; it covers a vast array,
Here, everything is joyful, and without dismay.

Nature is the best, and the most wonderful place,
It is sure to put a smile on anyone's face.

Chad Sullivan
Northlawn Middle School
Streator
Grade 6

Make a Choice

Tobacco, Alcohol, Drug Abuse
Changing our world with its constant use.
People dying and disabled.
Why don't we learn from reading the labels.
Warnings of dangers go unheeded.
STOP! THINK! Your life is still needed!
Change the world by changing your choices.
Let's stop the abuse by lifting our voices.
Don't drink and drive, inhale, or puff.
Shoot up, chew, sniff, or huff.
Make this world a better place.
Take a stand and win the race.
Drug FREE!
The way to be!

Jessica Evans-Becker
Grant Park Middle School
Grant Park
Grade 6

Leaves

Leaves come down to the ground.
Some turn red and some turn brown.
Leaves change colors every season.
And we know they have a reason.
Leaves are used to make cool stuff.
And some of them feel rough.
Leaves come down to the ground.
Some turn red, some turn yellow, and they all turn brown.

Perla Perez
Nixon Elementary School
Chicago
Grade 5

Hobbies

I love my hobbies.
Cheerleading is very hard,
But reading is fun!

Brysta Boyer
North Elementary School
Marshall
Grade 6

My Mom

My mom is really beautiful.
She is so nice.
I think she makes the sun shine.
That's my very nice mom.

Sean O'Connell
St John Fisher School
Chicago
Grade 4

Snowboarding

Snowboarding is such a thrill
Sliding down a snow-packed hill
Keeping your balance as you fly along
Even when the wind is strong
Finishing an exciting run
Makes snowboarding so much fun!

Steven Ainge
St John Of The Cross School
Western Springs
Grade 5

Summer

In the summer days
Children laugh with each other
And play with best friends

Sherry Graham
St Mary of Czestochowa School
Cicero
Grade 6

Nink

I went to visit the planet Nink
We were only allowed to eat ink
All we wore was orange and pink
We said "Hello" with a simple wink
And "Good-bye" with a blink
Why did I not stay there?
Well, I told the mayor to grow some hair
He told me to take a trip
Then, up I went on a rocket ship

That is the reason I forgot my homework.

Rebecca L. Bernhardt
Prince of Peace
Antioch
Grade 6

Holidays

There are many holidays in a year
None of them you should fear
All of which should be rejoiced
Be happy and sing out with your voice.

Jeannette Sims
Northlawn Middle School
Streator
Grade 6

School Doesn't Frighten Me at All

Noises down the hall,
Being hit by a spitball
School doesn't frighten me at all.

Bullies laughing loud —
Teachers in a crowd
School doesn't frighten me at all.

My grades are really lame
As I walk down graduates lane
No, they don't frighten me at all...

I go "Hi", make them fly;
I have fun, 'way they run
I go to play when they fray

In the new classroom where
Boys are mean
And girls
Are in tight little seams.
They don't frighten me at all

School doesn't frighten me at all.
Not at all
Not at all
School doesn't frighten me at all.

Sul Ahmad
Barbara B. Rose Elementary School
South Barrington
Grade 5

Drawing

I like to draw,
I think it is great.
People stare in awe,
At all the pictures I create.

Up in my room far away,
Is where I go each and every day.
My love for drawing will never stop,
Forever will my creativity always POP!

Suzi Johnson
St Irene School
Warrenville
Grade 6

Hummingbirds

Like humming birds fly backwards
And so must be able
To see what is behind them.

People this day think they are advancing
But unable to learn
From past mistakes.

Like people we could learn
From hummingbirds
Seeing what is behind them.

Mireya Valle
Nixon Elementary School
Chicago
Grade 5

Me

Megan is my name
Soccer is my game
I play it all the time
My mom says that's fine
It is very fun
I play it in the sun
It is very hot
But when you have a water bottle it's not!

Megan Ansley
McCray-Dewey School
Troy
Grade 5

The Way...

The way the water
greets the sand
The way the Earth
is in God's hand
The way the birds
sing their song
The way the lovers
stroll along
The way the children
like to laugh
The way the cow
treats her calf
The way the rainbow
cures the rain
The way God
cures our pain
The way we sleep
in merry play
The way we start
a brand new day

Sara Monson
Montini Catholic School
McHenry
Grade 6

Space

Space is dark, space is light.
Space is black, it is white.
Space is far,
It has many stars
Jupiter looks like a star,
We might get to live on Mars.
When you go into space,
Make sure you wear a helmet on your face.

Madeline Anne Martin
St. John Fisher School
Chicago
Grade 4

Flowers

F lowers are full of colors.
L ike red, pink, and blue.
O ur world is so beautiful.
W ith many flowers that bloom.
E arth is so big so many flowers that grow.
R ed, pink, and blue so many will bloom.
S o plant some flowers so the world will shine through,
  and feel lovingly and true.

Lisa Vaccaro
Our Lady of Mt Carmel School
Melrose Park
Grade 5

Me

You think you know me,
But all you really see, is only what I show
You think you understand me, but even I don't really know,
Just who exactly am I, who do you think I am?

I've tried so hard to cover up, who I really am
People say I'm stupid, people say I'm ugly,
Yet who are they to think I'm not a glam?
People think it doesn't hurt me, everything that they say,
But just because I don't show it, that doesn't mean I'm okay

I wish I could just stop, trying to be someone disparate,
But this mask I am wearing won't seem to dislocate

I wish I could be someone else,
Someone who is beautiful, smart, and athletic too,

People think it's unusual, what I want to do,
I try to be original, creating something new

And that is who I'd like to be, even though, it's already me.

ME

Desireé King
Channahon Middle School
Channahon
Grade 6

Pilgrims

In the early 1600's
The pilgrims sailed across the sea
They set foot on this land
And helped form what this country came to be.

Caleb Braun
Deer Creek-Mackinaw Middle School
Deer Creek
Grade 5

Life Is Like a Fun Game

Life is like starting a new game,
Rolling the dice
Not knowing how to play.
Just going along with it;
It is fun to start.

Life is like a long lovely game —
Advancing 5-10 spaces —
Getting to choose
Whatever toy or animal you want in the shop
It is fun to choose.

Life is like losing one's turn,
Receiving a penalty
Because you forgot to tie your shoelaces.
Ending up with a sprained ankle
It is a fun way to learn.

Life is like finishing the final game fondly,
Running the game —
With the game being long and great.
Knowing there is a better place.
It is fun to go home.

Kaitlyn Jansen
Barbara B. Rose Elementary School
South Barrington
Grade 5

Months

January = white for the snow.
February = pink for Valentine's Day.
March = green for St. Patrick's Day.
April = sky blue for rain.
May = raspberry for roses for Mother's Day.
June = light green for the grass in the meadow.
July = royal blue for the fireworks in the sky.
August = violet flowers in the meadow.
September = yellow for the leaves on the trees.
October = orange for the pumpkins by the front door.
November = brown for a turkey.
December = red for Santa's suit.

Mia Mazzone
Grand Prairie Elementary School
Joliet
Grade 4

Nature

One by one I hear footsteps...
pitter, patter, pitter, patter.

Rivers flowing...
shew, splash, shew, splash.

Rustling leaves from the trees...
sh, sh, sh,sh.

Wind making whistling noise...
wooo, wooo.

pitter, patter,
shew, splash.
sh, sh,
wooo.....

Meghan Connell
Montini Catholic School
McHenry
Grade 6

Spring

Spring flowers, rainbows
It's so colorful and bright
Blooming and growing
Jonathon Marcolini
St Mary of Czestochowa School
Cicero
Grade 6

Spring/Fall

Spring
flowers, warm
raining, playing, biking
fun, breeze, leaves, chilly
raking, falling, freezing
sick, cold
Fall
Paris Caldwell
Diekman Elementary School
Dolton
Grade 5

Spring

Spring
Warm, funny
Playing, growing, raining
Birds, happy, trees, people
Swimming, jumping, splashing
Hot, wild
Summer
Casey Nelson
Hyde Park Elementary School
Waukegan
Grade 4

Ice Cream Sundae

An ice cream sundae piled high,
Makes me feel like I could cry!
Cupcakes, donuts, chocolate galore.
Layers and layers, more, more, MORE!
Cookies and chips,
What a trip!
Blueberry pie,
Oh me, oh my!
If all of this was on my sundae,
It would be gone in the blink of an eye!
Samantha Wilkinson
North Elementary School
Marshall
Grade 6

Dreams

Close your eyes
And hold on tight
We'll ride through the day
And out into the night
Watch out for the shadows
They claw and bite

Dance in the darkness
Shout with all your might
'Cause nobody will hear you
When you're dreaming in the night

Look out for the rising sun
Whose rays are hot and bright
Hide beneath the covers
Hide from the light
Dreams are forever
Their promises are all right

'Cause nobody knows you, nobody cares
When you're dreaming in the night
Maggie Thomas
Channahon Middle School
Channahon
Grade 6

Looking

Looking at a seed you get a tree.
Looking at a tree you get wood.
Looking at wood you get a floor.
Looking at a floor you get a wall.
Looking at a wall you get a ceiling.
Looking at a ceiling you get a house.
Looking at a house you get a home.
Lucas Svehla
St Joseph Catholic School
Harvard
Grade 6

America

A fter every war, there are
M any memories that are
E verlasting—
R unning and being in the
I nfantry and many
C eremonies for the soldiers in the
A rmed forces
Jeffrey Thompson
Manteno Middle School
Manteno
Grade 6

Violence

Bats and brooms can give me wounds
and violence, the same.
For those of you who don't know me
I do not play that game.

And if you get in big trouble
you will be put in jail.
Don't you even think of it,
I'm talking about trying to bail.

And if you try to free a hair
I know someone will tell.
Then you'll end up in the chair.
Does that ring a bell?

Your mom and dad will cry
All day and night, just for your death
When the guy they really wanted
Looked like you; his name is Seth.

Seth lives in Indiana and
Is now a father of eight,
While you are sky high trying
To get past heaven's gate.
Thurayya Drew
Enos School
Springfield
Grade 5

Puppy

Puppy
furry, playful
jumping, begging, running
fur, tail, paw, whiskers
playing, fetching, chasing
cuddly, little
dog
Amanda Hyle
Stone Creek Elementary School
Roscoe
Grade 4

The Friend

She laughs
And laughs.

When I say something really neat
She usually falls off her feet.

When we jump up and down on something
It's usually in the very beginning of spring.

We smell the flowers
With all our powers.

Sometimes we talk together and play.
We always have something to say.

She is my friend
Until the very end.

Breanna Baker
Okawville Grade School
Okawville
Grade 5

Angels

These are the people who are so sweet,
Not only one will you ever meet.
Their kindness is a constant flow
That gives them a warm, kind, friendly glow.

Their smile is silver; their laughter is gold,
Their happiness continues from young until old.
If ever sad, go see them once more,
Afterwards, you'll wonder what you were sad for.

These are the people everyone wants to know,
If they want to be happy wherever they go.
So when you find any angels, don't let them leave,
For if you do, you'll forever grieve.

Diana Zimmerman
Northlawn Middle School
Streator
Grade 6

Day Dreams

You fell asleep, but not quite.
You are dreaming, but you're awake.
You are day dreaming.
It's a land of wonders.
Things are going in, and out of your head.
You are day dreaming.
You are comfortable just sitting there dreaming.
It feels of such freedom, but you are just dreaming.

Kelsey Harrington
Riverwood Elementary School
McHenry
Grade 5

Friends

Really, I have lots of friends.
Always around me to the end.
They all care, share, and love.
They all believe in God above.
Believe it or not, when I bump my knee,
All of my friends are there for me.
Even if I start to cry
They remove a tear from beneath my eye.
And they will me everything will be all right.
They never leave me in the cold,
And always make me feel like gold.
We do things and go places.
We find cool things and meet new faces.
But, no one could compare to my friend's place.
Deep in my heart, no one can take.
You know how precious friends can be.
They are very precious to me.
We will share lots of time and laughter
And always be together forever after.

Lindsey England
North Elementary School
Marshall
Grade 6

The Ocean

As I sit here on the shore,
Getting ready to snorkel like the many times before,
Thinking of all the fish in the sea,
And wondering if they're thinking of me,
They're filled with color green and pink,
Red, purple, yellow, and as blue as ink,
The coral is as colorful as the fish,
And helps them from being on someone's dish,
I hope this helps you understand,
what lies beyond the golden sand.

Maria Hinders
St Matthew School
Champaign
Grade 6

I Try

I try at everything I do
Even though sometimes that doesn't please you
The finger painting on the kitchen wall
I was bringing out my best work of all
My pet snake in big sister's bed
I guess I wasn't using my head
The sticky tack on Dad's work chair
I promise I didn't put it there
I know you say my head's in the sky
But really I do try

Samantha Smith
Kellar Central School
Peoria
Grade 4

The Sky

The sky is blue and hot too,
like a yacht in a hot spot.
It is hotter than the water
on a hot day laying away.

Mark Curboy
Tri-County Christian School
Freeport
Grade 4

Shopping

Every time you see me shopping,
Dollar bills are always dropping,
Clothes, shoes, lotions, more,
I'm not going too far,
People happy people bored,
I need to find my credit card,
Move people get out of my way,
There is no time to delay,
Clearances, prices, sales too,
Watch out for that sticky goo,
Mostly all the clothes are fitting,
'Cause I have no time for knitting,
Bags are getting very heavy,
I am so glad I drove my Chevy,
Feet are tired feet are weak,
I really want to go to sleep,
Day was successful day was great,
I had time to lose some weight,
I think the next time I go to the mall,
I will give you a call!!

Jessica Schmidt
Channahon Middle School
Channahon
Grade 6

Today, Today

Today, today,
Why today?
It doesn't matter,
Anyway.

It's chilly, it's cold,
I am really freezing.
I'll probably catch the flu,
And never stop sneezing.

Today I don't care,
I went to school in my underwear.
Stop!
It's not as bad as it may seem.
Don't worry,
It's just a dream.

Josh McGee
St Mary School
New Berlin
Grade 5

My Parent's Divorce

Their hearts were worn out,
For us, that's why they hide the pain from my siblings and myself.
For us, that's why they sacrifice their smiles.
Is love still lingering
Between their broken hearts?
My wish upon a star used to be
That they would fall in love all over again.
It is impossible. That's why it remains a dream.
When I made my wish upon a star
Had my selfishness fogged up my mind?
I could not see the sadness or anger
When their names were mentioned to each other.
Then I was forced to make a choice.
Who should I care about the most?
Where to go?
How to say goodbye?
But...I matured.
I do not want my wish.
Patience has overwhelmed me
And once again I see their smiling faces.

Amanda Turbyfill
Century Oaks Elementary School
Elgin
Grade 6

Baseball

B aseball is the greatest sport if you
A lways hit the ball.
S tealing bases is
E asy and fun.
B atting is good unless the other team catches the ball, or you strike out.
A lways be in your position if there is a ball hit to
L eft field.
L ine up with the ball when it is hit.

Jeffrey R. Schaffer
St. George School
Tinley Park
Grade 6

A White Bear's Winter

I am a polar bear.
There is snow and ice everywhere,
Cold and windy I don't fright.
I have a nice white coat that keeps me warm day and night,
Big wide feet help me swim, and then I build myself a little snow den.
I live way up north in the Icy Arctic,
Although my species is quite endothermic.
Seals and fish I do crave,
To keep my body fat and brave.
Winter cold does not bother me
My coat protects me from the icy sea.

Kaela Munster
St. Bede School
Ingleside
Grade 6

I Can Be

I can be an astronaut going into space.
I can be a movie star making big premiers,
Or maybe I can be a singer singing many songs,
Or just an athlete who likes to play ping pong.
I can be anything, anything at all.
I can be a famous writer writing all kinds of books,
Or maybe an artist who paints pictures of you and me.
I can be anything,
Anything I want to be.

Sarra O'Connell
Geraldine Kerkstra Middle School
Oak Forest
Grade 6

Baseball

On a summer day in July,
There is nothing I like to do more than catch a pop fly,
At a baseball game with the ball in the air,
I can hear the crowd cheer he's got it there,
When the ball is caught I don't just stop there,
Now is my turn to knock that ball in the air.

Brett Longton
St Irene School
Warrenville
Grade 6

Best Friends

Friends are always there for you
No matter what you do
Friends are there to care and comfort you
When you're feeling blue
Friends are there to stick up for you
But most of all friends never let you down

Melanie Mitchell
Manteno Middle School
Manteno
Grade 6

The Very Noisy Music Theatre

The bands and audiences in the music theater
Are so loud they are giving me a sore head,
I think I'm seeing red,
The music is so loud I'm turning insane,
How much noise can they make,
I'm thinking I'm losing my brain,
I wish they all would jump in a lake,
I should herd them all up and put them on a train,
The opera singers are so annoying I'm starting to crumble,
The haunting music is so creepy, I'm starting to tremble,
I hate the music because it's making my eardrums bleed,
The music makes me shake like a weed.

Shaye Pommer
Beckemeyer Elementary School
Beckemeyer
Grade 4

Jan. 22, 1988–?

Here is the tombstone of Jessica Brown,
Because of the ocean in which she did drown.
She swam and splashed for a very long while,
Having her fun in a quite neat style.
Then it came time for her to go,
But she swam away yelling, "No, no, no!"
No one has ever found her yet,
So alive or not her tombstone's set.

Jessica Brown
Grant Park Middle School
Grant Park
Grade 6

Friendship

Friendship,
A relationship that lasts a lifetime.
Nothing can keep you from happiness.
Friendship,
A time to treasure,
Someone to rely on for an eternity.
Friendship,
A gift from God,
A special gift,
One that lasts forever.
Friendship,
The golden light from the Arch to Heaven
Has spotted you and gives you a brand new life.
Friendship
Friendship
Friendship

Tyler Dameron
Indian Knoll Elementary School
West Chicago
Grade 6

Footprints

Whose are they, where do they go,
Those big white footprints in the snow?
Ah! They're following me!
Oh, gee! I forgot the footprints are from me!

Jamie Litteken
All Saints Academy School
Breese
Grade 4

Other End!

Have you ever wondered
what was at the other end?
Is there another beach, is there another state,
does it ever end?
What is at the other end?

Jenny Schess
Forest View Elementary School
Mount Prospect
Grade 4

Purple

Purple is a soaring gull
Flying across the sea,
Violet in the rainbow
For the world to see.
A sky with lilac clouds,
A mountain's purple head,
Sweet smelling orchids
In a lavender bed.
Purple is a grape
And other sweet things;
A multicolored butterfly
With silken mauve wings.
A twilight's dark evening
In an inky purple shade,
Long, stretched shadows
That the sun has made.
Purple is the royal color
For the queen and king.
It is the sparkling jewel
In an amethyst ring.

Lavanya Srinivasan
Steeple Run Elementary School
Naperville
Grade 5

Flying

If I had one wish, I say
Can I fly for just one day?
Oh, how I'd love to fly
Soaring in the bright blue sky.
Dipping, diving, through a cloud,
Trying not to be that loud.
If you had a wish too,
You would feel the way I do.
In just one day, my dreams come true.
If I had one wish, I'd say,
I'd love to fly for just one day.

Danielle Kile
North Elementary School
Marshall
Grade 6

A New Year

Yesterday is gone
A new year is here
We need tomorrow
For should we fear
The world is so full of beauty
For all of us to see
And we will all go into a new century

Amanda Christison
Virginia Elementary School
Virginia
Grade 6

Spring and Summer

Spring
beautiful, peaceful
singing, dancing, playing
birthdays, games, summer
people, animals, jump roping
bike riding, barbecuing, skipping,
bikes, toys,
Summer

Candice Clark
Hyde Park Elementary School
Waukegan
Grade 4

Mega Man

His shiny armor
Has no dents
And unlike a charmer
It can't be bent

His powers are strong and mighty
A virtual cannon of fire power
No one would want to fight
He's like no other power

His clever wits
And intelligence
Makes him not want to quit

With this mega man
Evil cannot stand

Kaushik Sarkar
Meridian Elementary School
Mounds
Grade 6

Summer

The sun is coming
Kids are getting out of school
I wish for summer

Virang Patel
North Park Elementary School
Chicago
Grade 4

Paradise

Blue skies above us
Green grass grows all around us
Ocean shinier than a star
Heaven all around
Where paradise is found

Meagan Gattis
Our Lady of Mt Carmel School
Melrose Park
Grade 5

Heaven

Heaven is light blue
It sounds like people laughing
Heaven tastes like bubble gum
It smells like a field of roses
And looks like forever
Heaven makes you feel free.

Lacey Koerkenmeier
Damiansville Elementary School
Albers
Grade 6

Wolves

Wolves are like dogs
They can find their way through
thick heavy fog.
A wolf would not live
in a murky, muddy bog.
You would never see a wolf
eat a big, green frog.
Wolves do not use cogs,
and live in buildings
Instead they live in a forest
filled with big round logs.

Michael DeWitt
Tri-County Christian School
Freeport
Grade 4

Boys

Boys are cute
Boys are fine
I need them all the time

If I can't have them
I'll cry, pout and whine
But that won't be a problem
Because they are around all the time

Stephanie Willhelm
Jefferson Elementary School
Springfield
Grade 6

My Dogs

Bella
playful, energetic
fuzzy, cute, nice
growing, learning, tiring out
larger, strong, guarder
intelligent, loud
Moochie

Carla Kariott
Emerson Elementary School
Berwyn
Grade 6

The Wind

The wind,
Singing to the trees,
Whispering to the meadows.

The wind so soft and gentle,
Like a beautiful bird's wings.

The only thing you can hear is her singing and whispering,
She is all around us,
Just singing and whispering.

But in the night,
When the moon is out,
And it is dark,
She gets scared and lonesome.

When the trees and meadows are asleep,
Sometimes in the night she cries.

But when the sun comes up,
And the trees and meadows awake,
There she is waiting for them,
She starts singing and whispering to them,
A different song and whisper each day.

And she dries her tears,
Because she knows it's a new day.

Chelsey Alderman
Red Bud Elementary School
Red Bud
Grade 6

The Game

This is a poem of my favorite sport
I could ramble on, but I'll keep it short.

My favorite sport is baseball see,
I practice every night hitting off a tee.

I dreamt of hitting a homer, to the top of Sears Tower.
But I don't think it's possible, to have that much power.

Last year I averaged over four hundred,
I'd get a good hit, and the whole team thundered!

Baseball is my favorite sport.
So don't think I'm playing on a court.

If I haven't yet made myself clear,
Baseball's my favorite sport each year!

Chris Beedie
St John Of The Cross School
Western Springs
Grade 5

Soldier

S oaring highly in the air, bombs exploding everywhere
O ver the ground are bodies that
L ay "Rest in peace, my friends," we say
D edicating bullets to them
I hear my friends drop ten by ten
E very war has an end but
R eal lives won't come back again

Brittany Molk
Manteno Middle School
Manteno
Grade 6

Softball

Softball is the game I love.
During the game I look above.
Birds and balls fly through the air.
A girl playing ball is such a dare.

I bat, I bunt, I run, run, run.
Softball is so much fun.
I'm out on the field ready to play.
Will this next ball come my way?

She's up to bat, ready to hit.
She hits so hard, I want to spit.
The ball is coming out of the sky.
If I am not careful, I might get hit in the eye.

My mother calls in a strong yell.
What is she saying? I wish I could tell.
The game is over, the day is done.
Softball is so much fun.

Kayla Schroeder
Wells Elementary School
Grayville
Grade 5

Untitled

Lying. Relaxed. Breathe, breathe.
Waiting to fall into my dreams.
As my eyes get heavy,
They drop.
And they begin.
Dreams.
My dreams.
Full of my imagination.
Not only thoughts that lie within my mind
But thoughts that lie within my heart and soul.
What are these thoughts you might ask.
For that is the secret that lies within my dreams.

Kelly Dedick
Jay Stream Middle School
Carol Stream
Grade 6

Rey

There once was a dog named Rey
Who ate from the garbage one day
She smelled so bad
And we really weren't glad
So we washed her off in the bay

Layla Frankel
North Park Elementary School
Chicago
Grade 4

Rainbow

Rainbow, rainbow in the sky
You are beautiful and colorful.
Clouds in the sky
Way up high—
Rainbow, rainbow in the sky
You are more beautiful than a butterfly!

DeAngelo Blatcher
Hickory Bend Elementary School
Glenwood
Grade 4

The Cooking Man

One day the cooking man baked a cake
He used white cake mix
The cake was a long football shape
When it came out of the oven
He used red and yellow icing
That was the very first cake
The cooking man baked.

Chad McClure
Hay-Edwards Elementary School
Springfield
Grade 5

Meg's Leg

I think I broke my leg.
I need a wooden peg.
That leg I smashed.
Maybe it was mashed.
Either way it hurts the same.
I think I'm going lame.
A check up. "No way she'll say."
How will I ever pay.
It's not broken; it is fine.
I think I've lost my mind.
He'll hurt me yes he will.
Then he'll make me take a pill.
He'll put a cast on my leg.
"Oh No!" says Meg.

Rachel Giovannini
Brick Elementary School
Beardstown
Grade 4

Home

Home, always over the river,
but under the heavens.
A place to be comfortable,
a place to relax.
This special place
may be far,
but always there.
To watch a family
grow and grow
to come from school
and tell what I did
But the best thing
about home you see
is that it is always there
when you need it!

Gia Ratoft
Parker Jr High School
Flossmoor
Grade 6

Unsupervised Equals Unsafe

Who's watching the kids?
  Nobody knows.
When parents aren't around,
  Anything goes.
Kids might be biting,
  they might be feeding.
Kids could be fighting,
  they could be bleeding.
Who will help them?
  Nobody's here.
Kids left unsupervised
  is a cause for fear!

Jack Lynch
Emerson Elementary School
Berwyn
Grade 6

Old and Young

When you're young,
  You play in sprinkles.

  When you're old,
    You worry about wrinkles.

  When you're young,
    You have fun as you
    Do when you're old.

    Now this poem is done.

Josh Henderson
Manteno Middle School
Manteno
Grade 6

My Cats

People love dogs but I love cats
Dogs are boring logs
Cats are playful
Unlike dogs
My cats are the best
That is why!

C ute
A ctive
L ovely
L azy
Y aps

A musing
N eat
D arling

P ounces
O utstanding
U seful
N ice
C ool cat
E nergetic
R ules

Jesse Askew
Bolin Elementary School
East Peoria
Grade 5

Homework Problem

Crumple, crumple my paper went.
Now I have nothing to present.

Up on the board my name did go.
Down went my grade to an all time low.

I have learned a lesson here
and to me it's VERY clear.

Catherine Roberts
Phillip May Elementary School
Rochelle
Grade 4

Varnack

Is sharp like a bad snowy day
on the 23rd of February.
It's so cold.
Very sharp pencil tips poke at your skin.
It is so red.
There's fire burning your flesh.

Christina Barbaro
St John Of The Cross School
Western Springs
Grade 5

I Wonder

I wonder if I'll ever be the same?
Be truly happy and not full of shame.
Can my true self be revealed?
Will I be allowed to say what I feel?
Can people see through my true hazel eyes?
Can I stop living in disguise?
Can I just be me?
The true person I want to be.
I wonder?

Amanda Dalessandro
Solomon Elementary School
Chicago
Grade 4

The Swamp Lizard

Swimming through the dark, noisy waters
   Hiding in the big, deep under water tree trunk
Eating slimy, smelly fish
   Playing hide and seek with no lights
Watching out for big, tall humans
   Thinking about eating huge, healthy fish
Dreaming about living like the king of the waters

Jamie Garwood
Wells Elementary School
Grayville
Grade 5

Reflection

I looked down at the water but what to see,
The image of a nearby tree growing straight and as tall as can be.
I looked up at the sky but what to see,
The image of a bird soaring gracefully above me.
I looked into a window but what to see,
A mother making sandwiches for her children of three.
I looked into a mirror but what to see,
The image of a face smiling happily at me.

Jamie Murray
Most Holy Redeemer School
Evergreen Park
Grade 5

Sleep

I love to sleep.
I go upstairs, and look at my bed.
I look at my fluffy pillows, and the warm comforter.
I love to sleep.
I jump in my bed and bury my head in my pillows.
I turn out the light, close my eyes and think of a dream.
In the warmth of my bed, I fall asleep.
I love sleep.

Kathryn Tuerk
St John Of The Cross School
Western Springs
Grade 5

Springtime

Springtime is flowers blooming.
People cleaning around the yard.
People loving and sending cards.
When people look gloomy it won't last long,
Their sweetheart will sing them a song.
Trees are getting leaves and when they are done,
My friends and I are having fun.
When it is over, I always save a four leaf clover.

Jacob Cashman
St John Fisher School
Chicago
Grade 4

My Cat

My cats are as fast as a cheetah running through the jungle.
My cats can eat as much as an elephant eating
20 pounds of peanuts!
My cats can sleep like a bear hibernating
in the winter.

Quinn Farrell
St. Richard School
Chicago
Grade 5

Color Poem

Red looks like a new shiny balloon,
Red smells like fresh-cut roses,
Red tastes like a big and shiny apple,
Red feels like a nice, warm and crackling fire,
Red sounds like a soft whisper to my ear.

Angelica Crouch
Shirland C C Elementary School
Shirland
Grade 6

Dr. Seuss

Dr. Seuss was a funny man
He wrote about Green Eggs and Ham
He wrote about a Cat in a Hat
Who else could think of something funny like that
His sense of humor was very funny
I bet he made a lot of money
He lived for 87 years
When he died, we all cried huge tears
He made writing books a sinch
Even when he wrote about the Grinch
The books he wrote took time
But they still rhymed
Dr. Seuss was a funny man
Even when he wrote about Green Eggs and Ham

Wayne Reynolds
Manteno Middle School
Manteno
Grade 6

Chelsie

Chelsie
Chelsie is a blessing.
She is like an angel sent from heaven.
She helps, jokes, and laughs.
She's my best friend!
Chelsie

Jennifer Lee
North Elementary School
Marshall
Grade 6

Stars

The stars know everything
In the whole universe.
There is a secret
That only they know.
What is it?
What do they know
That we do not know?
Seeing them glow
In that patch of dark sky
Makes you want to fly
And kiss each one of them.
There is a secret
That only they know.
What is it?
What do they know
That we do not know?
Maybe someday,
When the stars shine bright,
We will know what they know.
Someday,
Someday.

Danielle Palmer
St Mary School
Belleville
Grade 6

Nature

Nature is a wonderful thing.
The best season for Nature,
Is in the spring.

It's when the gentle wind blows,
And the North star glows
When the cornfields sway,
And the children play.

When the Cardinal sings,
And the birds flap their wings.

Oh, how I love the spring!

Stephanie Clark
Channahon Middle School
Channahon
Grade 6

Enchanted Night

On a peaceful midnight,
The silent village is slowly awakened
By a blur of mysterious, radiant light,
Illuminating the deserted cobblestone streets.
Venturing forth to explore,
People arise from their dreamlike slumber.
A shower of twinkling stars, fallen from the barren, lonely sky
Is scattered about the earth,
Seeming to whisper, "arise!"
People hesitate to become part of the glittering scene,
For they do not want to destroy this foreign beauty so near.
Not a single soul walks out among the stars.

Inside their homes they observe, out of fear, awe, respect.
Everything is wonderful.
The earth shimmers and the stars have kindled many a spirit.

Slowly the stars disappear,
For they long to enchant the lonely sky once more.
Everything is familiar on the cobblestone streets
And the secretive morning haze lingers.
Everybody drifts back into sleep,
And all is forgotten by the time the glowing sun pierces the horizon.

Alexandra DiFulvio
Quest Academy
Palatine
Grade 6

The Sea

Under the sun's beams it lies,
Still or waving.
The warmth of the sun surrounds the body,
As it tries to soak it up,
But never will because of the size.
The sand soaks up the warmth, also,
Making it warm to the touch.
Children laugh as they play along its shore,
The noise carries through the land,
Bringing joy and happiness.
When the sun fills the sky with a colorful scheme,
Contrasting perfectly with the deep blue of it,
The moon opens its eyes, and watches over it.
The coolness and crisp of the air is soaked up,
Leaving it cool to the touch, but soothing to the soul.
The giant arms reach out to grab the smooth rocks along the coast.
The sound of the crashing waves makes a humming music,
Its tone carrying through the darkness.
As the dawn arrives, it gets more active,
But it will never be too much to soothe the little girl's soul on the rocks.

Nina Luksic
Channahon Middle School
Channahon
Grade 6

My Dreams for this Millennium Are...
Not to pollute the air,
So there will be no bad smells anywhere.
To stop drugs and alcohol,
So people won't get addicted.
To take away all dangerous weapons,
So people won't get injured.
To help all the people who are poor—
To give them food and shelter.
To rid the community of street gangs,
So people won't live in fear.
These are my dreams for this millennium.

Brian De Leon
Solomon Elementary School
Chicago
Grade 4

Saying Bye With a Blast
Saying good-bye to the 20th century,
Was pretty easy,
And kinda cheesy,
They thought the computers would go mad,
There was no problem so don't be sad,
But there were other things that weren't so bad,
Like the invention of plastic bags named Glad,
So go on, complete your day,
Please don't delay,
Don't worry about saying good-bye,
Because time eventually does fly,
This event must be done,
It'll be loads of fun!

Shehbaz Sherwani
Schiesher Elementary School
Lisle
Grade 5

Over the Sky
The sun rises at the start of a new day.
The earth is not a well natured place.
Then all of a sudden,
the world is frozen.
At that exact moment the glorious gift of peace
is given to earth.
The earth is now a beautiful and wonderful place.

All enjoy life for its purposes.
All start a new life.
All living creatures on earth give glory to others.
A rainbow rises over the sky.
People watch the magnificent sky.
The sun sets to a glorious day.

Stephanie Mater
Meridian Middle School
Buffalo Grove
Grade 5

Winter
My favorite season is winter because of snow.
Snow is white and fluffy like a cloud.
In the snow we jump and play.
When in the snow it makes me feel like walking in clouds.
Snow is cold like an ice cube that just fell down your pants.
In winter you wear warm clothes so you don't get cold.
Winter is a season filled with fun.

Mike Ornelas
Iroquois West Upper Elementary School
Thawville
Grade 5

The Beach
So many waves, so much sun
Where are the kids, I want to have fun
I wake up early and put on my shades
B rush my hair and grab my blades
The wind is pushing me all the way
It feels like June, but it's only May
I hope it's like this all summer long
It reminds me of a Beach Boy song
My friends are here, some live far
Others near
All I know it's the best time of the year!!!!!

Alexandria Boyd
Most Holy Redeemer School
Chicago
Grade 5

My Grandfather
My grandpa is so special to me,
When I visit him he's filled with glee.

He tries so hard to make everything right,
But for him it is a terrible fight.

When he talks he sometimes mumbles,
And when he walks he sometimes stumbles.

Two times he has suffered a stroke,
Yet he laughs and plays and likes to joke.

Working hard to get through life,
He is an inspiration to all who face strife.

I am lucky and proud to have him around,
To hear his laugh, there is no better sound.

His message to me is to be my best,
If you trust in God, He will do the rest.

Emily Slavik
Immaculate Conception School
Elmhurst
Grade 5

Sailing

One day a man named Bob
Bought a boat to sail.
He'd go with his son
Some special time would not fail.
Many days it took to pack
Finally, they set out to sea.
Both with happy and anxious faces
A better time there would not be.
Later, the weather became stormy
The wind was so strong
Bob searched for his son
But found he was gone!
When Bob thinks of his Nick
It brings tears to his eyes.
What was meant to be fun
Was a tragedy in disguise.
Bob woke with a fright
How real it did seem —
"What a relief," he thought
It was just a bad dream!

Emma Day
Western Avenue Elementary School
Flossmoor
Grade 4

Animals

Animals here, animals there,
animals everywhere!

Up in the trees, down on the ground,
in the ocean, and all around.

They jump high, they jump low,
they even jump slow.

Morgan Anderson
St Jude School
Joliet
Grade 6

Chivalry

A knight must keep his word,
Must fight fair everywhere,
And respect women and elders.

He must not leave a man
To die on the battleground.

A page, a squire holds weapons,
Holds swords, but must not fight
Until dubbed a knight.

Matt Benegas
Manteno Middle School
Manteno
Grade 6

What Is Red?

Red is a rose, some peppers,
    a game piece in checkers.

Red is the color of your heart,
    that is apart, from any other.

Red is the color of spaghetti sauce,
    because I know, for I am the boss.

Red is an apple all fresh and clean,
    nice and tasty, it is supreme.

Red is a cardinal twittering away,
    oh how I wish it would stay.

Red is as red as it may be,
    red is the color for you and me.

Teresa Eck
St Tarcissius School
Chicago
Grade 5

2000 Is Here

A new number is here,
You may have fear
That 2000 is here.
There is no need to fight.
This is the big night.
10 seconds before midnight...
5, 4, 3, 2, 1...
Happy Millennium.
There goes the lights.

Mookdad Noah
Chaney-Monge Elementary School
Crest Hill
Grade 6

Spring

Spring sets your mind free.
All your worries and sorrow
drift away in the breeze.
Sweet music of larks and robins
fill your ears.
You are once again young at heart.
Spring,
the day when humans become
one with the animals,
the birds,
the bees.
Just watch them be.

April Crawford
Indian Knoll Elementary School
West Chicago
Grade 6

Summer Leaves

Leaves are so bright,
as bright as the light.
They swing and sway,
in the wind on a long summer day.

Luke Martens
Grant Park Middle School
Grant Park
Grade 6

Fall

As the leaves spiraled to the ground
I realized that time is flying by
So I stopped and looked around
At the beauty that is nature
The ground covered by leaves
All of nature, so beautiful
The trees so colorful

I can't help admire
The beauty that surrounds me
Nature is a wondrous thing
But this wondrous thing
Will escape our grasp

Because if we don't take hold
It will leave us forever
And if nature leaves us
We won't ever be able
To experience fall
Again

Norman Manos
Roselle Middle School
Roselle
Grade 6

Spring Has Sprung

Spring has sprung!
The rains have come,
Chicks are hatching
Bunnies are born.
Aren't we prayin'
For a warm country morn'.
Calves are resting,
Colts on the run,
Pigs in the puddle!
All are having fun!
All these animals
Without any alarm
Are happy and gay,
On our country farm.

Emily Maurer
North Elementary School
Marshall
Grade 6

Football and Homework Don't Mix

After school I like to play football.
it is really fun.
I ask my mom if I can go.
She says not until your homework's done.

I hurry up and finish.
I am not sure if it is right.
It's easier to get it done
Than mom and I to fight.

When I get home from playing football,
My mom is really mad.
She checked over my homework,
And it was really bad.

I had to do it over.
It took me all night.
When I woke up in the morning,
My mom said it was right.

Andrew Keener
Altona Grade School
Altona
Grade 6

The New Year

As we approach the new year,
We think of everything dear.
Computers and laptops,
Children's toys and spinning tops.
And as we invent new gadgets that are cool,
I hope we will still use some old fashioned tools.
And how we used to play in an old fashioned way,
We'll still be able to do, with everything new.
So as we go into the next century
We will still know what's elementary.

Adam Valdes
Schiesher Elementary School
Lisle
Grade 5

My Special Friend and Me

I have a friend named Brennan
We like to throw rocks in socks
Work on our fort together
Put nails in boards
Build a roof together
Play together in nice muddy weather
We like to spend nights at each other's houses
We like to spend lots of time together
And that's what we do together

Jeff Helfrich
St Mary-Dixon School
Dixon
Grade 6

Baseball

Baseball is the greatest game,
It requires a lot of skill and cunning.
You can play it in heat and rain,
Participants do a lot of hitting,
    throwing, catching and running.
Baseball is a complex game, even though
    it doesn't have a sophisticated name.
Baseball players play the game on a
    baseball diamond, not on a tennis court.
By the end of a baseball game,
You'll realize it's the most enjoyable sport.
But before a game can end, it has to start,
So, "Play Ball!"

Jordan Zucker
Meridian Middle School
Buffalo Grove
Grade 6

Pizza, Pizza, Pizza

Cheeses oozing in my mouth,
Sausage sizzling everywhere.
Pepperoni spicy hot.
A good pizza is never bare.
I like any topping except.
Ugly, wiggly, tiny fishes.
They don't make very good pizza dishes.
Sauce is always very good,
And usually bright, bright red.
But what would happen if it were dark, dark, blue!
That would be something to dread.
So next time you think of food,
Think of pizza, 'cause it puts you in the mood!!.

Brandon Scott
Bolin Elementary School
East Peoria
Grade 5

Friends

My friends are there forever.
No matter what is wrong,
They will be there forever.
Friendship is long.
Friends do their best for their friends.
My friends care about me
Even though our friendship may curve and bend
It'll always be us three.
Teresa, Kristen, and I, together we stand.
We are friends for ever and ever
I'll always remember them, and break apart?
We will never!

Samantha Davids
St Mary's of Kickapoo School
Edwards
Grade 5

Flowers

Flowers
Colorful, bright
Sprout, grow, bud, bloom, wither
Silky, velvety, flexible
Garden

Katilynn Kennedy
St Anthony's School
Streator
Grade 5

Basketball

I play basketball because it's cool,
this year, I played for my school.

It's not a really rough game,
if you're good, you'll find fame.

If you make a basket, it's 2 points,
if it's far enough, you'll get 3 points.

If you play hard and pass the test,
you will become the best.

Matthew Jarzynski
St Irene School
Warrenville
Grade 6

The Sandy Shore

Sand between my toes,
the fresh air up my nose,
walking along the sandy shore
along with my friend forever more
the two of us
walking along the sandy shore

Whitney Perry
Jonesboro Elementary School
Jonesboro
Grade 6

Farewell

Farewell to the 20th century
But please don't hurry
Through the 21st
We have learned many things
From technology, life, and even time
We will not stop learning
And use old knowledge
Farewell to the 20th century
With all we have learned and done
Farewell

Eric DiLegge-Castillo
Schiesher Elementary School
Lisle
Grade 5

The Mean Dragon

There once was a mean dragon,
purple, orange, and blue,
who lived in an apartment
on floor number two.

Her name was anonymous
and if you ask her why,
you'll have a black n' blue mark
'cause she'll punch you in the eye.

Victoria Cisek
St John Of The Cross School
Western Springs
Grade 5

Spring

Spring is a time for fun,
Playing with your friends,
Riding bikes and feeding ducks.
Spring is fun and I love spring.
That's why it is my favorite season.
Spring is a time when school is ending.

Dan Michalik
Most Holy Redeemer School
Chicago
Grade 5

My Friends

My friends are very nice.
We talk all day and night.
They call me in the morning
when the sun is very bright.
although they never call me late at night.
Sometimes when I cry,
They make me laugh inside.
I hope we never fight,
and always stay in sight.

Juliann Gusich
Our Lady of Mt Carmel School
Melrose Park
Grade 5

A Rainbow

In the sky
During rainy weather.
With many different colors.
Like red, orange, purple and blue.
The little raindrops
Reflect the light.
That makes such
A magnificent sight.

David Mihaila
Solomon Elementary School
Chicago
Grade 4

Sunrise

Fiery red
Pearly purple
Soft magenta
And golden yellow,

A bright yellow ball rises in the sky.
Puffy white clouds pass it by.
The sky is pale blue.
Here arrives the morning crew
And the beginning to a new day.

Sarah Treece
Iroquois West Upper Elementary School
Thawville
Grade 5

If I Could Change the World

If I could change the world,
I would get rid of drugs...
And guns would be no more.
There would be peace
Between all countries.
Everyone would share what he has
With those who have nothing at all.

If *I* could change the world!

Rabia Sadaqa
Solomon Elementary School
Chicago
Grade 4

Spring

S pring is my favorite season.
P retty flowers start blooming.
R ain comes and makes things grow.
I see more children playing outside.
N o more bad snow.
G reen grass starts sprouting.

Bridget Folliard
St John Fisher School
Chicago
Grade 4

Girls and Boys

Girls
Cute, sensitive
Caring, loving, smiling
Dreamy, awesome, dull, boring
Playing, fishing, racing
Handsome, rough
Boys

Jessica Krumrie
Manteno Middle School
Manteno
Grade 6

Wishes

Who cares about the world, right?
It's just our home, our base-sight.
Nothing to worry about, don't pout,
The world is nothing to cry about.
Our world is growing businesswise,
We worry about computer-eyes.
Do we care about our home,
About our sea, our land, our dome?
I don't think so, we don't yet,
We probably never will, I bet,
Until our world becomes a dump,
Where everything is just a lump,
From sitting playing computer games,
While you could be worrying about the plains.
Why not wish for the best,
To overcome all the rest,
To wish we had not been fools,
Worrying about our international duels.
We could be allies together, right?
To overcome this horrible fight.

Rebecca Schultz
West Middle School
Rockford
Grade 6

Penguins

Ever so gracefully across the ice,
Penguins waddle and slide so nice.
Heading towards the water, they say "Shake a Leg!
The last one in is a rotten egg!"

Ryan Rzeszutko
St George School
Tinley Park
Grade 6

Summer

Summer is my favorite season,
Because of this reason.
We go swimming in the summer,
When it rains it is a bummer.
I like this season,
Because of this reason.
We get out of school,
To play in a pool.
I like this season,
Because of this reason.
We go boating in the summer,
When our boat breaks down it's a bummer.
The reason I like this season,
Is because of all these reasons.

Jason Hill
New Hebron Christian School
Robinson
Grade 4

Dogs

Dogs
Fun, stupid
Barking, Rat Terrier, Rottweiler, Doberman Pinscher
Biting, growling, fighting
New, smart
Doghouse

Robert Cullison
Wells Elementary School
Grayville
Grade 5

That Special Someone

I will always remember,
watching the Cubs game in September.
It was so much fun,
seeing them hit homerun after homerun.
I watched them with that special someone.
She was just like my own mother,
and I always could hug her.
In December, she passed away,
and I still think of her every day.
I wonder if it will be the same,
as I watch all those Cub baseball games.
I will not cheer on my own,
for I know I will not be alone.
Yes, she is with me every day.
We will watch from different seats as the Cubs play.

Nicole Koehler
St Mary-Dixon School
Dixon
Grade 6

Brittney

Brittney likes
All bikes.

She is short and wears glasses
And in every grade she passes.

She has short hair and wears silver headbands.
She likes the Backstreet Boys for favorite band.

She wears colorful shirts
But never wears short skirts.

Brittney likes the candy Sweet Tarts
Her ears are pierced with hearts.

She has brown eyes
And they always spy.

Alisha Luebke
Okawville Grade School
Okawville
Grade 5

Fire

Hot burning logs
Ashes flying everywhere
Fire spreading quickly

Michael Waldo
Kellar Central School
Peoria
Grade 4

I Like to Play

My name is Robert
and I like to play.
I play basketball
and I'm always the same.
I play soccer
and I'm never so lame.
My name is Robert
won't you come and play?

Robert Rodarte
Nixon Elementary School
Chicago
Grade 5

Mom

My mom is so nice,
She's the best in the world,
She buys me cool stuff,
Even when she's real mad,
And she can get really mad.

Danny Roberts
Deer Creek-Mackinaw Middle School
Deer Creek
Grade 5

Independence

So many people went,
So little did return,
To their homelands,
Where they belong,
The bangs that were heard,
All of the cries of mercy,
Pleading to us,
Wars are dreadful,
But this one was our worst,
And our first,
All of the red,
Coats blood and all,
Bur our flag still stood tall,
We got what we deserved,
Freedom from the British,
No kings at all,
We shall always have that,
As long as our flag stands tall.

Kasey Kapitanek
Anderson Elementary School
St Charles
Grade 5

Anticipation*

The house is full of excitement
Tears of joy and fear roam through the air
Laughter and amazement shine through the eyes of those who look at his pictures
Guatemalan cultures and history becomes a part of our life
Children changing rooms
Cheerful decorations of colorful cars and cuddly animals brighten his room
A crib, a high chair, and a stroller fill the vacant corners of our house
Waiting for one important phone call
The anticipation will soon end and Samuel will be part of our family.

Cathy Gross
St Mary School
Alton
Grade 6
*Dedicated to Matt & Karen Gross

The Foxtrot

The music starts,
As the woman ice dancer skates with her heart.
She gracefully glides along with the steady Foxtrot song,
And smiles for it has been so long.

This woman met her partner who was her friend and husband many years ago,
And oh how on the ice they would lightly flow.
Her name, Eleanor and his, Ben,
Together their performances were worth a ten.

But the music and tens would stop soon,
For Ben was killed by a car under a full, dreadfully lit moon.
Oh how this mournful tragedy affected poor Eleanor,
But within her heart the memories and music would carry on forever more.

To this day Eleanor will remember the Foxtrot,
As she hears this musical dance play within her heart a lot.
For the Foxtrot dance was Ben and Eleanor's first,
And it was their last, but ice dancing for these two partners, friends, and lovers
Will forever be their thirst.

Alice Eileen Shallcross
St Irene School
Warrenville
Grade 6

Colorado

A lovely sight
A smear of colors—blue, gray, white and green
Seeing snow covered mountaintops high in the sky
Birds soaring through the bright sunlight
Hearing the sounds of birds chirping, waterfalls pouring, and coyotes howling
Smelling pine trees and wood burning
My trip to the Rocky Mountains

Jackie Dungan
Grand Prairie Elementary School
Joliet
Grade 4

Life

Life is like a pot of flowers
So full of many magic powers.

It makes you feel happy every day
It is a gift we should love and not throw away.

If we do not treat each other right
We have lost with no hope in sight.

Life is full of all sorts of greed
That we should not heed.

Sometimes we don't act as we should
And we turn to evil not good.

It is not a game to be thrown away
That is why we should care for each other
    each and every day!

Tim Lolley
St Mary School
Alton
Grade 6

Pool

In the summertime when it's hot,
I wake up and look forward to going to the pool a lot,
When the sun is hot and it makes me sweat,
I day-dream all morning until I can get wet,
The pool is great exercise by swimming a lap,
I know I can do it in a snap,
When my day of swimming comes to an end,
I dream about the pool and swimming again.

Sean Longton
St Irene School
Warrenville
Grade 6

Can You Capture a Star?

Can you capture a star,
Whether you're near or you are far.
A star is up in the sky
Or so you've been told
A star could be what you treasure,
Love or behold.
Shimmering and shining in the sky or your heart
Sometimes it's hard to be away or apart.
A star, a star, guides our way,
Through times of happiness and dismay.
So wherever or whoever you are
Do you have what it takes to capture a star?

Allison Hudson
Butterfield Elementary School
Libertyville
Grade 5

Flowers

Flowers are pretty.
Flowers smell good.
Flowers are the things that bloom
Outside when the time is right.
So listen up to what I have to say 'cause
Time is right for a bright and bloomy day.
Flowers are the things that make the sun bright.
Flowers are the things that stay up at night.
Flowers are pretty as you and me.
So that's what I have to say about flowers OK!
So if it's fine with me and fine with you,
So that's the story, that's what I have to say, OK!

Rebekah Andrews
Diekman Elementary School
Dolton
Grade 5

Earth

Earth is the third planet from the sun.
Some of the people who live on it aren't very fun.
People pollute the Earth every day.
In the future they will have to pay.

Every day the Earth gets warmer.
Some of the pollution is caused by farmers.
There is a hole in the ozone layer.
Some people blame their town mayors.

We should all take care of our fragile Earth.
The planet on which we were born at birth.
We all have to do our part to keep our planet clean.
I hope when you read this poem you see what I mean.

Aravind Bommiasamy
Northlawn Middle School
Streator
Grade 6

My Mother

My mother is sweet,
and very kind.
She gives me everything I ask for.
at the same time.
But when my behavior is out of control,
and I ask for something else,
she will not give it to me.
My mother is a very fair person.
And she doesn't play.
One thing about my mother that I really
like is how she takes very good care of us.
I love my mother very much.

Chastity Belton
Morton Career Academy
Chicago
Grade 6

What Is Black?

Black is an eight ball, opposite of light,
Black is a cave dark as night.
Black is death, black is evil,
Black is the color of a big black wheel.
Black is a cat, black is a crow,
Black is a bat, black is a bow.

Nathan Zarach
St. Richard School
Chicago
Grade 5

Out of the USA

Mountains, markets, arcades, beaches
People talking in another language
Green mountains
Blue sky
Yellow and gray clouds
Tacos, rice, enchiladas, cornbread
Sometimes wet because of all the rain
Mexico

Janessa Correa
Grand Prairie Elementary School
Joliet
Grade 4

There Is This Man

There is this man who is my friend,
He travels around from land to land.
He is a preacher,
Who preaches the Bible.
He is a teacher,
Who teaches what is valuable.
And that is what a real preacher is.

Bryant Attaway
New Hebron Christian School
Robinson
Grade 4

Green

Green's the fourth color
Of the rainbow.
It comes before blue
And it comes after yellow.
There are green grasses
And pens, and there are green ribbons
That you can win!
Doesn't the word "Green"
Have a wonderful ring?
Green's the most colorful,
Plentiful, fabulous thing!

Karlie Pleasant
Central Elementary School
Lincoln
Grade 6

What Is Blue?

Blue is the ocean
Blue is the sky that I see
Blue is my gym suit which I wear
My pen
My zipper case
My eyes when I am mad
My eyes when I am sad
Blue is the smell I smell
When I smell a blue flower
Blue is many, many things

Jessica Pitrowski
St. Richard School
Chicago
Grade 5

On the Sea

Sailing on the sea
It's like nothing's wrong
Nothing's going to happen
Going slowly in the water
Just thinking
Just wondering
Seeing the beautiful sky
With all different colors
You could be out there for hours
Just looking
Just staring

Melissa Robison
Tri-City Jr-Sr High School
Buffalo
Grade 6

Shane

His name
Is Shane.

His nickname is Baby Bubba Shane.
I go through work and pain.

He can be sweet, cute, funny, and loved
And just for doing that he gets hugged.

He is very tired
But isn't yet retired.

I tell him, "Time for bed!"
Then give him kisses on his head.

That is my brother;
I don't want another.

Amber Ganz
Okawville Grade School
Okawville
Grade 5

Fields

Fields, fields, fields, fields of dreams,
a place where dreams can come true,
a place to believe,
a place to love
a place to care,
a place to have fun.

Darryl Watkins
St James School
Rockford
Grade 5

Jennifer

J umping jack
E ducated
N ice
N ever gets in trouble
I ce cream is her favorite food
F antastic girl
E arly always
R eally friendly to my friends

Jennifer Robinson
Grand Prairie Elementary School
Joliet
Grade 4

Miles Away

I most think of you
When the sky is filled with stars
They shine and sparkle
As we grow miles apart

Anna Corcoran
Sycamore Trails Elementary School
Bartlett
Grade 6

Why People Like to Cry

People like to cry
cry, cry, cry
I don't know why people like to cry

They might cry in times of sorrow
hoping a better day will come tomorrow
that is one reason why
people like to cry

But instead, why can't people say hi
there is no reason why

So if you know, please tell me why
people cry

Jasper Taylor
Parker Jr High School
Flossmoor
Grade 6

School

Yellow bus
No fuss

Spelling, English, social studies, homework galore
Music, recess, art, and much more

Five days a week is much too long
Make it three and we'll sing a song.

One, two, three, four
Math never is a bore.

The best part is getting out
Go home! Play! Why not shout?

I see my friends
The fun never ends.

Kyle Meentemeyer
Okawville Grade School
Okawville
Grade 5

Spring

During the spring, you see lots of colors
Purple, green, yellow, and lots of others.

Spring is a time to have lots of fun.
You can enjoy the weather and the nice warm sun.

During the spring, you can hear the birds sing.
You can see the wonderful colors that the flowers bring.

Spring is a time to scream and shout.
And, that's what spring is all about.

Jamie Hertz
St Irene School
Warrenville
Grade 6

People

Around the world are people, like you or me
The people are all special,
As special as they could be
Around the world are people, caring, sharing, and good
Doing what God tells them
Trying as hard as they could
The people are in God's image
For example: you and me
We all live in this world together
As the happiest people could be

Bridget Garrity
St Philip the Apostle School
Northfield
Grade 5

The Game of Basketball

Basketball is an awesome sport,
It is for people who are tall and short.

There are rules you must follow in this game,
The referees are the ones to blame.

Boundary lines and technicals,
Fouls, turnovers, and time-outs called.

The team is in a huddle, the coach has a plan,
He names their plays, and calls in Stan.

Stan checks in, and hustles out,
And plays the game without a doubt.

He guards his man, like bees to honey,
He slam dunks the ball, and dances real funny.

Two points were scored down the floor,
Get the ball back and rally for more.

The scoreboard says, twenty to twenty,
Get that ball and score plenty.

The fans were roaring while we were scoring,
The team was hot, we could not be stopped.

We won the game, then hit the showers,
The coach came down with a bouquet of flowers.

Ryan Weppler
St John's Lutheran School
Buckley
Grade 6

Blue

Blue is like you're feeling down,
Blue as a queen's jeweled crown,
Blue is a really sad time,
It's feelings are like a mime.
Blue sounds like people crying,
But it looks like people trying,
And it tastes like rain on a warm spring day,
Trying to wash your troubles away.
The sky is blue,
And blueberries are too.

So think what things could happen to the world without blue,
Imagine what could happen to you.

Keep our world CLEAN!

Cynthia Leigh Gajeske
Hiawatha Elementary School
Kirkland
Grade 5

My Dog

My dog is very nice, caring, loving
Never bad.
That is why when she is limping
I'm very sad.
She loves to run
Playing ball and having fun,
And that's not all.
She's very athletic,
Jumping high and fetching sticks,
If we had a beach, I know she'd swim
All day playing fetch
And keep away.
Well that's
My dog through and
Through without my dog
I don't know what I would
Do. I love my dog.

Nic Tynczuk
Indian Knoll Elementary School
West Chicago
Grade 6

A Crime I Didn't Commit

I didn't do it, I'm innocent you know,
Don't arrest me, don't make me go,
Don't make me go to the judge,
I did not steal any fudge.
Please don't take me to jail,
Why do I have to eat out of a tin pail?
Why are you taking my blood cell?
Where are you taking it?
That is a crime I didn't commit.

Unique Goff
Plainfield Elementary School
Des Plaines
Grade 5

Outside

I see houses covered in white
some with wreaths, some with lights
It may be Christmas and time to share
but all I see are trees that are bare
Most of them covered in frost
because their leaves they have lost.

The snow covers the ground
and most everything around
Outside it may be cold
but here inside a blanket I hold
Oh, how I wish I could be home!

Brittany Bassett
St Mary-Dixon School
Dixon
Grade 6

My Dog Pooh

I have a dog whose name is Pooh
She likes to sit and stare at you.
She's a little dog with a lot of might.
She'll bark all day and sleep all night.
If you throw a toy, she'll start to run.
Playing with her is so much fun.

Sara Rakoczy
St Anthony's School
Streator
Grade 5

Yellow

The car is as yellow
as a ripe banana
that monkeys eat.

The sun is as yellow
as the butter we eat
on pancakes.

The Kool-Aid is as yellow
as the sour lemon
that is made into lemonade.

Zachary Jenskovec
St. Richard School
Chicago
Grade 5

Life/Death

Life
Good, sad
Interesting, long lasting, loving
Joyous, fun, nothingness, black
Frightening, decomposing, stinking
Cold, dark
Death

Jeanelle Nixon
Diekman Elementary School
Dolton
Grade 5

Horses

I got bucked off a horse.
It kinda hurt–of course.
I fell on the ground.
There were a lot of people around.
I never did cry.
The grass was still dry.
The horse was really bad.
Which made my dad mad.

Anthony Kaiser
Wells Elementary School
Grayville
Grade 5

Underwater

Children are like fish
swimming in the water,
playing and splashing
around each other.

Scuba divers under water
in the shiny suits sparkling,
are like scales of the fish
in the sun.

The waves of the ocean
sway me, like a wind
sways a little bird
that learns how to fly.

Edyta Slodyczka
St. Richard School
Chicago
Grade 5

Mom

My mom is hard working,
She supports us well,
If I'm sad she knows
How to perk me up so very well.

She's also on the go.
Junior League meetings
Work trips
Tribune meetings
And so much more.

But even so she's always there!

Drew Laue
Walker Elementary School
Evanston
Grade 5

Today and Tomorrow

There is always a today,
But it might not always be happy and gay,
There is always a tomorrow,
But it might be filled with sorrow,
There is always a today,
It's going to be happy and gay,
There is always a tomorrow,
It's not going to be filled with sorrow,
There's always a tomorrow and today,
Don't let it go by day by day.

Cara Feeney
St Matthew School
Champaign
Grade 4

Friends

Friends are people you count on.
Friends are people you care about.
Friends are people who can count on you.
Friends are people that help you out.
Friends are there to do you favors.
Friends can tell you any secret.
Friends can trust you in what all you are doing.
Friends are everything you need.

Lucas Minnich
Manteno Middle School
Manteno
Grade 6

Books

Books can take you to far off lands,
where kings rule the earth,
or where boats can fly.
Where a man is looking for one big whale,
or families are lost at sea on an isle.
But some bad things about books
are in this sentence right here,
some can be sad or full of fear.
Books can expand your imagination
because books make you think of thoughts
you never thought before.
Books are one of the best things in the world,
they can be fun or very funny or knowledgeable.
But one thing's for sure,
they're very interesting to read.

Brian Wendle
St Mary School
Alton
Grade 6

Summer

In the summer I can feel the hot sun,
I can smell the daisies and the woods.
I can hear dogs barking and children screaming,
I can hear the splash of water and children playing.

Whitney Cowdrey
New Hebron Christian School
Robinson
Grade 4

Football

Helmets collide;
The sound of shoulder pads hit (whoop, bam, crash!)
The receiver hits the ground like a rock (crack, smash!);
It's a touchdown; we win the game (woo, wow!)
The fans go wild.

Matthew Loepker
Beckemeyer Elementary School
Beckemeyer
Grade 4

My Dog Kiwi

One day I got a dog named Kiwi.
She was so small, I almost called her PeeWee.
Kiwi was tiny and, oh, so small.
You would have thought she was a little furball.
Her eyes and fur are very black.
Her fluffy tail even curls over her back.
Although she's a dog, she likes our cat.
When I give her a bath, she looks like a wet rat.
She's two years old now and is pretty big.
Sometimes when she eats, she looks like a pig.
I didn't know I could love a pet as much as I do,
But, Kiwi, I'm glad that I have you.

Rachel May
Wells Elementary School
Grayville
Grade 5

Edward

E ngineering
D oes the right thing
W orks hard every day
A nimal collector
R espects everyone in the family
D ouble-decker cookies n' cream milkshake for a snack

Eddie Montgomery
St John Of The Cross School
Western Springs
Grade 5

The Others

Have you ever thought about the others?
The others on the other side of the world.
They might be mean,
They might be nice,
They might be in between.
So have you ever thought of the others?

Adora Jones
Forest View Elementary School
Mount Prospect
Grade 4

Friends

My friends and I like to gab.
It does not matter if we are sad.
We like to party all night long.
We listen to our favorite songs.
E-mailing is quite fun.
Especially when you're online with someone.
We like to play many sports.
We love to play volleyball on court.

Tabitha Spencer
Wells Elementary School
Grayville
Grade 5

Flowers

Put seeds in the ground
If it rains the flowers will grow
The flowers look great
David Hunt
St John's Lutheran School
Buckley
Grade 5

Flowers

Through the meadow and over the hills,
There's roses, tulips, and daffodils.

Sunflowers in my garden,
Pansies in a vase,
They're so beautiful,
They put a smile on my face.

Blue ones, red ones, pink ones, yellows,
They're pretty enough for my fellows.

I want to cheer and say
"Hip, hip, hooray!"
If my mom asks for some
I'd say yes you may.
Shelly Warns
Westmore Elementary School
Lombard
Grade 4

Summary

Today, summer teased us.
She gave us warmth by the sun.
In the sun's baking glow,
Children went coatless and wore shorts.
Many walks were taken.
Elderly couples sat in the park.
People had picnics.
They played Frisbee with their dogs.
Children played tag and had fun.
Meanwhile summer had taken over, spring and winter fought.
March is a month when snow is melting
And flowers are just beginning to get ready for April.
Winter still wants his last lick,
While spring is very eager to begin.
Today we had our first of summer.
She has made us enjoy ourselves today.
Many will want this day to last forever.
This will not happen because spring will come
With her just-right temperature to make us not want summer to come.
But then summer will come, and once again,
We shall bask in summer's glow.
Elizabeth Bern
Parker Jr High School
Flossmoor
Grade 6

Silence

Silence is a sound itself,
an eerie sound.
Silence is a feeling,
suspicion.
Silence makes the clock tick louder,
silence is darkness.
Silence is an evil thing.
Julie Fry
Forest View Elementary School
Mount Prospect
Grade 4

Free

Soaring for miles and miles
My mind is flowing free
No hates,
no troubles,
while I'm flying over the sea.
But when I wake from
this wondrous sleep.
Everything will be different,
nothing will be free.
Jamie Schmidt
Indian Knoll Elementary School
West Chicago
Grade 6

On Buzz Saw Falls

I got in the cold damp seat.
It gave a kickoff and throws me back into my seat.
I was nervous by looking at the huge drop.
We went through fast rushing water. Waves were spattering me.
I got wet a little bit,
But I never threw a fit.
The ride started to pick up speed and in the woods we fled.
Around sharp turns, we flew under the bright blue sky.
We slowed down as we went up the hill.
The clanking tracks sounded like a clock.
We stopped at the top for others to go
As we watch their hats blow.
The tracks started clanking as we went up to the peak and stopped.
We heard a buzzer, and down we dropped.
Going down at what might appear
A speed so fast, the ground was getting near.
As the water grew closer, still I'd thought I would have to write my will.
When the ride was done,
I realized it was much fun.
I wish I could do it once more,
But waiting in the long line would be such a bore.
Matthew Tierney
Blessed Sacrament School
Belleville
Grade 6

The Contest

I've just won a contest
I've won 1st place
a long, sweet sounding, enjoyable song
I've played on my cornet
just Saturday morning
it seems as though I've just won a million dollars
though I haven't
it seems as though this poem is just about me
but it isn't
I couldn't have won if it hadn't been for all the people
working together to get the contest
plus there are the composers who wrote the songs
and the band teachers who taught the kids to play
so in a way, this poem is about me
and in a way it's not

Rebecca Tuley
Wells Elementary School
Grayville
Grade 5

Ruth

So sad
Not glad
And very bad
A friend gone
She lived so long.
She had to go.
We would not know.
For when she passed away
We went and mourned
And a new trust in God had formed
For all his love had seemed to drain.
She was like a grandma loving and warm.
I know I will miss her ever more.
Good-bye, good-bye, a mournful song.
Good-bye, good-bye to a loving lady, Ruth.

Amanda Stevenson
Nauvoo Elementary School
Nauvoo
Grade 6

My Big Brother

My big brother, better than no other
Cares, loves, joys, deals with all my noise
When I look around, he's always there
To be by my side, whenever I'm near
When I fall off track, he's always got my back
Crazy, you might say, he's always with my wicked way
My big brother, cares, loves, better than any other

Lindsay A. Dowdy
Diekman Elementary School
Dolton
Grade 5

A Soccer Ball

Black and white can give a fright,
Sometimes you're used at night.

Your checkered skin creates a bruise,
That kills the soul if you lose.

People do create a fuss,
When they're hit with a force like a bus.

Your patches cover your eyes,
So no one can see your cries.

It's only half time, you begin to weep,
You're only wish to go to sleep.

You hear a BOO from the crowd,
You see a player scream real loud.

You get a boot, it's just one on one,
You and the net, you have some fun.

You dodge the goalie, fake left then go right,
You see the nylon in sight.

You hit the net and touch the ground,
And then you see the goalie frown.

Finally the game is over !

Kyle Cassin
Kennedy Jr High School
Lisle
Grade 6

War

What is this world coming to?
We're fighting every day,
I wish an angel would come down and
take the weapons away.
We started out with arrows and now
we're up to nukes.
It seems that we're all madmen, about
to blow a fuse.
I did read in a book once, and it said
that it was so, only three minutes of peace
has been so of the globe.
I wish that war would vanish, into the
midst of air,
so only peace and harmony could be
found anywhere.

Troy Brundidge
Alexander G Bell Elementary School
Chicago
Grade 6

Late at Night

There was a poem that I had to write
So I waited until late at night.

I was going to write about birds,
But I couldn't think of any rhyming words.

I was going to write about my dad,
But that might make him mad.

So I finally got my homework done,
And it wasn't any fun.

Daniel Fuesz
McCray-Dewey School
Troy
Grade 5

My Family

The people who care for me,
Is my loving family,
It's me, dad, mom, and my brother,
That is it, there are no others,
I love them and they love me,
That is the way it will always be,
We are the Bournes family,
Just dad, mom, my brother, and me!

Justin Bournes
Marya Yates Elementary School
Matteson
Grade 6

My Brother Doesn't Frighten Me!

Screams and shouts...
So many pouts
My brother doesn't frighten me at all.

Pounding and yelling
Crying and sighing
My brother doesn't frighten me at all.

Getting his way;
Making my day
My brother doesn't frighten me at all.

Close to the wall,
Down the hall
My brother doesn't scare me at all.

Showing up everywhere —
Listening like a bear
My brother doesn't scare me at all.

My brother doesn't frighten me at all
Not at all
Not at all
My brother doesn't frighten me at all.

Kasia Sadlowski
Barbara B. Rose Elementary School
South Barrington
Grade 5

Index

Abene, Krissy 209
Adamji, Joseph 199
Adams, Brandyss 158
Adams, Christopher 89
Adcock, Amanda 110
Adefeso, Boye 294
Adorno, Dalina 187
Afante, Edwin 192
Aguilera, Laura 185
Ahmad, Sul 308
Aiken, Carmen 117
Ainge, Steven 308
Aiossa, Tessa 180
Alatorre, Jennifer 124
Albert, Savanah 166
Alderman, Chelsey 315
Aldridge, Tanya 99
Alexander, Julie 290
Ali, Zohaib 290
Allbee, Brittny 130
Allen, Alkedis E. 137
Allen, Emily D. 115
Allen, Marci 33
Allen, Rebecca 92
Almanza, Jessica 145
Altamirano, Rafael 45
Altamore, Anthony 56
Alvarez, Gena 163
Alvarez, Theresa 96
Amico, Gracey 34
Amstutz, Steve 31
Anders, Christa 270
Anderson, Brett 268
Anderson, Jessica 34
Anderson, Meagan 278
Anderson, Morgan 320
Anderson, Rachel 210
Andrews, Rebekah 325
Andriopoulos, Dena 172
Ansley, Megan 308
Araujo, Lyndi 267
Arellano, CJ 79
Arlen, Britt 137
Armbruster, Abbie 74
Arnold, Michael 274
Aronson, Alicia 299
Arroyo, Charlene 131
Ashmore, Joshua 218
Askew, Jesse 316
Atkinson, Michala 144
Attaway, Bryant 326

Atwell, Katy 157
Austin, Justin 179
Auth, Danielle 250
Autman, Destiny 235
Avila, Isis 81
Axel, Paul 249
Ayers, Kelly 305
Azar, Stephen 306
Bachmeyer, Karen 80
Baczewski, David 190
Bailey, Ricky 97
Baity, April 251
Baker, Breanna 311
Bakewell, Zack 299
Baldwin, Tyler 236
Ball, Erin 119
Ballard, Ryan 109
Ballou, Nicole Michelle 268
Balsam, Caitlin 80
Baltierrez, Jose 33
Baltimore, Loren 170
Bangert, Jennifer M. 31
Barbaro, Christina 316
Barker, Mike 130
Barlow, Andy 304
Barnard, Kin 268
Barnhart, Claire 264
Bassett, Brittany 328
Bauer, Alyssa R. 238
Bauer, Brian 209
Bauer, Tim 244
Bauman, Travis 169
Baumgartner, Alice 250
Bayan, Diahann 129
Bayley, Kimberly 46
Beals, Marci 145
Bean, Loralea 234
Beard, Jenny 296
Beard, Victor Q. Jr. 257
Becherer, Kendra 38
Bechtel, Alyssa 129
Becker, Brittany 44
Becker, Jake 20
Becker, Jessa 169
Bedeker, Jenny Louise 134
Beedie, Chris 315
Behrns, Kim 132
Bellgardt, Brittany 95
Bellinder, Jaclene 218
Bellis, Alicia 62
Belsky, John 203

Belton, Chastity 325
Benegas, Matt 320
Bennison, Jenna 288
Benson, Hannah 260
Berens, Mitch 167
Berg, Christine 111
Berghuis, Lindsay 263
Bergmann, Amber 294
Bern, Elizabeth 330
Bernhardt, Rebecca L. 308
Berns, Greg 253
Berry, Bob 20
Berry, Kristina M. 99
Berry, Nicole 55
Berry, Nikki 21
Berry, Sarah 268
Bert, Danielle 210
Beversdorf, Walter 302
Beyer, Alexis 58
Bhambri, Amit 31
Bialon, Darek 199
Biljan, Mirjana 123
Binder, Rob 292
Bird, Brittany 260
Biszewski, Matt 78
Bittle, Ryan 185
Black, Angela 102
Blackburn, Erin 171
Blackburn, Nicole 156
Blake, Bridget 185
Blake, Dan 123
Blank, Alexander 274
Blank, Samantha 159
Blaskey, Laura A. 283
Blatcher, DeAngelo 316
Blevons, Taylor 305
Blickhan, Synimin L. 92
Blumenstein, Kory 147
Blumstein, Jason 303
Bock, Katy 144
Boeger, Kasey 156
Bollinger, Jill 107
Bommiasamy, Aravind 325
Bonadonna, Michela 104
Bonds, Kristin 130
Bonheim, Christine 46
Bonner, Brandi Elaine 307
Booth, Brady 307
Borczon, Erik 132
Born, Matthew 18
Borst, Lauren 114

Boshart, Mace 16
Bosley, Amanda C. 200
Bounds, Heather 48
Bourland, Miranda 250
Bournes, Justin 332
Bouzi, Antoine 242
Bowers, Dave 100
Bowers, Roddrick 220
Boyd, Alexandria 319
Boyer, Brysta 308
Boyer, Sheila 275
Boysen, Amy 63
Bradley, Stefanie 98
Bradshaw, Marcus 268
Brady, Laura 256
Brady, Meaghan 176
Bragagnolo, Eric 77
Brall, Sara 244
Brandon, Jenna 300
Brandt, Liz 241
Brankin, Dave 295
Branson, Krista 146
Brant, Amanda Rose 140
Braun, Caleb 309
Brennan, Sean 293
Brickeen, Eddie 289
Bridgeman, Amanda 22
Brisuela, Anthony 56
Brooke, Stephanie 183
Brooks, Ashley Dawn 100
Brosius, Jacqueline 294
Brosnan, Kathleen 300
Brouette, Belinda 98
Brown, Candace 151
Brown, Danielle 105
Brown, Eboni 281
Brown, Heather 306
Brown, Jessica 313
Brown, Karissa 146
Brown, Nicholas 293
Brown, Rebecca 267
Brown, Whitney T. 193
Browning, Ashley 35
Brownless, Angela 131
Brundidge, Troy 331
Bruno, Patrick 137
Brush, Levi 241
Bryant, Mark 168
Brzozowski, Annette 209
Buckley, Bridget 265
Buhl, Philip 94
Buhle, John 88
Buhrke, Gretchen 266
Bumpus, Jim 37
Burke, Deirdre 274
Burzynska, Natalia 276
Buttle, Brittany 134

Cabanas, Kristal 155
Cabrera, Santos 205
Cacho, Danny 174
Cadwallader, Kerri 72
Caesar, Jamie 240
Cahue, Daniella 257
Calderone, Jesus 256
Caldwell, Paris 310
Camacho, Diana 206
Camacho, Rosa 297
Campbell, Marsean 45
Campos, America 113
Campos, Jonathan 92
Cane, Chrissy 76
Capron, Marcy 195
Cardella, Andrew J. 82
Carey, Brendan 289
Carlson, Justin 26
Carnahan, Kayla 264
Carpio, Marybel 161
Carrillo, Daisy 152
Carrizalez, Alejandra 197
Carroll, Jennifer 93
Carter, Kimberly 201
Carter, Shannon 276
Cartmill, Emily 267
Casey, Erin 267
Casey, Linda 82
Cashman, Emily 246
Cashman, Jacob 317
Cassin, Kyle 331
Cassista, Lisa 162
Cast, Crystal 301
Castillo, Andrew 136
Castle, Jesse 272
Castle, Nini 101
Castle, Shimon 280
Castro, Trevor 90
Caswell, Amber 174
Catlett, Alyssa 272
Caufield, Heath 117
Cearlock, Brad 32
Ceja, Desiree 143
Ceja, Guadalupe 101
Cesario, Tara 231
Chambers, Matt 275
Chamness, Blake 156
Chamness, Sarah 149
Champlain, Liam 286
Chapman, Lauren 249
Chavez, Kenia 192
Chazaro, Christian 183
Cheatom, Briana Chelsi 118
Cherry, Benjamin 6
Chhotani, Benazir 217
Chimino, Gina 120
Chmura, Mark 140

Christensen, Dane 136
Christison, Amanda 314
Ciardullo, Annamarie 213
Cicciarelli, Nick 138
Cimino, Alex 115
Ciomag, Estera 157
Cisek, Victoria 322
Cisneros, Guadalupe 22
Clancy, Caitlin 306
Clancy, Patrick 278
Clark, Candice 314
Clark, Stephanie 318
Clarkson, Megan 151
Clawson, Carissa 297
Cohen, Stacey 142
Cole, Ashley 178
Cole, Jame 123
Collier, Marvin 167
Collins, Aly 154
Comiskey, Bridget K. 126
Condon, Cara 101
Condon, Carly 305
Condon, Molly 272
Conlan, Tom 254
Conlin, Jessica 94
Conlon, Devin 106
Connell, Meghan 310
Conner, Julie 104
Cook-Banks, Tasheka 84
Cooling, Nate 250
Cooney, Michael 204
Corcoran, Anna 326
Corpus, Angela 39
Corradetti, Katie 287
Corral, Vanessa 234
Correa, Janessa 326
Corso, Alicia 75
Corzine-Migdow, Elizabeth 168
Cosgrove, Molly 139
Cotterman, Emily 213
Coulter, Andrea 234
Covaliu, Anca 277
Cowdrey, Whitney 329
Coy, Linus 133
Crawford, April 320
Creasey, Steven 192
Crinion, Julie 184
Cronin, Caitlin 235
Crosier, Stephanie 297
Crouch, Angelica 317
Cruse, Lauren Faye 42
Cruz, Maggie 218
Cudiamat, Nicole 73
Cuevas, Maria 304
Cullen, Colleen 155
Cullison, Robert 323
Cummings, Stephanie 84

Cunningham, Jemia 152
Cunningham, Raechal 179
Curboy, Mark 312
Curia, Mandie 132
Curran, Adam 298
Curry, Erica 273
Cusanelli, D.C. 260
Cuzzone, Francesca 140
D'Antonio, Joseph 150
Dacanay, Sean 82
Dailey, Craig 236
Dalessandro, Amanda 317
Dam, Kevin 271
Damato, Ashley 198
Dameron, Tyler 313
Daniell, Liberdy 286
Daniels, Greg 237
Dart, Ryan 248
Daum, Rachel 235
Davids, Samantha 321
Davila, Chris 154
Davis, Kelly 17
Davis, Kimberly 90
Davis, Missi 272
Davis, Wesley 121
Day, Emma 320
De Leon, Alysia 282
De Leon, Brian 319
Deacon, Kevin 278
Dearing, Joshua 39
Debes, Pier T.C. 221
Dedick, Kelly 315
Dee, Patrick 275
DeFrees, Reece 34
Degner, Tim 26
Deitz, Chelsea 157
Delaney, Erin 183
Delaney, Shannon A. 144
Dembkowski, Daniel J. 140
Dennis, Jaleigh 27
Desillier, Geoff 98
Dettmann, Amy 97
Devereux, Lisa 242
DeWitt, Michael 314
Diaz, Karina 128
Diaz, Ulysses 133
Dickerson, Alyssa 207
DiFulvio, Alexandra 318
DiLegge-Castillo, Eric 322
Dill, Ashley 33
Dimiropoulos, Ted 205
Dixon, Lauren 96
Dola, Adam 91
Dolan, Colin 153
Dolan, Danny 133
Don, Brent 174
Donahue, Lauren 125

Donahue, Mason 193
Donovan, Brian 128
Doolan, Mike 239
Dorman, Dave 193
Dorney, Greston 156
Dorworth, Mandi 234
Doty, Matthew 260
Dow, Mike 298
Dowdy, Lindsay A. 331
Drag, Chris 127
Drago, Matt 119
Dresner, Daniel 200
Drew, Thurayya 310
Droba, Walter 112
Drone, Stephanie 199
Dubree, Kelsey 277
Ducey, Austin 89
Dudlo, Adrienne 85
Duff, Chris 289
Duffey, Curran 84
Dulin, Brad 287
Duncan, Beth 7
Dungan, Jackie 324
Dunlap, Katy 283
Dunne, Molly 174
Duran, Anaese 242
Duran, Nicole 192
Durgin, Jackie 109
Dyas, Rebecca 174
Dzura, Vicki 129
Echeverria, Elizabeth 269
Eck, Brittany 91
Eck, Mary 132
Eck, Teresa 320
Edidin, Samantha M. 250
Edmonson, Danielle 147
Edwards, David 86
Edwards, Tara 207
Eggleston, Kyle 242
Eilers, Dustin 237
Ekstrom, Mary 150
Elam, Amos 284
Elizondo, Fransisca 285
Elledge, Jamie 53
Elliott, Matthew 271
Emlund, Tyler 188
Emmons, Margaret 143
England, Lindsey 311
English, Alexander 239
Epperson, Leroy 214
Erickson, David 84
Ervin, Kristi 164
Esquivel, Erik 286
Esrig, Valerie 58
Essenberg, Kathleen E. 110
Evans, Shauntia 188
Evans-Becker, Jessica 307

Ewell, Heather 213
Exposito, Jessica 108
Faculak, Natalie 252
Fagan, Bridget 118
Fan, Joyce 222
Fanucchi, Christina 233
Farrell, Quinn 317
Farris, Aaron 37
Faulkner, Alex 264
Fears, Jovon 247
Feazel, Fallon 86
Feeney, Cara 328
Fehrenbacher, Katie 234
Feicco, Thomas 272
Feighery, Ross E. 144
Feliciano, Alicia 298
Fenton, John 269
Fiedler, Marci 25
Fields, Emily 216
Fine, Katie 106
Fink, Kaitlin 223
Fischer, Paul 208
Fisher, Erin 202
Fisher, Jessica 196
Fisher, Molly 270
Fitzgerald, Elizabeth 142
Fitzgerald, Jennifer 137
Fitzpatrick, Jenny 167
Fleck, Justin 267
Fleming, Kellye 152
Flinn, Robert 51
Flood, Moira 103
Flores, Albert 79
Flores, Bridget 273
Flores, Jeanette 151
Flores, Ricardo 154
Flores, Valentina Lisa 143
Flowers, Sam 257
Foat, Katie 114
Fogarty, Kristeen 253
Fogerty, Ryan 87
Folliard, Bridget 322
Folz, Kathryn E. 253
Fonner, Heather 43
Fontanetta, Jackie 102
Force, Megan 272
Fortuna, Nicole 306
Fortune, Ariel 129
Foster, James 292
Foster, Shannon 121
Fourman, Karissa 214
Fournie, Lauren 189
Fouts, Elizabeth 142
Fouts, Jenny 27
Fox, Lauren 197
Frame, Andrew 290
Francis, Carrie 161

Franciscovich, Talisa 176
Frankel, Layla 316
Frantz, Carl 260
Frazier, Omari 121
Frederick, Amanda 208
Frederick, Toni 279
Fricks, C.J. 244
Fried, David 284
Fries, Matt 178
Friestad, Jared 36
Fritz, Dana 8
Fry, Julie 330
Fuesz, Daniel 332
Fujinaka, Amy 160
Fulton, Ari 171
Furkert, Karen 108
Furrow, Brent 18
Futch, DeAngela 277
Fuzak, Travis 145
Gabel, Amanda Danielle 204
Gaeta, Jessica 92
Gaines, Crystal 148
Gajeske, Cynthia Leigh 327
Galbavy, Patricia 24
Gallagher, Meghan 193
Gamber, Melissa 296
Ganz, Amber 326
Garcia, Adrian 172
Garcia, Benny 185
Garcia, Crystal 204
Garcia, Elvis 119
Garcia, Rogelio 88
Gard, Sarah 132
Garduno, Dulce 47
Garofolo, Jeffrey 31
Garrett, Katelyn 268
Garrity, Bridget 327
Garwood, Jamie 317
Gattis, Meagan 314
Gaytan, Arianna 290
Genge, Margaret 100
Gette, Matt 200
Gewarges, Maryann 290
Gher, Griffin 186
Gibbins, Danielle 290
Giblin, Betsy 131
Gielow, Ben 298
Gilbert, Chrissy 252
Gilbert, Kari 41
Gildehaus, Andrew 239
Gill, Emmy 53
Gillott, Michael 144
Gilman-Smith, Alex 75
Gilpin, Randy 257
Gimber, Eric 23
Ginsburg, Raphael 46
Giovannini, Rachel 316

Gish, Jonathan 77
Giza, Jennifer 161
Gluskin, Karen 292
Gnaedinger, Deanna 120
Goad, Sarah C. 215
Goedeke, Nichole 91
Goelz, Matt 115
Goetz, Amanda 181
Goff, Unique 328
Golchert, Ana 83
Goldenstein, Joel 250
Gomez, Jerry 162
Gonzalez, Luis 206
Gonzalez, Melissa 76
Good, Eleanor 247
Gosewehr, Alison 114
Gosewehr, William 95
Gotsis, Gregory 259
Goutos, Bianca 248
Gracia, Vanessa 76
Grady, Emily 190
Grady, Mary Beth 111
Graff, Nyssa 136
Graham, Sherry 308
Grandsart, Doug 159
Grandt, Sarah 93
Grant, Eboney 216
Grant, Mike 47
Grathler, Cory 105
Graves, Dameon 132
Green, Katelyn 287
Green, Michelle 141
Greenland, Elizabeth 208
Greentree, Logan 180
Grenning, Alyssa 32
Grentz, Kevin 171
Griffin, Dan 94
Grigg, Sarah 74
Grismanauskas, Julie 270
Groleau, Shireen 24
Gross, Cathy 324
Gross, Chris 34
Gross, Kathy 42
Gruba, Gabriel M. 112
Grujic, Bora 162
Grunloh, Danielle 254
Guallpa, Edgar 198
Gudewicz, Molly 165
Guerrero, Jose 279
Guess, Krystina 296
Guinid, Cherisse 203
Guizar, Stephanie 175
Gumm, Emily 248
Gunsalus, Kearney 33
Gurley, Rachel 188
Gusich, Juliann 322
Guthrie, Joey 215

Gutierrez, Seth 119
Gutierrez, Vanessa 197
Gutierrez, Yessenia 280
Guyer, Dessa Mae 175
Guzman, Lesly 74
Haas, Lisa Marie 30
Hacker, Lisa M. 49
Hackley, Andy 182
Hackley, Peter 280
Haeger, Valerie 189
Hagerman, Jamie 196
Haine, Joseph 265
Haine, Thomas 78
Hales, Molly 109
Halfpap, Rachel 82
Hall, Amy 153
Hall, Ashley 110
Hall, Kayla 79
Hall, Simone 279
Hall, Tiffany 230
Hallin, Sean 282
Halvorsen, Mallory 272
Han, James 56
Hand, Cody 100
Haney, Robert E. 183
Haney, Semaja 178
Hanik, Colby M. 48
Hankins, Erika 301
Hanlon, Terrence 125
Hannon, Heidi 105
Hansen, Dane 215
Hansen, Josh 74
Hanson, Lauren 19
Hare, Brittany 98
Harl, Jessica 173
Harmony, Erica 162
Harper, Malerie 29
Harrington, Caitlin 247
Harrington, Kelsey 311
Harrington, Maura 243
Harris, Nichole 268
Hartmann, Kristina 190
Hartnett, Arthur 72
Harvey, Lauren 89
Harweger, Jerica Lynn 236
Hasten, Jaimie 116
Hatzfeld, Cassandra 26
Hauffe, Drew 110
Hawkins, Ben 135
Haxel, Connor 298
Hayes, Ashley 180
Haynes, Brittney M. 245
Heafner, Tim 130
Hefner, Cal 127
Helfrich, Jeff 321
Helie, Daniel 73
Helmerichs, Ryan 124

Helsel, Anya 92
Henderson, Josh 316
Hendricks, Dusti Rose 206
Hendrix, Leslie 33
Hennessy, Elizabeth 113
Henrichs, Ashley 32
Henry, Allison 256
Henry, Jillian 293
Henry, Jon 180
Henson, Caitlin 245
Herbst, Grace 249
Herdes, Ryan 18
Hernaez, Joy 149
Hernandez, Alyssa 276
Hernandez, Jacqueline 244
Hernandez, Yvonne 104
Herrington, Kevin 103
Herskovic, Alex 64
Hertz, Jamie 327
Hesselbacher, Erin Louise 74
Hesselbacher, Michael 77
Hetrick, Lauren 251
Hickey, Samantha 244
Hicks, April 117
Hileman, Mandy 262
Hill, Angela 128
Hill, Jason 323
Hillman, Jim 198
Hilton, Ezra 107
Hinders, Christiana 266
Hinders, Maria 311
Hines, Hannah 177
Hitch, Ashley 282
Hochstetter, John 237
Hoeflich, Jacquie 286
Hoerr, Greg 247
Hoffman, Jessica 173
Hoffman, Rachael 194
Hoffmann, Chris 105
Hogg, Patrick 160
Hohenberger, Kurt Nicholas 113
Holcomb, Katie 203
Holcomb, Michael 236
Hollis, Kathryn 107
Hollock, Chris 198
Holm, Christine 276
Holman, Scott 26
Holmes, Michael 274
Holt, Cassie 255
Holtgrave, Amber 90
Homa, Emily 216
Hommadova, Anna 197
Hood, Shane P. 56
Hopkins, Mark 164
Hopp, Ashley 31
Hosty, Jean 156
Houpy, Candace 169

House, Jessica 164
Houston, Tamika 206
Howard, J.C. 40
Howard, Jason 140
Howard, Katherine 197
Howerton, Ashley 105
Hubbard, Mallory 94
Huber, Stacey 9
Hudkins, J. Taylor 301
Hudson, Allison 325
Hudziak, Ken 214
Huerta, Miguel 274
Hughes, Collene 172
Hughes, Danielle 277
Huiras, Nicole 120
Hunsinger, Tyler 231
Hunt, David 330
Hunt, Virginia 18
Hunter, Brandon 213
Hunter, Kristin 40
Hussain, Amara 141
Hutchings, Angie 155
Hutchison, Liz 96
Hutchison, Megan 194
Hutson, Megan 196
Hutton, Giana 307
Hyle, Amanda 310
Hyser, Natalie Lauren 22
Ianno, Aaron 92
Icalia, Vincent 97
Ince, Brittany 166
Ithal, Jeff 192
Izzo, Ellenia 136
Jacklin, Andrew 279
Jackson, Danny 106
Jackson, George Douglas III 125
Jackson, Marquis 148
Jackson, Sparkle 202
Jacobs, Emily 38
Jacques, Marilyn 242
Janes, Melissa 224
Jankowski, Jacqueline 225
Jansen, Ashley 103
Jansen, Kaitlyn 309
Jansky, Natalie 256
Jarema, Meghan 261
Jarzynski, Matthew 322
Javid, Kulsum 168
Jefferson, Katrina 272
Jenkins, Mike 254
Jennrich, Adam 54
Jensen, Erik 261
Jenskovec, Zachary 328
Jerome, Aubree 254
Jewell, Michael 171
Jiang, Jason 266
Johnson, Aaron 244

Johnson, Amber 237
Johnson, Brittany 126
Johnson, Jacob 256
Johnson, Karena 112
Johnson, Lorraine 58
Johnson, Michelle 92
Johnson, Nicole 106
Johnson, Suzi 308
Johnson, Tiffany 88
Johnston, Emily 182
Jones, Adora 329
Jones, Andy 250
Jones, Gregory 155
Jones, Markeisia 100
Jones, Tanishia M. 82
Jones, TaSheka 36
Jones, Tiffany 260
Jordan, Amy 79
Jordan, Robin 55
Joyce, Sinclaire 262
Judy, Sean 144
Julstrom-Agoyo, Wade 264
Kadakia, Jina 127
Kaiser, Anthony 328
Kaiser, Margaret 154
Kakumanu, Ruth 287
Kalmer, Travis 246
Kaminski, Kristen 37
Kampwerth, Danny 245
Kania, Laurie 113
Kantor, Crystal 119
Kapitanek, Kasey 324
Kaplan, Andrea 179
Kaplan, Stephanie 207
Kariott, Carla 314
Kash, Kristy 17
Kasperowicz, Matt 211
Kasson, Erin 274
Kato, Paul 253
Keane, Jacqueline 244
Keefe, Erin 55
Keefe, Tom 43
Keener, Andrew 321
Keigher, Rory 274
Keiss, Billy 240
Kellett, Jackie 156
Kellogg, Annie 255
Kelly, Brenna 198
Kelly, Bridget 238
Kelly, Lauren 294
Kelly, Mike 74
Kelly, Pat 116
Kelm, Jennifer 99
Keltner, Danielle 254
Kenealy, John 253
Kennedy, Clare 192
Kennedy, Katilynn 322

Kerber, Troy 167
Kerr, Kim .78
Kersey, Lisa 168
Ketterman, Larry 176
Keturi, Caitlin 244
Key, Charlene 291
Kilbride, Laura 159
Kile, Danielle 314
Kile, Dustin 29
Kim, Danny 57
Kincheloe, Whitney 236
Kindgren, Danny 129
King, Danielle 189
King, Desireé 309
King, Drew 46
King, Ronald 212
Kingman, Karleen 211
Kinney, Jennafer 181
Kinney, Kenan 304
Kinzel, Kara 65
Kipnis, Innessa 298
Kipping, Matt 298
Klein, Emily 116
Klein, Steven 281
Klostermann, Jonathon 185
Klostermann, Kyle 75
Knap, Margaret 127
Knisley, Rachel 254
Knoll, Ryan 126
Koblitz, Aimee 41
Koch, Susan 50
Koehler, Mike 299
Koehler, Nicole 323
Koerkenmeier, Lacey 314
Koester, Andy 112
Kofkin, Perri 234
Koganzon, Rita 138
Konow, Matt 176
Kopel, Catrina 191
Kopitke, Lauren 141
Kouba, Martin 203
Kraudel, Justin 57
Kreger, Chris 300
Krengel, Sunni 249
Krey, Mackenzie 262
Kroeplin, Kelli 191
Krol, Natasha 175
Krueger, Brian 25
Kruger, Kiley 262
Krumrie, Jessica 322
Kruszka, Andrea 196
Krystof, Emily 95
Kubal, Kristina 285
Kuchta, Meghan 261
Kuester, Kaila 295
Kuhl, Emily 260
Kunath, Kurtis 80

Kunke, Ashley 300
Kurt, Sarah 149
Kurtz, Steven 108
Kusar, Amelia 177
Laba, Kathy 230
LaBracke, Catie 21
LaMountain, Christie 177
Lampert, Amanda 126
Lancaste, Kelly 272
Lander, Eric 285
Lang, Brian 108
Lanter, Brian 216
Larkin, Casey 248
Larson, Jeremy 124
Larson, Richard 195
Laschinski, Garrett 17
Lasenby, Jonath 284
Laslie, Loren 188
Laue, Drew 328
Lauer, Dave 259
Lavitt, Adam 54
Laxpati, Leela 181
Lazar, Amy 32
Lazarus, Greg 86
Leach, Brittany 137
Leach, Megan 150
Leahy, Amy 132
Leahy, Megan 74
Leal, Jessica 254
Leamen, Alex 111
Lechner, Eric 248
Ledermann, Sara 41
Lee, Arthur 243
Lee, David 304
Lee, Jennifer 318
Lee, Rebecca 274
Lehner, John 142
Leinweber, Roy 202
Lembeck, Ariel 143
Lemons, Stephen 256
Lence, John 80
Leon, Jennifer 258
Leonard, Jamie 284
Leonard, John 52
Lessenberry, Rebecca 247
Levinzon, Olga 36
Lewis, Mandy 232
Lewis, Peter 195
Lewis, Victoria 181
Liametz, Samantha 276
Lievers, Ashley 200
Lima, Luigy 304
Lindholm, David 250
Lindsay, Rachel 43
Lindsey, Ashley 86
Lisch, Kevin 151
Lisch, Theresa 300

Liss, Allie .285
Litteken, Jamie 313
Little, Charcie 288
Little, Latariah 183
Littrell, Annie 256
Livingston, Abigail 242
Lizasuain, Priscilla 168
Ljubicic, Areta 47
Lo Destro, Grant 112
Loepker, Matthew 329
Logsdon, Amanda 132
Lolley, Tim 325
Longton, Brett 313
Longton, Sean 325
Loomba, Nikhila 87
Loomis, Tim 304
Lopez, Danny 147
Lopez, Priscilla 256
Lorch, Marinne 35
Losh, Kristina 204
Love, Kiani 273
Lovrant, Candice 158
Lowe, Jessica 281
Lowe, Tanya 99
Lowenstein, Sarah 212
Lowery, Bryan 291
Loy, Dennis 147
Lucas, Brittany 278
Lucas, Melanie 210
Ludden, Caitlin 199
Ludwigson, Tim 238
Luebbers, John 150
Luebbers, Theresa 160
Luebke, Alisha 323
Luevano, Juan 59
Luksic, Nina 318
Lupsha, Megan 134
Lynch, Jack 316
Lynch, Jessica 304
Mack, Chris 260
Mackley, Andrea 279
Mackowiak, Brittany 271
Madden, Bridget 186
Magat, Michelle 238
Maggio, Richard 135
Magnafici, Jaime 297
Magnusen, Chelsea 189
Mahan, Erin 248
Majka, Brittany 279
Makol, Jennifer 187
Maldonado, Mayra 296
Maldonado, Nicole 156
Maloy, Molly 174
Malycheva, Kira 138
Malzow, Angela 202
Manatt, Maryann 260
Mangum, Ashley 198

Manos, Norman 320
Manus, Sam 166
Marchese, Nick 274
Marcinkowska, Maggie 150
Marcolini, Jonathon 310
Marks, Ashley 295
Marler, Jessica 92
Marquez, Enedelia 81
Marquez, Julian 142
Marrs, Sarah 39
Mars, Ashley 139
Marshall, Amanda 76
Marshall, Danielle 241
Marshall, Sarah 205
Martens, Lauren 304
Martens, Luke 320
Martin, Angel 83
Martin, Cecilia 98
Martin, Cian 254
Martin, Julie 28
Martin, Madeline Anne 309
Martin, Mike 292
Martin, Philip 158
Martinez, Alma 217
Martinez, Elizabeth 48
Marzullo, Kimberly 292
Mashak, Jenna 118
Mater, Stephanie 319
Mathew, Ashley 270
Matias, Michael Q. 106
Matthews, Christopher 239
Mattison, Kristen 262
Mauhar, David 291
Maurer, Emily 320
May, Rachel 329
Mazzone, Mia 309
McAlpin, Jessica 209
McAlpine, Shannon 109
McAnelly, Jim 76
McBride, Angela 232
McBride, Tom 191
McCabe, Marin 124
McCall, Sarah 164
McCann, Aaron 242
McCann, Sean 160
McCarthy, Brett David 20
McCarthy, Liz 54
McCarty, Ashley 135
McClain, Emily 231
McClure, Chad 316
McCorkle, Rebecca 58
McCrary, Nathan 106
McDermott, Brittany Leigh 305
McDonald, Jessica 263
McDonald, Sade 125
McGee, Josh 312
McGhghy, Kristen 128

McGinnis, Amanda 235
McGowan, Steve 252
McGrath, Tom 45
McGuire, Lauren 207
McGurk, Brendan 100
McHugh, Patrick 168
McIntosh, Ian 145
McKay, Kyle 278
McKee, Charia 286
McKeever, Samantha 296
McKinley, Kristen 143
McLaughlin, Cassie 126
McLaughlin, Matt 125
McMillan, Nathan 20
McMillen, Megan 94
McNees, Brian 76
McNerney, Kevin 303
McNichols, Dustin 208
McShane, Katy 154
Meade, Andrea 178
Mears, Erin 204
Medsker, Morgan 52
Meehling, Amanda 23
Meentemeyer, Kyle 327
Meglio, Amy 19
Meier, Amanda 90
Meier, Carmen 147
Meirink, Erin 39
Meischner, Danielle 256
Melendez, Jazmin 52
Mellen, Jocelyn 287
Mellon, James 150
Mendez, Osvaldo 104
Mercado, Yolanda 286
Metz, John 240
Meyer, Billie 186
Meyer, Carrie 239
Meyers, Gerald 88
Michalczyk, Nicole 66
Michalik, Dan 322
Mihaila, David 322
Mihaljevic, Christina 149
Milender, David 79
Miles, Seth 29
Miletic, Katarina 260
Miller, Matt Lee 104
Miller, Pat 259
Milligan, Jessica 134
Minard, Aaron 273
Minard, Rachel 217
Minneci, John 132
Minnich, Lucas 329
Minor, Michael 190
Mitchell, Anthony 40
Mitchell, Katey 115
Mitchell, Meghan 261
Mitchell, Melanie 313

Mlot, Andrea 186
Moats, Shaun 211
Mocodeanu, Mary 155
Molitor, Margaret E. 284
Molk, Brittany 315
Mondane, Brittany 213
Monson, Britta 256
Monson, Sara 308
Montez, Diane 186
Montgomery, Eddie 329
Moody, Crystal 275
Moore, Amy 50
Moore, Molly F. 170
Moore, Nick 42
Morales, Angelica 198
Morales, Karen 180
Morales, Matthew 268
Moran, Christina 187
Moran, Leticia 114
Moreno, Andrea 286
Morgan, Cara L. 201
Moritz, Elizabeth 41
Morland, Brita E. 238
Morris, Amber 83
Morrison, Catherine 18
Moses, Karabeth 292
Mottet, Trae 265
Moya, Roy 245
Mucker, Clare 118
Mueller, Melanie 259
Muellner, Lauren 75
Mueth, Jonathan 189
Mulcahy, Jimmy 233
Mullen, Claire 238
Mullen, Emily 244
Mullins, Katie 96
Mulrooney, Melissa A. 206
Munoz, Eden 284
Munster, Kaela 312
Murphy, Becky 137
Murphy, Chelsea 78
Murphy, Mike 196
Murphy, Samantha 86
Murphy, Shannon 285
Murray, Jamie 317
Murray, Nick 212
Murrell, Angela 170
Muscarello, Andy 271
Musielak, Matthew 59
Musso, Maggie 296
Myer, Marcus 254
Myers, Peter 138
Naber, Andrew 290
Nagelli, Chris 101
Naughton, Shaila 273
Neal, Jonathon 301
Negroni, Eminia 212

Nelson, Casey 310
Nemecek, Scott 253
Newell, Elly 282
Newman, Kelli 187
Nguyen, Vy 206
Nichting, Brittany 226
Niewolik, Mark 99
Nisbet, Kristin 117
Nitzberg, Jacob 88
Nixon, Jeanelle 328
Noah, Mookdad 320
Nolte, Nick 80
Nootens, Nicolas 275
Norman, Jessica 245
Norman, Kris 292
Normann, Jami 280
Noronha, Tanya 75
Nosek, Liz .81
Novotny, Maggie 201
Nowaczewski, Matt 290
Nowak, Heather 196
Nowdomski, Kristen 169
Nowinski, Joe 148
Nudelman, Stephanie 248
Nugent, Nicole 238
Nuguid, Justine 290
Nuxoll, Roger 288
O'Connell, Sarra 313
O'Connell, Sean 308
O'Connor, Alexandrea 169
O'Keefe, Sarah 258
O'Neill, Anna 179
Oestreich, Nikki 22
Ofiara, Amanda 144
Olshefski, Andrew 244
Olson, Erik 34
Olson, Kimi 250
Olszewski, Lauren A. 122
Opalacz, Peter 173
Orlet, Anne 240
Ornelas, Mike 319
Orr, Casey 177
Orth, Colleen 120
Ortigara, Katy 293
Ortiz, Samuel 103
Ortiz, Stephanie 188
Osbourne, Ashlee 133
Osterholz, Anne 174
Otto, David 236
Ozarowski, Christine 237
Ozee, Lizzy 210
Ozga, Andrew 145
Pacey, Chad 304
Pagan, Kristie 144
Page, John 200
Palacios, Maria 29
Palma, Leslie 28

Palmer, Callie 171
Palmer, Danielle 318
Palmer, Melissa 145
Palmer, Nicole 296
Papadopoulos, Konstantinos 128
Papillon, Alexandra 158
Paplaski, Brian 217
Paris, Bree 116
Parker, Lydia 262
Parker, Ruth 42
Parkinson, Kari 73
Parks, Jason 28
Parks, Lawrence 284
Parr, Elizabeth 36
Parrish, Jessica 89
Parrish, Meghan 117
Parypinski, James 251
Pate, Josh 174
Patel, Dhruva 108
Patel, Raj 151
Patel, Swati 159
Patel, Virang 314
Patridge, Skylar 218
Patterson, Jamie 160
Patterson, Joshua 67
Paunicka, Liz 217
Pavel, Rachel 214
Paxson, Toni 133
Payonk, Barbara 262
Peacock, Ryan 198
Pearce, Ashley 98
Pearson, Emily 292
Pearson, Nikki 115
Peckenpaugh, Joseph 242
Pedroza, Christine 272
Pedroza, Natalie 57
Peinovich, Leah 275
Pelton, Nicole 243
Pendse, Emily 80
Pentek, Nick 206
Peralta, Patricia 253
Perez, Perla 307
Perizes, Fotis 80
Perkins, Russell 187
Perna, Lisa 73
Perrone, Lisa 120
Perry, Sara 154
Perry, Stephanie 123
Perry, Whitney 322
Pesek, Jon 162
Peters, Brock 89
Peterson, Katie 195
Pfeiffer, Elissa 162
Phelps, Doug 304
Pheteau, Stanley 241
Philbin, Tim 163
Piatt, Cara 19

Picchietti, Matt 210
Pickens, Brittany 85
Pieczynski, Stephanie 235
Piell, Amanda 148
Pieper, Elyse 280
Pierce, Christopher 286
Pifer, Angela 134
Pimentel, Erika 238
Pineda, Susana 73
Piper, Jason 241
Piriano, Dominic 142
Piskule, Michael 27
Pitrowski, Jessica 326
Pitt, Josh .289
Pittman, Brian 50
Piwowarczyk, Angelika 299
Pleasant, Karlie 326
Pliner, Kelsey 258
Pollock, Rachel 127
Polson, Kelsey Michelle 182
Pommer, Shaye 313
Porter, Cicero Jr. 261
Pospiech, Emily 98
Poston, Colisha 263
Potor, Corin 38
Powell, Jessica 19
Powell, Marquita 18
Power, Amy E. 121
Powers, Samantha 256
Pratscher, Cindy 262
Prebish, Liz 131
Prestridge, Morgan 198
Presutti, Marylyn 280
Prince, Cody 263
Prince, Emily 306
Prokopec, Nicole 97
Provost, Brandon 272
Puccinelli, Kara 282
Puentes, Carmen Grace 282
Pugh, Shannon 206
Pumpera, Amanda 156
Purdy, Tracie 24
Pursell, Brianna 301
Puttrich, Kelsey 284
Pycz, Jacqui 100
Quiter, Matt 267
Rachford, Dina 40
Raddatz, Samantha 132
Rakers, Brian 46
Rakoczy, Sara 328
Ramsey, Kandis 23
Randall, Annalise 262
Randall, Mike 233
Randle, Sara 141
Rangel, George 159
Rasmussen, Khristen 122
Ratoft, Gia 316

Rautio, Brittney 207
Razza, Anthony 162
Reboyras, Allyson 177
Redd, Emily 258
Redd, Jacquetta 303
Rediger, Laura 138
Redmond, Laura 172
Redmond, Michelle 293
Reed, Emily .68
Reed, Heather 258
Reed, Jessica 243
Rehage, Adam 152
Reich, Adam 69
Reid, Emily 289
Reinburg, Gina 22
Reishus, Kimberly 194
Reising, Elizabeth 100
Rembert, Shalisa 93
Renardo, Joe 236
Reschke, Erin 56
Reszke, Jennifer 80
Reyes, Virginia 283
Reyna, Daisy T. 216
Reynolds, Briana 123
Reynolds, Tee 211
Reynolds, Wayne 317
Reynoso, Doraliz 112
Rezansoff, Kelsy 230
Rhoades, Aubree J. 272
Rhoads, Celena 232
Rhodes, Nikki 269
Ribley, Connie 114
Richards, Sarah 92
Richardson, Keisha 45
Richmond, Taylor N. 186
Richter, Lucas 304
Riebold, Jennifer 246
Riggs, Robby 139
Ritzheimer, Jacob 92
Rivera, Angel Luis 52
Roberts, Catherine 316
Roberts, Danny 324
Roberts, Katie 155
Roberts, Katie 248
Roberts, Kris 276
Roberts, Megan 168
Robertson, Christina 182
Robertson, Tiffany 176
Robinson, Jennifer 326
Robinson, John Henry III 152
Robinson, Matthew 152
Robinson, Megan 81
Robison, Melissa 326
Robledo, Cristina 248
Rocha, Michael 284
Rockoff, Danny 288
Rodarte, Robert 324

Rodelo, Concepcion 215
Rodriguez, Abby 118
Rodriguez, Alma 41
Rodriguez, Juanita 70
Rogers, Earl 150
Rohrhoff, Annie 184
Rojas, Gladys 97
Rollason-Cass, Sylvie 178
Romero, Lyneth 54
Rosales, Gustavo 22
Rosario, Angelica Josephina 263
Ross, William Howard 257
Rothman, Julie 172
Rowe, Jeff .102
Rowland, Brooke 128
Roy, Justin 124
Roznovsky, Sandi 211
Rubino, Rose 120
Ruesch, Vanessa 274
Ruiz, Natalia 233
Ruiz, Rebecca 163
Ruiz, Ruben 27
Rupani, Zaheen 231
Ruppel, Rachel 106
Rusenovich, Jimmy 255
Rush, Allie 230
Russell, Erika 150
Russell, Mercedes 95
Ryan, Mike 241
Rzeszutko, Alyssa 10
Rzeszutko, Ryan 323
Saari, Cyndi 74
Sabatini, Olivia 139
Sabbs, Deonté 297
Sadaqa, Rabia 322
Sadler, Michael 230
Sadlowski, Kasia 332
Saez, Alejandro 121
Sagle, Jessica 303
Saint Germain, Marissa Rae 284
Salazar, Brenda 200
Saldana, Adrian 127
Salerno, Todd 284
Salgado, Liliana 201
Salin, Kara 257
Salunkhe, Aditya 242
Salvato, Vanessa 112
Sampson, Matt 255
Samsuri, Rajda 284
Sanchez, Bianca 241
Sanchez, Candice 270
Sanchez, Megan 303
Santora, Thomas C. 131
Sarkar, Kaushik 314
Savage, Katie 208
Saxour, Nichole 192
Scalero, Mary 53

Scalzo, Lauren 11
Scardina, Aimee 44
Schaefer, Heather 281
Schaffer, Jeffrey R. 312
Schermer, Gordon 50
Schess, Jenny 313
Schield, Sara 24
Schilling, Emilie 35
Schlarmann, Brent 198
Schleiss, Francesca 195
Schlueter, Brook 53
Schmid, Martha 299
Schmidt, Jamie 330
Schmidt, Jessica 312
Schmiege, Alyssa 268
Schmitt, Carrie 305
Schnepper, Linsey 35
Schott, Justin 286
Schrock, Evan 252
Schroeder, Alan 25
Schroeder, Kayla 315
Schuett, Nicole 250
Schulte, Kelli 172
Schultz, Kyle 204
Schultz, Rebecca 323
Schwarting, Abby 242
Schwartz, Jenny 184
Schwarz, Angela 251
Scianna, Mike 86
Scott, Brandon 321
Scott, Bruce 227
Scott, Chimere Lauren 212
Scott, Daniel 278
Scully, Amanda 165
Sebastian, Sam 178
Seber, Lauren 120
Sedano, Rebecca K. 192
Sell, Carla .149
Sell, Marie .161
Sendejas, Lizzie 205
Serling, Kate 26
Serna, Stephanie 262
Shah, Himadri 86
Shallcross, Alice Eileen 324
Shamberg, Melissa 231
Shanahan, Michelle 153
Sharp, Penina 176
Shawen, Chelsea 153
Shelby, Lashunda 57
Sheppard, Patrick 59
Sheridan, Brian 138
Sherwani, Shehbaz 319
Shevlin, Crystal 37
Shinnick, Kelly 105
Shotts, Christy 50
Shreffler, Kyle 38
Shyu, Esther 251

Siddiqui, Laila 16
Siebert, Carli 237
Siegert, Anthony 107
Sierminski, Rachel 43
Signore, Stephanie 245
Simek, Mark 294
Simmons, Shawna 35
Sims, Jeannette 308
Sinodinos, Mark 125
Siverly, Mandy 47
Slatton, Stacy 25
Slavik, Emily 319
Sloan, Billy 90
Sloan, Tricia A. 249
Slodyczka, Edyta 328
Small, Rhonda 34
Smith, Bridgette 296
Smith, Elizabeth G. 32
Smith, Erin 84
Smith, Jared 251
Smith, Jill 201
Smith, Kelly 29
Smith, Kevin 298
Smith, Megan 255
Smith, Romonica 83
Smith, Samantha 311
Smith, Tricia 144
Snethen, Steph 278
Snider, Danielle 85
Snow, Ryan 273
Snyder, Miranda 102
Snyder, Rachel 124
Solano, Evelyn 236
Soriano, Diana 102
Spangler, Julia 265
Spears, Devan 237
Spears, Jesseca 52
Spector, Robin 165
Spehn, Jimmy 106
Spencer, Brian 17
Spencer, Tabitha 329
Spiotta, Julia 248
Spivak, Ally 83
Springborn, Becky 162
Springer, Nicole 133
Springmeyer, Nathan 268
Spyrka, Pamela 238
Srinivasan, Lavanya 314
Stachnik, Savannah 71
Stanley, Erica 286
Staszowski, Jim 50
Steele, Matt 281
Stefanik, Stephanie 263
Steinwart, Erin 214
Stempinski, Kelly 112
Stenger, Lana 94
Stepanski, Christine 24

Stephenson, Neal 199
Stevenson, Amanda 331
Stiles, Andrea 168
Stinson, Taylor 295
Stock, Jeremy 179
Stodden, Felicia 37
Stoltz, Karissa 108
Stone, Stephanie 302
Stonewall, Nate 12
Strawn, Jonathon 249
Strickler, Casey 238
Strong, Lauren 93
Strozewski, Lauren 30
Stull, Joseph 81
Sullivan, Bethany 190
Sullivan, Chad 307
Sullivan, Kendall Rapheal 265
Sura, Poonam 157
Sus, Michelle 119
Sutfin, Virginia 236
Sutton, Leslie 55
Sutton, Teresa 48
Sutton, Trevor 283
Svehla, Lucas 310
Svehla, Spenser 305
Swan, Brianne 120
Swan, Ryan 49
Swanson, Ruthanne 187
Swantish, Laura 153
Sweeney, Susan 87
Sweetnam, Dale 51
Swiss, Greg 87
Syverson, Whitney 173
Szaflarski, Brittany 91
Szewczyk, Eddie 259
Szofer, Torrey-Paige 91
Szudarski, Adam 36
Szulyk, Natalie 291
Tanner, Cassie 135
Taylor, Jaclyn 278
Taylor, Jasper 326
Taylor, Kristin 247
Taylor, Ryan 184
Teel, Andrew Michael 59
Tellez, Eva Lezith 139
Tello, Veronica 126
Terry, Kelly Lynn 23
Teuber, Sarah 264
Thayalan, Vivek 173
Thayer, Jessica 47
Theobald, Benjamin 49
Theriault, Brian 141
Thibault, Justin 51
Thoele, Casey 246
Thoele, Courtney 175
Thole, Kim 101
Thomann, Holly 276

Thomas, Brittany Gail 115
Thomas, Claire 100
Thomas, Maggie 310
Thomas, Michelle 255
Thompson, Adam 26
Thompson, Brett 77
Thompson, Harry 188
Thompson, Jeffrey 310
Thompson, Jennifer 53
Tierney, Matthew 330
Tijerina, Ricardo A. 258
Tissiere, Travis 290
Tobar, Michelle K. 54
Todd, Mike 74
Toeller, Samantha 293
Toennies, Gabe 147
Toledo, Mike 298
Toler, Mary 296
Tolomeo, Madison 277
Tomich, A.J. 197
Tomines, Rhoda Faye 186
Topol, Lauren 113
Torres, Jennifer 192
Torres, Liliana 294
Torres, Noe 118
Torres, Virginia Lisa 191
Tosetti Winsloff, Jessica L. 21
Tovar, Brenda 208
Townsend, Carrie Renee 72
Tracy, Brennan 230
Treece, Sarah 322
Tresslar, Kelly 283
Trickie, Amy J. 122
Tripathi, Anuraag 289
Tronick, Peter 55
Trutman, Jordan 166
Truttman, Messina 135
Tucker, Caitlin Anne 270
Tuerk, Kathryn 317
Tugle, Shannon 21
Tuley, Rebecca 331
Tunstall, Erik 257
Tuntland, Lindsey 292
Turbyfill, Amanda 312
Turley, Amanda 27
Turner, Anne 233
Tutor, Tiffany 236
Twomey, Jenny 123
Tynczuk, Nic 328
Tyrcha, Melissa 101
Ubik, Ashley 236
Uhrich, Katie 51
Underwood, Courtney 231
Urban, Amanda 20
Urquhart, Rachel L. 58
Vaccaro, Lisa 309
Valdes, Adam 321

Valdovinos, Luz 182
Valle, Mireya 308
Valle, Nicole 281
Van Ryn, Rachel 218
Vander Zanden, Brad 246
Vandrevala, Cyrus 121
VanDuzer, Brandon 291
Vanick, Tiffany 110
Vann, Amber L. 261
Vargas, Cynthia 257
Vargas, Mayra 43
Vargas, Yesenia 205
Vargo, Jessica 303
Varndell, Tara 163
Vasquez, Pedro 288
Vasseur, A.J. 112
Veasey, Candice 109
Vega, Andrew 86
Velazquez, Sophia 165
Vera, Ishally 180
Vera, Monica 202
Vershay, Heather 111
Viehman, Faren 153
Villain, Chantal 162
Villarreal, Mirna 95
Villarreal, Steffen 51
Villegas, Yamilett 243
Vilutis, Art 130
Virgen, Fernando 86
Voaden, Laura 107
Voitik, Alex 136
Voss, Lauren 120
Wade, Courtney 28
Wagner, Heather 13
Wagner, Sara 113
Wagner, Zachary 260
Wakeman, Steve 243
Walat, Shauna 265
Waldo, Michael 324
Walla, Meg 156
Walrath, Jinger 302
Walsh, Amanda 228
Walsh, Erin 295
Walter, Ryan 14
Walz, Fred 111
Wanner, Brittany 297
Ward, Courtney 80
Ward, Frances 184
Ward, Jamie 180
Warner, Jake 138
Warner, Nikki 278
Warns, Shelly 330
Warren, Michael 15
Waspi, Kristen 19
Waterman, John 258
Watkins, Darryl 326
Watkins, Julian 168

Watson, Emily 58
Watson, Michael 243
Weakley, Peggy J. 144
Weathersby, Chandra 49
Webb, Megan 80
Weber, Jamie 246
Webster, Jeffrey C. 191
Wegmann, Brad 269
Wehr, Kimberly 264
Weidner, Andrew 251
Weiler, Katherine 23
Weirich, Kaci 286
Weisensee, Kim 148
Weiser, Brittany 184
Wells, Amy 248
Wells, Brooke 21
Wendel, Anne L. 138
Wendle, Brian 329
Wenerski, Amy 93
Wenger, Nathan 103
Weppler, Ryan 327
Werner, Kara 272
Werner, Samantha 236
Werntz, Ryan 260
Wertman, Katharine 140
Wesselmann, Ashley 84
West, Katie 277
West, Terra Lee 56
Westendorf, Drew 240
Westerdale, Becky 271
Wetzel, Greg 163
Whalen, Sean 256
Whitaker, Shaun 244
White, Courtney 301
White, Dane 143
White, Heather 30
White, Kate 254
White, Kathryn 157
White, Olivia 163
White, Trina 158
Whitehead, Daniel 193
Whitley, Shannon Lynn 291
Wibben, Brook 295
Wiberg, Eric 186
Wieneke, Shanna 20
Wilczak, Brittanie 184
Wiley, Kara 49
Wilke, Kristen 238
Wilkening, Mandy 78
Wilkinson, Samantha 310
Willeford, Bethany 215
Willette, Danielle 285
Willette, Nicole 17
Willey, Melissa 116
Willhelm, Stephanie 314
Williams, Abby 288
Williams, Adam 40

Williams, Lindsey 239
Williams, Stephanie L. 161
Williamson, Heather 167
Williamson, Meghan 282
Willis, Jessica 116
Wilson, Amanda 117
Wilson, Josh 218
Windom, Veronica 180
Wingren, Jessica 252
Winkeler, Phillip 269
Winsloff, Jessica L. Tosetti 21
Witt, Krissy 78
Wittrock, Bonnie 206
Wojciak, Crystal 299
Wolf, Jonathan 175
Wolfenbarger, Blake 87
Wollenzien, Kayla 103
Woodley, Melissa 85
Woolbright, Erik 148
Woolford, Stacey 114
Wozny, Carissa 278
Wright, Dana 135
Wright, Jeni 306
Wright, JuTaun 266
Wright, Michelle 164
Wruck, Tammy 233
Wurmnest, Jenna 283
Wyman, Kendyl 77
Wysocki, T.J. 165
Yambo, Esther 16
Yan, Frank 271
Yarrito, Sarah 166
Yatco, Brian 131
Yates, Ashley 269
Yates, Jared 181
Yniguez, Alejandra 252
Yocum, Jessie 236
Yoder, Adam 144
Yoder, Chad 141
Yost, Nicole 126
Young, Amber 110
Young, Natalie 104
Young, Rebekah 158
Yount, Emilie 48
Yuhas, Alison 229
Yun, Jenny 203
Zaccaro, Christopher 209
Zagajewski, Anthony 150
Zarach, Nathan 326
Zare, Stephanie 216
Zeanah, Christena 235
Zeller, Stacy 86
Zenteno, Diana 242
Zera, Michael 107
Zessemos, Christina 180
Zhang, Brandon 292
Zhao, Vivienne 252

Ziehm, Jennifer 57
Zieren, Sandra 20
Zimmerman, Diana 311
Zindel, Callie 293
Zingrone, Will 38
Zomick, Cory 281
Zorn, Alex 244
Zoubareva, Nadia 231
Zucker, Jordan 321
Zuniga, Erica M. 85
Zwickl, Kevin 240